How to Invest

MASTERS ON THE CRAFT

David M. Rubenstein

SIMON & SCHUSTER

New York London Toronto Sydney New Delhi

Simon & Schuster
1230 Avenue of the Americas
New York, NY 10020

First Simon & Schuster hardcover edition September 2022

For information about special discounts for bulk purchases,
please contact Simon & Schuster Special Sales at
1-866-506-1949 or business@simonandschuster.com.

The Simon & Schuster Speakers Bureau can bring authors to
your live event. For more information or to book an event, contact
the Simon & Schuster Speakers Bureau at 1-866-248-3049
or visit our website at www.simonspeakers.com.

Interior design by Lewelin Polanco

Manufactured in the United States of America

1   3   5   7   9   10   8   6   4   2

Library of Congress Cataloging-in-Publication Data is available.

ISBN 978-1-9821-9030-9
ISBN 978-1-9821-9032-3 (ebook)

*To Warren Buffett, the ultimate master of the investor craft,
and to Bill Conway and Dan D'Aniello,
who patiently showed me firsthand, for thirty-five years,
the craft of investing and the art of partnership.*

CONTENTS

Part III: Cutting Edge Investments

Introduction

M uch of life simply revolves around predicting the future and then taking actions that reflect the view of that future. Like everyone, I have made some good and bad predictions about the future, and taken some smart and not-so-smart actions based on those predictions.

I thought Jimmy Carter would beat Gerald Ford in the 1976 presidential election and, also believing he was the better candidate, went to work for Carter's general election campaign. Good prediction.

I thought Ronald Reagan was too old (69), too conservative, and too lacking in policy skills to beat Carter in the 1980 presidential election, and I did not plan for a post–January 20, 1981, forced return to private-sector life. Bad prediction. (I am now older than Reagan was then—he now seems like a teenager.)

I thought my Little League all-star skills at shortstop would not likely grow into a major-league career and decided to focus my efforts on improving my academic skills rather than my athletic skills. Good prediction.

I thought my hometown Baltimore Colts could not possibly lose to Joe Namath and the upstart New York Jets in Super Bowl III in 1969, and made a very large (for me) bet on the Colts. Bad prediction (and my last-ever sports bet).

I thought the private equity world would increase in appeal and that it was possible—with the help of talented investment professionals I was able to recruit—to build a global private equity firm from a Washington base. Good prediction (maybe my best ever).

I thought Mark Zuckerberg's company, created while he was in college, would not outgrow its college campus roots and thus would not be an attractive investment for me when presented by my future son-in-law. Bad prediction.

I thought Jeff Bezos's startup books-over-the-internet company could not possibly overcome Barnes & Noble, and told him that in our initial meeting at his cluttered first office space in Seattle, and thus later decided to sell our Amazon stock as soon as possible. Bad prediction.

Whether someone has predicted well or poorly about life events can be gauged differently by different people. In truth there is no single, universally accepted standard to gauge how successful someone has been in predicting and acting on the future.

In that respect at least, the investment world is wholly different. The skill of predicting the future, and taking preparatory actions, is quite measurable. In the investment world, achieving a profit—to a lesser or greater degree depending on the type of investment—is the essence of investing.

In working to achieve a profit, an investor is really making a prediction about the future—the desirability of owning a particular asset (stock, bond, house, currency, etc.) in the future, based on the likely future performance of the asset. Will the company attract new customers or invent a desired product? Will the economy at the time the investment is realized be strong or weak? Will interest rates be higher? Will climate change affect the value of assets? Will competition be less than might be expected?

Stated differently, are there risks that will possibly arise that could upset the investor's belief that an investment will work out and thus produce the desired outcome? And how great are those risks?

In life, there are always risks to be assessed, but the consequences may not always be measured precisely. In investing, the consequences can be measured quite precisely.

While investing today is a much more sophisticated process of trying to predict the future than it was in the past, the process of investing is centuries old, though by today's standards it was not all that sophisticated back then. Ever since money or its equivalent has existed, individuals have tried to take steps that will return to them more of something than they invested. In the United States, the country was basically started as an investment. The settlers in Jamestown, Virginia, arrived in 1607 because their financial backers in England expected the settlement would ultimately return multiples of the sums that were invested to get the settlers there. That turned out not to be a great investment for the initial backers.

In the past half century, the gold standard as an investor, and thus as a predictor of the future, has been Warren Buffett. He first bought shares of Berkshire Hathaway at $7.50 per share, and over the past sixty years the share price has compounded at an annualized rate of 20 percent. Others have made more money outside of the investing world. Others have had better investment rates of return over shorter periods of time. And still others have had more visible and spectacular investment returns on particular investments. But no other investor has achieved more over a longer period. Berkshire Hathaway now has a market value of $690 billion as of June 1, 2022. Thus Warren Buffett might be said to be the best long-term predictor of the future. For that is what he has in essence been doing all of these years.

I have interviewed Warren many times, as have others, and have always learned something new from him when interviewing him or reading the interviews of others. Those interviews made me think about the views of other great investors—how were they able to predict the future, in their own area of investment, and how were they able to act well or not so well on those predictions?

That led me to an effort to interview some of America's best investors to gauge how they prepared themselves to both predict the future and act upon it in their own area of specialty. The result is this book, which is a distillation of those interviews, with some of my own thoughts about each of the investors and their investment types, as well as some of my perspectives on investing. As with my previous books, the interviews have been edited for length and clarity with the permission of the interviewees.

Great investors have a number of skills and attributes in common, as I will discuss. But they also have skills and attributes unique to their particular type of investment area. A great venture investor may not have everything required to be a great distressed-debt investor, or to be a great real estate investor, or a great cryptocurrency investor.

So I thought that, to give a reader a meaningful sense of the varying skills and attributes needed for different types of investment areas, it would be helpful to have leaders in many of the different basic investment areas. I interviewed individuals like Jon Gray, who built the world's largest real estate investment business at Blackstone; Seth Klarman, who has long been, in his leadership at Baupost, one of the country's most respected value investors; Michael Moritz, who helped build Sequoia into perhaps the most successful of the large venture funds over the past five decades; Mary Erdoes, who has led J.P. Morgan's wealth management business into a world-leading position; John Paulson, whose bet against subprime mortgages between 2007-09 became known as the "greatest trade" in Wall Street history; John Rogers Jr., whose commitment to careful stock analysis led him to build one of the largest African American–owned and led investment companies; and Jim Simons, whose math genius enabled him to pioneer the use of "quantitative" investment strategies.

All of these individuals, along with the other great investors interviewed for this book, also have interesting life stories and investment approaches, which I have tried to bring out in the interviews. I have also tried to show, through a number of interviews, that the investment industry—long a white male preserve—is changing, and diverse investment leaders are now taking their rightful place in the investment world. But, as with my previous books, the interviews are really appetizers designed, in this instance, to whet a reader's interest in learning more about that particular investor and also that type of investing.

To simplify matters, I have classified all of the investors with whom I talked as being in one of these investment categories: Mainstream, Alternative, and Cutting Edge.

Mainstream investors include those individuals who specialize in areas that are relatively traditional—that is, part of the investment horizon for at least half a century or more: bonds, stocks, real estate, and traditional kinds of wealth and endowment management.

Alternative investors include those individuals who pursue investments in areas that were once considered (at least a few decades ago) quite novel or risky, though that is considered to be somewhat less the situation today. These areas, known within the investment world as "alternative," would include hedge funds, buyouts, venture capital, and distressed debt.

Cutting-edge investors focus on investments that are considered quite new by even the standards of what was once considered "alternative." That is to say that these investment areas are ones that may be only a few decades old (or even newer). These would include investments in areas such as cryptocurrencies, SPACs (special purpose acquisition companies), infrastructure, and companies focused on ESG (environmental, social, and governance factors).

Reading a book about these great investors will hopefully provide the reader with insights, perspectives, and inspiration—but, the truth be told, a book will not by itself make the reader a great investor any more than reading a book about Tiger Woods's secrets will make one a great golfer (as I have learned).

This book is designed to provide a glimpse into the investment thoughts and practices of many of America's leading investors. By doing that, I hope to help three different types of readers: 1) those interested in learning more about investing on their own; 2) those interested in learning more about investing through funds managed by professional investors; and 3) those who are students or young professionals interested in exploring an investment career.

Of course, no one book can perfectly satisfy the interests—or answer all of the questions—of these disparate kinds of readers, but I have hoped that the interviews in this book might enable them to at least modestly improve their investing knowledge and abilities, if not entice them into becoming professional investors.

I should add that the world of investing has probably changed more in the past three decades, and maybe even the past three years, than it had in the previous three centuries.

Investing was traditionally an activity pursued by professionals—those who invested for a living. Now investing is pursued by individuals whose professional obligations are in often unrelated areas.

Access to up-to-date information about public securities was traditionally not widely available. Now everyone can get instant access—on a phone—to information about stock and bond prices, private investment opportunities, and investment activities around the world.

And investing was traditionally an activity, with some obvious exceptions, pursued by individuals who had reached at least middle age. Now young individuals, in their teens and twenties, seem much more focused on this activity than anything witnessed before for their age cohort.

It may not wholly be a surprise that I have written a book on investing, for I have spent the past thirty-five years in the investing world, principally in the private equity investment world.

After leaving the Carter White House in January of 1981, I returned to the only profession I knew: practicing law, though in Washington rather than in New York, where I had practiced right after law school.

But I soon realized that I really disliked law practice (in no small part because I was not very good at it). I decided to try something seemingly more exciting—and most likely more lucrative. (I had never been that motivated by money, but I felt that law practice had become less of a profession than a business. And if I was going to be in business, I might as well try something with greater financial—if not also psychic—rewards.)

Inspired by former Treasury secretary Bill Simon's extraordinarily profitable buyout of Gibson Greeting Cards (his $330,000 investment turned into a $66 million profit in about 16 months), I decided the legal profession could survive without me, and I would try to build the first buyout firm in Washington. Since I had no professional investment experience (I had bought—at prices too high—a few stocks in my youth), I focused on recruiting a few individuals in the Washington area who had solid finance, if not investment, backgrounds.

Fortunately, while Washington was not New York, I was able to recruit several individuals who knew what they were doing when it came to finance and investing. Their backgrounds helped me raise $5 million, from four institutional investors, in 1987 to get the newly named The Carlyle Group going. We took that sum and built a firm that, as of June 1, 2022, manages $375 billion.

But that was not an overnight occurrence. And few in Washington (not to mention New York) took us seriously for many, many years.

Carlyle's growth in time occurred because our track record was at least as good, if not better in some areas, as our New York–based competitors. But we also developed a then-unique concept: building a diversified, multi-fund firm (i.e., investing through separate funds in other private investment areas—real estate, growth capital, infrastructure, credit, funds of funds, etc.), and, by doing so, building enough operational and investment talent to create an institutional-quality company. And we decided—also really innovative at the time—to globalize the firm by creating investment teams in Europe, Asia, Japan, Latin America, the Middle East, and Africa, using our developing brand and contacts to recruit investment professionals and to raise funds from all over the world.

As of June 1, 2022, Carlyle had invested $133 billion of equity in the corporate private equity area and had generated $256 billion of gains for investors. Over more than thirty years, Carlyle's annualized gross internal rate of return in corporate private equity has been approximately 26 percent.

I was not the individual at Carlyle responsible for its many-decades-long investment success. The credit for this achievement is really due to Bill Conway and Dan D'Aniello, my principal co-founders, and scores of talented investment professionals whom we recruited and trained in the Carlyle investment style (i.e., cautious, conservative, not high-flying). My contribution to the firm was more in the area of strategy, fundraising, recruiting, government affairs, and public relations. So I offer my own thoughts on investing with more than a bit of modesty.

That said, I did sit in several thousand investment committee meetings over a 35-year period, gave my perspectives, absorbed what the investment teams had to say, and learned a good deal. During that three-decades-plus period, the investing world changed dramatically. The level of competition (from domestic and foreign investors) increased manyfold; the amount of money chasing investments seemed to grow exponentially; prices grew to levels once thought unimaginable; the involvement of outside experts and consultants provided much more thorough analyses; and the interest of institutional as well as individual investors in private investments seemed to know no bounds.

Throughout this period, I came to greatly admire not only the skill sets and other qualities of the investors who were leading Carlyle's investments, but also the abilities of those who were leading our competitors' efforts. That led me, in time, to wonder more about the qualities that really separate the great investors from the average ones.

And that prompted me to want to use a practice I have pursued in recent years—interviewing—to hear firsthand from some of the world's great investors.

What did I learn from my interviews?

Great investors have a number of traits in common. Having these traits will not guarantee that one will be a great investor, but having them certainly improves the odds, if the life stories and skills of the great investors are any indication of what it actually takes to be a great investor. Let me encapsulate what the traits and skills of the great investors generally seem to be:

Background. They typically were raised in blue-collar or middle-class backgrounds; rarely are they from fabulously wealthy families, or families where there is a history of investing professionally. Of the investors interviewed in this book, none came from overly wealthy families, though many came from families with professional backgrounds.

Early jobs. While some investors created small businesses early, and a few dabbled a bit in investing when young, most came to investing after trying other professional endeavors, not always with the same extraordinary success as they later achieved in investing. That said, it should be noted: Jim Simons was a world-class mathematician; Marc Andreessen was a noted entrepreneur; Michael Moritz was a highly successful journalist; and Paula Volent was an accomplished art conservator.

Failure. Many of the great investors had career setbacks or major investment losses along the way. That may well have given them the drive to persist and ultimately to perfect their craft.

Intelligence. The great investors have a high degree of intelligence; and they tended to do well academically. While not all investors are math savants like Jim Simons, there is no doubt that an ease with numbers and math is common to the great investors, even if they happened to study social sciences or less math-oriented subjects.

Ultimate responsibility. It seems clear that the best investors want to own the final decision on investments of any importance. They tend to have self-confidence in their investment acumen and want to make the ultimate judgment on any investment matter of importance, as opposed to delegating the decision to their trusted lieutenants. And they are quite content to take the ultimate responsibility for that final decision.

Focus. The ability to focus on the most important factors in an investment decision is one that great investors tend to have in common. They are not as easily distracted by the unimportant factors, and have the ability to concentrate at unusually high levels. The ability to ferret out the key elements of an investment is something the great investors seem to be able to do exceedingly well.

Reading. Great investors seem to feel there is never too much knowledge one can acquire, and that some of that knowledge can help with perspectives on whatever issue might be raised by an investment. Great investors tend to be relentless readers of books, magazines, newspapers, and curated materials that fit their interests. Some may have had or have dyslexia; but these individuals tend to gather wide amounts of information through other means, often through frequent phone calls or video contacts with industry experts or other investment professionals. Stated another way, great investors have an enormous amount of intellectual curiosity, and want to learn as much as they can about any subject that might remotely relate at some point to their investment's activities. They seem to have a view that any piece of information can in time help shape a better investment decision, or inspire greater creativity or insight.

Battle of wits. When great investors become extremely wealthy, they still enjoy the game of investing—not because they really need more money, but rather because they view investing as a game of wits. They enjoy doing something others thought could not be done, or taking risks that might have been thought to be too great to take. The intellectual challenge of outsmarting others—or at least showing their own intelligence, cunning, and wisdom—is a gravitational force that keeps investors glued to their investment activities well beyond any need to earn more money.

Conventional wisdom. One of the easiest paths in life, and in investing, is to accept and follow the conventional wisdom. Why attract attention by going against the conventional wisdom? Why take a risk of being wrong by rejecting the conventional wisdom? No doubt life can be easier in proceeding along such a path. If you are wrong, you are in the boat with a great many others, and are less likely to attract unfavorable attention or be criticized.

But great investors do not accept conventional wisdom; they see what others do not; and they are prepared to take the risk of being proven wrong by going against conventional wisdom. No other characteristic of great investors is as important to their success as their willingness to ignore conventional wisdom, and to try something that others are afraid to try.

In the buyout world, the conventional wisdom in the 1980s and 1990s was that buyouts could not really work in the tech world. It was believed that technology could change so quickly that a buyout firm would not be able to pay down its debt before the buyout company's tech product would become obsolete.

But a current investment partner of mine, a technology expert who had worked at Oracle and Lotus, David Roux, disagreed. He started Silver Lake in 1999, with an intention to do technology buyouts. While I was skeptical this would work, in short order, Silver Lake achieved extraordinary returns by doing tech buyouts. Now almost any buyout without a focus on technology improvements is thought to be a likely failure.

Attention to detail. There are no doubt excellent investors who tend to focus on the big picture—where is the economy going? Are interest rates going to be increased? Is inflation likely to increase? But as a general rule, great investors pay an enormous amount of attention to the actual details of an investment. They want to know everything there is to know, and believe that a failure to pay attention to details is a prescription for failure. Thus they are sponges for information about investment opportunities.

Recognition of a mistake. Great investors can have large egos, but they are able to admit a mistake, cut their losses, and proceed with the next opportunity, largely without looking back unduly. That is certainly a trait I do not have. I am always looking back at the mistakes I made in not pursuing an investment or in pursuing an investment that did not work. But I am getting better, and only looking back now for a decade or so, rather than two or three decades.

Hard work. Great investors seem to have an obsession with what they do professionally, and thus tend to be, not surprisingly, hard workers who are willing to put in the hours necessary to master the skill set needed for their type of investing. It may be possible to be a great investor working a few hours a day, relying on others to do the hard work needed to understand an investment opportunity. But that is rare. Great investors tend to be workaholics, though they do not regard what they are doing as work. That is key—just as is the case with Nobel Prize winners. They regard work as pleasure, and thus do not feel the need to ease up all that much as they age a bit. They find investing a form of pleasure, and do not see a reason to reduce their pleasure because they already have a great deal of money.

Philanthropy. As noted, great investors tend to make considerable amounts of money, and may decide, at earlier ages than was the case decades ago, that they want to impress society not so much with the level of their wealth but with the level—and impact—of their philanthropy. The philanthropic instinct is partly stimulated by the social approval that accompanies philanthropy. Great investors are no different than others seeking social approval. And while there has been criticism in recent years of the way some wealthy individuals—and thus some wealthy investors—make philanthropic choices, generally there is social approval of philanthropic activity, and great investors enjoy that type of social approval (as would any human), and tend to be quite philanthropic. (Of course, they also believe their money will help address, if not solve, some social needs, and that is a large motivator as well.)

That great investors have many traits in common may not be a surprise. No doubt, the leaders in any profession probably have a fair number of traits in common.

But with almost any profession other than investing, there seems to be a readily apparent reason—other than simply the making of money—that draws people to that profession. While architects, lawyers, doctors, and corporate executives are well compensated, the making of money is rarely the principal purpose of the profession (or the sole draw of the profession to those who join it).

With investing, its raison d'être would appear to be almost always increasing the amount of money one has invested. Is that goal a worthwhile social objective? Why do so many talented people want to be in this profession? Would the world be better off if investors were compensated like teachers, presumably resulting in the many talented, highly motivated, and often quite well-educated individuals who become investors choosing a different profession? Would the world be better off if those with the talents to be great investors chose to pursue a profession of international diplomacy (hopefully resulting in fewer wars) or environmentalism (presumably resulting in cleaner air and water)?

There is no obvious, universally agreed-upon answer to those questions. It is impossible to know whether if someone with Warren Buffett's talents chose diplomacy as a profession, there would have been fewer wars or greater global harmony. (Warren Buffett would modestly say no as to himself—he thinks his skills are best applied to investing. Others may disagree.)

My view is that skillful investing, and thus skillful investors, perform an important role in allocating capital to companies or projects that perform valuable social purposes.

While the tech world and its companies are not without their flaws, it is difficult to say the world is not better off because of the investors who provided funds to get Microsoft, Apple, Google, Amazon, and so many other life-changing (and large-employment) companies off the ground. Or think of the investors who allocated money to Moderna. Clearly those investors helped facilitate a company that developed an extraordinary COVID vaccine in record time.

Capitalism has its flaws, for sure. It increasingly and sadly seems to be leaving people behind as it marches forward. But the overall wealth and employment created by capitalism, including the skillful decisions by investors about where, when, and how to deploy capital, cannot be underestimated. In the United States, the decisions by skilled investors over a great many generations—indeed centuries—have played a major role in enabling the US to become such a large, dynamic, and vibrant economy.

Of course, Alfred Nobel did not recognize investing as an achievement worthy of one of his prizes. Perhaps he did not think investors focused on the social impact of their decisions.

Indeed, until relatively recently, investors were in truth not obsessively focused on the societal impacts of their activities. Getting the highest rate of return or level of profit was the invariable goal. But that should not diminish the reality that just the practice of investing carries a valuable social purpose: jobs are created, companies are made more effective, an economy is more productive, and overall there are widespread resulting social benefits. The current focus in the investment world on having investors devote their attention, as well, to the ESG impact of their investments can only make the investment process—and investors—more helpful to society as a whole.

So, when you read the interviews of the great investors in this book, hopefully you will see them not merely as gifted capitalists, doing what they can to help or support themselves and their organizations, but rather as individuals whose skilled investment decisions have been vital forces in the country's social and economic growth.

Just as importantly, I hope you will read the interviews as illustrative of the kind of entrepreneurial and patriotic individuals who, beyond being role models for others, helped build the country by working hard to develop a unique and complex skill (i.e. investing), to perfect that skill, to then transmit it to their colleagues, and ultimately to give back to society through their philanthropic and educational efforts.

David M. Rubenstein
June 2022

David M. Rubenstein's
Notes on Investing

Over many years and in many different Carlyle investment committees—each fund has a separate committee—I have observed some extraordinarily talented investors present their recommendations. (In the private investment world, virtually all decisions to commit capital are made through committees—it is very rare for one individual to make an investment decision without the review and approval of others.)

And in recent years, I have also been involved in a number of other investment activities. In 2018, I created a family investment office, Declaration Capital, to invest some of my capital in areas not being pursued by Carlyle (with Carlyle's approval to avoid conflicts). Over the past few years, I have also served on the investment committees of the Smithsonian Institution, the Memorial Sloan Kettering Cancer Center, the Institute for Advanced Study, and the National Gallery of Art. And I have also served on the boards of trustees of Duke University and the University of Chicago and on the board of the Harvard Corporation. In these latter roles, I have been able to observe these organizations' own endowment investment activities (though I was not on their investment committees).

As a result of all of the foregoing activities, I have developed my own rules and perspectives on investing, and provide them here. While my focus has generally been in the private investment area over the years, these perspectives probably have, in my view, somewhat wider applicability.

Among the most salient of these perspectives:

Luck. Everyone has some good and bad luck in life, and investing is part of life. But counting on having good luck is a prescription for losing money. The investment gods do not reward those who hope good luck will provide superior investment returns on a regular basis. And, as with casino gambling, good luck at the outset of an investment process or career can actually be bad luck. One will think that genius rather than good luck was involved and will repeat itself, so a doubling down on the next investment will probably occur, typically resulting in losses greater than the initial gains. Hard work and rigorous analysis can, though, provide some luck from time to time (amazing how that is often the case); but just thinking that one is due for some good fortune is invariably a prescription for regular loss-making.

Price. For most investments, the best way to secure a transaction is, not surprisingly, to pay the highest price. The selling party may say it wants a responsible owner, someone who cares about ESG (environmental, social, and governance) factors; someone who will treat its employees well; someone who can get along with the management, etc. But in 99 percent of instances, the highest price (and the certainty of closing at that price) is principally what the seller really cares about when selling all of its stake in a company. I have invariably heard that the management team (rather than the owner) would prefer my firm as the investor, but if complete control is being sold by an owner, the preference of the management team is rarely dispositive, in my experience.

When a minority stake is being sold, the situation is a bit different, and an investor will find that other factors—typically the addition of value-added services or benefits—may play a real role. But still, these softer factors are often not enough to trump a much higher price. Around the margins, with price being relatively equal, these other factors can well make a difference to the seller, and should be emphasized by the buyer/investor.

But how does one know what is the right price to pay to secure a transaction and to later earn a profit? There are buyout, venture, and growth capital industry norms about what multiple of cash flow, or multiple of revenue in the case of some venture or growth capital deals, is the right price to pay. But a "right price" is really dependent on factors in the future: how will the management perform, what will competitors do, how will the economy perform, how will government policy affect the business—all factors not completely knowable at an investment's outset. But it is essential that the investor comes to a judgment about what the right value of an asset is to that investor, and do as much as possible to stick in that range, rather than let the seller's value dictate the price ultimately paid. Overpaying for an asset or company rarely has a pleasant outcome for the buyer.

Due diligence. For most things in life, preparation is a plus. My former Carlyle partner Secretary of State James A. Baker III had drilled into him by his father the aphorism that "prior preparation prevents poor performance." In the investment context, prior preparation is typically deemed "due diligence," which is to say the detailed work done analyzing a potential investment. With buyouts, that can entail six months or so of work, for there is an existing company and an enormous amount of financial data and related performance indicators to analyze. With venture capital, there is typically less data to analyze, and the due diligence often focuses on the quality of the entrepreneur leading the company, the uniqueness of the product or service underlying the company, and the size of the market opportunity.

For any type of private investment, the due-diligence process is designed to enable the investor to make an informed decision about the likely return that will be achieved at the price being paid. Good due diligence can also help an investor better prepare for likely future risks (or provide grounds for not making the investment).

My observation, though, is that the most detailed analysis, while helpful, does not always lead to the best investments. Due diligence cannot always adequately predict future management mistakes or departures, economic recessions, new competition, technological developments, regulatory changes, or emerging social changes. That said, due-diligence efforts are and should be extensive, though I have actually found that the high-quality depth and breadth of an investment committee memo (which can be 200–300 pages these days) does not guarantee the best investment outcome. Those who prepare these memos often seem to think the weight of the memo presages a good investment.

Instinct. The best investors invariably rely on their instincts or intuition—which is usually the sum of an investor's experiences and "gut" feelings—rather than exhaustive investment committee memos. Warren Buffett's decisions are rarely, if ever, premised on extensive investment committee memos. Of course, some investors overrate or overvalue their "intuition," and that can also be a problem. But there is no doubt that putting too much faith in projected rates of return down to the tenth decimal point seven years down the road are just as much of a problem. In my firm, and I suspect at similar firms, the detailed projections of rates of return seven years down the road (and this kind of analysis typically occurs in an investment committee memo) almost always miss the mark, and often significantly so—on the upside and the downside. No one can predict that well that far into the future. It can be self-deceiving to rely unduly on such computer-model projections (often put together by well-meaning but young analysts and recent MBAs).

Management. In due diligence, the quality of the management team, and especially the CEO, is usually a paramount consideration. A very good CEO for a company in which a private equity invests needs to not only have the normal good-CEO attributes—intelligence, hard work, focus, good communication, team-building skills, a vision for the company, a willingness to admit mistakes, and an ability to share the credit. In the private equity world, good CEOs also have to deal with their private equity investors, who are typically quite hands-on and strong-willed. (Private equity does not attract shrinking violets.)

Outstanding CEOs can make a gigantic difference in a buyout, but even those CEOs are not miracle workers. And while a CEO may seem quite outstanding in the beginning, a replacement will probably occur. In more than 50 percent of buyouts, before the buyout has been exited, the CEO will have been replaced. The turnover of CEOs in venture transactions may be even higher. But in venture, a great CEO can be even more valuable—though also much harder to find. Venture CEOs have the very difficult task of growing a young, often fragile organization. More venture deals fail than succeed—the opposite of buyout deals.

Realistic expectations. Invariably, an investment committee memo addresses the changes that should be made in the target investment, and while changes usually have to be made to increase value, sometimes the level and breadth of suggested changes may be unrealistic, at least in the available time frame and with the available financial and human resources. A key consideration for an acceptable investment result is to have realistic objectives, and therefore realistic rates of return. Some investments in the buyout world will produce five and ten times the invested capital. But that is rare—though in the recent two or three years, some great venture capital and growth capital investments done by the leading firms in these areas have far exceeded those multiples on their best deals. For Union Square, a leading venture fund, an early investment in Coinbase was worth nearly 2000x its cost when the company went public in 2021. (The post-IPO returns went down considerably in 2022 as the cryptocurrency market declined in appeal to many investors.) But that pre-IPO valuation was a once-in-a-lifetime rate of return; assuming that these kinds of returns may be readily or regularly achieved is a big mistake (though hope seems to spring eternal in the venture world at times).

Stated another way, with few exceptions, if the projected returns seem to be too good to believe, they should not be believed. If a proposed investment is that attractive, others will be pursuing it as well, the price will go up, and the returns most likely will come down.

Rate of return. In a typical buyout, the investor is seeking a rate of return, after all expenses and fees, of about 15–20 percent per annum, with the average buyout being about a five-year investment. Some highly specialized and smaller firms are often seeking and sometimes achieving net returns for their smaller buyouts of 20–25 percent per annum. About 75 percent of buyouts generate pre-fee proceeds in excess of what was invested. In venture capital, investors are often seeking to make net rates of return of 30 percent or more; but venture transactions have a higher failure rate than buyout investments, and only 40 percent of investments generate pre-fee proceeds in excess of what was invested.

In recent years, because of the overall increase in values, particularly in the technology area, venture investments tend to be profitable to a greater extent than the historic norm—but, as just noted, still more venture investments fail to be profitable than actually are profitable. The venture deals that get all of the high-return headlines are generally few and far between over the long term for most venture firms. That said, the past few years have been an historic wealth creation period for a small handful of leading venture firms.

Investors with realistic expectations of rates of return tend to be more successful. Investors who are chasing rates of return that are unrealistic—based on historic norms—will generally be disappointed. That became more apparent with the tech market declines in 2022. The large drop in values in this area tended to provide more reality to expectations of returns in much of the venture and growth capital worlds.

Commitment. There is no doubt that those who work on a potential investment and get excited about it can lose their objectivity, and might seek to pursue an investment in order to not feel that the due-diligence effort has been wasted. That can be a problem. However, a strong commitment to a transaction from an investment professional—someone who is truly excited about an investment and is pounding the table to get it approved—can be an important factor in deciding whether to proceed. An investment needs a strong advocate—someone who feels a personal obligation to make the investment work. Someone whose reputation—and future—is on the line will often be a big part of making an investment work well.

Value added. Companies that receive investments from professional investors are often seeking some value-added services from the investors—introductions to potential customers, assistance with potential acquisitions, help in securing board members, access to operational services, etc. To the extent that an investment firm can provide those services, the value of the investment can be improved. But it is important not to overpromise what can be delivered to a company in which an investment is being made; doing so often leads to real disappointments.

Timing of sale. In recent years, some investors who do not need capital back in the near term may be content to hold an investment for 8 to 10 years or even longer. (Warren Buffett holds some assets forever.) But the typical exit from a private equity investment occurs after about five years; by that time, the value-increasing activities should have occurred, and investors typically like to get their capital back in that period. Investments lasting longer are often ones that have had challenges getting the returns to the desired levels, and there is often the inevitable hope that things will get better if more work is done over the ensuing two to three years. In some cases, sales are delayed because the sellers have grandiose return expectations, and get greedy when not selling at normally acceptable levels. As a general rule, good investors know both when to buy and know when to sell; they tend not to fall in love with their investments, and recognize not only the value of buying at the right price but also, more important, of selling at the right time.

The above perspectives from a career spent largely in private investments may not provide the kind of generic investment advice new investors or prospective investors might be seeking. So I thought it might be useful to also provide below my basic investment advice for these individuals. And I have done so from two vantage points—investments being made directly by an individual and investments being made indirectly by an individual (i.e., investing through a fund managed by a third party).

Investing Directly

For nonprofessional investors who want the pleasure and excitement (though at times the risk and pain) of investing their capital directly, that is, picking stocks or bonds or doing buyouts, or venture or real estate investing directly, I offer these thoughts:

1. Do not risk more than you can truly afford to lose. Stated differently, for investments that have a realistic chance of losing all or part of the invested capital, make certain you have calculated that risk in your investment decisions, and know whether your financial situation can really tolerate that loss.
2. Diversify your investments. This principle is one of the key tenets of investing: do not put all your eggs in one basket. And, in that vein, try to have investments that are not completely correlated—that is, they all are likely to go up or down at the same time.
3. Do not think you are an expert or genius in investing because you are an expert or genius in any other area. Making a fortune as a manufacturer or artist or athlete will not make you an investment expert or genius, as many experts or geniuses in other areas realize relatively quickly in their investment efforts.
4. Have realistic return expectations. Having unrealistic expectations will inevitably lead to overly risky investments and real disappointments. For overall investment returns (assuming a mix of different types of public and private

investments), trying to continuously get annual returns above mid to high single digits is extremely difficult, certainly for a nonprofessional.

5. Read everything readily available about the investment being made. Make certain that the potential risks of the investment are as thoroughly understood and considered as the potential upsides. One cannot learn too much, read too much, or ask too many questions about the investment.

6. Talk to or consult with others who know the investment area or particular investment. More than one set of eyes and ears can be extremely helpful. And talk to those who have lost money in the area as well as those who have made money in the area.

7. Understand the public risks of the investment, and try to minimize if not eliminate many of those risks. For example, investing in a gun manufacturer or heavily carbon-emitting company may have adverse public consequences to a personal or professional reputation if the fact of the investment becomes public (and assume that it will).

8. Know your partners well. If the investment involves others as partners, make certain that everything relevant about those partners is known. An otherwise good investment can be ruined if an investment partner does not have a history of being a competent, solid, honest, and reliable partner. Unreliable, dishonest, or less-than-competent partners rarely get better in the future. Beware, as well, of partnering with "masters of the universe" who seem overly egocentric or unlikely to listen to advice or face reality.

9. Understand the tax consequences and regulatory constraints. Some otherwise attractive investments can be made far less attractive if the tax impacts or regulatory challenges of them are unfavorable. Make certain that sound tax and regulatory advice and planning are part of the investment decision.

10. Make certain that regular, reliable, and understandable information about the investment is made available, at least on a quarterly basis, and that there is a regular mechanism for questions to be asked and answered.

11. Do not be afraid to admit a mistake when an investment goes south (and thus be ready to cut losses), and do not be afraid to take a profit (out of a belief that profits can only get bigger).

Investing Indirectly or Through Funds

Much investing these days is actually done indirectly, by investing in funds where others are really making the investment decisions. This is the case in stock and bond index funds, ETFs, mutual funds, IRA and 401(k) funds, and the whole panoply of private investment–related funds.

With this type of investing, where someone else is really investing the money (once the basic fund investment has been made), my perspectives are these:

1. Make certain that the track record—assuming it is not a new fund—is fully understood, and preferably in the top quartile of its peer funds during the latest period for which data is available.
2. Make certain that the key individuals in the fund who have achieved that track record are still in the organization, and are reasonably likely to stay (i.e., are professionally satisfied and well compensated for their efforts). Also, determine if the key individuals—if legally permitted to do so—are investing meaningfully in the fund as well.
3. Ascertain whether the younger professionals in the organization—the ones who often do the day-to-day work—are also incented to stay because they are being appropriately compensated.
4. Determine whether the track record has been achieved in an area that is still likely to be growing and attractive during the period of the investment.
5. Determine whether the fund's terms are fair and reasonable by industry standards, particularly the fees (and make certain that the fees being charged are readily understandable).

6. Determine whether the organization sponsoring the fund has high employee turnover or a reputation for being sued regularly by investors for poor performance or unethical practices.

7. Figure out who the other investors in the fund have been or are likely to be. Smart money generally knows how to find the best funds.

8. Make certain that the relevant investment professionals are regularly available, if needed, to answer questions, and make certain that the information about the fund's investment performance is regularly provided, is accurate and under-standable, and, when appropriate, is verified by independent third parties.

9. If the fund is new, and thus has no relevant track record, make certain that the investment leaders had an appealing track record at whatever fund previously employed them (and that the investment leaders have some record of hav-ing worked together previously, and are also committing a meaningful amount of their own capital to the fund). Also make certain that the area in which the new fund is being invested is one that has a realistic chance of success.

10. Be certain that there are likely to be realistic, fair, and attrac-tive opportunities to exit the fund (perhaps through a "sec-ondary" sale of the investment) if there is a personal need for liquidity before the fund fully completes its investment mission.

The above rules will not ensure a great investment track record, but should be a brief guide to how one might make reasonable investment decisions without having to achieve the status of being a "great investor."

Investing as a Prospective Career

Some who may read this book are not yet ready to be investors, directly or indirectly. They may be students or young professionals still trying to decide on a career path.

There are an enormous number of attractive careers outside of

finance; inside finance, there are, similarly, an enormous number of attractive careers outside of investing. But for those who are interested
in considering or preparing for a career in investing, this book demon-
strates that while great investors have a number of traits in common, I
do not want to convey that having those traits is necessarily a prereq-
uisite to success as an investor. Also, one does not have to be a great
investor—a legendary performer—to enjoy the world of investing.
I have met countless investors over the years who would not be considered great but who are nonetheless quite successful and lead enormously fulfilling and gratifying lives.

And, perhaps most importantly, being at the top of any profession,
including one that is likely to yield considerable financial rewards, does
not guarantee happiness, presumably one of life's principal objectives.
Some of the wealthiest individuals I have ever met are not really happy
people. And some individuals with comparatively modest professional
and financial success are extremely pleased with their lives. So it is not
necessary to be a world-class investor to have a world-class life.

And it should be remembered as well that those who are in fact
interested in considering a career in investing, there is no ten-step plan
for guaranteed success. I wish that I had understood that reality when
I joined the investment world in 1987. I could have avoided many mistakes. But there are some strong principles that I have since recognized
as worth remembering, and pass them along for what they are worth.

1. Read as much as you possibly can about the investment area
   and other relevant subjects. Read more than newsletters or
   articles. Read books, for they tend to focus your attention
   better, and can have more lasting impact. You cannot read
   too much, or have too much knowledge about the world—
   and not just about the area of your investment focus.

2. Find an area that is of real interest to you—not necessarily
   one where you can possibly make the most money at the
   outset—and learn everything possible about that area. Ide-
   ally, the area will be a new, emerging one where the field of
   competitors is not yet that strong. The area has to be one
   that you ultimately, and hopefully in the near future, develop a passion to pursue. Working in that area should be

real pleasure and not just a job if you are really going to succeed.

3. Develop mentors—individuals who will help guide you through the challenges of building an expertise. Invariably, the path to success is eased with the guidance and support of mentors—individuals who are in your business or even outside it. Sage advice and helpful introductions never hurt. (In time, also pursuing the habit of mentoring the next generation can be just as rewarding and helpful to your own career.)

4. Seek one or two individuals who can partner with you as you build your expertise. Investing can be a solitary business at times, but talented investors usually have had partners to fill gaps in their own areas of expertise and knowledge. Do not assume you are an investment genius who needs no one to help you regularly.

5. Pursue a network of contacts in your general area of focus but also outside that area. A network can help you get better information when you need it, and can help provide opportunities, ideas, investors, colleagues, and exposure to a broader world. The best investors have a large and varied network of contacts at their fingertips.

6. Be prepared when you have—in person or virtually—meetings with colleagues, partners, and indeed everyone. Winging it might sound amusing or refreshing at times, but the truth is that the best investors—and professionals—are prepared for the many meetings and conversations they inevitably and regularly hold. They know what they want out of a meeting, and invariably get it.

7. Follow up on commitments and promises. A regular habit of doing this will enhance your reputation, but also make it more likely that your investors, colleagues, and mentors will want to work with you more closely. Failing to follow up, as promised, is one of the more common sins in the professional world, including the investing world.

8. Focus on developing a reputation for humility, cooperation, and ethical behavior. Arrogance is easy to achieve with professional success, and that may be particularly true in the

investment world. But a reputation for being willing to listen to others, accept advice, not brag, and help others will go a long way toward building a successful and admirable career. And do not be tempted to cross ethical lines—your reputation is the most important thing you carry around with you, and it can be destroyed forever by crossing ethical boundaries.

9. Learn how to admit a mistake and to correct it as soon as possible, with the least damage possible. Investors will always make mistakes, but the key for really good investors is learning when to admit them, cut losses, and go on to the next opportunity. And accept the blame, rather than regularly blame others (especially colleagues).

10. Find areas outside of investing that can enable you to broaden your scope as a human, and experience things other than the pursuit of money and professional success. Working around the clock just on investing is honestly not a prescription for success on a long-term basis in the investing world.

Perhaps all of the above is obvious. But sometimes the obvious may be overlooked. I often wish that I had taken all of these steps when I was preparing for and starting my investment career. I would have avoided a great many mistakes.

Again, undertaking all of the above steps for a young investor or prospective investor will not ensure success, but these steps will generally not get you in trouble or hurt your career. They will almost certainly help.

A final note. You will find a career in investing much more rewarding if you believe that this kind of activity is beneficial not only to you but also beneficial to your society, your economy, and your country. If you see investing only as a way to make more money than is possible in another profession, you will never have the intensity and drive and joy needed to be successful in this line of work. And you will miss much of the joy of investing (and life). In the end, it is not only about the money.

PART ONE

Mainstream Investments

Perhaps the most common investment historically has been cash—just holding the money one owns, satisfied that inflation will not eat away its value and that it is readily accessible to the owner.

Of course, as individuals decided that holding cash (stuffed under the proverbial mattress) may not always be the safest decision, banks arose to hold one's cash, at times paying modest interest rates as the inducement to provide that cash to the bank (or equivalent institution, like a savings-and-loan organization or credit union).

Today, holding cash in a bank or equivalent organization is still an investment decision, and there is competition for sure among institutions to gain individuals' cash to manage.

There are, of course, individuals who are skilled at getting the maximum return for their cash, and in doing so in ways where—in the United States—the federal government guarantees the principal up to certain levels. I did not include such individuals in this book, and decided to focus on individuals who are able to achieve extraordinary returns compared to the average investors. Such disparities in returns do not usually occur in just managing one's cash.

So I have focused this section on those who invest in three other kinds of traditional investments—fixed income, public equities, and real estate—as well as those who have traditionally invested in these areas (like endowments or family offices).

When Americans in the 1700s first began to seek returns better than those offered by cash, they invested in fixed-income instruments like government and corporate bonds. These investments were designed to provide the investor with an attractive and predictable annual income, with the principal being repaid in time.

This kind of investment was thought not to be unduly risky. Government bonds were thought to be little to no risk, though governments did default from time to time, or high inflation could reduce the effective value of the principal investment when its repayment was due.

A somewhat riskier investment was thought then to be stock, or part of the equity, in a company (private or public). There was no guarantee of a repayment of principal, but the ultimate return to the investor was thought to be higher (albeit less assured than that of a bond). Bonds and stocks (along with some cash) were generally considered the backbone of an investment portfolio for most of the time others entrusted professionals to manage their money. (For many years, a common standard for investors was 60-40—60 percent in equities and 40 percent in fixed income.)

Real estate was often the third part of the triad of investments that could well be called traditional. For most individuals throughout history, real estate (typically a home) was their most valuable asset. By the late eighteenth century, American investors began to purchase or invest in real estate not needed for their own living or basic business purposes. Real estate, like bonds, was widely considered a reasonably safe investment if not purchased (or invested in) with unsafe amounts of debt.

In recent decades, as real estate opportunities have become more complicated and varied, and the returns much more attractive than traditional, basic real estate, some investors have come to regard much of real estate to be more "alternative" than "traditional." For the purpose of this book, since the vast bulk of real estate investing is not what is called "opportunistic" or "value added," I have included real estate in the "traditional" category.

These three pillars of traditional investing—bonds, stocks, and real estate—were the areas that wealth managers typically pursued for their clients. The same was true for other large pools of capital, like university endowments or pension funds.

Fixed Income

LARRY FINK

Chairman and CEO, BlackRock

> *"If you focus on the needs of your clients, and if you can create something that is better than what the ecosystem provides, you have a huge opportunity to grow dramatically."*

In many ways, the most important and influential investor in the world in recent years has been Larry Fink, who co-founded and still leads BlackRock, initially a fixed-income investor but now the world's largest asset manager. The company manages $9.6 trillion* of its clients' assets, investing on their behalf in every major asset category—fixed income (i.e., debt of one kind or another, such as a bond), public equities or stocks, ETFs (exchange-traded funds), private equity, and real estate, among other areas. Looked at differently, BlackRock isn't just the world's largest investment firm, it's also among the most important.

But Larry's influence is due not only to the size of the company he helped build from scratch in 1988. His influence stems as much from his thorough, indeed encyclopedic knowledge of where assets are moving around the world and what investors are doing with their money.

In recent decades, Larry has also become a trusted advisor—at times formally and at other times informally—to a great many heads of state, central bankers, and finance ministers. Indeed, he is so conversant in this world, and so respected, that it has been discussed in the financial

---

* As of March 31, 2022.

world that he should at some point become secretary of the Treasury or chairman of the Federal Reserve Board.

Such a result might not have been predicted for Larry when he was growing up in a middle-class household in Los Angeles, or when he became a bond trader at First Boston after business school at the University of California, Los Angeles, where he focused on real estate. Or even when he became First Boston's youngest managing director and youngest member of its management committee. There are many Wall Street wunderkind who do not go on to build a company like BlackRock.

I know I did not think great things would happen to BlackRock or Larry when I read that the firm had raised its first bond fund in 1988. I would not have actually paid that much attention to another new firm raising a bond fund, but one of my colleagues from the White House, Ralph Schlosstein, was a co-founder, and I remember thinking how ironic it was that the young Carter White House aides—like me—who knew so little about the arcane world of finance in our government days were now involved in Wall Street. That said, I thought—undoubtedly like many on Wall Street—that this would be just another bond firm seeking its place in the sun. I did not think it would in time actually become the sun.

I have interviewed Larry on many occasions, and have served with him for many years on the board of the Council on Foreign Relations, where I regularly see how the most prominent names in finance and foreign policy listen carefully to whatever he says on any subject. I interviewed Larry virtually on June 30, 2021.

DAVID M. RUBENSTEIN (DR): The firm you started in 1988 and still run is the largest manager of investment assets in the world, and thus also the largest investor in the world, with $9.6 trillion currently and growing. In your wildest dreams, when you started the firm after leaving First Boston, did you think this result was possible? Was it even conceivable?

LARRY FINK (LF): When I started the firm, I didn't know what $9 trillion meant. I didn't know what $100 billion meant. The idea was to do something that was unique, emphasizing risk management [i.e., assessing the possible downside risks and preparing actions to minimize if not avoid completely those risks]. That practice had not always been followed by Wall Street firms eager to close a deal or make an investment. Eight friends came together and worked together, but the objective was to build a good firm. I was a builder at First Boston, and I am a builder here. The objective was to build a firm to be proud of, to get rid of the politics of a big firm and focus on the needs of clients, and the results would be the results.

One thing that differentiated us from so many financial services firms is that there was not one person among the founders who had any financial ambitions. I don't think there was anybody who believed that the path of BlackRock was to be wealthy. Wealth is an outcome of success, but there was not one person among us who was motivated principally by material possessions and achieving great wealth. It was about building something that we would be proud of.

DR: You grew up in Los Angeles in a middle-class family that was not involved in the financial or investment business. After getting undergraduate and graduate degrees from UCLA, you headed to New York and First Boston. What prompted you to do that? What did your family think about your moving across the country?

LF: I was always planning to go into real estate in Los Angeles. I happened to meet a number of partners from Goldman Sachs in my last year of school and I became intrigued with Wall Street. I began a process of interviewing, and I was offered a job from First Boston in trading. At that moment, I had no idea what trading was. But it just felt right, more than anything else. When I was interviewing in New York, that was the first time I was ever in New York City. That was the first time I ever saw snow fall, and it just felt right. My parents were very enthusiastic. When I told my father that my starting salary was $20,000, he said, "You don't deserve that much. You're still a punk." That's how I remember my father.

DR: What was your specialty at First Boston? When you are trading bonds, do you consider that investing in some way, or just finding a buyer and a seller?

LF: My first job was in mortgage-backed securities through my background in real estate finance. Wall Street is not about investing. Wall Street is about velocity of money. That's one of the corrupting things about Wall Street because it's not about the long term, it's about just facilitating the trade.

My first day on a trading desk in mortgage-backed securities was about education, because no one knew about these kinds of securities. Fannie Mae and Freddie Mac were not issuing mortgage-backed securities until 1981, '82, and '83. The foundation of my career was about educating clients about this new class of assets, and as that asset class grew, we were able to expand. The foundation of my growth at First Boston became the foundation of our growth at BlackRock.

DR: You helped invent the business of securitizing mortgages and other assets not previously available to be sold to investors. Was that the innovation that changed Wall Street in many ways? Did it get carried away and lead to the securitization of assets at inflated prices?*

LF: Generally, good things turn into bad things. That's what markets do.

This story is not being told as much as it should be. In the late '70s, the spread [or difference in interest rates] between mortgages at the consumer level and the 10-year US Treasury bond was about 450 basis points, or four and a half percent. Through securitization, we brought down that spread to about 150 basis points, or one and a half percent. When you think about the savings of America and the mechanism for home ownership, securitization was a foundational reason why more Americans were able to buy homes.†

Changes to government-influenced underwriting characteristics, which first occurred in 2004, focused on having more people have home ownership and on reducing down payments. The result was that individuals with lower-quality credit would be able to get mortgages that

---

* Securitization began in the United States in the 1850s, but it ended with the Panic of 1857 (when many mortgages associated with railroad financings collapsed). Securitization was revived in the early 1970s when government-affiliated entities started packaging home mortgages into securities that provided predictable interest rates and repayment of principal dates.

† A basis point is a measurement frequently used in financial markets, most commonly when measuring interest rates. One hundred basis points is equivalent to 1 percent; 25 basis points would be 0.25 percent.

previously would not have been available to them. These were typically called "subprime mortgages." That led to the financial crisis. The structure of mortgage-backed securities remained strong and good and helpful for society. All good things, if not properly governed, can lead to bad outcomes. That's what really happened. But if you add up, even with the financial crisis, the savings for Americans in terms of enjoying a single-family mortgage spread roughly 150 basis points over the 10-year Treasury bond rate, that's an amazing accomplishment of securitization.*

DR: You were a superstar at First Boston. Why did you decide to leave and start a new firm called BlackRock? Did your colleagues on Wall Street wonder what you were doing when you left?

LF: I became the youngest member of the executive committee when I was 31 years old, and at 34 I became an outcast at First Boston because of a large loss my group experienced. This is one of the foundational reasons I left. We did not have risk management at First Boston. I blame it on me more than I blame it on the firm. We were trading big books of assets. We were the most profitable division in the firm for multiple years, until we weren't. One quarter our group lost $100 million, and I was blamed for the loss. I never forgave the firm for a lack of partnership. In a brief moment, this whole concept of partnership and friendship turned out to be false.

That was in 1986. It took a year and a half for me to determine what I wanted to do. A year and a half later, I left to start BlackRock in partnership with Blackstone.

DR: What were your ambitions when you started BlackRock? Why did you do so with a $5 million line of credit from Blackstone in return for about 40 percent of your company? Did you ever use the line of credit, and what was your initial focus?

---

* The 10-year Treasury bond is the traditional benchmark for the safest fixed-income investment, and thus the US Treasury can comfortably sell these bonds at the lowest interest rate of any fixed-income instrument. The 10-year bond is in effect a gold standard of fixed-income securitization. An interest rate of only 150 basis points, or 1.5 percent, over the 10-year Treasury rate is a very low rate for an instrument not guaranteed by the US government.

LF: That whole episode at First Boston crushed my self-confidence. I had a couple of friends who were going to fund me to start my own company. I was intrigued by Steve and Pete [co-founders Stephen A. Schwarzman and Peter G. Peterson] at Blackstone and how they talked about partnership. I became the fourth partner at the Blackstone Group. I felt like there was going to be a strong partnership and friendship that I was searching for.

They provided a $5 million line of credit for, as you said, 40 percent. I think we drew down $100,000, then we were making money and by the end of the year, we tore up that line of credit and Blackstone was able to get their 40 percent for nothing. We subsequently grew rapidly. We were very successful, even in the first six months. This is where I give Steve Schwarzman a lot of credit. He had more confidence in me than I had in myself. Our rapid growth was the genesis of our separation from Blackstone a few years later.

DR: You showed your savvy as an investor in buying along the way Merrill Lynch's asset management business and Barclays Global Investors. Were those investments helpful in growing BlackRock from a bond-investment business to a public equities and ETF business?

LF: We were essentially a bond firm [a firm that raised funds to invest in corporate and government bonds]. When we did the IPO in 1999, we had about $300 billion in assets. That was all organically growing. We were the dog of the IPOs that year. This was the dot-com era. In fact, the IPO was so unsuccessful that we had to bring down the range, and we were priced at four multiple points below the industry [i.e., asset management companies were trading at a price-to-earnings, or PE, multiple of 20x, while BlackRock was priced at 16x]. That's how badly received the IPO was.

People didn't want bond managers, and they didn't want institutional managers. We then had the dot-com crisis, and equity and mutual funds got crushed. Importantly, we did everything we said we would in terms of our growth rates. Within three years, we went from a four-multiple-point discount to a four-multiple-point premium [i.e., our PE was 22x when our competitors were at 18x] while the rest of the asset management industry did poorly as we were doing well.

Over the early 2000s, we started talking to different firms. Clients were looking for a more fulsome relationship with BlackRock. We had conversations with five or six different firms across the board, and we became close to a few different asset managers.

The first big transaction was acquiring State Street Research from MetLife in 2005, which was the foundation of our growth pattern. It was through State Street Research that we saw we could do an acquisition. We could assimilate it. We could put State Street on our platform. Less than a year later, we did Merrill Lynch, and Merrill Lynch provided us global equities and an international footprint, which BlackRock did not have. It was not only an accretive acquisition at our purchase price; it gave us the foundation of international growth and of becoming an equity manager.

Then we had the financial crisis. At that time there was a view that index or passive investing is a different culture than active investing. I always wondered, "Why is it different?" If your clients are using all these different types of products, whether index or passive or active strategies, why can't we have a holistic conversation with them? Every transaction was motivated by "Can we expand our footprint? Can we provide a more complete array of investment choices to our clients?"

When Barclays put its flagship iShares ETF unit up for sale in 2009, we negotiated to not only buy iShares but the entire asset management business, Barclays Global Investors (BGI). Although we paid a big premium for it, it was still an accretive addition to our PE. One of the most important differences between our acquisitions and what others had been doing is that a year after we acquired Merrill Lynch and a year after we acquired BGI, we had 1,000 more employees.

In both cases, we did these acquisitions for growth and product, not for expense reduction. It was all about building our footprint and our platform globally.

That is the biggest differentiator. Even today, with all the acquisitions being done in the asset management business, most of them are just consolidation plays. Our acquisitions were based on growth and building deeper relationships with our clients.

We had tremendous conviction in our acquisition of BGI, including iShares, and that's been justified. In 2009, iShares had $340 billion in client assets. As we speak, we're close to $3.1 trillion.

DR: Other than the acquisitions, is there something that was your secret sauce? Was it the unique or non–Wall Street culture of your organization—the way your employees relate to each other and to your investors and shareholders—or a vision that enabled you to become the biggest asset manager in the world?

LF: Culture is what binds an organization. Culture is what makes an organization differentiated and unique. I spend at least 30 percent of my time focused on our culture, if not more.

One of the major cultural foundations is having one technology platform. When you look at financial services, of all the mergers of banks and insurance companies, one of the outgrowths of that was a financial crisis, because many financial services firms never consolidated onto one common platform. We've always had this foundational belief that we're going to have one global platform worldwide. A big reason we were able to do these giant acquisitions is because we have this technology platform.

The other thing is that I had a view that the global capital markets were going to be the engine for economic global growth. I still have that view, despite some fears that the globalization we have experienced over the last three decades is changing.

That fundamental belief was the foundational reason we did these acquisitions. When we did the BGI transaction, everybody said we were going to be too large. At that time, we had $2.7 trillion in assets. That represented 1.6 percent of the global capital markets. Today we're $9.6 trillion, and we're about 1.9 percent of the global capital markets.

The reality is that we could not be the scale we are today if the global capital markets didn't grow. Many banks own 10 or 12 percent of deposits in any one state. Many financial service companies control 30 or 40 percent of their ecosystem. Even as large as we are, we only control assets comprising 1.9 percent of the ecosystem.

DR: By being global, do you have insights in what's going on around the world that are helpful to the investing you do?

LF: Unquestionably. By having offices and managing client assets in various parts of the world, and having deeper, broader dialogues with more clients and listening to their needs, we have unique insights, and those unique insights translate into our alpha [the investment return above the market average return for a particular type of investment over a specific time period].

DR: Has your early use of the latest technology given you an advantage? What is Aladdin, and how hard was that to develop?

LF: The foundation of Aladdin [BlackRock's proprietary software platform for risk management] was my failure at First Boston. By having our own risk-management platform, we could better understand the risk that we're taking on. Aladdin evolved not just from a risk-management platform, it became the heart of the firm. It pumps the blood throughout the whole organization. It's truly a back-, middle-, and front-office technology platform. It's much broader than risk analytics. It creates great efficiencies and a better dialogue. It enhances our culture. It came from our foundational belief that technology was going to shape who and what we are.

In the new world of work created by the pandemic, having a technology platform like Aladdin at the center of everything we do is a key differentiator. It has given us the flexibility to pivot our business model—enabling a smooth transition for our employees to work remotely, making it easier to connect with clients anywhere in the world, giving us the ability to reach every financial advisor so that we can help them in doing their business better. Having technology to create model portfolios, to democratize investing, and to create customized liabilities or indexes gives us a unique advantage. We can work with every client and try to shape their desires into portfolios.

DR: When people entrust money to you, are they mostly interested in rate of return, risk-adjusted rate of return, good tax records they can use, or just nicer hand-holding and advice? What is it investors really want when they entrust you with more than $9 trillion?

LF: Some clients are looking for total return. Some clients are looking for tax-adjusted return. Some clients are looking for safe hands. Most importantly, clients are looking for somebody they can trust and who can help them in their financial futures.

Two-thirds of the assets we manage are retirement assets. It's not about the trade. It's not about the meme stock. It's not about cryptocurrencies. It's about helping our clients on their path to retire with dignity. We persistently talk about the long term. We don't get into the debate about the tick-tock of the market and the ups and downs. We don't get involved in the stock of the moment or the IPO of the moment. Our dialogue with our clients is all about how to shape a portfolio to meet their intermediate and long-term needs.

DR: Is there a big difference between what institutional investors want and individual investors want?

LF: Years ago I would have said yes. I would say individual investors and financial literacy are growing. Institutional investors, we are all looking for relative performance versus liability. More and more, though, institutional investors are looking for long-term returns. They're also interested in absolute returns. The individual investor is more focused on absolute returns on a risk-adjusted basis. Now, through our technology, we can show them that. We can model how their portfolio is going to look in different interest rate scenarios, different economic scenarios, so they can make a judgment: can they live with that type of volatility or risk? There's a blending of desires into one common style across the world and across all investors.

DR: You have been a leader in the ESG world, even saying that companies in which you invest should have good ESG practices, which include good diversity practices and good environmental practices. Why have you been doing that? Has it helped your business, hurt your business, or had no impact?

LF: I don't think I was uniquely prescient on this. In 2019 I saw a dramatic change in the shape of our conversations with our clients. Thirty percent of all dialogue in 2019 was about sustainability and governance. It was clear to me, as somebody who's been in finance now 40-odd years, when finance recognizes a problem, we bring that problem forward. It was clear to me that this was going to be as big as mortgage-backed securities were in the '70s and '80s—that this is going to transcend like so many other trends we're accustomed to. We rebooted the entire firm in 2019, and it accelerated our growth considerably.

Today, more and more clients, accelerated by COVID, are looking at sustainability as a major foundation of how they want to shape a portfolio. This is where we're going to be going. I think sustainability will be no different than another risk-management measurement.

This is why, at BlackRock, we have been investing more than any investment management firm in the world in technology to analyze climate risk on a portfolio level, climate risk at an individual asset level, climate risk on an individual corporate level. We all have to live under the fiduciary standard rule in the United States. You need to document and justify all investments. We have been investing heavily so we could have the best analytics to understand climate risk and transition risk across all asset classes. We're doing this because we believe in it as an investment risk. More and more clients are looking for this, and it's been a real accelerant to our growth.

DR: Warren Buffett popularized the idea of having a letter to his shareholders telling everybody what he thinks. You have, with him, become probably the most prominent person who writes a letter to shareholders. How long does it take you to write that letter, and how much time and thought do you put into it?

LF: It's hundreds of hours. I generally don't put pen to paper until September, but it's a dominant component of September through January in terms of my life.

The dominant conversation in financial media is about the markets, the tick-tock of what's going on. We've lost the narrative of long-termism. We've lost the narrative of what's important to all the men and women who are trying to build to live in retirement and dignity. The first letter, in 2012, was all about long-termism. Then in 2018, I wrote about stakeholder capitalism, why that's important for long-termism. I get lots of hate mail, from both the far left and the far right. But my letters are well received by our clients, and I do believe it helps drive the success of the firm.

DR: Do you consider yourself now more of a CEO, a corporate manager, or an investor? Are you still involved in strategic investment decisions?

LF: I don't run the firm day-to-day. That's been years now in the making. I have great managers. I'm not a scale operator. That is not my strength. Strategy and culture are the two foundational things that I do well, and still do well today. I'm very good at client relationships. The big strategy—where we're going to go, what we're doing in ESG, all the acquisitions—that's what I focus on.

My hope now, in my later years at BlackRock, is that other people can take over those responsibilities for me. I spend a lot of time with the board focusing on the organization. This is the most important part of the spirituality of a leader—how to make sure the organization does well without the founder. One of the main reasons why the firm has been so successful? I know my weaknesses, and I have a lot of weaknesses. I've built a talented bench behind me.

DR: You have been an informal advisor to central banks, chief financial officers, and heads of state on finance and related investment matters. How complicated is that for you to do? When COVID came, did you have to do this by virtual means? Is that an important part of the insights you get around the world, talking to these ministers?

LF: I get my most important insights by going to one country, having 10 meetings a day, getting on an airplane after dinner, flying to another country, having 10 meetings, and speaking with our clients, regulators, policymakers, or a head of state. When you're on an airplane, when you have downtime, you try to accumulate all those conversations you had. Is there a common idea that's translating from country to country, from client to client, from policymaker to head of state? Those are the kind of insights it is only possible to get through in-person conversations or meals, and I dearly missed a lot of that during COVID. We had a lot of Zoom calls, like we're having now.

I just came back from Saudi Arabia, and the two days there were probably my most favorite days of the year, because of what I learned in those two days on Middle East politics and on energy. I'm going to be in Europe all next week. This is what gives me the juice to determine policy strategy, insights. It furthers my conversations with government leaders and clients. It's all additive. It's like a sedimentary rock—a layer here, a layer there, and soon enough you'll have some substance.

DR: People entrust you with a great deal of information. What's the trick to engendering confidence in your ability to keep this information confidential? How do you deal with all those pieces of information? Is that a hard thing to do?

LF: Not at all. It's trust that allows us to have so much share of wallet, trust that allows us to have these types of conversations with heads of states and regulators and policymakers. We have proven to be a fiduciary in every way.

We have a lot of naysayers. Our reputation, like in every company, is so important. What I try to tell everybody is we earn basis points on managing people's money. We don't have a balance sheet; we don't invest for our own benefit. All the information we have as a fiduciary is directly for our clients. I'm a beneficiary of some important conversations throughout the world, and it's about trust. You break trust once and then you don't have the trust. I want to give more than I get. When I'm asked for my opinions, it's about giving information, not getting.

DR: As the CEO of the largest investment firm in the world, you must have some well-developed thoughts about investing. Are there certain general rules or maxims you have developed or apply to BlackRock's investing activities?

LF: Yes, but I haven't been on a trading desk in years. It's all about culture more than anything else. We try to develop and grow the best investors. We built an organization around sharing of information that is public and sharing insights. I do believe that is the foundation of why we are having a lot of success, some of the best in our history, on active returns. That took a long time, because historically investors wanted to create their own silos. We didn't want anybody who would create a silo. The key to our success is that community of information.

DR: What are the most common mistakes you see investors making? They put too much in one thing, or they rely on the newspaper headlines?

LF: They may be making this mistake right now. We get accustomed to an economic environment, and we assume that kind of environment will last forever.

Right now the challenge is going to be inflation. For 30 years, we've had a deflationary environment, and that is over. We have also had a time of enormous liquidity and low interest rates. That may be over as well.

Investors should not assume that what we perceive today is going to be the same in seven years. I felt that in 2004 and 2005. It generally comes down to liquidity and leverage that creates failures. Then, obviously, we have political issues. We have environmental issues.

DR: I assume there's somebody at BlackRock who manages your money. Is that an easy job? People want the job of managing the boss's money?

LF: I'm pretty good at managing my money.

DR: You manage your own?

LF: I do, yes.

DR: Is there some new product coming out that's going to be equivalent to ETFs? They changed the investment world in many ways when they first appeared in the late 1980s and early 1990s. Do you foresee anything like that on the horizon?

LF: The reason why ETFs became transformational is because they're a better product than mutual funds. We saw that in 2007. You can manage your tax basis with ETFs. With mutual funds, you can't. ETFs have bid/ask spreads [the difference between what a buyer will pay and what a seller will accept for a particular ETF] throughout the day; mutual funds all accumulate the withdrawals and the additions at the end of the day. This is one of many reasons why an ETF is just better than a mutual fund.

We are working right now on something called "LifePath Paycheck." We believe the biggest silent crisis in the world is retirement. We've worked on a new way of refocusing defined contributions, to make something a little more like a defined-benefit plan for the participant when they retire. We believe what we're doing is going to reshape retirement, and it's going to reshape the defined-contribution business. Once again, it's focusing on the needs of a client.

Not enough people are paying attention to the retirement crisis. If you focus on the needs of your clients, and if you can create something that is better than what the ecosystem provides, you have a huge opportunity to grow dramatically.

DR: What is so exciting about a career in finance or investing? Why should a young, talented person want to go into finance or investing?

LF: It's not for everybody. If you're going to be successful in finance and investing, and if you want to have a long career, you have to be a student your entire life. You have to be reeducating yourself every day about what's going on in the ecosystem. I love markets, because they're changing. I may not look it, but I feel young. I'm challenging myself every day. That's why I said it's not right for everybody.

A lot of people don't want to continue to grow, they want to just enjoy. But for those who love the challenge of change, for those who love that the global capital markets are the engine of economic activity globally, it's a remarkable career. The joy comes from the desire of learning and reeducating and staying relevant and staying current.

When we have our young trainees who are joining the firm every summer, when I'm onstage talking to all of them, I say, "For those of you who think your education is over, BlackRock is not right for you. If you are going to have a bright career in finance and investing, you are going to have to challenge yourself every day and grow and learn. The moment you stop growing and learning, someone's passing you by."

DR: What do you think you'd be doing if you hadn't gotten into finance?

LF: That's an intangible I don't ever want to think about. I would have probably been in real estate.

DR: You'd be the biggest real estate developer in the world?

LF: I don't think so.

Public Equities

RON BARON

Founder and CEO, Baron Capital

> *"I don't regard investing as gambling. I regard it as trying to take care of you and your family for the long term."*

I n recent years, many individuals and institutions interested in participating in the rising value of public stocks have gravitated away from
traditional equity mutual funds and moved toward market index funds
and exchange-traded funds (ETFs). These are funds that simply track
market performance; do not attempt to pick the best stocks or bonds;
rely heavily on computer-driven models rather than human judgment;
and can be purchased and sold through a public exchange at extremely
small fees. The view has taken hold, for many, that public markets are
very efficient and that it is generally hard to beat them on an ongoing
basis. So rather than try to do so, through the stock-picking capabilities
of an equity mutual fund, a great many investors now believe it is a bit
safer, and far less expensive, to capture the market's rise for one's portfolio by purchasing market index funds or ETFs.

However, despite this view, there are some stock mutual funds
(which cannot be readily traded throughout the day) that have consistently been able to beat market averages, and such funds have thrived
despite the appearance of ETFs and other very low-fee index funds.
One such family of funds is led by Ron Baron, whose Baron Capital has,
since its founding in 1982, seen its funds outperform their indexes by on
average about 500 basis points annually. The result is that Baron Capital
manages more than $50 billion, with a dedicated following among its

investors, more than a few of whom have been investing with the organization almost from its inception.

How does Ron Baron, trained as a lawyer and stock analyst, manage to create such attractive returns (and a loyal following)? His technique is patterned after Warren Buffett's—find businesses with strong franchises and solid management (preferably with a meaningful ownership stake in the stock), buy their stock, and then hold it more or less forever, thereby avoiding transaction costs and tax impacts. Ron and his firm's analysts like to focus on long-term trends in technology, consumer preferences, and demographics. He is most definitely not a short-term market trader.

Of course, his technique is a bit more complicated, or everyone would be doing what he does. He does an extraordinary amount of research on the companies in which he invests, and he tends to support them through thick and thin, selling infrequently, typically just when, due to the stock's appreciation, future returns will likely be "average," or when there has been a major unanticipated problem at the company.

This approach recently worked quite well for Ron when he decided to follow one entrepreneur, Elon Musk, and became an early and large investor in Tesla. He has also been a large investor in SpaceX, though that company is not yet public; but this investment is part of Baron mutual funds' private equity portfolio that Ron offers his investors as well.

I first met Ron when Carlyle was going public in 2012, and I saw him on our road show. I was surprised the head of the organization was doing the detailed due diligence; he took copious notes and asked quite well-informed questions. He bought the stock and became a large shareholder. The stock did not increase in price on a sustained basis for a good many years (though the dividends were attractive). But Ron held on, and when Carlyle's share price, including dividends, increased more than 16 percent per year from the IPO to the time of this interview, Baron's investors were the happy beneficiaries.

Ron treats his firm's investors well in another way. At his annual meeting, held at Manhattan's Metropolitan Opera House in Lincoln Center, he personally pays to have superstar entertainers perform for his investors. It is rare that a mutual fund offers annual meetings with performances by Barbra Streisand, Bette Midler, Paul McCartney, Billy Joel, or Elton John. Baron Capital does.

But it is Ron's returns for investors that keep them so loyal, and satisfied. I interviewed Ron at his home in East Hampton, New York, for the *Bloomberg Wealth* show on August 26, 2021.

DAVID M. RUBENSTEIN (DR): You were a big believer in Tesla and in SpaceX before everybody else went along. What did you see in Tesla early on? And what do you see in SpaceX now?

RON BARON (RB): In Tesla, early on I thought the opportunity was to convert the cars that we make in the United States and the world from gasoline to electric. I was betting on Elon Musk. Most people bet against him. In order for Tesla to be successful, Musk had to be a spectacular engineer, a great leader, and had to have an unmatched understanding of technology. Then he had to fight entrenched interests, the car dealers and the automobile companies and the oil companies, the energy businesses. To be successful against those odds, you can understand why people would sell it short. We invested $380 million between 2014 and 2016, after thinking that we shouldn't invest in it, which was 1.5 percent of our assets at the time. We've made $6 billion in profit so far, and I think we're going to make another triple, maybe four times over the next 10 years.

DR: What about SpaceX?

RB: It's the same idea. You're disrupting an industry that relies on cost-plus contracts with guaranteed profits. The space industry didn't want to innovate. They had a business that was producing rockets, and they felt if they used rockets over and over again, there wouldn't be strong demand for new rockets.

As a result, there was no innovation. They would subcontract out the work they did on these rockets with the result being that they would become more and more and more expensive, and the government would just pay for it. Then they exercised monopoly power. Lockheed and Martin formed ULA, United Launch Alliance. When they did that, the price Lockheed and Martin told the government would fall actually went up.

Elon comes along and he says, "I've got a cheap way to get to space, and the cheap way is by using the rockets over and over and over again." Everyone else said that was impossible. As a result, no one else tried to accomplish that remarkable feat.

But Musk did. He's now able to get to space cheaply. And now, due to inexpensive launch, there's an opportunity for a trillion dollars of revenues from satellite communication broadband to your home. Half the people in the world don't have broadband. This will be a real big cash-flowing business. He's got about 2,000 satellites now, cheap satellites, and will ultimately have a 30,000-satellite constellation. When you can use the rocket over and over again, launch is inexpensive. That gives you a chance to put up a lot of satellites and serve a need for humanity.

DR: And do you have a Tesla?

RB: Yes, three of them. Four of them.

DR: And when you drive them and you say, "Maybe something could be better," do you call up Elon and say, "Can you fix this?"

RB: Actually, we do. When we bought the first one, my wife complained about the makeup mirror on the sun shade. "There's no makeup mirror here." I said, "How can there not be a makeup mirror?" We had just been to visit their engineering plant with the individual who designs the cars. I called him and said, "My wife is complaining there's no makeup mirror." He says, "Yeah, we've had to do a special edition Tesla" where they put in that extra mirror. That was my wife's idea.

DR: Let's talk about how you got started in the business. Did you grow up in New York?

RB: New Jersey. Asbury Park.

DR: And did you say, "I want to be in the investment business" when you were growing up? Or did you want to be a professional baseball player like many young boys?

RB: My parents wanted me to be a doctor.

DR: And what did you say to your parents?

RB: One summer I worked as a lifeguard in the daytime, nine to five, and then eleven to seven I worked in the emergency room of a local hospital. People would come in and they'd have been shot or stabbed. And I'm a skinny kid. I had to hold them on a gurney until the next of kin gave permission to operate. Patients died while I was holding them.

That was one job. Job number two was they would bring in drunks who would mess up bedpans. I had to clean the bedpans. And job number three, when people expired I had to wrap them and put them into refrigerators. So that was my experience. I hated it.

DR: So you decided not to go to medical school.

RB: Right. I didn't get into medical school. And then I said, "I didn't really want to do that anyway."

DR: So where did you go to school?

RB: I went to Bucknell University. Undergraduate chemistry major. Then I had a fellowship at Georgetown in biochemistry for a year, because I didn't want to go to Vietnam. I was a waiter, a bartender. I was making $1,600 a year in a fellowship and living in a basement in Rock Creek Park.

Then that summer I was selling Fuller Brushes door-to-door to make extra money. I knock on a door and a guy answers the door. Changed my life. He answers the door, and he's wearing real clothes. He has a suit, slacks, and a shirt. He has his wife cooking dinner for him in the kitchen, and windows with a view. I said, "What do you do? How come you're not in Vietnam?" And he says, "I'm a patent examiner. It's a draft-exempt job. My salary is $11,000 per year!" I said, "How do you get to be a patent examiner?" He says, "You take the law boards, and if you get a good grade, you apply to the United States Patent Office, and you can get a job there. It's a draft deferment because it's a critical skill."

I'm a chemistry major, so I take the law boards. Got a good grade. Got into George Washington Law School. Went to law school at night and worked in the Patent Office in the daytime. So this guy changed my life.

DR: How did you go from George Washington Law School and being a patent examiner, to the investment business?

RB: After my bar mitzvah, I was interested in the stock market because I had friends who had been given stock, from their grandparents who were successful, in Eastman Kodak and Polaroid. Polaroid was a $250 stock, and Eastman Kodak was $40 or $50, the bluest of blue chips. And that was for their college. And I said, "I want to do that." My father said,

"We can't invest in stocks. We've never done that." In fact one of the ideas behind my business is that I wanted to be able to have people like my parents be able to invest in the stock market.

I had $1,000 at the time. And he said, "If you show me why you want to invest in a company, I'll open an account for you." I would go to this brokerage firm called McDonald & Company, right by Asbury Park High School. I would go there after school, and all these guys, old guys 40 or 50 years old, they would be sitting there on these green chairs and looking at a tape that hardly moved. I think the New York Stock Exchange was 25 million shares a day and the American Stock Exchange was a million or two million shares a day. I got a report on Monmouth County National Bank. It was around the corner from where I lived in Allenhurst, outside of Asbury Park. I told my father why I wanted to invest in it, and he let me invest. And the stock was $10 a share, 100 shares. Every day for the next six months, seven months, every day the stock either stayed the same or went up an eighth. Then it was acquired at $17 a share. So my thousand dollars became $1,700. I said, "Man, there's nothing to this. I want to do this."

DR: What year did you start your company?

RB: Nineteen-eighty-two. I came to New York in 1969. I'm in debt. I'm living in my friend's basement in New Jersey, unemployed for three or four months. I thought I was never going to be able to get a job. I was thinking about opening up a bicycle shop outside Central Park.

I told my dad, "I'm never getting a job with all these people unemployed who are analysts and have all been fired." My father said, "You've always wanted to do this. You can't stop. You have to try." Ultimately I got a job as an analyst.

DR: At a brokerage company?

RB: Janney Montgomery Scott. I worked for a man named Tony Tabell in Princeton, New Jersey. He would choose stocks for me, and I'd go visit those companies every week and write a letter that went to their salesmen. They had 250 brokers. I was the entire research department.

DR: How many years did you do that?

RB: One.

DR: And then you said, "I'm going to set up my own company"?

RB: No. Then I was fired!

DR: You got fired? Why did you get fired?

RB: Because Tony was picking stocks, and then I had this idea about General Development, a Florida land developer. I thought that, due to inflation, they hadn't provided enough to develop their properties. I wrote a report expressing that opinion and it was published in the *Wall Street Transcript*. General Development stock was 32 or 33 and started falling. The chairman then called me up and said, "What are you doing? You're wrong." That afternoon, I was fired. This was even though General Development ultimately went bankrupt.

Alan Abelson was receiving my weekly letters. He was an editor of *Barron's*. I called him to see if he could recommend me for another analyst position. I don't know why I called him. But I called him, and he invited me to come visit them. He offered me a job as a reporter. He really liked how I wrote and how I thought. And I said, "Thank you very much, but I have always wanted to be an analyst." He said, "Put my name on your resume as a reference, and I will recommend you." That helped me get my next job.

Suddenly I became an institutional analyst. Then I joined a friend from law school, and we worked together from 1973 to 1982, selling research to hedge funds. We had 100 clients. We would recommend stocks to them, and they would buy them or not. My income was based on brokerage commissions. My negative net worth in 1970 increased significantly by 1980, when I became worth a million dollars. In 1982 I started Baron Capital.

DR: You started with how much capital?

RB: Baron Capital was really Baron lack of capital. My firm had $100,000 book value and three employees, including me. Our first month in business, we made $30,000.

DR: Today, in 2021, you're managing assets at Baron of what?

RB: Fifty-five point three billion dollars. And we made our clients over the years $51.5 billion of profits. My family and I are the largest investors. More than 6.5 percent of the assets we manage are ours.

DR: From $100,000 more or less to $55 billion under management — not bad.

RB: Now my dream is to see if in the next 10 years we can reach $200 billion.

DR: Is it a mutual fund?

RB: Yes, mostly. Of our $55 billion, I'd say maybe $48 or $49 billion are mutual funds — 17 funds, 18 funds. And the rest of it is in separate accounts.

DR: That's invested mostly in publicly traded shares?

RB: All but about $900 million.

DR: We met when my own firm, Carlyle, was going public. They said, "You need to go see Ron Baron because he buys publicly traded shares when they go public." So I met with you, and I was surprised that you had a pen and you were taking detailed notes. I said, "He's the head of the company. Doesn't he have somebody else doing this?" But you were taking notes. And I assume you wrote them up and then you assessed it. You gave us very detailed questions. Do you do that with all the people going public that you think might be interesting?

RB: Yes. Everyone whom I think is interesting. That's what I do, except I don't use the pen and pencil anymore. Now I use the computer. The 40 analysts I work with do the same thing.

DR: When you do this, what are you looking for? You are known for having a long-term hold position. You told me this when we were getting ready to go public — that if you bought our stock, which you did, you'd hold on for a long time, which you have. What is your theory about holding on for a long time? Why not just sell and take a profit?

RB: First of all, you promised me I was going to make money. That was a promise. You said, "Buy my stock. Wall Street does not understand the value of this business." The stock was $22 at the time when you went public. And now it's $49. And if you compound it, including the dividends, we would have made 16.1 percent investing with you from the time you went public. Why didn't we buy and sell?

Because if you buy and sell, you pay taxes every time you do that, number one. Number two, what makes me think I'm so smart that I'm going to be able to figure out the exact top and the exact bottom, buy here, sell there? That didn't make sense. Plus I didn't have any confidence that anyone was going to be able to predict what the stock market was going to do. I lost confidence in market predictions from watching Alan Greenspan describe "irrational exuberance" in 1996 that caused the market to be "too high." The market then went up 80 percent the next three years.

DR: For any SEC [Securities and Exchange Commission] commissioner who's reading, I didn't promise the stock would go up. I said I was hopeful that it would go up, or whatever I legally was able to say, just for the record.

RB: You were definitely within the framework of what's legal.

DR: Good. To be very serious about it, when you have that much money, $55 billion under management, you've got a lot of responsibility. Every night, do you worry that the stock market is going to go down and your assets will go down? Do people call you to complain? Or they basically say, "I'm happy"?

RB: They mostly say they're happy. My picture's in our quarterly letter. I get stopped on the street almost every day. People come over to me and say, "Thank you." Last night we were at a dinner in a restaurant. As we were walking out, a man walked over to me and said, "Thank you very much. You paid for my daughter to go to college." I get that all the time. It's the most unbelievable thing. That's my job.

DR: The publicly traded stock market, over the last hundred years, probably has returned 6 percent or so a year, more or less. If somebody invests in one of your funds, which are publicly traded stocks, they're presumably going to do better than 6 or 7 percent?

RB: If they didn't, they wouldn't invest with us.

DR: So what do you think about index funds? Some people say, "Just buy an index fund." Presumably, people are buying your funds because you're going to do better than the indexes?

RB: Yes.

DR: How do you try to outperform an index by 200 basis points or 300 basis points?

RB: We've outperformed indexes by about 500 basis points annually since inception. We've earned annual returns in the low teens, mid-teens. Baron Partners Fund, for example, has a better performance record than any mutual fund since 1992 of the 2,200 or 2,300 funds that we compare against. This is though it was a partnership from 1992 to 2003 when it charged higher fees. Since it converted from a partnership to a mutual fund in 2003, it is the number one-performing mutual fund. Baron Growth Fund is in the top 2 percent of funds since 1996.

It's very rare that mutual funds outperform their index. The index is the passive benchmark, and so it's very rare that outperformance happens. That's because everyone thinks they know better and that they can predict when the market's going to go up or down because they know what interest rates are going to do.

They know whether we're going to go to war. They know who the president's going to be. They know what monetary policy is going to be. And because they know things and they're so bright, they believe that they can do better than the market. They don't, though, because they buy and sell and they don't have any information that's any different than everyone else's.

But it's rare that they're going to be able to take advantage of any information sufficiently to be able to do better than the market. Hardly anyone outperforms.

DR: Suppose somebody comes into your office. They're going to go public. They want to meet you because you're known to be a long-term investor. What do you look for when you're looking at a CEO who's coming in to pitch you on his or her IPO?

RB: I want someone who's really smart, works really hard, has integrity. I trust them. They have a vision for their business. They're good leaders.

DR: Let's suppose somebody has these qualities and you like them. But you buy their stock and it performs really poorly. Do you ever give up and just say, "I've got to get out of this stock"?

RB: In general, I give up because we made a mistake on the business or the person, not because a stock doesn't perform. The stock performance isn't a measure of whether the business is successful or not. The stock performance is just the measure of the stock performance during a discrete period.

The way I think about it, the reason we've outperformed is we have the same kind of outlook and the same way of looking at businesses that you do. Why does private equity outperform? Because what they do is take the profitability of a business and invest in that business so it can become larger.

DR: A CEO comes in and makes a presentation and he or she impresses you. What are the qualities you're really looking for?

RB: The businesses in which we're investing we think are competitively advantaged. There's something about those businesses that makes it very difficult for someone else to compete against them, like I was describing to you before about Tesla and SpaceX.

So at its heart, it's competitively advantaged, has great people, and there's big growth opportunities. That's what makes us invest. When we make a mistake, we sell. As fast as we can, we sell. And making a mistake does not mean that the stock isn't performing. It means that we've been mistaken about the people or about the business. The stock price reflects what people think about it at that point in time. It doesn't reflect what the value of that business is at that point in time.

DR: But generally when you buy a stock you intend to hold on to it. If you are not happy, do you hold on for a year? Or two years? Three years? What is the average time it takes for you to say, "I made a mistake and I want to get out"?

RB: It's not the time. It's the fundamentals of the business. I could own a stock for a number of years and not make a return on it, and that wouldn't bother me as far as making me think I had made a mistake. We were an investor in Tesla for four or five or six years and didn't make a return. Then, all of a sudden, we made twenty times our investment in a year. So it's not the time that does it. It's the fundamentals.

DR: Your investors are individuals more than institutions?

RB: Half and half.

DR: You're famous for your annual shareholders meeting in New York.

RB: People call it my annual bar mitzvah.

DR: You've had very famous people there. They're great entertainers.

RB: Paul McCartney, Barbra Streisand, Billy Joel, Elton John, Jerry Seinfeld. I pay for that. Investors, if they have at least $25,000 invested in Baron funds, they can come to that meeting.

DR: Is it easier to negotiate with a CEO or Paul McCartney or Barbra Streisand?

RB: You can't believe what it's like to negotiate with performers.

DR: Let's talk about what investors really want. When somebody invests with you, what they want is a return that's better than an index fund. They want low fees as much as possible, I guess. After all the years that you've been doing this, what have you learned about what investors most want and how to deal with them?

RB: Most people want to have their money grow consistently every day and make high returns and low fees without volatility. That's what they want. That's obviously not what they get from equity investments.

DR: Do you have investors stay for 10 years? Twenty years or so?

RB: I have people who stay in our funds for decades. The longer someone stays, the longer they will stay, because they look at the returns, and accountants tell them they've never seen multiyear returns like that before from stock mutual funds. Our long-term holding of stocks and our deep level of research really helps us achieve attractive returns.

We are dealing with individuals. We have financial planners. We have salesmen around the country. We sell indirectly through RIAs [registered investment advisors who are professionals representing individual investors] and through brokerage firms as well as directly to wealthy families and foundations.

DR: What's the pleasure for you of investing? What is it that you like about investing?

RB: I love what I do. When I get to meet and talk with people who run businesses and who are changing the world and explain to me how they're doing it, it is so much fun. My wife says, "All of my friends, their husbands don't work anymore. How come you work? Why are you doing this?" They all play golf or cards. I think that if anyone had a chance to do what I'm doing instead of playing golf, they would choose to do what I'm doing.

But it takes a lot of building to get to this point. You don't just say, "Okay, I'm going to do that." Their job was to make enough money so they could retire and live comfortably. My job is different. I'm trying to build an institution that's going to last for a hundred years.

DR: If somebody wants to invest with you, how much do they have to invest to be in one of your funds?

RB: The normal minimum is $2,000. But you can invest for as little as $500 and $50 a month. No fees to buy or sell. But if you sell within three months of purchase, then we regard you as a trader, and you're not going to be allowed to buy with us anymore.

DR: It sounds like T-R-A-I-T-O-R.

RB: I think of it that way.

DR: You're content to do this for as long as you can do it? You're not slowing down. You're not going to go play golf full-time?

RB: As long as I'm healthy.

DR: Did your parents live to see your success?

RB: My dad lived to 95 and my mom lived to 93. My dad gave me $5,000, when I started, to invest for him, and it became several million dollars.

DR: When your father invested with you, did you give him a discount on the fees?

RB: No. It's the same fees for everyone, including me.

DR: Right now, many people think the stock market's pretty high. Fully valued, many people would say. Are you nervous about that? You're not in the shorting business, which is to say taking protections against the market going down. How do you protect investors against a downturn, and do you worry about a downturn?

RB: I don't worry about that. December 1999 through 2008 were a really difficult eight or nine years for the stock market. The stock market was down 30 or 40 percent, 3 or 4 percent a year for eight or nine years. We didn't make a lot of money in that period of time, but we didn't lose. We were up 25 percent over that eight- or nine-year period of time, which was really terrible for the market. Since then, of course, we've done really well. My big picture of the world, the only things I am certain about are I'm sure our economy will grow; I'm sure our country will survive; and I'm sure inflation will persist.

I think that the value of my money will fall by half every 14 or 15 years. Everything I want to buy is going to double in price every 14 or 15 years. I regard stocks as a hedge against depreciation of my currency. I want to own stocks, shares of businesses that can outpace inflation.

No one can predict what the market's going to do. No one can tell you when it's too high or too low. I'm just taking what's coming at us. When the market falls, for example, like right now, there's been a rotation out of the kind of companies we've invested in that have done so well for the past couple of years into cheaper "value" stocks. We didn't change how we invest when this occurs. We just try to keep moving forward.

DR: What do you think about cryptocurrencies?

RB: That's a commodity. We don't invest in commodities. We don't own gold. We don't own cryptocurrency.

I always worry if you have cryptocurrencies and they get to be real valuable, why is the government going to allow private enterprises to have control of their currency and their economy? In 1932 or '33, people were afraid of leaving their money in the banks. They took their money out of the banks and bought gold. Then President Franklin D. Roosevelt made it illegal to own gold. You had to turn in all your gold. Why do I think that that same thing couldn't happen with crypto? That government could ban ownership, which could occur even if blockchain does not give up secrets—most citizens will not want to break the law. I'm not saying it will, but I think there's some risk it could.

DR: Have you had role models as great investors over the years?

RB: Everyone has Buffett as a role model, but he's not as growth-oriented as I am. But I like reading his letters.

DR: He writes his letters. You write your letters as well?

RB: Yes.

DR: If you are talking to students at a university who want to be professional investors, what would you tell them are the most important things to do to prepare? Be well-read? Be smart? Hardworking? What are the most important skills?

RB: All those things. Three or four years ago, at Rosh Hashanah, the rabbi gave a sermon that touched me. He said, "Would your younger self be proud of you for what you've accomplished in your life? Would your younger self be proud of you for what you've done?" That's a good guidepost. Looking back at everything you've done, would you be proud of your younger self at some future point?

What students should be doing is they should only do things that they feel would make their family proud of them.

DR: For students who say, "I want to be the next Ron Baron if not Warren Buffett," what do you recommend that they do to prepare to be a good investor?

RB: First of all, they should study the businesses in which they're investing or in which they want to invest and why they're going to invest in them; and they should understand that with the economy, there will be changes. Change is what's happening everywhere. All the growth in the world has taken place in the last 200 years. And that growth is now accelerating. You have to understand what's happening in the world around you, what's happening in our country. Not that you're going to make decisions on a short-term basis. But I tell the young people who work with me what they should be thinking about is this: if the well-being of their families was dependent upon their being right on the business in which we're investing on their recommendation, what would they need to know to be able to make that recommendation?

If everything you have is dependent on your being right about that business and its executives, that doesn't mean you have to be right all the time. But for the well-being of your family, what do you have to know? That's the question that you need to ask. Not about the next quarter.

DR: What is the best investment advice you've ever been given by anybody?

RB: I learn from watching people as opposed to someone saying, "Do this. Do this. Do this." I'm just always trying to learn. How does something work? What's good or bad about it? And what makes what you're doing different than anyone else?

No one's ever said, "You should do this and that will make it better." One person, when I came to New York, told me something I thought was very interesting. He said, "Don't worry about earnings per share. They make up those numbers. Worry about sales." That made sense to me. The only way you're going to get fooled by that is if it's a fraud. It's just little things that you pick up all the time.

DR: What is the most common investment mistake people make?

RB: They think that because they can open up an account at a brokerage firm, they can buy and sell stocks and do as well as anyone else. Just like I wouldn't want to fly an airplane or be a dentist or even cut my hair—what I have left of it. People have an understanding that they can buy and sell stocks successfully just because they can pick up a phone and do it, and they can't.

DR: If I said, "Ron, I have $100,000. I'd like to invest it somewhere," where would I put that $100,000, on your recommendation?

RB: Baron WealthBuilder. That's a fund of Baron Capital with only five basis points of expense.

DR: And if you were to advise somebody today about opportunities to invest, you would say public equities are good places to invest?

RB: For the long term. But just invest the same amount every year. Don't think about it as "This is an investment I'm going to make." You should think, "For the security of my family and myself, I should invest. I should figure out how much I'm going to invest, and do it every single year."

DR: Is there something you would tell somebody not to invest in? It sounds like crypto is one of them.

RB: I'm not investing in crypto. But that doesn't mean it's not a good idea. There are really smart people who have big investments in crypto. I study it periodically and I choose not to because it's a commodity. I'm not interested in investing in commodities. I'm interested in investing in businesses that grow. Businesses that grow, with great people, competitively advantaged and for the long term.

I don't regard investing as gambling. I regard it as trying to take care of you and your family for the long term. And you do it by investing similar amounts every year for a long time and living to be old. And then you get to be rich.

DR: What are you most proud of that you have done with your life?

RB: I'm really proud of what we've accomplished. My business, of course. And my children. We all live together, and I'm proud that they want to live here in our weekend home in Long Island. And I'm especially proud of how hard they work. I'm proud of the values my family has.

JOHN W.
ROGERS JR.

Founder and co-CEO, Ariel Investments

> *"You have to have the courage to go in there and buy when everyone's sitting on their hands or selling."*

S hortly after graduating from Princeton University (where he cap-
tained the basketball team), John Rogers had an audacious idea—
with only two years of work in the financial services sector under his
belt, he would start an equity mutual fund in his hometown of Chicago,
and in so doing establish the first African American–owned and led
money management firm in the United States.

That was 1983. Today this firm, Ariel Investments, manages more
than $17 billion and is one of the country's largest African American–
owned and led investment management firms. It has achieved that status by relentlessly pursuing its "value" investment approach, and not
chasing the latest fad in investing or pursuing expensive ("nonvalue")
investments.

Getting to that level was not easy. Nor was raising the initial capital. But perhaps the biggest challenge was surviving the severe financial
downturn of the Great Recession, when the firm's assets under management dropped by more than half. However, under John's leadership,
and with the support of the charismatic and highly talented Mellody
Hobson (also a Princeton graduate and now Ariel's co-CEO), the firm
has prospered. And that is despite the fact that its investment approach,

value investing, has been harder to execute well in recent years, for stock prices have been so high that there are fewer and fewer "values" (low-priced stocks) to be found in the market.

For many African Americans in the investment world, John has been a role model and mentor for more than three decades. Through tough and good times, he has been a steady, low-key, and focused investor in stocks that he thinks are undervalued; he still does the detailed due diligence on stocks himself, frequently meeting with CEOs of companies of potential investments.

His love of investing began when John was a boy. His father would give him stocks for birthday and Christmas presents, and John would learn everything he could even then about the underlying companies. It would have taken something extraordinary to lure him away from investing. When his good friend and fellow basketball player Barack Obama became president, John did not think for a second about going into the government. He is an investor, and nothing gives him greater pleasure—other than perhaps visiting his favorite McDonald's almost daily. (He is a board member and perhaps its most loyal customer.)

I have known John for many years and have most recently spent a good deal of time with him on the board of trustees of the University of Chicago. His parents were graduates of the university's law school (as was I) and he went to the university's renowned Lab School before going to college. I interviewed John virtually on September 3, 2021.

DAVID M. RUBENSTEIN (DR): You have built one of the largest investment companies owned and led by an African American. You started the firm in 1983 at the age of 24. Were there many African American–owned investment firms in 1983? What made you think then that you could build a firm like Ariel?

JOHN W. ROGERS JR. (JR): We were the first African American–owned mutual fund and money management company when we started in 1983.

What gave me confidence was two things. The first was coming from a town like Chicago, where so many great African American entrepreneurs started their companies at a young age. John Johnson had started

Ebony and *Jet* magazine through Johnson Publishing. He was a fantastic role model and inspiration. Another gentleman named George Johnson, no relation, built and created Johnson Products, which sold Afro Sheen and Ultra Sheen haircare products. They were the first Black-owned company on the American Stock Exchange. He was an extraordinary success. In his free time, George Johnson started *Soul Train* with Don Cornelius and started Independence Bank, the largest Black bank in the country. Those role models made me feel confident you could start a business at a young age if you had a product that you deeply believed in.

Second, we were one of the original small-cap to mid-cap value managers when we started in 1983. We thought it was important to have a product and a strategy that wasn't being emulated by many people at that time.

DR: Had you been in the financial world long before you started your firm? Did you not think more experience would be helpful?

JR: My father thought it was important to get more experience. But I was confident in the investment strategy and philosophy. I thought we had an original approach to small- and mid-cap value investing, and so the time was right to get going. The markets were starting to come out of the economic doldrums during that period. The wind was at our backs. I really felt comfortable and confident.

The other reason I was comfortable and confident, of course, was the stocks I'd been picking in my job at the investment banking and financial services company William Blair, going out and doing my own research. Those stocks had performed very well. Those early wins made a difference.

Then, finally, my father bought stocks for me every birthday and every Christmas after I was 12. By the time I was 24, I had 12 years of experience of making a lot of mistakes before I started Ariel.

DR: Where did you learn initially the art of investing? Being a young boy getting stock from your father? Is that where you learned the art of investing?

JR: You learn from a lot of different folks. My dad was very conservative, and he just bought blue-chip stocks for me that paid a hefty dividend. It whetted my appetite. He introduced me to his stockbroker, Stacy Adams, who was the first African American stockbroker on South Street here in town. He was a gold bug, of all things, and taught me a lot about commodity investing.

What had the most influence is that when I was at Princeton, Burton Malkiel was the chairman of the economics department, and we had to read his book *A Random Walk Down Wall Street*. That book is all about efficient markets, but at the same time, he does an extraordinary job telling you about some of the great bubbles that happened in history—the South Sea Bubble and the Roaring Twenties and what happened in the '70s. He goes through all these different bubbles and then the bubbles bursting.

It started to sink into me that the best way to be a successful investor was to be a contrarian, to not follow the crowd. Reading that book, I understood how the madness of crowds can take over markets and force inefficiencies into some very efficient markets. I remember when I went to see him in 1979–80, the markets weren't too good then, and he told me, "It's the time to buy." Professor Malkiel had a lot of early influence on me.

DR: Did you consider yourself a value investor from the start?

JR: Professor Malkiel was the start of me thinking about value investing. Then John Train came out with his book called *The Money Masters,* and I started to learn about these great investors like John Templeton, who famously bought stocks when World War II was breaking out. He was my first role model. Then, as I learned more about Warren Buffett, he became my second role model. He was always so thoughtful and so eloquent about how he described value investing.

I wanted to focus on small- and mid-cap value investing with this idea of investing like John Templeton, when things are out of favor, or like Warren Buffett, who talked about buying great businesses while they're out of favor. Being greedy when others are fearful was one of his key themes. Sir John Templeton always said, "You want to buy when there's maximum pessimism." Those two themes resonated with me. I was comfortable thinking differently than the crowd. I was comfortable being willing to lean in when others were fearful. That was the starting point.

For me, value investing meant buying not only stocks that were selling at low prices relative to their earnings and their cash flow. The EBITDA [earnings before interest, taxes, depreciation, and amortization] multiples had to be cheap. We wanted to do our own independent analysis to determine what the value of the business would be if it was sold.

DR: Are you surprised that there are still not more African American–owned investment firms?

JR: I am surprised. When I started 38 years ago, Harold Washington had just been elected mayor here in Chicago. Maynard Jackson, the mayor of Atlanta, had been a hero of mine. I thought doors would start to really open up in major cities for African American entrepreneurs, in particular for African American entrepreneurs in money management. I thought not only would the public funds open up but enlightened corporations would open up. I especially thought universities, hospitals, museums, and foundations would be open to having minority firms manage their endowments. Those institutions talk about diversity and inclusion. They were talking about it 40 years ago. They're talking about it today. I just assumed there was going to be this huge tailwind. All these institutions that had never had a Jackie Robinson moment would finally hire their first minority firm, their first African American firm. I thought, "This is going to be a great business model," but it just didn't happen. The doors were very slow to open. They are still very slow to open in the nonprofit world.

There were also two terminology problems that came up when someone wanted to hire a minority firm. One was they wanted to hire an "emerging" firm. The definition of minority firm was an emerging firm. But who wants an emerging doctor when they go to the hospital for heart surgery? You want someone who's good at what they do, not someone who's emerging. With "minority" and "emerging" being synonymous—and "emerging" means $2 billion or less in assets under management—when any firm got a little bit successful, they were deemed too large, and people stopped working with them.

Second, many universities and hospitals do what they call "supplier diversity." They were used to hiring African Americans to do construction, catering, low-margin supply-chain opportunities. They would give the financial opportunities, the high-margin business, to established private equity, hedge funds, venture capitalists. People didn't think about African Americans in those worlds. Implicit or unconscious bias was another big reason why we didn't have the growth that I anticipated 40 years ago.

DR: Ariel is set up in a mutual fund structure. Why did you select that structure? Are all of your funds in that format?

JR: It's roughly half and half. We'll be $18 billion pretty soon. We're getting some nice growth, and hopefully it will be $20 billion by the end of the year. Roughly half of those assets are in mutual funds. Our flagship Ariel Fund is by far our largest fund. It's a little over $3 billion. We are the only mid-cap value fund in the Morningstar and Lipper universes that goes back to 1986. It's rare to have the same portfolio manager that entire 35-year period.

We love having mutual funds, because individual investors can use us. Minority individual investors can use us. It's easy to add us to a 401(k) plan or a 403(b) or a 529 plan. Mutual funds give us a lot of flexibility to go along with our separate-account money management, where we manage separate accounts for institutions.

DR: Has it been hard to be a value investor in recent years? What about now?

JR: Our recent performances have been exceedingly strong. It's a wonderful time to be talking to us. This is a humbling business, but we are having tremendous performance for the year to date. We're actually ahead for three years, five years, 10 years, and 35 years after fees in our flagship Ariel Fund. The performance has been quite strong relative to our benchmarks. It's rare to have this long-term track record.

Our performance this last year has been helped by doing what we started the firm to do—to be greedy when others are fearful. A year and a half ago, the market was cratering because of COVID. We were in there buying favorite names that had gotten hammered and finding brand-new ideas about stocks to buy for the first time that were meeting our valuation disciplines. Names we'd been looking to own for 10 years, 15 years, finally came into our valuation parameters at the height of the COVID crisis.

When I look at our performance over this entire 38 years—35 years with the Ariel Fund—it's been built around periods when the inefficiencies are there because there's some kind of panic in the marketplace. In 1987, when the market crashed 22 percent in one day, we were calling clients, telling them to send us more money. This is a once-in-a-lifetime chance to buy bargains.

Then 2008–09 was a second-in-a-lifetime chance to buy extraordinary bargains as the financial crisis hit and lingered into the spring of 2009. We kept buying our favorite names as they got cheaper and cheaper. We've been number one in our category in the Morningstar universes since the March 9th lows of 2009 because we were buying. Then this third-chance-of-a-lifetime came last spring.

Those are the things that have had a major impact on both our one-year numbers and also our long-term numbers. It's this ability to execute value investing in what we call "crunch times," when there's an enormous amount of stress. You have to have the courage to go in there and buy when everyone's sitting on their hands or selling.

DR: Since your start, how has the overall performance been?

JR: It's been tremendous. We're number one in our category, depending on which month you look at. At the end of July 2021, our Ariel Fund had compounded, after fees, 11.67 percent since November 1986—so, over almost a 35-year period, an 11.67 percent performance ahead of all the relevant benchmarks, from the S&P 500 to the Russell 2500 Value Index. We're proud of that long-term performance, but it's not straight up. We've had some bad periods. Calendar year 2008 was, bar none, the time when we disappointed people significantly on the downside. We learned lessons during that period, and hopefully we improved, because that was a really rough year.

DR: During the Great Recession, your assets under management went down by about roughly half. Were you worried about your firm's ability to survive?

JR: We were confident we were going to survive. I have this extraordinary business partner, Mellody Hobson, who's been with us 31 of our 38 years. We're both conservative, and so we had always saved money for a rainy day. My father pounded that into me. Mellody's mom pounded that into her. We had a real nice nest egg to survive for several years, even if we had very little revenue. We weren't worried about the survival of the firm, but it was extraordinarily uncomfortable. Having to have the first layoffs in the firm's history was heartbreaking and brutal. It was heartbreaking to lose clients you thought believed in you. When the tough times got going, they just left.

We saw all these bargains. The reason I was so confident is that it was like being a kid in a candy store. Here were these great companies selling at extraordinary discounts, some of them 70–80 percent discounts from what we thought the private-market values were. It was so much fun to be an investor then, even as we were suffering financially. But we knew, in our core, the market should come back and our favorite bargains would come back. We kept buying them as they got cheaper and cheaper. We were lowering our average cost substantially, which meant that performance coming out was going to be fantastic.

DR: Are you still deeply involved in the investment process?

JR: I'm doing that every single day like I have for the last 38 years. I spend my day talking to management teams, visiting with them every quarter, and then talking to competitors to hear what they think about the industries and companies we invest in, talking to the sell-side analysts to get their perspectives. This is my life's work. This is what I do.

DR: Let's go back to your days at Princeton. Why did you go to school there? Did you want to be a basketball coach then? What happened?

JR: I wanted to play Division One basketball. That was my dream. The idea of places like Princeton and Penn were intriguing for someone who wasn't good enough to play at North Carolina or your alma mater, Duke. I wasn't going to get recruited to places like that.

But the cool thing about playing basketball at Princeton is you got to play against some of those teams. I went to Princeton because it was a great program. They were ranked regularly back then in the top 20 in the country. Ivy League basketball was at its peak at the end of the '70s. A lot of players went to the NBA.

I often tell people it was like going from third-grade math to calculus. A lot of people are good at math in high school and college, and you realize there's no chance you can become a PhD in math because it's so hard. It gets so complex as you go higher up the food chain. Fortunately,

I had this other hobby of being in love with the stock market, because I didn't have the skill set to be a basketball coach (my real ambition). My parents were disappointed I didn't follow their footsteps and go to law school. But they were understanding that I loved basketball. I'm sure they thought I would grow out of it.

DR: When you graduated, what did you do?

JR: I went to work at William Blair. It was a classic kind of Princeton story. My mom was friends with a Princeton alum named Tilden Cummings, from Continental Bank. Tilly called Ned Jannotta, a well-known Princeton alum. He was the managing partner at William Blair. He introduced me to the folks in the wealth management division. Back then we were called stockbrokers. They hired me. I was the first African American they'd ever hired in a professional position at William Blair. They very rarely hired someone right out of college. I think they saw something in me. They saw my passion for the markets, how much I loved it, how much I loved reading about it, how I was developing an approach to investing. They could tell I wasn't like everyone else. I was growing up as an only child in a community of independent thinkers, so I learned to think for myself.

DR: You left at the age of 24 to start Ariel. Where did you get the name Ariel from?

JR: It's a silly story, but I used to like to watch *The Waltons*. John-Boy, the star of the television show, was in love with a woman named Ariel in one episode. I wrote it down. "If I ever have a daughter, I'm going to name my daughter Ariel." The company came seven years before my daughter was born, so, my daughter's Victoria and Ariel is the company name. I loved the way it sounded, and it wasn't popular back then. It was well before *The Little Mermaid*.

DR: Where did you get the capital to start Ariel?

JR: I went to all of my high school buddies and asked them to give me checks from $10 to $20,000. I had clients from being a stockbroker. Those that believed in me, I went to them. I went to my neighbors like Valerie Jarrett's parents down the block on Greenwood Avenue in Hyde Park where I grew up. Finally, I went to my mom and my dad. I always tell people, my mom gave me all of her liquid cash, and my dad made it clear he was giving me what he could afford to lose. That was my original seed capital.

DR: It worked. How was your performance in the early years?

JR: It was really good. It was important in those first years that our stocks performed well. We came up with this newsletter idea called *The Patient Investor,* to remind people that we were prudent, long-term investors and we were not going to take undue risks with people's money. In this newsletter that came out every month, we would talk about our favorite stocks and then we would list their performance on the back page. That enhanced our credibility, because people could see the arguments we were using to justify a stock system selection and then see whether those selections actually worked or not. After the first six months we had been in business, we got this $100,000 from Howard University—our first institutional client—and we grew from there.

DR: How has the firm changed since you began it?

JR: It's changed dramatically. In the beginning, you had to hire people who were available. I had a great high school buddy who quit her job and joined me as my number two person. The number three person was a guy I met selling dictionaries door-to-door. I thought, if he's a good salesman of dictionaries, maybe he'll be a good salesman for Ariel.

The firm's grown from the three of us that first year to now over 110 people, with offices in San Francisco, New York, Chicago, and Sydney, Australia. We have an enormous amount of multigenerational depth and a lot of talent.

In the old days, I had to make all the decisions. Now I have a team of great leaders that help us make these decisions and help us run the firm. It's so much fun. I can actually be a little bit of a coach.

DR: How has your investment approach changed since the outset?

JR: The core values are still there of buying wonderful companies that are undervalued, that have great management teams, strong balance sheets. Among the things that have evolved over time, one is we created our own proprietary debt ratings over the years. My colleague

Charlie Bobrinskoy led that effort to improve our ability to see what the margin of safety was on the balance sheets of the companies we invested in. That's been an important thing for us. The second thing is that we've worked hard at learning about behavioral finance. I got to know Daniel Kahneman through being on the Investment Committee at Princeton. We got to know Dick Thaler, because he's right here in our hometown, and we have a love for the University of Chicago and a commitment to it. [Both Kahneman and Thaler have won the Nobel Prize for economics.]

These behavioral finance leaders have transformed the way that we think about how we work day-to-day—trying to understand our behavioral biases, which of us have confirmation bias, which of us are anchoring in old estimates, which of us have recency effects [i.e., a preference for recent events]. This tremendous push on behavioral finance is important to us. We think that's helped make us better by understanding our behavioral biases.

The other key area of improvement is in our questioning. We use an outside company called BIA [Business Intelligence Advisors]. They're former CIA agents and government officials who help clients be better questioners and better listeners, and understand whether people are being direct with you or not in their answers to your questions. They've been helping us coach each other on how to use our time with management more effectively.

DR: What have been the most important lessons you have learned as an investor over these many years?

JR: One is to work on this idea of confirmation bias. It's so easy to search out people who agree with you on a thesis. You have to be willing to hear all different sides, make sure you're talking to competitors, to suppliers, to other money managers who don't like that industry, to push yourself to have nonconfirming information to help you make decisions. It's so hard to do. I'm pushing myself always to ask questions in a way that doesn't lead to an answer I want to hear but to ask the right questions that force people to say what's really on their mind to the best of their abilities.

The second lesson is that the ability to stand alone and not feel pressure to be like everyone else is critical. I grew up as an only child. I grew up in Hyde Park. I'm kind of like you, I think, a quirky kind of different kind of a person.

DR: I'm an only child, too. Maybe it's being an only child?

JR: You don't feel like you have to follow the traditional rules in any way. That's critically important to successful investing. I learn more and more to embrace my quirkiness and not try to feel a pressure to be like others. I don't email. There's many things that I don't do like everyone else does.

DR: Why do you not email?

JR: I don't email because it sucks up an enormous amount of time, and it allows people to control my time. If every moment something's beeping at you, instead of being able to read and concentrate and think about the long-term values of companies, you're constantly swept up in the current noise. I have friends who spend hours returning emails every evening, and that time can be better spent reading and thinking about the markets.

The final lesson I would reinforce is not a new lesson. It's one that has been reinforced these last 38 years. Warren Buffett talks about how in the last century, the Dow Jones started at 66 and ended at over 11,000. He reinforces over and over again that we had a Great Depression, we had several recessions, we had a pandemic, we had deaths of presidents that were surprising and shocking and heartbreaking. We had World War I, World War II, the Vietnam War, etc., and we always march back. Our country is the best capitalist democracy ever invented. That ability to remind myself to think long term about what's going to happen up over the horizon and not get swept up in the headlines in the daily news is a lesson that's been reinforced over and over again, and fits nicely with our patient-investor, turtle theme.

DR: When you buy a stock, how long do you typically hold on to it?

JR: It's typically five years, but we have a lot of names that have been in the portfolio for 10, 15, or 20 years. We lighten up when they're expensive and buy more when they get cheap. Management teams love having us for shareholders, because they say we're really rare, owning their stocks for so long.

DR: To be a good value investor, what do you think the most important attributes are other than patience?

JR: The ability to stand alone is critical because of the pressure to follow the crowd, particularly at crunch times. In 2008 and '09 everyone thought the world was coming to an end. We thought last year, with the pandemic, the world was coming to an end, and who knew how long this virus was going to destroy our economy. It was the quickest recession ever. Those are the times we think you can make the most money, when you have the courage to buy when everyone's panicking or sitting on their hands. Markets are just like I learned from Professor Malkiel 40 years ago—they're extraordinarily efficient. But there are times when doors open and windows of opportunities arrive, and you've got to be ready to jump in there and buy aggressively. That ability to think independently—there's nothing more important than that to being a great investor.

The final thing is the ability to look out over the horizon to try to imagine the future three years from now, five years from now. Most people just can't help themselves. They get fixated on what the headlines are, not understanding that this too will pass. If I can look out beyond that, I can have an opportunity to see things that others don't see.

DR: When you think you've made a mistake in deciding to buy a stock, do you sell or do you try to change the management? What do you do if you think you've made a mistake? Or do you not make that many mistakes?

JR: We've made many over the years, and we sell. We're not going to try to change management or get into that game. That's just not our game.

DR: If someone who wants to invest their own money, do you think they can just pick stocks and do well? Is it much safer to give that money to professional investors?

JR: For sure it's much safer to trust professional investors, and you'll most likely get an average return. The only way you can make money, I think, as an individual investor is to stay within your circle of competence. Invest in industries that you know extremely well, because maybe you built your career there. You've worked in the pharmaceutical industry for 30 years or worked in a specific part of the tech industry for 30 years. Then maybe you'll have that ability to see things that others don't see. But you've got to be specialized in your investing to be successful as an individual investor. Otherwise, you're always going to be at a disadvantage to the pros, who are true experts in many sectors.

DR: Who manages your money?

JR: The vast majority of my money is in my shares in Ariel Investments, my shares in our flagship fund. I have significant ownership in the companies whose boards I'm on. So I guess I manage my own money. I don't have anyone else I've entrusted it to.

DR: In recent years, the index funds have done quite well. It's hard to beat them, certainly on price. What is your view of stock index funds? Do you offer only traditional mutual funds?

JR: We only offer mutual funds that we manage ourselves here at Ariel. We eat our own cooking. It all comes down to the skill sets of the portfolio managers.

DR: On stock index funds, do you think that they actually are good buys? In effect you're saying you can beat the stock index funds.

JR: We think there's a handful of funds out there that can outperform. We believe in ourselves and think we are one of those funds, but with the vast majority, you would do better if you put your money into index funds. We don't offer them here at Ariel. We offer our own funds that we manage ourselves. But we do believe the vast majority of people would be better off putting their money in index funds, and the vast majority of institutions would also. A lot of money is being spent paying high-cost fees when it might be better just to buy the index.

DR: You now offer private equity funds. Why do you invest in that area?

JR: We've been saying over the last year, if you can't beat them, join them. Some of our largest positions in our Ariel Funds have been in the public/private equity funds. We believe in the industry, and decided that not only would we invest our clients' money in the publicly traded private equity funds, we would start our own. We felt we could do something in this era where there's so much interest in diversity and inclusion and helping to solve this huge wealth gap between the African

American community and the white community. If we could create a fund to invest in African American and Latino and Latina entrepreneurs who are building businesses of scale, not only would it be a great performance vehicle for us and a great diversification move for us, we would also be helping to create opportunities for real wealth building in diverse communities.

DR: What's the pleasure that you get from investing?

JR: I'm extraordinarily competitive, and this has been a really fun game. When I wake up in the morning, I can't wait to turn on CNBC and see how the market's opening up. I get the early indications from my deputy portfolio manager of what's moving the markets. He sends me all the new research reports on all the various companies and industry sectors that we follow. I love reading about it. I love studying it. I love getting out there and competing against all the other mutual fund managers and portfolio managers. It's just so fun.

Of course it's really fun when you're outperforming, but I love the game. It's like looking for that needle in the haystack. It's like being a treasure hunter out there looking for buried treasure, looking for wonderful companies that have been misunderstood and misplaced and misallocated. There's nothing more rewarding than taking a contrary view on one of these neglected stocks and seeing it work out and enhance the performance of your funds for you and your customers.

DR: Do you recommend this area of finance to young professionals looking for career advice?

JR: I tell young people the best way to get exposed to the markets is to work in the investment offices of the university that they happen to be a part of. I wish I had known to intern at the Princeton Investment Company when I was at Princeton. I was a vendor at Wrigley Field selling Cokes, beer, popcorn, and hot dogs. I never knew there was an endowment office where I could learn about all the different asset classes that are available.

Every time I talk to young people I say, Go to your local endowment office. Volunteer to work during the school year. Get an internship during the summer. It will be the best place to learn what part of the money management industry you want to be in.

DR: How do you keep informed about investment trends, new stocks, market trends? What is it that you do to keep yourself informed?

JR: I tell people that what I do all day is read. I start out with the five newspapers [the *New York Times, Wall Street Journal, Financial Times, Chicago Tribune,* and *Chicago Sun-Times*]. I started watching CNBC in the morning and seeing what latest trends are happening, and the latest news. I read as many books on the market as I can. More and more I've been focused on behavioral finance books. Annie Duke, who's an extraordinarily successful women's poker player, has a recent book out and a podcast. We've been studying her work. There's *Think Again* by Adam Grant, which is so important because it teaches you how you've got to learn to be flexible and change your views on the markets or an individual decision. Too many people get locked into a decision and can't adjust.

I've tried to build a great network of investors that I respect a lot. I build relationships with them so I can talk with them and learn about what's happening in the markets from their perspective, what they're worried about, what they're seeing that we're not seeing. That's something that I tell young people, too—build relationships with your peers in business school so that you can talk to them 30 years, 40 years later, when you need independent advice on a tough decision you're making in the markets or out of the markets.

DR: What do you do for rest and relaxation? Do you play basketball still?

JR: No. After my hip replacement, I can't run any longer. I started from scratch taking piano lessons about three and a half years ago.

DR: I always wonder whether anybody could learn at midlife to play piano and really master it. Can you?

JR: I've got an extraordinary teacher from the People's Music School here in Chicago. She's the CEO there, and I think I'm getting better.

DR: If I ask you to play "Rhapsody in Blue," you can do that right off the top of your head?

JR: I would need the music in front of me. I could, I think, learn to do that one. I'm playing "What a Wonderful World" now. I'm pretty good at "Twist and Shout," the Beatles' old song, and "I Want to Hold Your Hand" and John Lennon's "Imagine."

DR: That's pretty good. Do you still eat one meal a day at McDonald's?

JR: I've got my McDonald's Diet Coke here. It's not always a meal. Sometimes it's a biscuit and a Diet Coke. Sometimes french fries and a Diet Coke. Sometimes it's a McFlurry.

DR: You do that because you're on the board?

JR: It's a tradition I've always had. After college, I loved to get away and read the newspapers at a McDonald's. I also meet some friends who are there every day. It's kind of my home away from home. I've always loved it.

DR: Do you use computers at all?

JR: I did learn to use an iPad for this new world that we live in with Zooms and the like. But no, I've never used a computer.

DR: When people want to reach you, how do they get messages to you?

JR: I do have a cell phone. People can call me directly on the cell or call me at home or call me at the office. I tell people my phone number is listed—John Rogers on East Delaware Street in Chicago. You call 411 and you'll get connected to me.

Real Estate

JON GRAY

President and COO, Blackstone

> *"The best thing is to be a high-conviction investor. When you dabble and just put a bunch of money on things you don't know or understand, it tends to work out badly."*

From the beginning of time, real estate has actually been the principal investment asset for most individuals in the world. Their home, land, farm, or ranch have often been their principal—if not sole—asset.

Individuals have traditionally felt some security in being able to see and touch this asset and understand its value. For most individuals, pieces of paper (such as stocks or bonds) do not carry the same emotional connection as a physical asset they regularly use, see, and enjoy.

As some individuals acquired wealth in Europe and the United States in the 1800s and 1900s, they felt there was value in buying real estate (land or buildings) occupied or used by others. Such assets were easily understood. And the current income (from rents) achieved from such assets, and the profits often achieved upon a sale of such assets, tended to produce solid, relatively predictable returns.

As populations increased and businesses increased, there was more need for various kinds of real estate, and investors began to increasingly view real estate as an important type of investment—not high-yielding like a great venture capital transaction, but also not so subject to failure.

In Europe and the United States for most of the twentieth century, "core" or traditional real estate was seen as a relatively safe, single-digit-return kind of investment.

In the late 1980s, when the savings-and-loan (S&L) crisis occurred in the United States, the federal government ultimately assumed control of the real estate of the S&Ls that failed. In short order, the federal government sold these real estate assets to investors at what turned out to be very low prices relative to the ultimate resale value.

The result was that the purchasers of these real estate assets achieved attractive double-digit returns. That spawned a new type of real estate investing—"opportunistic," which is to say buying at low prices, adding considerable value to an asset in need of some rehabilitation or value-added service, and achieving buyout or venture-type returns for the investors.

Opportunistic real estate investing (with the higher returns) typically allows the firms pursuing this kind of investment to charge a profit-sharing "carried interest" to their investors. The result has been the entrance into the real estate world of large private equity firms, which have long histories of providing value-added, "carried interest" services to their investments.

This is illustrated by the rise of Jon Gray and Blackstone in the world of opportunistic real estate investing (though Blackstone later expanded into more basic or "core" real estate as well).

When Jon joined Blackstone in 1992, fresh out of college at the University of Pennsylvania, the firm really did not have a real estate investment business. Today, as a result of Jon's leadership, Blackstone operates one of the world's largest and most profitable real estate investment businesses, with more than $290 billion in assets under management.

How did this occur? And how did Jon pull off two of the most legendary deals in the history of real estate investing—deals that cemented his reputation and enabled him to build Blackstone's extraordinarily large and successful real estate business? The first, the purchase of Sam Zell's Equity Office Properties, was the largest real estate transaction ever—a $39 billion acquisition. Although the acquisition was done at the top of the market in 2007, Jon cleverly presold the least-desirable assets and created a multibillion-dollar profit for Blackstone from those that remained.

The second of these deals, the purchase of Hilton Hotels, was a combined real estate and private equity deal, but it was Jon's idea, and it was his skill that helped save it during the rough patch for hotels during the Great Recession. The end result was a $14 billion profit—the most profitable buyout in history.

In my discussion with Jon at the Blackstone headquarters in New York, he was too modest to say that his success is due to his remarkably high intelligence, incredible work ethic, and engaging personality, or to his exquisite sense of timing. But Jon not only anticipated the likely collapse in commercial office space during the Great Recession, he also foresaw the enhanced value likely to accrue in recent years to single-family homes, apartment rental units, logistics warehouses, and Indian commercial space.

But these are the attributes that many of Jon's colleagues and his competitors in the real estate world would cite as the reason for his ascent from a young college grad doing the tedious work of a staffer in Blackstone's investment banking business to his current position as the firm's president and chief operating officer.

I have known Jon for a number of years from our nonprofit and business interests, which have at times intertwined, and I have always admired the personal qualities just described. But I have also admired his disarming modesty—often not a quality one associates immediately with someone who built and led for many years one of the world's biggest businesses in any area.

Although Jon's current responsibilities entail overseeing all of Blackstone's myriad investment activities, I wanted to focus my discussion with him on the area where he became the world leader—real estate. I interviewed Jon in person at the Blackstone offices in New York on June 7, 2021, for the *Bloomberg Wealth* series.

DAVID M. RUBENSTEIN (DR): You made your name in the investment world as a real estate investor, and you've built the largest real estate business in the world. Did you always want to be a real estate investor growing up?

JON GRAY (JG): I did not start out as thinking I would be a real estate investor. I had grown up in suburban Chicago. I'd never really been to the East Coast prior to going to college at the University of Pennsylvania.

And when I got to college, I decided that I really wanted to be an English major. I wanted to be a journalist is what I thought. I wrote for the

Daily Pennsylvanian. And about a year into school, I realized a bunch of my friends, fraternity brothers, liked business. They were in Wharton [the University of Pennsylvania's business school], and I owned a few stocks. I liked numbers, so I decided to get a dual degree. My senior year, I met a young woman who was an English major also. A few weeks later, I got a job working for a small investment advisory firm.

That was about 30 years ago, and that was Blackstone, and that was my wife, Mindy. I started at Blackstone in the private equity area and in the M&A [mergers and acquisitions] area. I was mostly running numbers, doing pitch books for clients, and ordering dinner. I had to make sure the associates got their food by 7 p.m.

About a year in, the real estate market collapsed, and the visionary founders of Blackstone, Steve Schwarzman and Pete Peterson, said, "Real estate is a place we should go." They formed a real estate business, and they had virtually no people. I had been helping them draft the private placement memorandum for the first real estate fund. And they said, "You seem like a reasonable person. Do you want to move over and join this group?" I talked to Mindy, I talked to my parents, and I came back and said, "Yes." That's how I ended up in the real estate business.

DR: You talked to your parents about whether you should go from private equity to real estate? You must be very close to your parents. And your wife said, "I don't know if it's a good area to go into"?

JG: My wife and my parents said, "What do you think?" I said, "I really love the idea of doing principal investing." I loved the idea that we could control whether we made the decision to invest. I also was thinking, "They may make me want to go back to business school if I stay in the private equity area." With real estate I didn't think I'd have to go back, so I said, "Sure." I say to my kids all the time, "Luck is a core competency," and this was definitely the case.

DR: What did you all do in the beginning? Did you have money to invest? You didn't have a fund, I presume, in real estate. So what did you do for money?

JG: We used a little bit of capital from the firm. We did one deal using the private equity fund, but the investors were insurance companies and

Japanese investors who'd been hurt by the US real estate market. So we had to raise the money. We just did little deals to begin with.

The first deal I worked on was a shopping center in Chesapeake, Virginia, the Great Bridge Shopping Center. It was a $6 million transaction. We borrowed $4 million, so it was a $2 million equity check. You would have thought I was buying the island of Manhattan. I was down there for three weeks. I met every tenant, I was counting the car traffic, I was learning the business.

It was an amazing experience because I was the chief bottle washer, I was the waiter, I was the maître d'. We were this tiny little business, and I was learning it firsthand.

We did an $11 million hotel deal in Colorado Springs, a Marriott. When I look back at that, I say, "I shouldn't have been doing all this work," because it was back at a period of great distress. We were buying that Marriott for a third of the cost they'd built it for just a couple of years earlier. I should have just said, "How do I sign the contract?"

But it was an incredible education. I loved the real estate business. I got out from being behind a desk, I got to get on an airplane, I got to meet people, I got to learn about different places, and, because it was such a small business, I got to touch everything. It worked out wonderfully well for me.

DR: Today nobody asks who Blackstone is. In those days, when you were showing up to buy things, did they say, "Who's Blackstone?"

JG: They would say, "Who's Blackstone?" And I would say, "It was founded by Steve Schwarzman, who ran M&A at Lehman Brothers, and Pete Peterson, who was formerly secretary of commerce."

DR: Let's talk about two deals you did that became two of the best-known deals in the history of US real estate. The first is EOP, Equity Office Properties, built by Sam Zell. Can you explain what that was, why it was so risky, and why it turned out to be, for you, a very good deal?

JG: We grew the business a lot from $6 million deals to EOP, which was a $39 billion transaction that we closed at the beginning of 2007. How did we get there? The biggest thing that changed the business was in the early 2000s. After the dot-com bubble and 9/11, we went into a recession. It was a pretty shallow recession, but Alan Greenspan [then chairman of the Federal Reserve] cut rates dramatically.

Real estate weathered that recession and the decline in rates well, so a bunch of money flowed in. We were opportunistic investors, saying, "How can we find value?" Because the buildings seemed to be very expensive.

I stumbled on the public real estate markets, where there were companies that owned real estate trading well below where these buildings traded individually. Then we said, "There's this new commercial mortgage-backed securities [CMBS] debt," which is much lower-cost than leveraged loans and high-yield loans that you typically used in a buyout.

We convinced the banks to let us use that to go buy real estate companies. Beginning in late 2003 through 2007, I think we did 12 of these deals where we started buying these big public real estate companies. We used the public CMBS debt, and, in many cases, we would sell off pieces.

Think about it like a fruit basket: you'd sell the grapes to the people who wanted them, sell the bananas over here. That's what the Equity Office deal was all about. We bought the biggest collection of office buildings in the United States. When we started on it, the deal was $36 billion.

Vornado, run by a very smart real estate investor, Steve Roth, decided to compete with us. The problem was we had a plan to sell off a third of the real estate, but, as the price started to move up, we didn't want to take so much inventory risk.

So I went to Sam Zell, who's obviously very savvy, and I said, "Sam, if you want me to compete here, you've got to let me talk to some of the downstream buyers." And he let us do that. It was like running a store where at the front end you're taking in the merchandise and at the back end you're selling it.

We ultimately won the auction. We sold almost two-thirds of the real estate. We paid down our debt and we ended up owning great real estate. We kept assets in California and New York and Boston. Had we kept suburban Chicago and Stamford, Connecticut, it would not have been so good. At the end of the day, it was a wholesale-to-retail arbitrage, but the key was what we kept. We ultimately tripled investor capital.

DR: Ultimately, you sold about two-thirds of what you bought. How do you explain to an investment committee, "I'm going to go buy a company and I'm going to sell two-thirds of it right away"? Does that make it hard to explain to people?

JG: No, because that had been our business plan. Typically we were selling a third, but in this case we knew what we were doing. As the price was getting bid up, we had done a presale, so we knew a bunch of these deals were going to happen at the time of closing or shortly thereafter. What we were saying was, "We'll still end up with $13 billion of real estate that's very high quality at a basis well below the market, because we'll have sold off the weaker assets." So people were comfortable.

DR: In the end, it turned out to be a great deal for you. It wasn't so good for the people you sold the real estate to, because the real estate market collapsed more or less when you completed the deal. Did you ever buy some of that stuff back?

JG: We ended up buying some of it back. A lot of those people are my friends. No one knew at the time the music was going to stop.

DR: Let's talk about another deal you did that turned out to be the most profitable buyout of all time. Right before the market crashed in 2007–08, you bought the entire Hilton Hotel Company. Was it a real estate play or a corporate play?

JG: It was a bit of both. We did the transaction with our real estate private equity funds and our corporate private equity fund. Hilton owned great real estate, like the Waldorf-Astoria and the Hilton Hawaiian Village, but it also had this amazing management franchise business— Hilton, Embassy Suites, Hilton Garden, Doubletree, and so forth.

It was similar to the Equity Office transaction in that we thought we could buy something because of the scale and, because it was in the public markets, more inexpensively than we could buy these assets individually. We also believed that the multiple was reasonable. We were paying 13 or 14 times cash flow for what we thought was a great business.

Our mistake was that our timing was terrible. We closed on the transaction at the end of '07. In less than a year, Lehman Brothers would collapse, the global economy would be melting down, global travel would decline dramatically. The company's revenues would go down 20 percent, cash flow would go down 40 percent, and we marked our largest investment ever as a firm down by 71 percent. That was not a good feeling.

But we believed in the business. We still saw tremendous opportunity to grow the company around the world: China, the Middle East, Europe, even the United States. And we believed the decline was cyclical in nature. So we invested $800 million more at the bottom, we stuck with the company, it started growing. There was a cyclical recovery. We ultimately took it public. We broke it into three different companies — a management franchise, time-share, and real estate business — and we made $14 billion for our investors. So it ended well.

DR: When it wasn't looking so good, did you go home to your wife and say, "You told me to go into real estate, and maybe it wasn't such a good thing"?

JG: In a period of time when things are stressed, having people you can rely on and talk to, and who still believe in you, is really important. And it was hard. Because you felt terrible, you felt badly with your colleagues, with your investors. But we never lost faith.

For me, that searing experience with Hilton was probably the most important thing for me as an investor. We bought at the worst time possible, and we ended up having the most successful deal of all time. What that said is we had bought a really great business in what we call "a great neighborhood." It had terrific tailwinds. Global travel's a growth industry. These brands were super valuable.

Too often when we invest capital we focus on what I'll call the individual house, not "Am I in the right sector?" or "Do I have those tailwinds?" Hilton was a fundamentally great business, and we could afford to have paid too much and to have done it at the wrong time. But, ultimately, with the right management team, the right financial support, we made a bunch of money. That has impacted everything I've done since then.

DR: After the Hilton deal, the real estate market in the United States got better, but while it wasn't so great, you decided to buy a lot of houses that had been defaulted on, so they were very low-priced. Was that a good decision?

JG: It was a very good decision. The core of our real estate business was to buy hard assets at a discount to replacement cost. If it costs $300 a foot to build an office building, can I buy something at $150 a foot or $200 a foot? That tends to be a good approach as a value investor in real estate.

After the housing crisis, the largest private asset class in the world, single-family homes in the United States, had declined by 30 percent. After 60 years of going up in price every year, in some markets like Phoenix and Las Vegas, home values declined by close to 50 percent. The question was, How could we take advantage of this?

We realized there were 13 million single-family homes in the United States available for rent. In most cases, a doctor or lawyer owns their home, they own another down the street, they rent it out. They don't provide much service, they don't invest a lot.

We said, "What if we started buying homes at scale? What if we created a company that provided real professional service, invested in the assets?" We had this idea that we would buy big swaths of homes from banks. That never happened. What we ended up doing was buying individual homes. We bought them vacant, post-foreclosure. We didn't want to foreclose on people.

We ended up buying 50,000 of them, building a company. The housing market came back, we took it public, we ultimately sold our shares, and we built something that we're incredibly proud of.

DR: What are the types of real estate? As I understand it, you have core real estate, core-plus, value-added, and opportunistic. What are those four different categories?

JG: If you think of investment-grade bonds like Procter & Gamble and IBM, they're perceived as very safe. The returns are lower. Then there are high-yield bonds on leveraged companies, less mature companies, where you get paid more.

That's similar in real estate. When you think of core real estate, think about an asset that's leased long-term to a credit tenant. There's not much risk. With opportunistic real estate, at the other end of the spectrum, we talk about, "Buy it, fix it, sell it." It's an empty building, it's run-down, it needs capital, you fix it up, and then you turn around and sell it. Core-plus and value-add would be somewhere in between. The rates of return differ based on the risks.

DR: What rates of return are you trying to get in the opportunistic real estate world?

JG: You're trying to produce 20 percent gross, 15 percent net to the customer. Which is what we've done for 30 years in our real estate business.

DR: Let's talk about two different types of real estate—residential and commercial. Is residential less risky than commercial?

JG: If you talk about for-sale, single-family housing, there's probably more risk, in the sense that you're building something and selling it, and it's a function of the market. If you're talking about rental housing—think about an apartment complex—that tends to be less risky, because it's less cyclical. People don't give up their apartments. There's some volatility, but nothing like, say, office buildings or hotels.

I would say residential real estate is safer, less volatile. Commercial real estate involves office buildings; warehouses—that has been the biggest theme for us over the last 10 years—hotels, shopping centers, senior-living facilities. All of them have different risk returns, depending on geography.

DR: Another way of looking at real estate is "things that already exist" and "things to be built." Is it riskier and higher reward to build something, or are you trying to buy things that already exist?

JG: We generally are in the business of trying to buy existing real estate at a discount. So we bought the Cosmopolitan hotel and casino in Las Vegas for less than half of what it had been built for, because it was built during the financial crisis. That, to me, is ideal. Occasionally we'll build things. But in general we like to try to get into real estate when it's already producing income. The problem with development is it's a bit like saying, "I'm going to IPO three years from now." When you go to lease out your building, it could be in a different economic environment, and you might not have tenants, you might not have revenues. So we're generally biased towards existing real estate.

DR: As a rule of thumb, real estate prices generally go up. Values increase. Why is it that sometimes you read about real estate developers going bankrupt?

JG: The classic sin in real estate is you have long-duration assets and people finance them short-term. For developers, who often rely on a lot of leverage, that can get them into trouble. The other thing that could impact real estate, particularly today, is changes in technology, the ways we live and work.

If you think about enclosed shopping malls, they were, from the postwar period until a decade ago, the best assets. A large shopping mall, anchored by department stores, lots of retailers, a food court: Those grew in value 5 percent a year unleveraged for 40, 50 years, because they were very hardy. They were fortresses. What happened is that the internet showed up, e-commerce showed up. That's impacted those businesses, and we've seen sharp declines. But that happened over a long period of time. The bigger thing generally has been leverage.

DR: Why are interest rates so important to real estate? Is it because people borrow so much money when they make investments in real estate?

JG: Part of it is that real estate, as an asset class, is perceived as safer. And it is if you're a lender. You can get more leverage against a real estate asset, and therefore a larger portion of the capital structure is through debt. So if rates go up, that certainly has an impact on value.

The other reason is that some real estate is more bond-like. If you own a building and it's leased for 20 years to the government at a flat rent and rates go up, that building's worth less. That's different than, say, hotels, where you're leasing them out, essentially, every night. But that does make real estate a little more interest-rate-intensive.

DR: I've noticed that some people "sign for" the debt. They personally guarantee the debt. I assume you don't personally guarantee anything.

JG: No personal recourse. That was the lesson most of the developers learned in the late '80s.

DR: One of the most famous sayings in the real estate world is "Location, location, location." You might also say it's "Local, local, local," because most people make real estate investments in the area they know. You've made investments all over the world. How do you, sitting in New York, know about the value of real estate in Europe or in Asia?

JG: The key to that is to have a global footprint. We have a major business presence across the United States, in London, across eight different offices in Asia, and tens of thousands of people across portfolio companies as well. It took us a long time to do it. We've been at this for 30 years, and you really need talented people on the ground. You need local people who know the markets.

The one thing that is advantageous about real estate is that so many of the trends we're seeing, particularly driven by technology, are the same around the world. When we started buying warehouses back in 2010, we noticed there were these e-commerce tenants showing up, and we started buying more in the US. It wasn't a big leap of faith to say, "The same thing's going to happen in Canada, it's going to happen in the UK, in continental Europe, and across Asia."

If you have the skill set, you can evaluate, plus you travel a lot. I'm on planes a lot. I no longer run the real estate business day-to-day. My colleagues have done an amazing job. They have teams around the world on the ground, and we're local in those markets. You cannot buy real estate in Mumbai the way we have done flying in and flying out of New York.

DR: Suppose someone on your team comes to you with a deal, you sign off on it, then it doesn't work out so well. Do you say, "Let's get rid of the person who suggested it"? How do you save a deal when it doesn't look as good as you thought?

JG: We see investing as a team sport. Somebody may have championed a transaction, but there were plenty of us who reviewed it and ultimately signed off. To blame an individual, I don't think that's a good practice. You're trying to build a real sense of team.

When things go wrong, what you try to do is not get caught up in the fact that you put a lot of money in before, but look at things where they sit today and make a hard choice. So you bought something, you invested money, you think the equity's now gone. The question is: from here, do you think there's appreciation? Or are you putting in good money after bad? A disciplined investor will leave that old choice in the rearview mirror, and look at this soberly.

DR: What's the pleasure of being a real estate investor? What is it that you like about real estate that kept you in it?

JG: I love the people. I love learning about all these different places. I got to see all of the United States, virtually all of the developed world. There's something really tactile about it, where you can go and say, "How does this neighborhood feel?"

When you're investing in pharmaceutical businesses or other companies, it's harder to say, "I have real expertise about the efficacy of this drug versus that drug." But as an individual you can say, "I've been in the neighborhood here. I'm in Oakland today. It feels a lot like Brooklyn did as it started to gentrify. I'll connect the dots and do this." The tangible nature of it, the experience—if you love to travel, if you love to see places, real estate's hard to beat.

DR: Where do deals come from? People call you all the time? Or do you come up with the ideas yourself?

JG: In many cases, we're the first call, because we buy and sell more real estate than any firm. It was a challenge as we were building the business—flying out, giving them your business card, saying you have capital. Once you've been at this for a long time and people know you, you tend to get to the top of the Rolodex.

DR: For the individual investor, what is the best way to invest in real estate?

JG: There are a couple of ways. There's a public REIT [real estate investment trust] market where you can invest in some excellent companies here in the United States. There are REITs around the world.

Another way to do it today is we have things called private REITs. We at Blackstone have a vehicle called BREIT, which owns primarily logistics and rental apartments across the Southeast and Southwest. Historically people did not do a great job offering private real estate to individual investors. We've focused on trying to deliver a first-class product. There are others who offer similar products.

For investors who are more adventurous, they can partner with local developers. The challenge I worry about with that is misalignment of interests and liquidity. You're generally not getting a lot of diversity in that approach.

DR: Are you worried about the economy now? It's been pretty good, but it probably will head down at some point. Economies always correct. If I want to invest in real estate, is now a good time?

JG: I think it's still a pretty good time for real estate, for a couple of reasons. The warning signs for real estate are twofold. One is too much leverage, too much capital. We don't really have that in the real estate system today. The other is too many cranes, too much building. We're actually below historic levels, in terms of new supply.

The other thing I'd point out is that if you look at the S&P 500, it's delivered something like four times the return of public REITs since the beginning of 2020, before COVID. So real estate is lagging coming out of the recovery, because obviously people have been concerned about the physical world.

I think that, as the economy reopens, as people go back into spaces, real estate is going to see a little bit of a bounce. One positive thing about real estate is that inflation drives up the replacement cost of buildings. That gives you a little bit of a cushion on existing real estate.

DR: Do you expect that people will come back, work five days a week, and use all the office space in New York and similar cities that they did before? Or is there going to be a need for less office space?

JG: I think there will be some need for less office space. There'll be some hybrid arrangements, some people who may work permanently remotely. But there is a tendency, sort of a "recency bias," to assume that because we've been home, that's the way it'll be.

When we think about our company, we know we're better together: we're better at being creative, we're better at solving problems, we're better at training our young people. It's an apprenticeship business, learning how to invest.

And so I think being together matters. Some companies will conclude they don't need quite as much space, and that will create some additional vacancy. People will be concerned about owning office buildings, and that may create an opportunity. Because there'll be some headwinds for a number of years, and then, over time, things will recover.

I would point out, though, outside the United States, for instance in China, buildings are back to full capacity. And in Europe, people don't have as much space in their home lives. Hybrid is harder to do. So not all geographies are the same. Even here, I think there'll be a bias toward going back towards the office, though it won't be like it was before in full.

DR: A lot of people have moved to Florida and Texas, maybe for warm weather, maybe because those states don't have income taxes. Do you think that trend will continue? Is that a good place to invest in real estate now, because more people are moving there?

JG: I would say it's a bit of both—the weather, the lower cost of living, lower taxes, particularly in a post-SALT [state and local tax deduction] world, concerns about quality of life, crime. Texas is one of the fastest-growing states in the country. That was accelerated by the pandemic.

On the other hand, New York City, San Francisco, these are amazing places. When you think about technology and innovation, entrepreneurship, immigrants—people are going to come to these cities. They want to live there. With the right policies, these cities can really thrive.

DR: Blackstone, like other large private equity firms, worries about ESG [environmental, social, and governance factors] these days. How do you deal with environmental concerns when you're buying existing buildings?

JG: We've said to our investors, "Every asset we buy, going forward, we want to reduce hydrocarbon emissions by at least 15 percent." We've set that out as a goal. There's a bunch of things you can do around building management systems, windows, where you set temperatures.

We also, at specific projects, have done big things. At Stuyvesant Town, the largest apartment complex in America, we did an urban solar project that is the largest in the country. We're doing a bunch of things on our investing side in terms of credit and energy investing in these areas. Real estate consumes a lot of energy, and in many cases buildings like this can be inefficient. We're trying to do our part by being a force for good, helping the planet.

DR: When you were growing up—and certainly when I was growing up, I'm older than you—people really wanted to own their own house. It was part of the American Dream. But you've been buying a lot of rental housing now. Is that because you think young adults want to rent now?

JG: There could be some of that. Home ownership rates have gone down a bit. There is this sharing economy, the Airbnb/Uber world we live in. But in the last 12 months, during COVID, there's been a surge in people wanting to own homes.

Our investment in rental housing is based on the fact that we just haven't built a lot of housing since 2008–09. We've averaged less than a million homes built in the United States during that period, versus probably the million-five we need to keep up with population and obsolescence. That's created support for single-family-home values but also for rental values. As the economy reopens here, the shortage in housing will become more acute. So we continue to like it as a sector to invest in.

DR: What's the best investment advice you ever received?

JG: I don't know if it's advice or what I've learned along the way, but definitely the best thing is to be a high-conviction investor. When you dabble and just put a bunch of money on things you don't know or understand, it tends to work out badly. But when you see something — single-family housing, global logistics, the movement of everything online — and you lean into that, that's when you have the best outcomes.

DR: What is the worst investment you ever made in real estate?

JG: When I was young and enthusiastic, in 1999 we bought some office buildings on North First Street in San Jose. There was, at the time, a dot-com bubble. I didn't recognize it. There was a building where the main tenant was called "Gobosh.com" — GoBigOrStayHome.com. And I should have stayed home. We bought the building for probably twice its physical replacement costs. The tenant went bust three months after we did the deal. It was a small investment, but it was so painful.

DR: If I said to you, "I have $100,000 and I want to invest it in real estate or something else," where should I put my $100,000 today?

JG: In real estate, we love what we're doing in the private REIT space. You can invest in a good basket of public REITs as well. More generally, I think the S&P 500. Even though values have moved a lot, the market's trading in the low 20s [average PE multiples], and when you compare that to where the 10-year Treasury rate is, I think you'll do fine over a long period of time. Plus there's a lot of exposure to fast-growing tech companies in there.

DR: Where should I not invest my money?

JG: You should stay away from buggy-whip businesses: you should stay away from landline phone companies and some of the legacy retailers, some legacy media businesses. You want to focus on the future.

On real estate in particular, if I had one piece of advice about where geographically, it would be to go where the creative and technology types are, because those are the markets where there'll be the most economic activity. So the West Coast of the United States; Austin, Texas; Cambridge; Shenzhen; London; Amsterdam; Tel Aviv; Bangalore. Tech is driving so much of the growth in this global economy, those are the most interesting places to invest.

DR: Do people come up to you and ask you for investment advice?

JG: They often ask me about residential home prices, which is not my area of expertise. What I tend to tell people is, "Focus on the longer term." The insta world we live in—the Snapchat, TikTok, meme-stock thing—is dangerous for investing.

What you want to ask is, "Is this fundamentally a good business? Is it in a good sector? Is this a good piece of real estate, where supply is limited, demand is favorable?" And if you own something good, hold it for a long period of time. Find those right neighborhoods to invest in, deploy your capital, and then be patient.

SAM ZELL

Founder and Chairman,
Equity Group Investments (EGI)

> *"Knowing what you're putting at risk is ultimately the most important thing you can do."*

Before the investment world became so organized, computerized, and buttoned-down, there were larger-than-life figures who were outspoken, who relied on their gut rather than investment memos, and who were unafraid of any challenge. Indeed, the tougher the challenge and the more impossible the mission, the more they thrived.

One such figure still remaining in the investment world is Sam Zell, long considered by many as the smartest, toughest investor in real estate and in a good many other areas as well. He has consistently been willing to take risks that others thought it best to avoid, and his risk-taking seemed to work—often with a Midas touch. In fact, in 2017 Sam was recognized by *Forbes* as one of the 100 Greatest Living Business Minds.

Sam once labeled himself "The Grave Dancer" for his unique talent at finding and resurrecting investment opportunities where others had failed (and figuratively had gone to their grave trying).

Although educated as a lawyer, Sam only practiced law for four days, preferring to manage and then buy real estate properties. He did so well at this undertaking that he ultimately built the largest publicly traded collection of office buildings in the United States (Equity Office Properties) and sold it at the absolute top of the market in 2007 after running an auction that secured a price even he had not thought was possible. (Blackstone was the winning bidder but—as noted in the Jon Gray interview—it wisely sold two-thirds of what it had bought within months of the closing, retaining the best properties, and ultimately doing quite well; those who bought from Blackstone did not have the same good fortune.)

Sam is legendary not only for his investment acumen and timing but also for his blunt and "colorful" language. His autobiography is appropriately titled *Am I Being Too Subtle?* But Sam's blunt language seems not to have cost him any admirers or friends. He has legendarily close friends and investment partners throughout the world, and with some of them he regularly goes on extended motorcycle trips, where his fearlessness is even more apparent.

I have known and admired Sam for many decades, though we have never invested together. We have been on investment conference panels together and have in common one important view—the legal profession is better off when certain law school graduates spend their professional time not practicing law.

The Sam Zells of the world may be a declining breed, but fortunately there is still at least one left—the original; and he is going strong at an age where others might spend time on less arduous pursuits than grave dancing. I interviewed Sam virtually on May 20, 2021.

DAVID M. RUBENSTEIN (DR): You're famous for buying things when they are out of favor. Right now, what are you buying? What do you think is out of favor and has been beaten down because everything seems so expensive right now?

SAM ZELL (SZ): The answer is that pricing reflects reality, and I would imagine that cheap things are cheap because they're not very good. What we've found is that there's more than just price. We've spent quite a bit of time in the last three or four years doing what I call generational investing, where there's an existing business and maybe one generation, one person, runs it, and then there's an aunt and a sister and people who want liquidity. We've been, in effect, putting up 75 percent of the money and allowing the operator a role while we participate in the growth of the company.

DR: In 1976, you wrote a famous article called "The Grave Dancer." It was about how you're basically dancing on the grave of assets that had lost favor. When you show up to buy something, do people say, "If Sam is coming to buy it, must be we're selling it at too cheap a price"? Does that reputation as the Grave Dancer hurt you or does it help you?

SZ: Probably 50/50. Some people are intimidated. Most people have enough self-confidence that they feel comfortable dealing with the approach. Yes, I wrote the article called "The Grave Dancer," but what I was really trying to point out was that buying distressed assets requires you to walk very close to the graves, and that if you weren't careful, the best of intentions could have you falling in.

DR: You grew up in Chicago. Your parents are Polish immigrants. You didn't grow up in a wealthy family. When you were growing up, did you say, "I want to be the Grave Dancer when I grow up and be a famous investor"? When you were a boy, a young man, what did you say you wanted to be?

SZ: I was sure I should be a fireman, then I thought about it and I expected to be a lawyer.

DR: You went to the University of Michigan undergrad. How come you left the state of Illinois?

SZ: Michigan was truly an extraordinary school. I thought that I could get a broader exposure at a higher-quality school.

DR: You then went to the University of Michigan Law School as well. So you must have thought you were going to be a lawyer. I assume you had parents who said, "My son is going to be a nice Jewish lawyer," and they were happy with that, right?

SZ: The advice from my parents was very single-minded, and that was you have to have a profession so that you could always work for yourself and make a living. They encouraged me to go to law school. I'm the classic story of "What is a lawyer? A Jewish boy who can't stand the sight of blood." Medical school wasn't an option. I wasn't interested in it. But the legal world held some attraction.

DR: When you went to law school, did you enjoy it or did you say, "This is pretty boring"?

SZ: I thought it was horrendously boring. The three years I spent in law school were definitely the lowest point that my pulse rate was in those years.

DR: In my own case, my mother wanted me to go to law school. When I got to be a lawyer and I started Carlyle later, she said, "Keep your law license because you need something to fall back on."

SZ: That's right.

DR: I'm still a member of the DC Bar.

SZ: Your mother and my mother could have known each other.

DR: While you were in law school, you had an opportunity to buy an apartment building, is that right?

SZ: I started out when I was a junior. I visited a friend of mine who was living in a house. He said that the owner of the house had been there the night before and had bought the house next door and was going to build a 15-unit apartment building. I said, "Why don't we go pitch him? We'll run it and we'll each get a free apartment." We did it, and we did it very successfully. Then we got another building, another building, another building. Then I started buying a couple of buildings. I spent a year buying a square block, and I was having a great time.

DR: Did you ever pass the bar? Did you ever take the bar exam or not?

SZ: Yes, of course.

DR: Did your mother say, "You should be practicing law, not buying these buildings"?

SZ: No, she didn't. I was doing all this stuff before I was out of law school. So, I was theoretically going to law school at the same time, which I was, and I graduated.

DR: You had a partner, somebody I guess you met in law school — Robert Lurie?

SZ: As an undergraduate.

DR: When you met him, you just said, "Let's go into business together"?

SZ: No. He was my first employee when I was building the management company when I was an undergraduate. By the time I left Ann Arbor, he was running a significant portion of this business, and I sold it to him. I said to him that when he got through playing around with these little guys and wanted to come play with the big boys, he should call me. Three years later, he called me and I said, "Sure." And we built a spectacular relationship.

DR: What is it about real estate that made it appealing to you? Real estate is different than buying securities or companies. You've done that, and we'll talk about that. But what is it about real estate that you find makes it appealing as an area in which to invest?

SZ: First of all, I doubt there is any other area of commerce where more leverage (or debt) is available than in real estate. And most of that leverage is nonrecourse [meaning that the lender, upon a default, cannot seek recovery from the borrower's personal or corporate assets; recovery can only occur from the value of the assets against which the loan was made]. For someone intent on building a net worth as opposed to an income, the role of leverage in real estate was extremely attractive. I don't know whether I sat down and figured out the numbers specifically, but I felt as though I had a better opportunity in that arena than in any other to make multiples of invested capital.

DR: With real estate, you borrow a lot of money. That gets some real estate people in trouble from time to time. But you have to have some equity. Where did you get your equity from? Was it public markets or friends or your own money?

SZ: Initially I had made a little money. The first building I bought was $19,500. It was $1,500 down and $18,000 land contract. There were a bunch of those deals.

DR: In real estate, you had many different vehicles at one time. Was it difficult to have that many different real estate vehicles at once and keep them all straight and make everybody happy?

SZ: It was amazingly conflict-free. Buying an office building was not anything that anybody at Equity Residential [EQR], our residential company, or Equity LifeStyle Properties [ELS], our mobile home park company, could be concerned with. Buying a mobile home park couldn't possibly be a conflict with EQR. So, in effect, the arrangement of having three major views on the asset class in proximity to each other was very positive. I think it created more opportunity to find new deals and better opportunities to operate.

DR: My experience is that at Carlyle, we often have these young people prepare deep investment memos, 100-page memos, to convince me to do something or convince our investment committee to do something. But I've often thought that the best investors in the world used their intuition, their gut, and they don't rely on 100-page investment memos. When you were deciding to buy real estate over the years, did you do the due diligence yourself? What made you decide to buy something or not buy something?

SZ: I for sure didn't call for 100-page memos because, number one, I'd be suspect of anybody who could write a 100-page memo, and two, I'd be suspect of whether I could read it and not fall asleep. We did due diligence on everything that we bought, but due diligence was a couple of days of a couple of smart people going to Tucson and checking what they were buying in an apartment project, checking occupancy, talking to the brokers, getting a sense of what new was being added to the market. That's an appropriate amount of due diligence. Now, with the internet, so much information is available that any young analyst can do due diligence on a city or property they're pitching relatively quickly. Then they come in and make their pitch, and I sit there and I go back and forth and I challenge them on it. If they succeed in the challenge, then we buy the property.

DR: You did one of the most famous real estate transactions in the United States. You built a company called Equity Office Properties, known as EOP, a publicly traded REIT. Then some people decided that they wanted to buy it from you—CalPERS initially—and then you had a bidding war. It turned out at the top of the market. Why did you want to sell then, and how did you run that auction?

SZ: I very much like to take credit for catching the top of the market. I promise you it was accidental. I never even thought about it from that perspective. But with all of our REITs, every 90 days we do our own internal analysis of what they're worth, just so that we always know. We did the same thing with Equity Office. When we got the first inquiry, we were a little stunned, because we thought we were too big to be bought. So we never even thought about it beyond the fact that somebody actually inquired.

Fortunately, at the time their price was materially below our own analysis, so we just rejected it and went back to business and forgot about it. And then there was this famous line where somebody called from one of the brokerage firms and said to me, "What would it take?" My answer was, "It would take a 'Godfather' offer." That led to the first offer from Blackstone and eventually, with another company competing, the total deal went from $36 billion to $39 billion.

DR: The original offer that you got was probably 20 percent or 30 percent below what you finally got by running an auction?

SZ: Yes, that's right.

DR: As it turned out, the people who bought it bought at the top of the market. And, fortunately from their point of view, Blackstone resold a lot of it. But had they not, they would have made some mistakes for sure.

SZ: Blackstone sold over two-thirds of the portfolio, and every one of the Blackstone buyers didn't make it.

DR: You've bought a lot of things in recent years that are not real estate. How did you decide to get comfortable buying non–real estate companies?

SZ: Back in 1981, my partner, Bob Lurie, and I were sitting there and ruminating about the fact that we didn't like the big commercial real estate market. We started talking about the fact that as long as you weren't designing rocket engines or biotech or something like that, the rules of the game were basically one-on-one with supply, demand, market share. It was all logic. We said to ourselves, "If we've been as successful as we are in real estate, we ought to be able to take that success and apply it to the business world and be equally successful." We made a kind of pact and said, from 1981, in 10 years we wanted to go from 100 percent real estate to 50/50. We more than did that, and continue to more than do that. Today the ratio is probably 70 percent non–real estate/30 percent real estate with great diversity, including logistics, healthcare, manufacturing, energy, and agribusiness.

DR: Were you still a grave dancer in non–real estate assets as well?

SZ: When there were grave-dancing possibilities. In 1990, we raised that $1 billion fund. In 1990, a billion dollars was what a billion really should be. We raised a billion dollars and the investment goal was "good company, bad balance sheet." Over the next eight years, we invested and harvested that money and we took great advantage of the opportunity.

DR: Over the years, you went to some large institutional investors, the same ones that I often went to. What was it like? "The Great Sam Zell, Mr. Grave Dancer" going and asking for money from young investment professionals who were managing these big pension funds—was it difficult to go ask these people for money?

SZ: Probably no more difficult than it was for you.

DR: But you're more famous.

SZ: Both of us succeed with a combination of ego and humility. We succeed because we're able to adjust that ego and humility backward and forward to achieve our objectives.

DR: What would you say is the skill you have that has been helpful? Is it finding the deals, negotiating the deals, financing the deals, adding value to the deals, or all of those different things?

SZ: I'd like to say that all of those things are relevant, and to some extent they probably are. If I had to make a determination, I would say that it starts with some kind of innate recognition of what kind of deal was worth pursuing. I had a banker in the '80s who had an orange sign on his desk that said, "Fastest no in the west." I'll never forget that, because more than anything else, what I'm really good at is not spending time on something that won't lead to fruition.

DR: Nobody in the investing world makes every deal work perfectly, and you've had some deals that didn't work out.

SZ: Without question.

DR: Do you say, "What did I do wrong?" Do you blame somebody else? How do you deal with the fact that you lost some money?

SZ: I've been losing money ever since I started. All I can do is remember that in baseball they pay a guy $25 million a year to hit one out of three times. What I want to do is be right 60 percent or 70 percent of the time, but wrong in a controlled fashion. Knowing what you're putting at risk is ultimately the most important thing you can do.

DR: One of the most visible deals you did that didn't really work out was the *Chicago Tribune*. What made the deal not work out so well?

SZ: In the most simplistic form, we underwrote the deal on the assumption that there would be a 6 percent per annum suppression in revenues in the newspaper business. And instead of six it was 30. Everything else was irrelevant.

DR: Let's talk about the appeal of investing. Obviously, others of us in the investment world find it intoxicating to do. Find a deal, do a good deal. Is it like a high that you get from doing deals? Is that why you like it?

SZ: That's not a bad description. Long ago, any one deal wasn't going to change who paid for jet fuel for my plane. What motivated me was figuring out how to do things and how to make 1+1=6. The reality is we both work for charity, because ultimately I'm giving away whatever I make anyway.

DR: I understand the feeling. Somebody reading this might say, "I want to be the next Sam Zell." What skill set would you tell young professionals they should have to be the next Sam Zell?

SZ: I answer that by saying, "Sam Zell is a professional opportunist. He's an entrepreneur. As an entrepreneur, he has a lot of self-confidence, justified or not I can't tell you, but he has a lot of self-confidence. Failure is not in his lexicon. Sometimes it doesn't work out, but never fails. Sam sees problems and sees solutions, and in the same manner. A character like Sam is a great observer, whether you observe by watching or reading or both, but a great observer of a huge volume of facts and the ability to sort through them and find relevance in making decisions."

DR: Let's suppose somebody says, "I don't think I can be Sam Zell, but I have a lot of money and I want to invest in real estate." What do you recommend they do with their money that they want to put in real estate? Give it to people that have experience, maybe like you?

SZ: I definitely would, assuming they acquired all that money because they did something else. The highways are strewn with the skeletons of people who said, "I'm a businessman and I can do real estate the same as the next guy." I invest with other people in real estate today because they do things much better in real estate than I would do, or they're at a different scale. To the extent that somebody has serious money and is looking to diversify into real estate, there are plenty of money managers out there who specialize in real estate and who I think do a very good job.

DR: If somebody wants to invest in real estate as opposed to buyouts or venture capital, what do you think is a respectable rate of return? Is that 8 percent, 9 percent, 10 percent, something like that?

SZ: That actually is generous today. The cap rates for real estate properties today are probably closer to 5 percent, and getting to 10 percent for an overall return might not be easy.[*]

---

[*] In real estate, the cap rate, or capitalization rate, is the annual return on the overall investment in a property from a property's income sources after all costs have been paid. If an office building was purchased for $1 million and the available cash each year after payment of all expenses to operate and insure the building is $50,000, the cap rate would be 5 percent. Upon the sale of the property, if market conditions have improved, a buyer might be prepared to pay a higher price than $1 million. That higher price would increase the return on the investment above the 5 percent cap rate.

DR: When you're looking for people to hire, what is the skill you're looking for? A high IQ, a big work quotient, a great education? What is the skill that makes you say, "I want to hire that person"?

SZ: I'll start by taking the last of the items you mentioned. I don't remember ever concentrating on where anybody went to school, either plus or minus. I've had too many Harvard grads come in who I don't think were very good. I've had local kids who did terrific. And as far as IQ is concerned, if I'm looking for people to work for me, I want them to have an above-average intelligence quotient but not to be too smart. I'm much more interested in energy level and motivation. The most successful people who have worked for me have had the highest degree of motivation.

DR: Are there any investors that over the years you have particularly admired? People who are not in real estate, or maybe they are in real estate.

SZ: The single biggest business role model I ever had was Jay Pritzker. Jay was just the smartest businessman I've ever met since, before, after, and then. I worked with him for 20-odd years and it was truly a pleasure.

DR: Your personal style, I think it's fair to say, is not buttoned-down. You're not a Wall Street kind of guy. You're not a suit kind of guy. You're iconoclastic. Has that been helpful to you? Were you always that way or did it just come along in recent years?

SZ: I've always been that way. My office went casual in 1969. We have investors in deals who used to come over to our office because they just couldn't believe that you could excel and dress funny at the same time. More than anything else, we were always out to prove that. We felt that if we created a unique environment we could excel, and we have.

DR: Do you own any ties?

SZ: Yes. As a matter of fact, at the end of my closet I have a tie rack. And every month or so I go and I move them around. It's like pop art.

DR: You have a very well-developed sense of humor. Did you get that as a youth? Did you develop it later in life? Does it come back to haunt you sometimes if you make a joke and somebody doesn't like it?

SZ: Oh, sure. I'm learning how to be better. I've always kind of shared what's in my head with whoever is standing next to me, and sometimes I'm sorry. But there's never an intent to offend people. And over the years I think I've succeeded because I've always been intense, and I've always been observant. If I make a mistake, I catch it rather than let it fester.

DR: You wrote an autobiography called *Am I Being Too Subtle?* The title's a reflection of the fact that generally you do tell people what's on your mind. You're not beating around the bush. That's been successful for you, more or less?

SZ: Yes, I think so.

DR: If you had to do your investment career all over again, is there anything you would have done differently, or you're pretty happy with the way things worked out? Not every deal worked out. Any regrets?

SZ: No. That probably has more to do with the fact that my personality doesn't have regrets attached to it. I've never been the kind of person who looked back and said, "I wish I had done this" or "I wish I had done that." I've always been confident in what I do. I'm sure sometimes I wish I'd done it better. Sometimes I wish I skied down the hill better than the last time I did. But I've never really thought, "I wish I had done this" or "I wish I had done that."

DR: You have a lot of people depending on you. Investors give you money. Banks lend you money. But you are a big motorcycle person, and you ride around the world on your motorcycle at very fast speeds, as I understand it. Isn't it a little unsafe to do that?

SZ: I have a lot of confidence in my ability to ride. I've been riding since I was 18. I think I'm a pretty good motorcycle rider. If you look at the statistics, the great majority of motorcycle accidents occur within the first six months of a person getting the bike. The history says that the longer you ride, the safer you become.

In the end, I give life an awful lot. I give society a lot of things. I work for society. I'm philanthropic. I've got to do what provides freedom to me, and I always will. Motorcycling is just an example of it.

DR: Some people in the investing world like to watch computer screens all the time. When you're riding your motorcycle around the world, it's hard to keep up with what's going on. You worry about something happening when you're riding your motorcycle around the world?

SZ: No, but I keep in touch. In the old days, we'd go for two weeks, and maybe we'd have a phone call to check with the office once every couple of days. It was a very different world then.

DR: If you were to summarize what you would say to somebody who wants to be a successful investor, what would your advice be in a couple of sentences?

SZ: Good investors focus on risk. Risk is the downside. Bernard Baruch said it well when he said nobody ever went broke taking a profit. Those who focus on containment ultimately have a greater percentage of succeeding. My own orientation is that if I wanted to be an investor today, I would be an observer. I'd study. I'd think. I'd see. But I'd ultimately look at the world and say, "What could go wrong?" And deal with that rather than take a positive attitude and get disappointed or be unprepared.

Private Wealth/
Family Offices

MARY CALLAHAN ERDOES

CEO, J.P. Morgan Asset & Wealth Management

"The best wealth managers in the world do much more listening than they do talking."

For several centuries, banks and related financial institutions have helped the very wealthy manage their money and other assets, and helped facilitate the transfer, and continued stewardship, of that wealth for future generations.

But the number of individuals and families needing these services was small compared to the overall population. In recent years, though, as the wealth in developed markets and in so many emerging markets has grown exponentially, so has the demand for these types of services, often now called "wealth management."

The services that wealth managers provide their clients have expanded in recent years, as the challenges of having wealth have increased. Traditionally, wealth managers would manage the wealth of their clients by recommending investments to be made (or, with appropriate authorization from the client, make the investments directly).

But wealth managers now do much more. Their services include advice about income taxes, especially trust and estate taxes; bill payments; philanthropy; divorce; and intra-family challenges. Wealth managers are generally focused on enabling a family (or extended family) to maintain and protect their wealth, and hopefully as well to enhance that wealth.

Not surprisingly, many specialized wealth management firms have arisen around the world to meet this demand, though banks still are the single most significant provider of these types of services. For many, the gold standard of these banks is the J.P. Morgan Asset & Wealth Management division, now entrusted with more than $4 trillion in client assets globally.

Clearly, money has been attracted to the name J.P. Morgan for more than a century. But many other well-known names have fallen by the wayside in the competitive wealth management business, in part because they did not provide the investment opportunities and returns sought by increasingly sophisticated clients. J.P. Morgan has been able to do so in no small part because of the leader of its wealth management business—Mary Callahan Erdoes.

She joined J.P. Morgan more than a quarter of a century ago, after getting degrees from Georgetown University (where she was the only female math major in her class) and Harvard Business School. At J.P. Morgan, Mary was quickly recognized for her financial skills and investment acumen. She rose quickly to the top of J.P. Morgan's asset and wealth management arm despite the fact that, like so many parts of the financial services world, both the asset management and wealth management industries were heavily male-dominated.

In addition to her role in overseeing the wealth management business, she is a member of the J.P. Morgan Operating Committee, and has been a trusted advisor for more than a decade to J.P. Morgan's legendary CEO, Jamie Dimon.

I have known Mary for a good many years, as a very satisfied client of her wealth management division and as a colleague on the New York Fed's Investor Advisory Committee. It has been rumored that she might one day succeed Jamie Dimon. Selfishly I hope that does not occur, for I really like as a client having her overseeing the wealth management business. For the celebration of her twenty-fifth anniversary at J.P. Morgan, I forwarded a note that I had received from heaven from Mr. J. P. Morgan himself, saying that she was actually his favorite employee of all time, but asking her not to tell Jamie. I interviewed Mary in person on June 7, 2021.

DAVID M. RUBENSTEIN (DR): When you were growing up, did you say, "I want to manage $4 trillion when I am an adult"?

MARY CALLAHAN ERDOES (ME): I wish I had had that clairvoyance back then, but no. My first foray into the money management business was my grandmother asking me to balance her checkbook. She actually paid me a couple of dollars every month to do that.

One day she said, "I think you need to get a real job," and sent me downtown, to the city of Chicago, to look for a job. I found one in the mailroom equivalent of Stein Roe & Farnham, which was an investment management house. The mailroom equivalent was the computer room, where you ripped off the pieces of paper for the big portfolios, then you walked the different floors and delivered them to people. Over time, a few of them took interest in explaining to me what I was delivering to them every day.

That's when I fell in love with markets, and understood that every day was different, that all of the brokers managed portfolios in a different manner. I also learned about the concept of overtime, so that was pretty cool, too.

DR: You went to college at Georgetown University in Washington, DC, where you're now on the board. What did you major in there?

ME: I majored in mathematics, with a minor in French.

DR: Were there a lot of women in the mathematics major?

ME: No. I was the only one at the time. That's changing, with all of the great work that people are doing to promote STEM [science, technology, engineering, and mathematics] in universities across the country. But I was the only one, and I didn't know where it would take me.

I found myself on Wall Street, and went through the analyst program at Bankers Trust. Those training programs have a way of accelerating learning in an intense period of time.

DR: After doing that for a few years, you went to Harvard Business School. Were there a lot of women in your class then?

ME: We were fewer back then. But it was a wonderful experience. It opened the world up to the different kinds of things you could do and the training that you needed, not just to be a financial analyst but to be a manager of people. The organizational behavior class was probably the single most important one that I took.

DR: Now you've been at J.P. Morgan for about 25 years, and you run one of the most important parts there, the Asset & Wealth Management business. What is wealth management, and how is that different than asset management?

ME: The two are often used interchangeably, but they have distinctions. The asset management business is where we manage money on behalf of individuals, institutions, sovereign wealth funds, pension funds. We manage them in mutual funds. We manage them in ETFs. We manage them in single stocks, single bonds, hedge funds, private equity, and the like. That is the heart of the fiduciary business that we run here at J.P. Morgan. Wealth management is that plus understanding someone's entire balance sheet.

With the individuals we manage money for, we also help them with their mortgage. We help them with a loan they might need. We help them with their basic credit card. Wealth management is trying to help someone with their entire life, both their assets and their liabilities, their planning, their gifting, the legacy that they want to leave for their families, the 529 plans they need to prepare to get their kids through college. It's a great insight into people's entire journey.

DR: Many organizations like J.P. Morgan have wealth management businesses. Some are bigger, some are smaller, but basically you're managing money for wealthy people?

ME: Yes, although many of the successful wealth management firms today have figured out how to take all of those great things they do with very wealthy people and package them for people who have their first paycheck and want to be able to save a little bit of money. We've been able to do what we do for a super wealthy family and package it into a bite-size option, where you can walk into a Chase branch and get some of the same advice.

The most important thing is to be able to save early. Look at an average investment over the past 20 years. Take a balanced portfolio. It's about a 6.5 percent average annual return. The problem is that most individuals' actual return is less than 3 percent, so it's less than half. Why? Because they make emotional decisions when markets are one way or another. They get caught up in the hype of things. It's super important to have that advice as early on as we can give it.

That's the rewarding part about this business—being able to try to help people through all of those different journeys they have, and help them to do it in a way that would be better than if they did it on their own.

DR: So what you're saying is that the average person, if he or she says, "I'll manage my money myself," that person generally is either selling at the wrong time or buying at the wrong time? Or at least they're not getting the returns they could get if they had a professional manager helping them?

ME: Some people are very successful investors in their own right. What I've seen over the 25 years I've been doing this is that most people make great sums of money by doing one thing really well. When they master that one thing, like maybe running one of the largest and most successful private equity firms in the world, nobody can beat them in that space. That's the way they make their money. Then, to keep their money and continue to grow it, the trick is diversification. Diversification comes with having to master lots of different things. Generally, people find it hard to master lots of different asset classes, sectors, areas to invest in, because they don't have the time to do that. So being able to get other people to help with those components is the way most successful people have handled this situation.

Now, that doesn't mean they are just farming it out and saying, "Call me in a year and let me know how it goes." Many people are actively involved. Some give full discretion to a wealth management firm. No two clients ever, in my history, have walked in the door with the same amount of money and at the same place in their life, and decided to do the same things with their wealth.

DR: Your point is that some people can be geniuses in building a tech company or something else, but they're not generally going to be a genius at investing because it's a different kind of skill set?

ME: It takes so long to master a field. I think of it like being a specialty doctor. If you're a heart surgeon, you work to become the best in the business, but that doesn't mean you would go and try to be a doctor in all the other fields. That's what we find in the money management business. It's incredibly complex. Our job in wealth management is not only to help a client to figure out what pieces they need, but then to access those great managers around the world and get exposure to different places and different experts.

DR: Somebody reading this might say, "I don't have $25 million or $100 million, so J.P. Morgan wouldn't want me as a client. Citicorp wouldn't want me." What does it take to be a client of the wealth management group of these large banks?

ME: Large banks used to say that if you didn't have a certain amount of money, you wouldn't be able to be covered by them. That has completely changed, because of the fractionalization and the digitalization of everything we do. So you can have your first hundred dollars and get exposure to some of the best money managers who have a balanced mutual fund. It's about starting early, getting access to advice, and finding your way through that journey. The earlier you save, the earlier you learn, the earlier you have your stumbles, the better it is. The very successful wealth management firms can help you in that regard.

DR: Let's suppose somebody makes a big fortune and he or she all of a sudden becomes a billionaire. Do they just call you up out of the blue? How do you get very wealthy people to be your clients?

ME: This business is based on trust. You don't wake up one morning and find yourself with a great sum of wealth and then just go trust someone you haven't known for years.

It is a long journey to get to know people, to get to know their families, to help them with a piece of something along their journey. The more you do that, the more you can find your way and be able to give them the proper advice.

The advice can be, Stay in cash. Or monetize. Or do nothing. It's not as much about managing your money as it is talking about structuring your money. Let's figure out where we're going to hold it. Let's figure out how much you're going to give away, how much you're going to keep for your family, how much taxes are involved.

DR: Let me give you my three rules of money management and see whether they comport with yours. Number one: Don't lose what you have. A lot of times my observation is people think that they made a fortune and they can double it or triple it, and they're willing to take risks that might make them lose everything.

ME: "Don't lose what you already have" is a very good way of thinking about it. We always say to clients, "Try to figure out what sum of money that, if you were to have it, you wouldn't change your lifestyle. Everything else beyond that, there is room to be more aggressive." It would be unfortunate to find yourself in a downturn not being able to live the life you had worked so hard to achieve.

DR: My second rule of money management is: Diversify. Don't put all your eggs in one basket.

ME: One hundred percent. We see it all the time. You can see it in today's market environment. Some of these things look very easy to make money in, because there's so much froth in the markets. There's so much liquidity that's been pumped in by governments all around the world. And so what's seemingly easy may not be. One of the jobs of a good wealth manager is to always stress-test a portfolio and to say, "Are we sure we want to be holding on to that outsized position?"

DR: My third and final rule would be: Have realistic expectations about what rate of return you're seeking. Be realistic about what you're going to get. Do you tell people that there are different asset classes with different rates of return and they should be realistic about what they're going to get? Or do they all think they're going to double their money if they give it to you?

ME: It's such an important question, especially with interest rates where they are today. If you use the 10-year Treasury bond as a marker at 1.5 percent, everything above that is additive. If you go to a client and you say, "I can get you 1 percent over Treasuries," it's not very exciting, especially when the markets are providing 10, 20, 30, 40, 50 percent returns on some of these asset classes for a short period of time.

If you look over the past 20 years, the average balanced portfolio has had a 6.5 percent return. But a 6.5 percent return compounded each and every year for 20 years is a very sizable return. Over the past year, many people have had average balanced portfolios up 30 percent, and they have become accustomed to those returns. They want to hear from someone who's going to say, "I can get you another 30 percent." But if something sounds too good to be true, there's a high likelihood that it is.

DR: Let's talk about how somebody becomes a wealth manager. I don't know if there is a special course at Harvard Business School or other places on how to be a wealth manager. What kind of people do you hire and how do you train them?

ME: Training on Wall Street, specifically in wealth management, is a very long process. It begins with a two- to three-year training program. Yet it is a constant education, each and every day. Every morning we start with an eight o'clock meeting. I call it a mini university. It's not just about what you've read in the newspapers as to what happened overnight, it's about understanding how all of those components fit together in a client's portfolio. You're synthesizing all of that information every morning, then you're going out and figuring out how to apply it to each situation.

DR: If you go to a meeting with a wealthy family and they've got their children there, maybe the grandchildren, do you realize they don't talk to each other about money very much? Or they have different views?

ME: I've never met a family that has the same views universally. That's what makes this business so interesting. Every single day it's something new. Every family has a new set of questions. The dynamics are different. Some people want to be involved. Other people don't. Some people want to give all their money away. Other people don't. Some people want to spend a lot of time thinking about giving back to the country.

DR: Patriotic philanthropy.

ME: Philanthropy is, in and of itself, teaching families how to think about the mission. Getting everyone to come around and join in on that same thinking is not an easy task.

DR: Do clients come in and basically ask your advice? They tell you what they want? Or they just say, "I don't really know what I want. Tell me what I should be doing"?

ME: The most successful rarely say, "I don't know what I want." But it's a long journey from what they think they want versus where they may end up. Most clients have a mindset of how to express their risk and reward. "I don't want to lose any money." "I need this kind of income." "I only want to invest in these countries." "I only want to invest in these sectors." "I'm very interested in environmental issues and I want to double down there." Each has a separate and distinct path. The best wealth managers in the world do much more listening than they do talking.

DR: When does somebody establish a family office? What kind of net worth does one typically have before you set up a family office?

ME: A family office can be relevant and important for any size family. It's about having people surrounding you. They can work directly for you or they can work at an outside firm. I like to think of J.P. Morgan as an outsourced family office.

There's no hard-and-fast number as to when that makes sense. It's all personal preference. We have some people with multi-billions of dollars who have no family office, and we have people with $10 million who have their own family office. It's all where you want to put your efforts.

DR: Who manages your money? I'd hate to be the person who has to come to you and say, "Well, it didn't work out so well." How do you select the person who's managing your money? I presume you're using J.P. Morgan.

ME: We have always had J.P. Morgan manage my family's wealth. But it's very important that I don't spend a lot of time doing that myself. I don't think our clients would like me spending a lot of time thinking about my own portfolio.

I also think it's very important to be able to invest in everything you are thinking that your clients should invest in. I'm generally a first buyer of most everything that we offer at J.P. Morgan.

DR: Let me talk about the great wealth transfer. My generation, the Baby Boomer generation, is aging a little bit. It's thought to be the wealthiest generation in our country's history, but eventually, this generation is going to be giving a large part of its wealth to its children.

Is that a difficult thing for a family to deal with? They come in and say, "I don't want my children to have too much money," and they say that in front of the children? Or they say, "My children don't know anything about money. Don't let them make any decisions"? How do you deal with those intergenerational issues?

ME: Intergenerational issues are probably one of the toughest challenges. They morph and change over time. There are basically four places you can give your money if you live in the United States of America. You can spend it yourself. You can give it to your children. You can give it away to charity. Or you can give it to the government. And you have to figure out which of those four buckets you want to have weighted in which manner.

There's no right answer. There's no wrong answer. You work so hard to make the money, trying to figure out how to impart your values to the next generation or on philanthropies, or how you're going to live your life.

That's not for any wealth manager to say. Our place is to figure out how to ferret out answers to those questions, then be able to apply a plan and work through that plan over time.

DR: One of the most difficult things for wealthy people to decide, I've found, is how much money to give to their children and also how to deal with their own estate. Is it awkward sometimes when you have to ask people about their will and what they're going to do? Do you ever find out that one spouse hasn't told the other spouse where the money's going?

ME: That happens a lot. It's not about not telling. It's about not really understanding the mechanics of what happens when. We spend a great deal of time putting on one piece of paper a nice picture of what's actually going to happen when.

The hardest conversation to have is when a client says, "If I die." We first have to work through that thought. These are awful conversations to have to think through. But if you think about it early enough, it becomes much less emotional.

DR: I won't mention his name, but one of the wealthiest, most famous investors in the world has told me that he's redone his will 17 or 18 times, almost every year. Then he shows it to his children to get their judgment. Do people typically show their will to their children? Or is it kind of a guessing game?

ME: Changing it every year would make for an interesting annual meeting with the family.

The most important thing is just talking it through and working through those issues, and understanding the responsibility that comes with wealth. Because wealth isn't about just getting the money as a next-generation person as part of this great wealth transfer you mention. It's about preserving wealth. It's about doing the right things for your community and for the things that you care about deeply.

Sometimes we're the catalyst for those conversations, because it's not something you want to talk about every night at dinner. It can be a little awkward.

DR: Do you sometimes feel like a psychiatrist when you're listening to these family issues?

ME: A little bit. As a wealth manager, we get to see so many families, not just in the United States but in Brazil, in Europe, in Asia. Our job is to bring to the client all the collective experiences we've seen, and to say, "Here's how it might work if you do that." We often put families in touch with other families and say, "Let me call and ask if they'd be interested in talking." Those are probably the best pieces of advice we can give.

DR: Howard Hughes famously died without a will. Most of the people that you're talking to, do they come in and have a will?

ME: Not all come with a will. We think it's a very important part of our role to make sure that we've gone through the checklist of things you should do in your life, and that's certainly one of them.

DR: Let's talk about the environment we're in now for managing somebody's money. Interest rates have been low for a long time. The government has stimulated the economy a lot, and prices are pretty high. Are you now telling people to be careful because the economy might slow down? Do you give them geopolitical advice as well as financial advice?

ME: Yes. Every day that's a different conversation. As you say, the markets are very healthy right now, given the liquidity that has been infused. We had a recession that was five times greater than the average recession. It happened so fast. Yet our response to it was to add deficits to the

United States government that were greater than the last five recessions and the deficits that came about then. We've had policy responses that are unprecedented here, and now we're seeing that play out in the marketplace. When you have something like Dogecoin that was created as a joke and now has $30, $40 billion worth of value [now worth $11 billion as of June 1, 2022], you have to ask yourself, is it the liquidity that is sloshing around in the system that's causing this or are these real, new things that are happening?

Only time will tell. But it goes back to one of the most important things you pointed out, which is diversification. There's just no way to be able to know everything that's going to happen in the future in every single asset class. And so the most important answer is proper diversification of these portfolios.

DR: If somebody comes to you and says, "I want to invest in cryptocurrency," do you say, "You shouldn't do it" or do you facilitate it?

ME: Blockchain technology, which is the underlying piece of all of this, is very real and is changing all of the ways that we digitally interact with the different financial markets. Digital currencies are new. In general, it's being debated whether digital currencies are an asset class or not.

A lot of our clients say, "That's an asset class and I want to invest." Our job is to help them to put their money where they want to invest. It's a very personal thing. We don't have Bitcoin as an asset class per se. Time will tell whether it has the store of value. The volatility that you see in it today has to play itself out over time.

DR: You and I both were in the financial services world during the Great Recession of 2008–09. Were clients in the wealth management division of J.P. Morgan calling up and saying, "I've got to jump out the window. I'm losing all my money"? Was there panic? How did you deal with calming people down? It was a pretty difficult period.

ME: A very difficult period, the seeds of which also played out during the pandemic that we are still going through today. The Great Recession we experienced in 2008 was a quick, rude awakening to the safety and security of assets.

It was the first time in a long time where people not only said, "Oh gosh, the markets can go down and I can lose money," they also started to ask themselves, "Where is my money being housed? What's commingled with other assets? How do I think about that?"

I remember at one point in the fall of 2008, with all of that frantic movement, there were billions of dollars being moved around each and every day. There was a run, mentally, on "Where do I want to put my money?" About a billion dollars a day at one point was coming into the bank.

Trying to help people understand the safety and security of their assets and understanding diversification is key. You have to ride through these times. You can't be emotional, because at the end of the day, a lot of wealthy people don't need their money tomorrow. It's for many decades in the future. Trying to keep that long-term focus is probably the most important thing that we do.

If you fast-forward to the pandemic, many of the same things happened. If you look back to March 2020 and all the volatility then, a lot of people thought, "I should sell all my assets. The whole world is going to change." Other people thought, "Whoa, I can take advantage of these opportunities and think about all of this money I don't need daily liquidity in."

Again, safety and security of assets also came into play. Now you're seeing a constant flow of money to the firms where people are giving the good advice, helping think through the long-term issues, not being short-term about how they manage the assets.

DR: During the Great Recession, many people thought major banks were going to fail. J.P. Morgan was generally seen as the safest bank, so people just took their money from everywhere and just gave it to J.P. Morgan. Could you manage all that money easily? Were you surprised at how much money was flowing in that quickly?

ME: I was as surprised by how many people were uncomfortable with their money being held and managed at other places. The lessons learned as we went through that Great Recession and the leadership that Jamie Dimon showed all of us who were working at JPMorgan Chase were lessons that we will never forget.

We had tremors in the summer of 2007. We had the Bear Stearns event in 2008 where we helped that company and absorbed it into JPMorgan Chase. By the time we got to the fall of 2008, we already knew how you run the play. You meet, as a management team, three times a day, at 9 a.m., noon, 5 p.m. You go around the world, understand what issues are on the horizon. You try to ask the questions.

There's an old saying, "Always ask five 'whys' to be able to try and figure out why something is happening." We were at about 50 whys on the different mechanics of parts of the market. It helped us have a faster and better understanding of what was happening in the markets, and to be able to play that back to our clients to make sure that they were properly diversified.

We used that same playbook as we came into the global pandemic. You have to figure out, "What is changing? What do I know? What have I learned from different parts of the world?" Being able to use the power of a big global firm to bring that advice to bear for clients is one of the things we do very well.

DR: Do you have to keep up with everything going on in the economy and Washington, DC? Do you get briefed several times a day about what's going on to be able to answer questions?

ME: The job of any money manager, or anyone working in any field where they're responsible as a fiduciary for other people's money, is that's your life journey. You are constantly trying to understand all of the components of what's happening.

No one person at J.P. Morgan has to do that for every asset class. We have subject matter experts in each and every field. We have people we turn to in order to understand the nuances of the different things that have changed in the past year. All of that we synthesize each and every day and try to bring that back to our clients. It is a 24/7 process.

DR: When you first got into this business, would a wealthy man come in and say, "Can I have a man be my wealth manager?" I assume it doesn't happen today. Is there discrimination against women who are wealth managers?

ME: Thankfully, that never happened. I don't think that J.P. Morgan, even back then, would have ever stood for that kind of demeanor. That doesn't mean that clients don't have preferences of who they want to manage their money. If you and I meet and I say, "This is the way our firm manages money," you may like what I said about the firm, but we may not have a personal connection.

The job of a great wealth management firm is making sure that you have the proper fit. Because it's a long journey, and you have to trust somebody. That needs to be flexible. That needs to be flexible for different family members, too. Not every family member wants the same person helping them with their wealth. The true strength of a company is being able to be very flexible in how you cover the client.

DR: Let me ask you a few lightning-round kind of questions. What's the best investment advice you ever got?

ME: If it sounds too good to be true, it probably is.

DR: What is the biggest investment advice you would give to people about something they shouldn't do?

ME: You should never invest in something that can't be simplistically explained to you. One of the problems on Wall Street is that people use lots of acronyms and make it very complicated to explain something. The good investment advisors can take complex matters and make them simple.

DR: If somebody called you up tomorrow and said, "I'm not that wealthy relative to all your clients, but I do have $100,000. I'd like to put it somewhere." Where would you tell that person to put $100,000?

ME: In a balanced portfolio, well diversified, that they can store away for a long period of time, and hopefully it compounds healthily for them.

DR: What would you say to somebody is the most important thing they should *not* do with their money?

ME: They should not put all their eggs in one basket.

DR: My producer here would like to retire at the age of 40. Do you have any good investment advice about what she should do?

ME: Invest every single dime you have as early and as often as you can. There's a question, "Would I rather have a dollar double every day or get a million dollars?" A dollar doubling every day over a month would give you more than a million dollars. Investing and compounding — that's the answer to every question.

DR: You're running one of the biggest wealth management operations in the world. What's the pleasure of it as opposed to the frustrations of it?

ME: The real pleasure is helping the big pension funds that we manage. Each and every little decision that we make now for someone's retirement 30 or 40 years from now can mean an extra couple hundred dollars a month for every year that they're in retirement. That can fundamentally change someone's life.

DR: Would you recommend this as a career choice for young people?

ME: Wealth management is an important life component for everybody, because the more responsible you are in understanding how to invest money can help you, can help your family, can help other people you're advising. You don't need large sums of money to be able to do that and to do it well.

DR: I've said many times that private equity is the highest calling of mankind. But you would probably say wealth management is the highest calling of mankind, right? Because you're preserving people's money and enhancing it.

ME: That's exactly right. The value of the work that we do to help people to hopefully have a better retirement in the future, that gives me great joy.

DAWN FITZPATRICK

CEO and chief investment officer,
Soros Fund Management

> *"We're all wrong sometimes in this business. You only have to be right a little more than 50 percent of the time to do really well."*

For nearly a century, the wealthiest of American families—the Rockefellers, Mellons, Phippses, Vanderbilts, Kennedys—have had family offices, managing the families' money as well as dealing with philanthropic, real estate, bill-paying, insurance, legal, and estate issues. These offices often provide the same services as a wealth manager like J.P. Morgan. But families with enormous wealth seem to prefer to create their own internal wealth manager, to ensure greater control, privacy, and focus on their specialized needs. In a family office, all of the professionals in the office usually focus on the interests and needs of one family, though increasingly this becomes an extended family as the years pass by.

Typically, the focus was on wealth preservation, and the investment arms of the family offices were quite conservative. The offices were often created long after the initial creator of the wealth, if alive, was still active in the financial or business world.

In recent years, the creators of considerable wealth, at relatively young ages, have built family offices to manage their own affairs as well as the needs of their heirs. And when the wealth creator is still active in the financial world, these family offices have become more than collectors of dividends. Instead, they have created large new pools of wealth for the family by investing in private equity, venture capital, and growth capital vehicles, often being the lead investors in these funds. Most recently, some of them, like the Dell and some Pritzker family offices, have also raised large sums of money from other investors to supplement the capital they are deploying in new and potentially quite lucrative investments.

As a result of these trends, the family office has become an increasingly important part of the investment world. Typically, a family office can move quickly, without regulatory or bureaucratic constraints, and can add real value to an investment from its insights, contacts, and reputation.

After stepping down as co-CEO of Carlyle, and becoming co-executive chair of the firm, I followed the lead of many of my peers in the private equity world and also created a family office, Declaration Capital, to diversify my assets, to pursue areas that Carlyle does not pursue, and to involve my three children in some of my investment activities.

But my effort is modest compared to some others who have long preceded me in this area, who have much more to invest, and who may be seen far more as an investment leader than I am.

One of those investment leaders who have placed their assets in a family office investment vehicle (though most of the assets are now also in a foundation) is George Soros, the pioneering hedge fund investor and successful wealth creator for his investors over many decades. Before hedge funds were that well known or a constant, major presence in the investment world, Soros created hedge funds in 1969–70, and was the very active, hands-on leader of those funds for decades.

The results were so spectacular that Soros became one of the wealthiest professional investors in the world. He did invest in stocks and bonds, but his strength was generally his ability to spot macro market trends and to invest heavily in those trends. In recent years, as he has generally handed over the reins to others, his own money is being managed through a family office, as Soros has generally focused more of his time on philanthropic and political activities.

Currently, he has entrusted the investment of his family and foundation assets to an extraordinarily well-respected investor, Dawn Fitzpatrick, who has been a trailblazer among women investment professionals.

And while Soros is generally not managing his considerable wealth, his reputation for exquisite market timing and sagacity ensures that his family investment office will still attract considerable market attention. That can place enormous scrutiny on Dawn's investment decisions.

Dawn is a graduate of the Wharton School, and started her career at a proprietary trading firm, O'Connor & Associates, and stayed there when UBS acquired the firm. In time, she became the chief investment officer for O'Connor and ultimately the head of investments for UBS Asset Management, where she oversaw the investment of more than $500 billion. Her strong performance there attracted many suitors, including my own firm, but the winner of that effort was George Soros, who was willing to turn over the reins of managing his considerable personal fortune and the assets of his personal foundation, one of the country's largest foundations, to another extraordinary investor.

I have served with Dawn on a New York Fed Investor Advisory Committee, and it is clear from the way that the others on the committee and the New York Fed officials listen to her that she commands enormous respect within the investment community.

Her investment secrets are not complicated—a sensitivity to the Soros legacy, high intelligence, driven work ethic, not being intimidated by the large sums she is given to invest, willingness to listen to colleagues, and perhaps as well her commitment to running every day (a legacy of her time at Penn when she was on the track and cross country team). If I thought taking up running would also clear my mind and thereby improve my own investment skills, I would consider it. But I think it is her other qualities that are the key to her investment success. I interviewed Dawn virtually on June 22, 2021.

DAVID M. RUBENSTEIN (DR): You are now the chief investment officer for the Soros family office and for foundations in which George Soros has given a significant amount of his assets. Are you accountable to him, to his family, to the foundations' board, or to an investment committee?

DAWN FITZPATRICK (DF): I report to a five-person investment committee for the foundations. The committee comprises a select group of sophisticated investors from a variety of different asset classes.

DR: George Soros has had a number of outstanding investment professionals work for him over the years, but of his most senior investment professionals, his chief investment officers, you are the first woman. What prompted you to take a position that some in the investment world say has had a high turnover?

DF: Undoubtedly there's been a lot of turnover in the seat that I have. I was confident that I had the skills both to manage money and to manage the team. Going in, I asked for a construct where I could set the platform up for long-term success. I'm the first CIO at Soros Fund Management (SFM) who's also the CEO. When you think about this kind of investing, it's more than just your front-line portfolio managers that impact the returns you can deliver. Even with good investment performance, success was far from guaranteed; and thus it was not a given that I would survive. But as investors we're in the business of taking calculated risks, and I thought this was a risk well worth taking.

DR: Previously, you worked for a publicly traded company where short-term profits and quarterly numbers are the coin of the realm. What is it like overseeing the investment of funds for a large family office? You have a longer-term perspective. Is that much different than what you did before, and is that a problem or not?

DF: It's a significant advantage. A lot of the asset management industry that focuses on public markets, whether it's hedge funds or long-only managers, has to manage returns week to week or month to month. Because of that, you see some behaviors that are counterproductive. For us, having a single really sophisticated investor or client in the foundations, who have a medium- and longer-term investment horizon, is a monumental advantage. I push the investment team to think about how to capitalize on that advantage. We can lean into dislocations in ways that I think some more traditional asset managers have difficulty doing.

DR: Do you focus on many different types of asset categories, from fixed income to currencies to private equity to growth capital? Is there anything that you expressly do not pursue in the best-known categories of investment?

DF: No. Our investment mandate is broad, and we can pretty much invest in any asset class anywhere in the world. We try to be intellectually honest about where we have advantages or edge and where we don't.

An example might be commodities. The vertically integrated investors and traders in that space are massively advantaged; so we might make a directional investment in commodities but we're not going to trade relative value or in ways that are complex. It's important to us that we avoid investments that are inconsistent with the values of the foundations. We won't fund a private prison, for example.

DR: Do you do the investing directly, which George Soros used to do, or do you essentially outsource the investments to managers and you manage the managers?

DF: The beauty of the SFM platform is we can manage money internally and we can allocate externally. Since I joined SFM, we've actually been moving more towards direct management, because we can play to our strengths. When you invest assets with an external public-market hedge fund or long-only fund, they have to manage the utility curve of a hundred or a thousand investors versus a single investor. For us, there are white spaces in between how third-party asset management products are constructed. The opportunity set in those white spaces is outsized. We try to identify and capitalize on them given our uniqueness. Being able to deliver solutions to companies and projects that span debt and equity with a single partner also creates opportunities.

About 70 percent of our public market exposure right now is managed directly internally. Ninety-five percent of our private credit exposure is managed internally, and that's because we can affect outcomes. If something goes wrong, we can hold and manage through that. The only place where we have a majority of our assets allocated externally is private equity and venture.

DR: Is there a certain rate of return you are seeking to achieve overall each year?

DF: Managing to a specific return each year is dangerous, because it can lead you to take outsized risk at exactly the wrong moment in time. That said, we are benchmarked or judged against a couple of different numbers. We compare ourselves to big college endowments and the returns they're producing. We look at a simple, passive 60/40 portfolio [60 percent public equities, 40 percent public debt], and then we have our own policy portfolio that's set by our investment committee. That policy portfolio has your standard cap and growth bucket [large capitalization and growth public stocks], capital preservation bucket, and real asset bucket. We measure ourselves against those three groups—peers, passive, and a custom benchmark—and that's how we decide if we're doing a good job or not.

DR: How did you get into the investment business at the outset? What prompted you to want to be an investor?

DF: I'm naturally curious and I'm naturally competitive. When I was a little kid, we lived in a neighborhood of close, split-level '70s houses, and all the doors to the different houses were open. I used to wander down to my neighbor Marty Atlas's house and he taught me how to read the stock pages and follow companies at a young age. When I was 12 or 13, he gave me *Reminiscences of a Stock Operator* [Edwin Lefèvre's Wall Street classic], and I was hooked from there on out and was focused on becoming an investor.

DR: Was your family in the investment business as well?

DF: No, not at all. My grandparents immigrated from Ireland, and my father was in the computer consulting business.

DR: Did you go to Wharton with the expectation you would someday become an investor?

DF: Yes, absolutely. Wharton was the school I wanted to go to more than anything when I was in high school, and as soon as I got there my focus was on finance. I joined the Pennsylvania Investment Alliance and learned as much as I could from teachers and from fellow students.

DR: What did you do right after Wharton? How did you enjoy your days in the Chicago trading pits, and were there many women there with you then?

DF: Right out of Wharton I went to a proprietary trading firm called O'Connor & Associates. They specialized in derivatives, across asset classes, and they were the first firm to use big computing power to devise relative-value trading strategies. It was a meritocratic firm and there was a lot of intellectual firepower, so it was a great place to work. I was a clerk on the American Stock Exchange and then I went to be a trader on the CBOE [the Chicago Board Options Exchange], down in the trading pits, and it was a great place to learn. There weren't a lot of women there.

But when I was growing up, girls' sports teams were not as ubiquitous as they are today. I come from an athletic family and most of them are well-sized people, but I am very small, was always the smallest in my class. My parents would throw me on a sports team with boys if there wasn't a girls' team, and I was expected to compete. No tears, no excuses. That mindset has served me well, so when I walked onto the trading floor or any room I walked into in this career, I've never felt like I didn't belong.

DR: I assume you went to that firm because O'Connor was a nice Irish-sounding name?

DF: It happens to be my mother's maiden name, as coincidence would have it.

DR: What's required to be an outstanding investor? Are there certain qualities that you think are essential to being an excellent investor?

DF: I talked about being curious. You can't take an answer as a given. You always have to ask why and keep asking why and go down rabbit holes. I also think you have to be self-aware about what you're good at and what you're not good at, and willing to surround yourself and develop teams and talents that can make up for your shortfalls. In this industry, you make money by having a view that's not the consensus and, over time, becomes the consensus view. You have to have the confidence to have opinions and be an independent thinker and then be willing to bet on them.

The last thing I would say is we're all wrong sometimes in this business. You only have to be right a little more than 50 percent of the time to do really well. You have to have the discipline and humility to recognize when you're wrong, cut the position, and move on.

DR: In your current position, you're overseeing managers in many different areas. How do you decide what percentage of your assets go into one particular asset class versus another, and what are the qualities you're looking for in managers you hire?

DF: It's about the opportunity sets. You're thinking about the potential return stream and what are the risks associated with that return stream, and then you want to think about how many other return streams look similar to that. If you can have two attractive return streams but they look very different—in other words, one makes money on a day when the other might not be—that's obviously that much more attractive.

In terms of what we look for when we're allocating money or hiring a portfolio manager, we talked before about self-awareness. When I sit down with a manager, I want them to be able to explain to me what their edge is and why it exists. I don't like managers who always tell me their opportunity set is a 10 out of 10, because that is never the case. You want managers who fiercely want to win, but they have to be able to lose and learn from their losses, because losing is inevitable in this industry.

When we hire a portfolio manager, we hope they're going to be with us for the rest of their career. That said, sometimes opportunities just disappear for regulatory or other reasons. What we also see too often is where a good manager gets too focused on asset gathering vs. generating value-added returns. Investment strategies are almost invariably capacity-constrained—taking in assets past a certain point simply erodes the quality of returns. Sometimes, worse than that, managers start investing beyond their competency and in ways they have no skill in.

It is important that whomever you hire—whether directly or an external fund—puts the client interest first. That should always be a given, but I think we both know it isn't.

DR: If a manager is not performing, how long do you give them before they're discharged? Is it a year, five years? How long do you wait?

DF: A manager not making money might not necessarily be a reason we'd separate with them, and in fact could actually be a time when we want to double or triple our capital allocation. What we tend to evaluate is whether the returns, given the market backdrop, look like what we would expect. Sometimes you have a manager who's making significantly more money than you would expect, and that's actually a red flag. Sometimes you have managers who lose money for the right reasons and it's actually an opportunity. You want to be able to see that, and the longer you're invested with a manager, the more confidence you have to flex in with that manager. Then you have managers who lose money for the wrong reasons. They get fired, and they deserve to get fired.

DR: In your experience, the best money managers have what attributes, generally?

DF: I would say they understand the edge that they might have over the average investor, due to their experience, knowledge, or vantage point. They have a healthy respect for markets. They're calm under pressure and they're intellectually curious. They're great aggregators and assimilators of information. We all have confirmation bias, so they invest with that knowledge and with understanding of where that is. They're open-minded. They don't get wedded to an opinion in the absence of supporting facts.

DR: For those who are not quite as wealthy as George Soros but have enough assets to organize a family office, what are the important qualities for a family investment office to work well? Are there offices you have admired over the years?

DF: First of all, you need to understand the objectives of the family office. How much money do they intend to spend from the family assets each year? Do they want a type of slush fund in case there might be an extraordinary spend? It's important to understand the generational transitional plan. A lot of times, people focus on the returns that someone wants to make. But on the flip side of that, you have to understand the drawdown tolerance, because in the absence of understanding that, you could be in a situation where you hit it and all of a sudden you're selling at the worst possible moment. Have those conversations up front, so when you hit a moment in time when a portfolio is losing money, which invariably will happen, it's a way easier conversation to have. I also think that these days you need to have a conversation about ESG. What do they want to lean into in that regard? What are the red lines and areas they absolutely do not want to include in the portfolio?

DR: You focus on ESG for your own organization as well as for the managers you invest with?

DF: We focus on both. A lot of this is about transparency and accountability. A lot of the measures around ESG are nascent. They're developing.

So it has to be a conversation. Generally what we find both at the manager level and at the companies with which we invest is that everyone wants to do this well. Sometimes they just don't have the tools or know where to get started.

We really are trying to be part of the solution. We think this is a journey, and we want to be on that journey with the companies and with the managers. You have to report your DEI [diversity, equity, inclusion] numbers, you have to report your climate numbers, and you have to show progress.

DR: When you are managing money in the way you are as a fiduciary, do you feel it is appropriate to take the kind of bold bets that George Soros did such as his famous bet against the British pound in 1992, or is that too risky or outsized a bet to make when you are managing someone else's family office money?

DF: There's a great story about George when he was making a bet against the British pound. One of his trading heads turned to him and said, "You know we could lose everything on this?" George turned back to him and said, "That's okay. I can make it all over again."

I genuinely think that's the case. He is a force of nature. He's 91. He's tireless. In terms of aggregating and assimilating information, no one does it better. Running the foundation assets, I don't think I have the liberty to lose it all and make it back again. That's why, with the investment committee I report to, we talk about drawdown tolerance and liquidity needs, and we manage the portfolio in the context of that. That said, one of the interesting things is when I came into SFM, the portfolio was overdiversified. When a portfolio's overdiversified, you're guaranteed mediocrity, so we've concentrated the portfolio more since I've arrived here.

DR: What's the pleasure you get out of managing money in this manner? Is it the wide array of asset classes, the access to top managers, the ability to invest in novel areas?

DF: What I enjoy most about this industry is that every day you come in and your challenges are different and there's something to learn. When it comes to the SFM platform, in terms of solving those challenges, we have more degrees of freedom than any other pool of assets, especially relative to our size. That's really fun, and we have a dedicated team that works together. With the tools we have and the foundations we serve, it's the best job in the world.

DR: George Soros coined a word, "reflexivity." He was saying that when things go in one direction, they're going to go in that one direction more than you might expect before they rebound, and therefore you should make big bets in areas where you think you've spotted a trend. Is that something you have followed as well, or you don't go into something as boldly as he did when he was managing the money himself?

DF: We look at that. It's hard not to be watching cryptocurrencies in that context, and I can tell you George is. It's catching his attention in exactly the context you just spoke about, but the game and markets in that context have changed a little bit. It used to be easier for assets to move in those ways, because there was more asymmetry of information. There were a greater number of currencies. Central banks were less so-phisticated. That's a long-winded way of saying we don't do a lot of that. We make money in different ways, but the opportunity set in markets is very different than when George made his billions. I think if George was investing today, he'd make his billions differently than he did back in his heyday.

DR: How do you measure your success in doing this? Is it a certain rate of return, multiples of invested capital, pleasing the investment commit-tee? How do you measure your success when you're running a family office?

DF: Obviously I want to please George and the investment committee that I report to. I mentioned that we are measured against the bench-marks of the big college endowments, 60/40, and our policy portfolio. But at the end of the day, it's about making sure the foundation has the billion-plus a year to spend on all the good work they do. They're the largest private funder of human rights initiatives.

When it comes to success, the returns produced while I'm here are important, but I also want to create and build an SFM that's durable. In other words, I want to make sure that there's talent and a process and teams that produce good returns while I'm here and for decades after

I'm gone. Sometimes people root for things to fall apart when they're gone, because it shows their worth, but I disagree.

DR: Any regrets about not pursuing some other career?

DF: No. I feel so lucky to be in this industry. I bounce out of bed every day. I do daydream, one day when I'm retired or semi-retired, about teaching. That's something that I might do in the future, but I'm right where I want to be.

DR: What do you do to clear your head outside of the office? Sports? I know you were a great track star when you were younger. Hobbies, philanthropic interests—what is it that you do outside the office?

DF: The job keeps me busy. I also have three school-aged kids, and I do two boards. I do one school board and I'm on Barclays' board. I'm a big believer in "Everything you do, do well," and so that takes up a lot of time. That said, I still love to run. It's my version of meditation. I run pretty much every day, and I can still run a pretty fast mile. I also like to read. I have a library that my grandparents gave me, and I enjoy that.

DR: I think about running. I've been thinking about it for about 50 years, but I haven't actually done it yet, so I don't want to injure anything. Are your children going to go into private equity or the investment world or not?

DF: They all seem intrigued with what I do for a living, and the past year, the meme stocks and cryptocurrencies have captured the attention of our youth. I think at least one of my kids will go into trading and investing.

DR: I don't know if I failed or succeeded as a parent. All three of my children are in private equity.

DF: I think it's a good sign. They like what their dad does.

Endowments

PAULA VOLENT

Vice president and chief investment officer, The Rockefeller University; former chief investment officer, Bowdoin College

> *"I don't believe in waiting out mistakes. Once you make a decision that you've made a mistake, or you've lost conviction, you need to act."*

In the late 1800s and the early 1900s, US college and university endowments were comparatively modest, certainly when compared to the endowments of leading British universities. In 1900, Harvard's endowment was $13 million; Yale's was $5 million.

In those days, the relative cost of operating a college or university was much smaller—fewer buildings, students, faculty, and scholarships, and far fewer regulatory and administrative costs. So most colleges and universities were not focused particularly on the size of their endowments, or the need for meaningful and steady income streams from those endowments.

That changed in the 1930s and 1940s. Colleges and universities realized that large endowments gave them a competitive edge in the quest for academic distinction. And these institutions' costs increased with so many returning soldiers using the GI Bill to get higher-education degrees.

In the late 1940s and early 1950s, Paul Cabot, Harvard's treasurer, began investing its endowment in publicly traded stocks, producing a much higher rate of return for Harvard than would otherwise have been the case. (US college and university endowments had largely been fixed-income or debt investors.) Other universities and colleges followed suit, and public equities became an increasingly important part of university endowment investing.

But beginning in 1985, university endowment investing was changed forever by a 31-year-old Yale PhD in economics, David Swensen, when he was placed in charge of investing Yale's endowment. Over the ensuing three decades plus, David became the gold standard in this rarefied world, achieving consistently above-average rates of return while transforming the way that university and college endowments invest.

From the time David began leading the endowment in 1985 until his untimely passing in 2021, he achieved an annualized rate of return of 13.7 percent (through June 30, 2021), generating $50 billion of value relative to the mean return of college and university endowments, as tracked by the consulting firm Cambridge Associates, during his tenure.

David Swensen's singular innovation, initially thought to be too risky, was to invest heavily in illiquid assets—private equity, venture capital, real estate, hedge funds, among other assets—and to do so by utilizing outside money managers who were new to having their own funds, with the result being that Yale could be a significant investor and perhaps get lower-than-normal fees. As noted, the results over an extended period of time were outstanding. Once again, other universities as well as other nonprofit endowments in time followed suit, and the consequence was the "endowment" approach to investing, i.e., heavy on the illiquid but generally higher-performing assets. In fiscal year 2021, this approach yielded spectacular returns for Washington University in St. Louis (65 percent), Bowdoin (57 percent), Duke (56 percent), Massachusetts Institute of Technology (56 percent), Princeton (47 percent), Yale (40 percent), and Harvard (34 percent).

In the view of many, David Swensen's equally transformative accomplishment was training a generation of university, college, and endowment investment professionals who have led other significant endowments. Among the most successful of them has been Paula Volent, who led the Bowdoin College endowment from 2000 to 2021. She now manages the endowment of The Rockefeller University. During her years of leading Bowdoin's endowment, her returns exceeded the returns of every single Ivy League endowment, including those of her mentor.

Paula did not come to the investment world in a traditional way. She was trained in college and graduate school as an art historian and art conservator, and thought her career path would take her, in time, to leading an art museum. But a once-unexpected interest in finance led her to the Yale School of Management, an internship with David Swensen, and then some time helping with his classic book, *Pioneering Portfolio Management*.

When she started managing the Bowdoin endowment, it was comparatively modest in size—$465 million. That provided a challenge in getting the best investment managers to want to develop a relationship. Perhaps a bigger challenge was that very few women were running college or university endowments at the beginning of Paula's tenure, and it was not as easy to be taken seriously in the then male-dominated endowment investment world.

But Paula's drive to succeed, razor-sharp intellect, and willingness to take risks on new investment managers proved to be a winning formula. And she would have been content to continue applying that formula for many more years on behalf of a college she had come to love. But the pull of helping a university doing cutting-edge biomedical research proved irresistible, and Paula accepted in 2021 the position of managing The Rockefeller University's endowment.

I came to know Paula when I was seeking talented investment professionals to serve on the investment committee of the National Gallery of Art. Because of her interest in art and some brief time spent working at the National Gallery in her pre-investment days, she seemed an ideal choice. The only problem with her work on that committee is that the chairman has to spend time wondering how long it will take before everyone at the Gallery realizes she and her colleagues on the committee, including Kim Lew (also interviewed in this book), know much more than he does about investing. Much more. I interviewed Paula virtually on June 11, 2021.

DAVID M. RUBENSTEIN (DR): Most outstanding investment professionals I've met over the years seem to have had a love of investment almost from the time they were a child. They spent a lot of their college and postcollege years learning how to be an investor. Your career was originally in art, which is unusual for somebody who's a professional investor later on. How did you gravitate from being an art-related person to being somebody in the investment world, and did your interest in art help you become a good investor?

PAULA VOLENT (PV): I am a first-generation college student. My father had severe dyslexia and didn't even get through the third grade. They kicked him out. He was very creative and very artistic. He painted, he was an inventor, he was curious about a lot of things. My mom was a housewife, didn't go to college. At a really young age, I was curious and a big reader. I would read every book in the bookmobile. Throughout my career I've been very curious and I read a lot.

I feel deeply about the importance of education, especially for financial aid, which is one of the reasons I am so proud of what I've done at Bowdoin. I started at Emerson College in Boston, thinking I was going to be a speech therapist because I could work and get married and do that whole thing. While I was there I had to take an art history class. I had to write a paper, and by chance I ended up in the Fogg Art Museum [at Harvard], looking in the door at Marjorie B. "Jerry" Cohn, who was the paper conservator at that time, just about to dip a drawing in a bath of water. She looked up and said, "Don't just stand there. If you want to come in, come in and watch what I'm doing."

I always tell students that you never know when serendipity and being at the right place will happen. The encounter with Jerry Cohn instilled in me a curiosity about restoration of works of art. I loved art. I spent a lot of time in museums, so I ended up leaving Emerson. I worked for a while, and then I got in-state tuition, because I was paying for college by myself, and went to the University of New Hampshire. I majored in chemistry and art history because I was so interested in conservation. When I graduated from the University of New Hampshire with a major in art history and a minor in chemistry, I was approached by both Brown University and Bowdoin College to work in their museums. I worked at Bowdoin right after undergrad as a curatorial assistant.

DR: You eventually went to the Yale School of Management. How did you go from this to doing that?

PV: After Bowdoin I worked at the Clark Art Institute for a little while in the conservation lab, and then I went to the Institute of Fine Arts at NYU and got a master's degree in art history, which I loved. In art history I focused on the study of northern Baroque drawings and contemporary art. I also got a degree in art conservation from the Conservation Center at NYU. I interned at the New-York Historical Society, then I interned in the paper conservation studio of the Palace of Fine Arts in San Francisco; followed by my final internship in the paper conservation laboratory at the Los Angeles County Museum. After the completion of my internships, I went and worked with a couple of LA-based private conservators. I worked with a lot of galleries, private collectors, and artists.

Then I started running a private practice working with artists and with collectors on restoring their works of art. When I was running a business, I realized I needed to know a little bit about finance. I had a staff, a payroll. I had insurance.

I started taking business classes at night at UCLA, and my professor said, "You're pretty good at this. Did you ever think about doing something in business?" I had thought about the problem of how I had restored all these works of art and how, with some of them, people couldn't pay for the treatment, or you would go in and see these little museums with artifacts falling apart. I got interested in doing something a little more than just fixing artwork. I thought I would be a museum director with a big focus on preservation.

My professor at the night school at UCLA knew one of the recruiters from the Yale School of Management. At that time Yale SOM had an MPPM, a master's in public and private management. Tom Krens, the director of the Guggenheim, went to the Yale School of Management. So there was an art-career connection there.

I applied to Yale. I got in early admission, and they said, "You better come now because you're getting older." In that same time frame, I got an offer from the National Gallery of Art to take the William R. Leisher Fellowship. Bill Leisher was a paintings conservator who died of brain cancer, and the Gallery set up a fellowship in his honor.

I turned down Yale and went to the National Gallery, and in addition to working on the conservation of primarily contemporary works of art, I worked on collecting historic artists' materials from all over the world, documenting and analyzing them. It was fabulous, but I talked to

Tom Krens again and he said, "You have this option to go to Yale. You should take it."

I decided to go to Yale. My husband and I had been trying to have a child, and we just decided, "Okay, it's not going to happen," and, of course, it was instant pregnancy. I got to Yale, and my daughter was born in February. They said, "Can't you just take a couple of days off and come back?" And I said, "No."

When my daughter was about a month old, I was restless. I wanted to keep learning to be a museum director. I knew that museums rely on endowments. I went and I knocked on David Swensen's door, and he was great. We had a conversation. He looked at my resume, commenting "You know you don't have anything that is relevant to investing, but why don't you come in and start filing and let's see what we can do?"

So I worked with David. I started filing investment pitchbooks, legal documents, investment memos. I started organizing their due-diligence process and, little by little, David started giving me projects. Because I was trained as an art historian, I'm a good writer. In art history research, you have to piece together all these disparate pieces of information. In art conservation, you do lots of research. You study and test before you do an invasive treatment on a work of art, because you have to understand what could go wrong.

There's a direct parallel to what I bring to due diligence on investments. I try to piece together all these different parts and then make a decision on whether to make an investment and also think about what could go wrong with it. There's a left-brain/right-brain thing there.

I went back and finished my degree at the Yale School of Management. I worked at the investment office the whole time, and I also was David's teaching assistant. He brought in Seth Klarman, Michael Price, all these investors to his class at Yale College. I also spent a summer internship at the Getty, working in the investment office there. David wanted me to see what a traditional portfolio was versus the way that he was managing the Yale endowment portfolio. I worked with the Getty to help them on due diligence for their first private equity investments as well as carrying out a big project on cash management.

I graduated from the Yale School of Management with my little daughter on my hip as I marched. Seth Klarman's book on investing,

Margin of Safety, was getting lots of attention and it was a big success. David was a little bit competitive and he wanted to write a book, too, and he knew that I was a good writer. I had accepted a job at Disney to go back to LA and work in their investment office. David asked me to stay for a couple months longer to write a book, *Pioneering Portfolio Management.*

Obviously, that took longer than three months. I turned down the job at Disney and David offered me a senior associate position in the Yale investments office. We worked very closely together for about a year on that book. I always thought *Pioneering Portfolio Management* was a crazy name, but now I think it's perfect for what he was doing.

When I was at the Yale investment office, David was investing in private equity and venture capital and all these new asset classes. He came up with the name "absolute return," thinking about what hedge funds should really do. The Yale investments office, under David's leadership, was doing all these innovative things.

I started at Yale with no background in finance. I didn't know what a basis point was, and I had to go to baby math when I came to the Yale School of Management. I had a little baby and it was challenging. But it was so exciting, all the things that I was doing, and David loved to teach and mentor. No question was too basic.

DR: Did David tell people what to invest in or did he kind of wait for people to bubble up ideas and he would approve them or not? How would that work?

PV: There was always someone coming through the investment office in New Haven. Fund managers would make the trip up to New Haven. Yale professors such as Bob Shiller and Steve Ross would come and have lunch with the staff. It was collaborative, but David was the one who really saw opportunities.

One of the things he taught the Yale team was to look for inefficiencies, to look where other people are not looking, and also to back smart, innovative people who are going to "eat their own cooking." He didn't like big asset gatherers that got rich off charging an asset management fee. He wanted smaller managers, especially in the real estate asset class.

The final decision went to him, but we also had to present investment recommendations to Yale's investment committee. We would bring discussions and big memos to the committee, and they would discuss them and vote on them. I brought that discipline and process to Bowdoin as well. Although a lot of work went into writing due-diligence memos and it was a critical part of the investment decision making, a lot of times we would work on a big memo and a recommendation and then at the last minute I would say, "Now that we've done all the work, it's not as compelling as it was."

DR: How many years were you there at Yale?

PV: I was at Yale from 1996 to 2000.

DR: After four years, did you say, "I'm now ready to go on my own"? How did you get the position at Bowdoin?

PV: Ellen Shuman was one of my colleagues at Yale. She was a Bowdoin alumna and she said, "You know, Bowdoin never had a dedicated investment person." They had the treasurer and they had the investment firm Cambridge Associates as a consultant, but they didn't have anyone internally that oversaw the investments. Stan Druckenmiller, at the time I arrived, was the chair of the investment committee. He was early to put hedge funds into the portfolio, but there wasn't an internal process. Fund managers would be invited to a meeting, and then the committee would vote after the meeting with not really a lot of analysis.

Ellen asked me to talk to a couple of the people at Bowdoin. My family is from Maine, and I thought it was a great opportunity. I came to Bowdoin, I interviewed, and I thought it was innovative. It was really entrepreneurial.

The endowment was $465 million that June. I joined in July 2000, just when the dot-com bubble was starting to break, and so, during my first year, the endowment went down to about $400 million. The first year all I did was listen and get to know the portfolio. One of my keys to success was figuring out, "What is the risk profile of the investment committee? What is the risk profile of Bowdoin? This is different than Yale. Fewer zeros and a completely different risk profile."

DR: You had the advantage of having worked with two of the most famous investment professionals of our lifetime, Stan Druckenmiller and David Swensen. How were they alike and how were they different?

PV: First of all, they were both amazing mentors. David had such a big heart. He instilled a love of doing something for a university. He could have run a hedge fund. He could have made much more money, but he loved Yale. He loved the fact that he was working with students. He loved the fact that we were making money for financial aid. And he did instill a curiosity in us. He was tough on writing skills and critical thinking. We did these memos and he would mark them up with red. He made you a really good writer.

Stan has the biggest heart, and he's amazing. A man of few words a lot of the time, yes or no. Very bearish a lot of times. Brilliant about market transitions. The thing I learned about with Stan is risk management. If you don't know something, you have to say, "I don't know, I'll get back to you," rather than try to smooth it over. You need to get into that investment committee room with everything in your back pocket to make the recommendation.

David was the same way. You had to have done your work. This was important money for an institution, and you weren't just going to sprinkle it around. You needed to be thoughtful about where you put it.

No one in the investment community knew Bowdoin when I came there. They thought we lived in the Arctic or something because we have a polar bear for a mascot. No one knew Bowdoin at all, so my job in the first five years was to go out to the top managers and tell the story of Bowdoin and what the money would do for financial aid.

Bowdoin College is still need-blind, no-loan—one of the few colleges to do that. The college has illustrious alumni and a long history of commitment to "the common good."

In the early years of my tenure at Bowdoin, I had to go out and sell the brand of Bowdoin and try to get access to the top investment firms. We had no venture capital. Zero. So I figured out the best venture capital firms and I started going out and visiting them. Finally at Sequoia they were so tired of seeing me, they said, "Okay. You can have a $500,000 commitment in our new strategy, the China fund." I brought it to the investment committee and fought for it, and now Sequoia is one of the college's largest and most successful relationships. Bowdoin has a great brand now in the investment community.

DR: When you started in 2000, there was $465 million in the endowment. You left in 2021. What was the size of the endowment then?

PV: Around $2.72 billion.

DR: During that period of time, am I correct in saying that Bowdoin outperformed the major Ivies on an annual basis? I read that you've had a higher internal rate of return than the Ivies.

PV: Yes, that's true. David sent me a beautiful letter with a quote from Leonardo da Vinci: "Great is the student that excels the master." One time he was in my office and he was looking over my shoulder. David was really competitive. He said, "Oh my God, you're beating Yale."

The risk profile and our manager selection at Bowdoin was very different than a lot of our peers'. For instance, over the past 10 years I have had very little in fixed income. I typically ran the portfolio fully invested. Don't hold a lot of cash. Really focus on liquidity with a laser eye. Through June 30, 2021, Bowdoin was in the top decile of endowment returns for the 1-, 3-, 5-, 10-, and 20-year time periods, knock on wood.

DR: For people who aren't familiar with college endowments, what purpose do they serve? People in Washington, DC, in the government, sometimes criticize these colleges and universities for having big endowments. What is their main purpose?

PV: It's for perpetual support. David always used to say that Benjamin Franklin said, "You can't get away from death and taxes, but endowments can." Although some college endowments are paying taxes now because they have over $500,000 per student. [An endowment tax was imposed by Congress on certain college and university endowments in 2017.]

An endowment is perpetual support. At Bowdoin they still have the James Bowdoin III endowment. He gave a tract of land and some library books and something like $1,000. We protect the original value of the gift, and then you can spend returns.

About 40 percent of Bowdoin's operating budget comes from the endowment, and 81 percent of the financial aid support comes from endowment payout. I agree that some endowments are really large. But there's fluctuations in the market, and so an endowment, as David's book will tell you, protects you from relying on student tuition. [Student tuition, on average, often covers less than half of the cost of educating a student at many colleges and universities. If endowment income, government support, or philanthropic support in the form of scholarships were not available, colleges and universities would have to set tuition prices—to cover costs—at levels that the vast majority of students could not possibly afford.]

You see a lot of institutions that go under when, during periods like a pandemic, tuition goes down and they don't have the support from an endowment. It also supports you so you can do innovative work without having to rely on government grants.

DR: The way it works is you have the endowment and you're trying to get a certain rate of return each year. Risk-reward appropriate return. Is there a number you have in mind each year that you're trying to get? How much do you have to pay out to the college each year for their expenses?

PV: Bowdoin has a spending rule that uses a 12-quarter average, taking the endowment value for 12 quarters and then averaging it. That's the number you use. We take 5 percent of that. We're trying to get that 5 percent plus inflation. At The Rockefeller University we use a different spending rule that takes into account the previous year's spending, adjusted for inflation as well as a small component of the 12-quarter moving average.

DR: If I have my history correct, it was in the late 1940s that Paul Cabot of the Cabot family became the treasurer of Harvard and, as a treasurer—it was a part-time job, as I understand it—he decided to more actively manage the endowment, which was then maybe $200 million. That began the process of endowments being more actively involved in investments. Is that how it happened?

PV: Absolutely. Bowdoin had a relationship with Cabot, because when Cambridge Associates was formed, it was Bowdoin, Harvard, and a couple other schools, but Cabot was instrumental in starting to use active management before that. Prior to Cabot, most college and university endowments were primarily invested in income-producing assets: faculty mortgages, railroad stocks. You'd also have lots of bonds, because you could only spend current income. Then in the '70s, the Ford Foundation did a big report on equities and the concept of a total return policy where you could spend gains as well as income, and people started doing more active management and spending from gains as well as income, so that changed the focus from fixed income to doing more equities.

DR: To continue the story, David Swensen's innovation was going into "alternative" investments (private equity, venture capital, growth capital, distressed debt, etc.) at a much higher percentage than people had traditionally done. Is that what drove his high returns?

PV: David went into alternatives because he understood that you could take advantage of inefficiencies and get paid a liquidity premium [meaning that assets that are "inefficient" or not readily tradable are generally valued at a lower price than assets for which investors are paying a "premium" for the liquidity or efficiency of being able to sell them readily]. David also was a really good market timer. He was brave. During market downturns he would go in. He was very good at rebalancing. A lot of times he would be rebalancing on his BlackBerry while he was traveling. He was passionate about markets. He was early to see the rise of China. That's one of the things that I think attracted me to David—his curiosity and his willingness, his bravery, to do new things. The economist John Maynard Keynes was one of his heroes, and one of his favorite quotes from Keynes was: "Worldly wisdom teaches that it is better for reputation to fail conventionally than to succeed unconventionally."

"Alternatives" is a giant umbrella. It can be private credit. It can be hedge funds. It can be a buyout fund. It could be a guy in a garage making an invention. David was willing to go across that whole landscape. David was an unconventional investor.

DR: There are two big decisions people have to make with an endowment: What is the allocation between, let's say, fixed income, equities, alternatives, and so forth, and who will be the outside money managers selected to invest the endowment's funds? Which is harder for you, and what's more important? Is it the allocation between classes or is it the selection of the money manager?

PV: In business school you learn that asset allocation accounts for the majority of returns. But as the endowment world has become more sophisticated, the difference between asset classes has blurred. In venture capital, for instance, a lot of their portfolios are holding public stocks, post-IPO. Then you see these hybrid funds run by managers like Viking or Lone Pine that are holding private positions in their marketable portfolios, so it's getting very blurred.

I would say Bowdoin's success has been in manager selection. We carried out an asset-allocation study every year, and we used metrics to help us analyze whether we should regularly adjust our commitments to an illiquid asset class like venture capital or private real estate. You can't really rebalance illiquid alternative investments yearly, because it's the manager who decides when to send you back money. The more you go into alternatives, the more you have to think about the ability to generate liquidity to fund capital calls and the spending draw of the institution.

You need to be in equities. Why do you need fixed income? Is it for liquidity? Is it a deflation hedge? Is it an inflation hedge? There's reasons for different asset classes. For Bowdoin, and probably for Yale, too, the manager selection is up there with the asset allocation, maybe even a little bit more important.

DR: What are you looking for in a manager you want to back?

PV: A lot of the work that we do is looking at different themes. I read the *Wall Street Journal* and the *Financial Times* every morning. Seth Klarman always said that the best ideas he saw were on the back of the *Wall Street Journal.* You're like, "Oh, that's interesting." Then you think about where the opportunities for returns could be, where there are inefficiencies.

I like to meet with as many managers as I can. A lot of times you'll hear the same thing from managers in a specific thing, and then you hear someone who has a different view, a different perception of markets. I look at how the team is set up. A lot of times you might meet a manager and they need their analysts by them to feed them the information you're asking for. I'm looking for a manager that knows their stocks really well, back and forth, and has good due-diligence processes.

Lately we are asking fund managers about the diversity of their team. That's going to become an increasing thing. I have, at Bowdoin, carried out long due diligence on a fund and then, when we're in, we're in and we're going to be loyal investors unless there's a big change.

I like managers who give money back when the opportunity doesn't happen to be attractive. I also like managers who call me when they're pounding the table about the opportunity set, saying, "I want new capital to take advantage of an inefficiency." Some of the most successful investments I've made have been when managers have had their worst performance period and I've added capital because I understand the portfolio and have a good line of communication with them.

DR: Have you found your returns are better with the managers who already are oversubscribed? Or is it better when you find people who are trying to get you to come in because they need the money? Where do your returns come out better?

PV: For 20 years, I've run a farm-team portfolio. Stan Druckenmiller used to call me up all the time and say, "I met this great young person who could be a great addition to the endowment portfolio," but it would be hard to do the due diligence. No track record. You don't know how the person is going to be able to run a business. So we started a farm team. That has been really successful and a source of good returns.

It's also sort of pattern recognition. A lot of people can be good portfolio managers but they have no clue how to run a business, and so the investment firm breaks up because of disagreements or something like that. A lot of my success has been either getting early into a manager and watching them and then adding over time, or getting into a really good manager because we told the story of Bowdoin and the mission of the institution and the manager wants that kind of investor.

DR: Let's talk about ESG and diversity. When you started, there weren't that many women running college or university endowments. Did you find a prejudice against you, when you were trying to do the job? People talked about "Women can't do this," or it wasn't a problem? Is it still a problem today, or not anymore?

PV: It definitely was an issue I had to deal with. I would go to meetings and there would only be a couple of women. I don't think it's solved. I'm active on empowering young women and women in the asset management industry. Seema Hingorani started Girls Who Invest, and I've been there since the very beginning, working with them. I also work with 100

Women in Finance. I am coaching and mentoring a number of women and venture capital firms that are run by women. I'm trying to bring visibility to that.

It's a little bit better, but it's not solved. For instance, women venture capitalists are having a really hard time raising money. I go to Yale School of Management or to Bowdoin, and I tell women, "You can have a career in asset management. This is a viable career for you." The one thing I don't want to see is institutions take a Girls Who Invest person or an intern and then check the diversity box and think they are done. You need to have a path up to the C-suite for young women.

DR: If a manager comes to you today and has an incredible track record but is all white men, will you say, "I'll come in but can you hire somebody else?" or would you just say, "We're just not even going to consider you"?

PV: I would have a dialogue. That's what I want to do. I want to open up the dialogue.

We had a Girls Who Invest intern last year who went through all of our managers and looked at their org charts and where the women were. A lot of them were in compliance and accounting and in admin, but not in the portfolio managers. We shared that with our managers and had a discussion.

DR: Some people would say, "Having diversity, gender, and ethnic diversity is good social policy." Other people would say, "It's also likely to lead to better returns." How do you respond to the idea that it will lead to better returns?

PV: Diversity is important, culturally. It depends on the people, on their strengths. For the opportunity to run a portfolio, I'm not going to hire a woman who hasn't had an opportunity to run a P&L. I need to have some experience and invest in firms that are willing to give women the chance to develop into a great investor. In certain sectors, like in some consumer sectors and VC, women bring something as a consumer to that sector that a man might not have.

As our society becomes more diverse, and that diversity is reflected in the way companies operate and change, a manager who reflects society's diversity will, in my view, be better attuned to which companies are likely to prosper in that environment.

DR: Some investors, like me, look back at the deals that got away and kick themselves. They also spend a lot of time thinking about the deals they did that didn't work out. Do you ever think about the ones that got away? Do you kick yourself about the ones that didn't work out?

PV: I do both. You start getting pattern recognition and see your biases sometimes, things that you missed. Learning from your mistakes and learning from your successes is a really important part of going further. In one real estate fund, we went in and I felt like, "Okay, I'm going to give this manager one more chance," because I liked the manager. I didn't appreciate the fact that the fund was breaking up and that the opportunity wasn't attractive. I definitely do a postpartum look at all of our investments.

DR: When you make an investment and you realize, maybe a year into it, that you made a mistake, do you say, "I'm getting out of this tomorrow"? Or do you say, "I'll ride with it for a while"? How do you get out of mistakes?

PV: First, I would do a lot of meetings with the manager and try to understand if it's a mistake or if it's just a market fluctuation. I don't believe in waiting out mistakes. Once you make a decision that you've made a mistake, or you've lost conviction, you need to act. You seldom make your money back if you stay in. That's a bad strategy.

DR: When you run a college endowment, your compensation is generally known to the public, and the amount is modest compared to what you could make doing this in a hedge fund format. Why is this an appealing career path?

PV: As I said, I was a first-generation college student. I relied on financial aid throughout, even in graduate school. I've always worked for not-for-profit institutions. There's this amazing feeling that you're doing something for society when you're running an endowment or a foundation where the money is going to make the world a better place, to bring in students that couldn't ever think of having an education at a place like Bowdoin or The Rockefeller University.

Running an endowment is entrepreneurial because every day you're thinking about different asset classes. You're thinking about the balance between generating money for future endowments or future students versus the students of today. It's intellectually interesting. I know you could probably do that in a hedge fund, but I find that the mission here makes a difference.

DR: Suppose somebody is reading this interview, and they say, "I want to be just like Paula. How do I get trained? Should I go to art school and learn art conservation? What should I do to kind of prepare myself to get a job in the college or university endowment area?"

PV: Serendipity and openness to experience, to opportunities. I think a liberal arts education is really important—learning how to write, critical thinking, curiosity. A lot of people in the endowment management industry have art history or history or English degrees. In undergrad, you need to be curious and explore all areas. I don't think everyone has to have an MBA, but mine changed my life.

DR: Let's talk about the next five years or so. How are college endowments, university endowments likely to change the way they invest?

PV: The pandemic is going to cause a lot of changes in how colleges think about education. There's going to be hybrid learning and more technology.

The market is pretty frothy. Some of the venture deal pacing and valuations are huge, and you wonder how long it will last. Kevin Warsh [a former Federal Reserve Board member] wrote me an email saying, "The end of the gilded age is coming." A lot of people entering the investment world right now have never, except for a couple of days right at the start of the pandemic, experienced a down market or high inflation.

We have to have a diversified portfolio now. We have to realize that globalization is taking a step back, and that some of the strategies and the themes we had in the past aren't potentially going to work. We also have to realize that innovations, whether it's blockchain or advancement in biotech discoveries, are here to stay, and that you need to get a foot in the door and start learning about that.

I think about the blurring of asset classes, where you have public and private together and multistrategy things. It's going to be hard, going forward, to make the returns that we've had over the past five years.

DR: What's a down market? I don't remember a down market. [I remember them now, post-May 2022. —DR]

A final question for you. Do you regret that you're not the first woman director of the National Gallery of Art? That could have been you if you'd stayed in the art world. Do you have any regrets about not staying?

PV: No, I love what I do. It's so interesting. I volunteer on a lot of investment committees for small institutions, and I love doing that. I still collect art, my friends are artists, and all that. But I love figuring out, every day, where there's an opportunity or where there's a challenge. I don't have any regrets, but I do say to students that if you had told me 30 years ago I was going to be sitting here, talking to you, I would not have believed it.

KIM LEW

President and CEO, Columbia
Investment Management Company; former chief
investment officer, Carnegie Corporation

"We're building for the long term."

For decades, large foundations invested their endowments as universities did—initially in conservative bonds and then in relatively safe public equities (i.e., "mainstream" investments). But just as major universities a few decades ago began seeking higher returns for their endowments, and thus began investing in "alternatives" (i.e., investments that are riskier but potentially able to provide higher returns), so too did large foundations. With the mounting pressure to increase returns, both universities and foundations turned to building alternative portfolios that leveraged the long-term nature of their underlying assets. Given the complexity of managing these investments, the larger universities and endowments with bigger investment teams led the way, and smaller institutions have followed.

Colleges and universities have endowments to provide relatively predictable annual income to support student scholarships, research, capital projects, faculty, and student activities. A percentage of the endowment's annual income is usually provided to support these kinds of needs. Even though student tuitions are seen as high and growing by 2 to 4 percent annually, tuitions pay only a modest fraction of the actual cost of a student's education. Foundation endowments actually have a much greater need for steady, predictable returns to honor long-term grant commitments (and they cannot count on steady tuition inflow to provide that income).

One of the leaders of her generation in endowment investing, particularly in the alternatives area, has been Kim Lew, who led that area at the Ford Foundation and then became the chief investment officer for the Carnegie Corporation. In 2020, she assumed the position of president and CEO of the Columbia Investment Management Company, which manages Columbia University's endowment.

While foundations and university endowments have many similarities in their investment approach, universities have alumni contributions and government grants to help deal with their financial needs. Foundations typically are solely dependent on their endowment for needed funds, and thus must be particularly sensitive to cash needs. I thought Kim could well address the foundation-university distinction, among other subjects.

She did not initially see the nonprofit investing area as her career path after graduating from the Wharton School and Harvard Business School. A Wall Street career, with its much higher compensation, prestige, and better professional opportunities, seemed more likely. But an unexpected meeting with an officer at the Ford Foundation led her to see this area as a better career path—though any career path, for a woman of color in the investment world, faced challenges then.

Kim's father was Chinese; her mother was African American. Her parents were both 17 years old when she was born, and both parents' families were not at all pleased with the marriage and birth. But her parents stayed together, and raised an incredibly bright and highly motivated woman who has succeeded at every academic and professional challenge she has faced. And the challenge of being a professional investor who was female was certainly one of the challenges when Kim was starting her investment career. When I was seeking last year to add an experienced professional to the investment committee of the National Gallery of Art, Kim (like Paula Volent) was recommended by everyone I consulted.

This interview occurred as part of my *Bloomberg Wealth* TV series, and was conducted outdoors at Columbia University, with the sirens, overhead aircraft, and nearby construction reminding us constantly that we were in New York. I interviewed Kim in person on July 30, 2021.

DAVID M. RUBENSTEIN (DR): The Columbia endowment is roughly what size?

KIM LEW (KL): Approximately $14.3 billion.

DR: Why do universities have such big endowments? They all seem to be bigger than they used to be 20 or 30 years ago.

KL: The universities' endowments are used both to fund student needs like scholarships as well as larger university needs like faculty research and capital projects such as building construction.

Those needs are growing every day. For instance, Columbia University is trying to tackle the climate issue, no small endeavor. It has a lot of research behind that, as well as a number of students to support in order to find solutions. The endowments grow to solve some of these big problems and to educate the students that are going to be the leaders of tomorrow.

DR: The rates of return have been very good for university endowments recently. Is that because the investment managers are so smart, or the markets have been pretty good?

KL: It's a combination. We hope we are picking managers that are particularly smart and doing even better than the markets. But the markets have been strong. There's so much technology that makes it more efficient to do a lot of different things, and doing so introduces a lot of new ideas and opportunities.

Now everyone's looking for equity options in order to meet their returns goals. They're making a lot of relative decisions about the best places to put their money. That means all the good ideas get bid up. There's just a lot of money out there managed by institutions who have high return hurdles that are looking to invest, so you see some of the best ideas getting more and more expensive.

DR: When university endowments were first starting, let's say in the early part of the twentieth century or earlier, they were very modest. Gradually they began to invest in more than fixed income and bonds. Now a large percentage are doing what's called alternatives. Why are alternatives such an important part of the endowment process right now?

KL: Increasingly, alternatives are not alternatives, they're core parts of the portfolio. They were considered alternatives at one point because it was unusual for people to invest in them. But they're particularly a great investment for a foundation or an endowment because they are a long-duration asset. You can't get your money back right away. It really is an investment for the future. It's a great opportunity for us to leverage the fact that we're long in nature. Columbia University expects to be around for hundreds of more years, so having investments in things that probably won't mature for 10 or 20 years is fine.

DR: Typically, a university takes a certain percentage each year out of the endowment to pay for operating costs—maybe 4 percent to 6 percent. That's what Columbia does?

KL: Yes.

DR: So each year you need to make at least 4 percent to 6 percent or whatever your payout ratio is?

KL: The board determines what the payout is. We are not involved in that. What is important for me to be successful in my job is that I can get that payout plus whatever inflation exists, because to pay for those same students a year from now will be more expensive than it was to pay for them this year. I want to make sure that I return whatever the payout is plus the inflation rate.

DR: In the Trump tax cuts, there was a provision that said endowments from universities should pay a tax for the first time. Some universities have been doing that. What is the theory behind why a nonprofit university endowment should be taxed?

KL: I think Congress increasingly felt that universities haven't had to devote all of their resources to their missions in the same way as before, because they've been growing their endowments at this high rate and not being taxed on endowment profits.

A lot of people look at the endowments and think, "They're so big, they're not taxed, that's an opportunity to support the government." But there's tons of research that's being done here. There's all this work to support society in meaningful ways. Sometimes that gets lost when people think about the tax.

DR: Do you manage your endowment by hiring outside money managers to invest the money or do you hire employees and have them do the investing in-house?

KL: We use outside managers.

DR: When you're hiring managers, are you looking at their track record, their diversity, their commitment to ESG? What is it that you're looking for?

KL: I start by looking at their strategy. Is their strategy unique? Does it offer the opportunity for them to make outsized returns? Then I look at their organization. Have they created and built an organization that supports their strategy and makes sense?

Then I look at their alignment. Are they aligned with me and Columbia? Are they treating us as partners? Do they have high integrity? Are they committed to the values that we are committed to? And are they thinking about the long term in the same way that we're thinking about the long term?

We then look at the track record to support whether or not the analysis that we've done about all those other things has been shown to be true. A lot of times people start with the track record, but track record just tells you what a manager did with the circumstances that existed in the past. I want to know what they will do going forward; so let's think about what it takes for them to be successful going forward. Then I look at the track record to see if they have those skills.

DR: Let's suppose somebody calls up and says, "I'd like to make a presentation to the Columbia endowment. I'm a prominent Columbia graduate and I'm a big donor to the school and I have a lot of Columbia graduates working in my firm." Does that make a difference?

KL: It is our responsibility to meet with all of our alumni and to make the best decision for the long term for the benefit of the organization. Columbia does a great job of educating people and of creating creative and talented people. But first we serve the interest of the endowment, making sure we are doing things that create the return that we need and that support the values of the institution.

DR: You came to Columbia after having served as the chief investment officer of the Carnegie Corporation, a large foundation. What's the difference between overseeing investments for a university and for a foundation?

KL: There are two distinct issues. At a foundation, the principal problem, the thing that we're trying to solve for before anything else, is liquidity. There are no inflows of capital, so we need to make sure that we can meet our obligations. That includes the payout to fund grants and our unfunded commitments from our alternatives portfolio and any rebalancing that we need to do in order to manage the portfolio.

At a university, there are inflows. There's tuition, there's gifts from alumni, there are other sources of cash. There are reserves the university has. So the principal problem is not liquidity. The principal problem is volatility, because the university bases their budget on an expected return, and drawdowns put the university at risk. So you're trying to solve for different problems.

DR: Universities can decide what percentage of the endowment to provide to the university each year to help support the university's ongoing cash needs. The percentage paid to the university each year (the "payout ratio") might be 4 percent, 5 percent, 6 percent, depending on various things, including the investment performance of the endowment. The decision on the right payout ratio is made by a university's board of trustees. Foundations, by contrast, are required by federal law to pay to the foundation's grantees at least 5 percent a year of the foundation's endowment?

KL: Five percent.

DR: Do you invest differently when you know you have to pay out 5 percent a year?

KL: Yes, but the difference is that we have to pay out 5 percent of what we have. So if there's a market drawdown, the amount we have to pay out reduces. So it really is about controlling your fixed costs. There are very few fixed costs in a foundation that's run well, because most of your payout is grants. We never want to cut grants, but we can. But with a university, almost all of the costs are fixed, so it's much harder to cut your payout.

DR: Sometimes alums and others say, "Universities should not invest in oil or in gas or in other kinds of things that are socially controversial." How do you deal with those issues?

KL: It is very important for the investment arm of any institution to be aligned with the values of that institution. On the other hand, as a chief executive officer of the endowment, I want to have as few restrictions as I possibly can, because my principal goal is the return. But I don't think we can do that at the expense of values.

Columbia has been very clear that they have a value around sustainability. They have a Climate School, they have an Earth Institute. When the board of trustees made a decision to commit to solving this type of world problem, they decided it was a value of theirs. When I was interviewing for the job, they made it clear to me that it was important. I didn't argue about it at all, because of course I want to make sure that the endowment is managed in a way that it is completely aligned with the university.

Similarly, the university has, over the course of time, made a real commitment to diversity, equity, and inclusion. They've thought about it strategically and asked each of the departments and the faculty, the staff, the vendors they support to think strategically about how to support the community. Similarly, we will be doing that at the endowment. We're going to look through and try to make sure that we build out the amount of diverse managers that we support, and that we reflect the nation.

DR: What's the appeal of a career being an investment manager for a university? Is it better than private equity?

KL: This is the most amazing job that exists. We are obviously a wonderful institution which does great work that a lot of people want to support. We are able to talk to all sorts of people that, growing up, I never imagined I would ever have access to. And we have a wealth of expertise here in the university. Every day you learn a little more. Every day you get to make an impact on an institution that is doing great work and is mission-based. I can't think of a better job. Every day I'm smarter and every day I feel good about what I'm doing.

DR: Let's suppose a donor says, "I'm willing to give a large amount of money to Columbia University, but I want to make sure it's well invested." Is there pressure to make sure you don't lose money?

KL: Anybody who has the capacity to give a large investment to Columbia University understands markets and they understand that there is volatility in markets. We're building for the long term. Of course no donor should want to invest in a place that does not produce an appropriate risk-adjusted return. If they felt that they could invest and just support specific causes, they would do that. But we're able to invest in things that an individual couldn't. We're able to invest in places with opportunities that might be difficult for an individual to do. The argument is always, "You're making a long-term investment in the growth of this institution, and we're going to invest it to the best of our ability."

DR: Let's talk about how you came to this position. Your father is Chinese, and your mother is African American, and you were born when they were teenagers.

KL: Yes. It was very controversial in the family. Seventeen-year-olds having a baby is never something that you want. My father was estranged from his family for a long time as a result of it. But my parents had a strong foundation as a couple. They had a real commitment to education. As a result, my brother and I have both done well.

DR: Where did you grow up?

KL: I was born here in Harlem, so it feels like I've come home. Born in Harlem, and stayed here for a number of years living with my grandmother. Then we moved to the Bronx when I was about six years old.

DR: You went to high school where?

KL: Bronx High School of Science.

DR: That's a pretty good high school.

KL: Others will disagree, but I think it's the best one in the city.

DR: You must have done pretty well, because you wound up at the Wharton School. When you went to Wharton, did you say, "Wow, these people are pretty smart and they have wealthier, more privileged backgrounds, such as prep school, than I do"? Or you didn't say that?

KL: No, you absolutely say that. I didn't just grow up in the Bronx, I grew up in the housing projects in the Bronx. There were very few people that went to college, let alone a college like Penn, where there are people from all over the world. Penn was the first place I'd ever traveled to. The first person I met at Penn came from Alaska. That was shocking to me. People came to Penn from all over the world, with very different economic backgrounds, although I think that that wasn't so obvious back then. We all lived on campus, we all stayed in the same dorms, we all ate in the dining halls. It is much more apparent and much more challenging for students who come from poor backgrounds now than when I was there. The wealth is conspicuous now in a way that wasn't the case back then.

DR: When you graduated, did you say, "I want to become a chief investment officer for a university"?

KL: I was an accounting major, because I understood what that meant. I thought I was going to be an accountant. I went to a few accounting interviews, and it was clear to me that this culture probably wasn't the most appropriate for me. So I asked around, "What do you think is a possible thing for me to do?" And they were like, "With an accounting major, you can go into banking. You can be a credit analyst or you can go into investment banking." I chose to go to a commercial bank, and I went to Chemical Bank, which was one of the most amazing credit-training programs that existed at the time. It was a wonderful decision.

DR: You ultimately went to Harvard Business School. Was it hard to get into HBS or not?

KL: It was challenging. I had a number of different business schools to choose from at the time. I made the decision to go to HBS largely because they challenge you to speak up in class and to express yourself and be able to support your ideas. At the time, I struggled with public speaking. I felt HBS was going to give me that opportunity to learn to express myself better and build confidence.

DR: Did going to Harvard give you more confidence?

KL: In some areas it did. In some areas it was just intimidating. You are at a place with people who are competitive in the same area of the world you're competitive in. For many, it can be really challenging. You have to find a support system. It's important to have administrators and faculty that care about you and are committed to doing what they need to do to help you feel like you belong. HBS did do that for me.

DR: When you graduated, what did you decide to do?

KL: I went to Prudential and Prudential Capital specifically, in the private placement group, which is sort of the next level of credit.

DR: After that, you ultimately went to work for the Ford Foundation. How did you get that position?

KL: Largely luck. I had a classmate at business school whose mother was the director of research, the technology analyst, and the alternatives director at the Ford Foundation. She wore many hats, and she was making the decision to transition out of the role as the stock picker in technology and insurance. He knew that they were interviewing. He said, "My mom does investing, you do investing, you should reach out and talk to her." So I went to talk to her. She was a woman named Betty Fagan, who has turned out to be the best mentor I've ever had.

We got along really well. She introduced me to the chief investment officer at the time, a woman named Linda Strumpf, and the person who headed the public equities group, a gentleman named Halliday Clark. I had wonderful conversations with each of them. If HBS doesn't teach you anything else, it teaches you to convince people to let you do a job that you arguably are not qualified to do. So they hired me as an equity analyst with no experience in the equity markets and no experience in technology—in 1994, right at the start of the best run in technology ever.

DR: Ultimately you left to go to Carnegie?

KL: I did, in 2007. I was in charge of private equity and I went to work for another wonderful woman, chief investment officer Ellen Shuman. She had a very different investing philosophy than the Ford Foundation. When I was at Ford, they ran a traditional portfolio, largely public equities and fixed income. Conversely, Carnegie ran what is in common nomenclature known as the endowment model, or the Yale model—a portfolio that's heavily alternatives. It was an opportunity for me to learn. It was also an opportunity for me to go to a place where they encouraged all of us to talk across asset classes. I knew that I would be able to learn how to be a CIO there.

DR: And ultimately you became the CIO. Was rising up to be the head of Columbia University's endowment hurt by the fact that you're a woman or a person of color, or it didn't affect you at all?

KL: There are many challenges for women and people of color to get opportunities in this space, because it tends to be relationship-driven and network-driven. For someone like me, from a background where I didn't know anybody growing up that had relationships in this area, your name is not as well known, or you're not as easily identified or as easily due-diligenced as others would be.

Fortunately, I had been at a place that encouraged us to get out there and to cultivate our expertise and be known as thought leaders in the industry. As a result of that, I was known to the people that mattered at Columbia. But that's unusual, and it's tough for a lot of women and people of color who don't get the opportunity to do that.

DR: Many people are excited about cryptocurrencies. Do you have a view on that?

KL: It is important for endowments, especially endowments like Columbia's, to have a view on it, and to start to think about whether or not it is going to be a viable currency or strategy for the future. We make some modest investments so that we can follow it closely.

I think it will have profound effects. There are many different avenues. There's stablecoins, there's NFTs, there's the blockchain, different layers. People are using it for so many different things. Clearly it's here to stay. Clearly it's going to play some role. It's not clear what role it will play. It's important for us to dabble a little, so that we make sure we have relationships with people who are going to develop expertise, and we can leverage that expertise and decide which way to go.

It is not something that we would invest a lot in at this point. It has a lot of volatility. There's a lot of risk, which is not something we're necessarily getting paid for right now. But we have the ability, because we are long-term investors, to explore new roads, and cryptocurrency is one of them.

DR: Inflation has been very low, near 2 percent or below per annum, for 25 years, and there has not therefore been the inflation-related concern that a company's products or services will cost much more to produce than the price at which they can be profitably sold. Now, because of COVID and supply-chain challenges, inflation's coming back at 1970s-type levels, at least 6 to 7 percent per annum. How are you going to deal with that? How can you pick companies in which to invest that can safely meet higher costs by passing those costs along to their customers with higher prices?

KL: Many of the tools we've historically used to battle inflation no longer work in the same ways they used to. People oftentimes thought of retail and real estate as a way to hedge against inflation. That's less and less possible. Commodities, similarly, have been thought of as a way to hedge against inflation, but there are challenges. Over the long term, equities have been a hedge against inflation. We will continue to do what we have done in the past, which is build a diversified portfolio where there are many different opportunities that have the possibility of hedging against inflation.

Different types of inflation have to be hedged in different ways. So if it's a quick increase in inflation as opposed to a slow rise, is it temporary or is it a long or persistent type of inflation? I never model myself as an economist who can predict where inflation is going. What I need to do is build a diversified portfolio where there are different options that can fight the different types of inflation, and to pay close attention to it.

DR: The US government has a lot of debt—about $28 trillion. [As of June 1, 2022, the US national debt was $30.4 trillion.] It's added about $1.5 trillion this fiscal year. Does that worry you?

KL: For a long time I was worried about the debt because of the potential impact on inflation and the value of the dollar, but I wasn't super worried about it. But we're starting to see capacity constraints, which have a much larger impact on inflation. That's a mounting worry. But other places and markets trust the United States, because the currency's backed by the promise of the government. I think we continue to have a place in the world where people feel confident about us. But there are other powers rising every day. We have to be conscious of that. And we have to be careful. The debt level is something we have to watch and pay attention to. But if you can print dollars, you can pay your debt.

DR: Suppose the president of the United States called you up and said, "What can I do to improve the US economy?" Do you have any recommendations you might give him?

KL: The wealth divide is a challenge. I don't think an economy can be sustainable if there are so many have-nots and so few haves. Efforts need to be made to make sure that we have a more equitable society. Institutions like Columbia, which are trying to equitably educate the world, are playing a part to try to do better on that. But the economy needs people who can buy. We need consumers. Very wealthy people are not consuming all the goods that we need to sell. That's something we need to work on, which means that we need to deal with the issues around bias and who gets opportunities and who doesn't. It's a huge problem. I don't think that it is an easy fix. But none of the problems that we have right now are easy fixes.

DR: Universities like yours have been investing heavily, as we mentioned, in alternatives, but the returns have been so high that this cannot be sustained. Are you beginning to say, "Maybe we should lighten up or hedge our positions in alternatives"?

KL: I think alternatives will continue to be a viable investment. Alternative and private investments are going to continue to be a major part of our portfolio, and major generators of return.

I do think you're going to have to be selective. There are people who use debt in strategic ways to create value. I don't think there's anything wrong with that. I want to invest with people who are skilled at doing that.

DR: University endowments have been doing quite well in recent years, in part because of alternatives. Right now, if you wanted to buy a stock market index, you could easily do it, or buy a fixed-income index. But suppose somebody says, "I want to replicate what Columbia does." There's no way to buy an index that reflects that, is there?

KL: Not currently, although there are people out there who are trying. There are people out there trying to pull apart all the different components of value creation in a private market and create baskets or structures that allow you to leverage all those different opportunities. It's challenging. People are working at it. I don't know whether I believe that someone has it exactly figured out right now.

In reality, you actually wouldn't want passive exposure to private markets. Passive performance is generally average performance, and the average performance of private equity doesn't compensate you sufficiently for the illiquidity risk you take on. Instead, you want to invest in the very best managers, the top quartile performers. This requires active manager selection. You have to determine the characteristics of the most skilled managers in each asset class, get access to those managers, and then convince them to let you invest because they are often oversubscribed, meaning more people want to give them money than they need.

DR: When you pick outside managers to invest part of your endowment, they have discretion to invest the funds you have allocated to them. [An outside manager makes the investment decisions—someone like Kim reviews the manager's overall performance but does not second-guess the manager's decisions day-to-day.] You have selected them, presumably, because of their area of focus and track record. Let's suppose you decide to invest with manager A. They make a great sales pitch to you. They have a great track record. They're good on ESG. They're Columbia graduates. But their performance is not good after one year. Do you say good-bye or do you give them two years or three years?

KL: For me, it's always "Is the underperformance explainable?" Every strategy has a good time and a bad time. Just because they are underperforming the market doesn't mean that they are not a good manager. We choose managers for specific strategies, so we want to look at whether they are performing appropriately for their strategy. Were they underperforming for an odd reason, an idiosyncratic risk that was not predictable? Or yes, they underperformed, but they recovered from it strongly. Then you give them more time.

It's a matter of understanding what created the underperformance and whether it's something that shows an erosion in their ability to outperform. If it doesn't, you stay committed. That's one of the things that we have the benefit of doing, because we have diversified portfolios.

DR: Today, as you look at the investment environment, what makes you the most nervous and what makes you the most optimistic?

KL: I'm most optimistic always about technology and how technology is solving so many of the world's problems. I do believe that we're going to see solutions to the climate issue. I do believe that there are going to be solutions to lots of medical issues. The biotech field is awash with wonderful opportunities and brilliant people solving problems. That makes me incredibly optimistic.

I'm most pessimistic about the fact that so many world problems are not things whose outcome we as investors can predict. Since we can't predict the outcomes of these global geopolitical issues, we're trying to invest around them and trying to hedge as best we can.

But it's hard to predict. I think a lot about the relationship between different governments. I think a lot about rising debt levels and the impact that will have on the long term and on the stability of the economies.

Investing implies a level of predictability. It implies a level of trust and an ability to analyze. So many of these problems are idiosyncratic and not predictable. We don't control the outcomes. That worries me.

DR: When you go to a cocktail party—they're coming back—do people say, "What do you think I should do with my money?" Do people ask you for advice all the time?

KL: I say "The cobbler's children have no shoes." I'm an institutional investor. I'm not a retail investor. The risk tolerance and duration of a Columbia University are very different than those of the individual, so I don't give stock advice or market advice.

DR: What is the best investment advice you've ever received?

KL: The best investment advice I've ever received is that we are in the business of taking a risk. If you want to produce returns, you have to be willing to take a risk and you have to be willing to analyze and mitigate that risk the best you can, and to make sure that the return potential of an investment is equal to the risk. But you can't avoid risk.

DR: What is the most common mistake investors make?

KL: The most common mistake is following the herd and doing what everybody else is doing, not making sure that an investment is appropriate for your institution. There are a million ways to make money. There are a million strategies that can work. Not every investment is consistent with your strategy. There's a lot of herd mentality. That's a huge mistake.

DR: Let's suppose your oldest child came to you and said, "I made $100,000 by doing something creative. You're an investment professional. Mom, what should I do with $100,000?"

KL: I would tell her to go to a professional who deals with retail investors and make sure she invests it. Young people need to invest in their future. For different young people, it's different things. My daughter wants to be a lawyer. She should pay for law school. That's a great use of that capital. Other people aren't sure what they want to do and they need to park the money someplace while they think about it. They should go to a talented individual who is very good at retail investing and have them invest their money for them until they figure out what they need to use it for.

DR: Is there one thing you would say, "This is something you should absolutely avoid. It's the worst thing to do with your money right now"?

KL: The answer to that question is, do they need that $100,000 to live? If you need that $100,000 to live, you should not be investing in cryptocurrency. It is way too volatile. If this is just play money, perhaps you should invest in it. It depends on their risk tolerance.

DR: Compared to earlier in your career, do you think women have greater roles in the investment world? Do you think that's going to get even better than it has been?

KL: Yes. We are increasingly seeing that the way diverse types of people think about the world is different than the way traditional investors have thought about it. Whether it's true or not—it's hard to tell—the perception is that women think more long-term than men, and they think more about investing as beginning longer-term partnerships as opposed to shorter-term, transaction-only investments. It's debatable. What I do know is that you invest according to how you came up and your experiences. There's a real understanding of markets that traditional investors maybe don't have a window into, and those are the markets that are probably underfunded. So there's an opportunity to make money there.

Increasingly, as people acknowledge that diversity is important along all different dimensions, you'll see women and people of color get more opportunities, and you'll see better performance. I fundamentally believe that.

DR: Columbia's most famous graduate, other than Warren Buffett, is Alexander Hamilton. If Alexander Hamilton were to call you up and say, "How is my investment endowment doing?" what would you say?

KL: I think Alexander Hamilton would feel proud of the fact that Columbia has done as well as it has done and that it has educated as many talented leaders as it has. He was incredibly focused on opportunities for all types of people, and he would be thrilled at what this university has done and the role that the endowment is playing to support that.

PART TWO

Alternative Investments

Following World War II, the investment world changed forever with the creation and growth of investments designed to yield much higher returns than the traditional bond, stock, and real estate investments. These new kinds of investments were often called "alternative," which is to say they were alternative to those traditional types of investments.

The theory behind these kinds of investments was that the investment professionals would be actively involved in trying to add value to them. They would be doing more than simply picking stocks or bonds. They would get involved with management. They would serve on the boards. They would help with acquisitions or industry contacts. They would recruit management talent. And so on.

For these "value-added" services, the "alternative" investment professionals would share in the investment's profits, often at a 20 percent level (if not higher at times for extraordinary alternative investment managers).

The first of the types of alternative investment managers was in the venture capital area. It may be apocryphal that venture capital was initially dubbed "adventure" capital, but there is no doubt that the risk of creating and growing new companies was considered at the time a true adventure.

The first modern venture capital fund, created in the late 1940s, was followed shortly thereafter by another "alternative" investment vehicle, the hedge fund. Hedge funds were initially called "hedged" funds, for the fund was permitted to "hedge" the possible downside of an investment through a variety of techniques (e.g., shorting a stock).

The 1970s produced another kind of alternative investment fund, the buyout fund, where considerable leverage was used to facilitate (and enhance the returns of) a buyout of a company.

Initially, these kinds of alternative investments were considered quite risky, and it was not until 1979 that the US Department of Labor considered them to be sufficiently "prudent" for private pension funds to invest their capital in them. Public pension funds followed a bit later.

With that ruling, and with the quite attractive returns being achieved by these alternative investment vehicles, the alternative investment world grew exponentially. Other alternative areas of investment were later created as well—growth capital, distressed debt, private credit, and secondaries, among other areas.

Today, nearly a half century since the Labor Department effectively allowed the growth of this industry in the US, the alternative investment world has almost become mainstream itself, for most investors feel a need to have a responsibly good-sized component (5 to 35-plus percent) of alternatives in their portfolio. Today, more than $11 trillion is committed to or invested in alternative investments.

Hedge Funds

SETH KLARMAN

Founder and CEO, The Baupost Group

> *"Value investing lies at the intersection of economics and psychology. I've joked that it's a marriage of the calculator and a contrarian streak."*

An informal survey of the world's greatest investors about who they most admire is likely to include one person who is probably not—by design—a household name: Seth Klarman.

For nearly four decades, and largely out of the public eye, Seth has led Baupost, a Boston-based, value-oriented hedge fund. During that period, the fund has had a compound annual total return of more than 15 percent with only four down years—an almost unmatched record over such an extended period.

What has been the fund's secret? To begin with, Seth is brilliant by anyone's standards. He is also a voracious reader, absorbing enormous amounts of information that often leads to valuable, not-always-apparent investment ideas. He is also quite patient, waiting for the right opportunity, even if he needs to keep cash on the sidelines as he waits. And perhaps most important, he has built a formidable investment team of over 60 people to whom he delegates significant responsibility.

While standard investment categories are not always perfect fits, it is probably fair to call Seth a "value" investor—someone who wants to make investments at a discount to underlying value. He is unwilling to chase the latest investment fads or trends, and willing to hold on to an investment for quite some time. The most famous value investor of all time is Warren Buffett, and that is someone with whom Seth Klarman is frequently compared.

Seth wrote about his investment approach in *Margin of Safety,* published in 1991, and that book has become an investment classic, rivaling Benjamin Graham's *Security Analysis*. Seth has not yet updated his book, and copies are hard to find, for the book has long been out of print. They apparently sell for thousands of dollars on Amazon.

The fact that Seth has not updated such a well-received book probably reflects the fact that he is not really interested in publicity about his investment approach. He is more public about his philanthropic interests, which include the preservation of democracy and children's health.

It was on the latter subject that I first met with Seth. He asked to interview me in connection with an event for Boston Children's Hospital. I told him that was a role reversal, and that the greater appeal to his audience would be hearing him be interviewed. In the end, we interviewed each other.

In preparing for the interview, I realized that we had both grown up in Baltimore, and probably lived only a few miles from each other. But our paths had never crossed, to my dismay. Had I met him sooner, I no doubt would have learned a great deal more about investing many years earlier. I interviewed Seth virtually on July 1, 2021.

DAVID M. RUBENSTEIN (DR): You and Warren Buffett, with whom you have often been compared, are probably the two best-known and successful value investors. What precisely is a value investor? What skills are required to be a successful value investor?

SETH KLARMAN (SK): The basic practice of value investing is trying to buy dollars for 50 cents, sometimes 60 or 70 cents—in effect, buying bargains. Early on in the 1920s and 1930s, Benjamin Graham wrote about value investing. The idea is that markets are affected by human behavior, by greed and fear. They sometimes overshoot, both too high and sometimes too low, and that a value investor who appraises the worth of a company or its assets can find bargains that will produce good returns.

In terms of the requirements to be a value investor, the skill set, first of all, people need to be patient and disciplined. There aren't always bargains. You have to wait for them. Intellectual honesty is unbelievably important—figuring out what you really think, always reflecting and pivoting and, if you're wrong, learning from mistakes.

Deep curiosity benefits all investors. Attention to detail, pattern recognition, having a lot of ideas around any specific situation—all of those are requisite skills.

DR: How has value investing evolved since it first emerged as an investment approach?

SK: All of investing has evolved over the last 80 years. Investing basically was the Wild West. There were really no professional investors a century ago.

There's more sophisticated analysis now, for sure. Obviously, computers have been introduced over the last 50 or 60 years and play a big role, along with the steps that we all know—the introduction of spreadsheets, lately big data, artificial intelligence, Michael Porter's "Five Forces" that act on businesses. The understanding of businesses, and of technological forces that disrupt them, is way more sophisticated these days. [Michael Porter, a prominent Harvard Business School professor, created a way to analyze the five key forces—competition in the industry, the power of customers, the power of suppliers, the potential for new entrants, and the possibility of substitutes—that always affect a company's performance.]

Ultimately, value investing lies at the intersection of economics and psychology. I've joked that it's a marriage of the calculator and a contrarian streak. While value investing has evolved in the sense of achieving greater sophistication, along with the rest of the investment business, the basic principles—the idea of investing with downside protection using numerous methods to assess value—have stayed the same.

DR: In the current high stock market situation, the high-growth economy, are there many opportunities to be a value investor? Is it like being the Maytag repairman, a bit lonely being a value investor now?

SK: I have at times felt like the Maytag repairman, but at this moment I don't really. The first thing I'd say, and it's important for people to understand, is that a value investor doesn't need the whole market to be cheap. A value investor needs a handful of investments to be bargain-priced, to be inefficiently priced. You can build a portfolio on 10 great investments. You don't need the whole market.

That said, the markets are clearly expensive by historical standards. People who have said it's as high as it can go have been wrong over and over. I'm not going to make any heroic statements about where the market should be. But one of the things our firm has found is that value investments don't just reside in stocks, as Benjamin Graham focused on, or even bonds, but also in other areas of the market such as private investments, real estate, structured products from time to time. [Structured products are investments such as mortgage securitizations, and sometimes involve the use of "derivative" instruments like puts or calls.] Right now we're finding a fair number of things to do in most of our areas of opportunity. So the answer to your question is, I'm not the Maytag repairman right now.

DR: Is it hard to resist the temptation to buy the latest high-tech, cryptocurrency, software, and e-commerce companies? In what areas are you finding value today?

SK: I don't find it hard to resist any of those temptations. A value investor has a certain discipline. When something just doesn't make sense, you can't figure it out, you don't play. I'm not drawn to hot areas or to what other people are doing. Obviously, I want to see if I'm missing something, but I haven't been able to find opportunity in areas like crypto, and have no interest in chasing things just because they're going up.

That is, in many ways, the psychology Ben Graham has taught—that you're not trying to chase the market, that stocks are a fractional interest in companies, and if you can figure out what a company's worth and buy it for significantly less, that's value investing. In terms of the areas of opportunity, parts of the equity markets are overlooked. Certain sectors come into favor and others go out of favor; so we do have some equity opportunities.

We have been finding opportunities, as you can imagine, over the last year and a half. Parts of the real estate market have become challenged or distressed. COVID caused construction delays, and nobody was signing new leases for a while, so there's a lot of opportunity for a value investor in real estate at this point.

Again, in private investments, there are many situations where people are in need of capital, even though it seems like capital is ubiquitous. Nevertheless, there are individual situations where companies have trouble accessing capital, accessing how much they want when they want it, and that leads to an opportunity to inject capital.

DR: Do you keep a good deal of your funds in cash, waiting for markets to break and for distressed opportunities to come along?

SK: We view cash as a residual [whatever is left over after you have made all the good investments you can find]. When we find great opportunities, we buy them, and when we don't, we hold cash. We don't choose to throw it into things that are not undervalued or mispriced. So our cash is a residual, and from time to time we have meaningful cash. Right now, it's toward the low end of historic, which is counterintuitive given the level of the markets. But when we find excellent opportunities, we make investments. We're bottom-up investors, not top-down, which means looking stock by stock, security by security, investment by investment, rather than developing a macro view of where the market should be.

DR: You published a book in 1991 called *Margin of Safety*. What does "margin of safety" mean to you?

SK: I blatantly stole the title from Benjamin Graham's work *The Intelligent Investor*. It was the title of a chapter. "Margin of safety," in Graham's words, means that you leave room for error, room for bad luck. It means that, with a focus to the downside, you're buying for less than something's worth, and when you buy it cheap enough, even if something goes wrong, you still have a chance to get your money back or even make money.

Over time and with a sizable portfolio, the margin-of-safety concept is critical. One of the things investors must deal with is how are they going to behave when they're going through a rough spot, and if they buy with no margin of safety and they hit the rough spot, it can be very paralyzing for them. The margin of safety, the willingness to have some dry powder from time to time, can lead an investor to stay in a good psychological place when the markets get rocky.

DR: Any interest in writing an updated version of your book? What have you learned since 1991?

SK: I think about writing an updated version or a companion edition. I haven't gotten around to it, I'm so busy with my day job and my other activities, but maybe at some point.

I've learned a huge amount since 1991. I was 10 years into my career at that point, and now I'm almost 40 years into my career, so hopefully I've learned a great deal. The updates I would make if I were updating the book? The initial idea of value investing was framed around the public financial markets, around stocks and in some ways bonds, and I would expand that because, as I said earlier, we find opportunities in private assets, in private equity, in real estate, in private structured credit. That is now a meaningful part of our investment fund. Those are all things I've come to appreciate, areas of opportunity and edge where we could build sourcing networks and we could develop real capabilities, real experience, that would let us invest intelligently and successfully in those areas.

I also would write about the criticality of team. Who's on your team? How do you motivate them? Culture is critical for every organization. The investment process is important, and consistency of process is a major thing. In Daniel Kahneman's new book [*Noise: A Flaw in Human Judgment*, coauthored with Olivier Sibony and Cass Sunstein], he talks about noise, and noise, in some ways, is the inconsistency of process.* It's important that, as investors and as leaders of a firm, we're making the same decisions on Tuesdays as on Thursdays, in January and in July, whether we're up or down and whether the markets are up or down. Process is crucial in applying investment principles.

DR: If you were to summarize, for anyone reading this, the main principles of investing you would like them to take away from this interview, what would those be?

SK: The two really important principles are taking a long-term approach and getting as flexible a mandate as you can. Having a flexible mandate basically means you're not looking at one thing. You're not narrowly confined in a silo, but rather you're looking across markets, across geographies, and across different types of investments, because you never know what's going to be mispriced, and so the wider you look, the better the chance you're going to find a real mispricing.

---

* Noise, in this analysis, is the inconsistent and thus flawed way decisions are made as a result of such factors as human bias, group dynamics, or emotional thinking.

But then you have to retain the ability to dig deep, to make sure that you know what's going on and that, as Warren Buffett would say, "You're not the patsy at the table." Besides those, risk aversion is crucial, the margin-of-safety concept, along with a disciplined approach to buying and selling. A lot of people forget to sell, and it's important when securities or investments reach full value that you move on. Then there's the criticality of independent, and sometimes contrary, thinking.

DR: To find investments that meet your standards, what do you do? Research, talk to friends, have ideas brought to you by colleagues, watch the Bloomberg terminal, or just think? [The Bloomberg terminal is a desktop computer that is the favored source of up-to-date financial information and market data for professional investors, particularly traders.]

SK: My colleagues and I scour the landscape for potential opportunity. We conduct extensive due diligence. We discuss and debate the attractiveness, the downside, and the upside of our ideas. Part of investing is also filling your inbox with interesting ideas that may turn into investments in the portfolio. Filling your inbox means developing pipelines of potential investments, across markets, trying to think about not just whether something's cheap but also why it might be bargain-priced.

DR: As a value investor, are you always hoping that prices go up, or do you also go short with assets you think are too expensive?

SK: We don't short really much at all. It's tempting for people to think that shorting is always a risk-reduction activity—that it is the mirror image of going long, and it just isn't. If you go long, all you can lose is the money you've put up. If you go short, you can lose an infinite amount, and so we really are loathe to short. But even given that we're not shorting, we don't always hope the markets go up. We know that when you make an investment and it goes down, it becomes a better bargain if you've done your work properly. When we own something that drops, we check and recheck our work, and if we have the opportunity we add to the position. That's a way of turning lemons into lemonade.

DR: How did you deal with COVID-19? Did that hurt your portfolio, or did it give you an opportunity to buy many things cheaply?

SK: The first thing to say about COVID is what a tragedy it's been for the world. So many people lost their lives, lost their health, lost their jobs, and are suffering.

COVID is one of those outside-the-box eventualities that investors need to be prepared for. It's an example of one of the reasons that you don't get over your skis. You don't leverage your portfolio, you don't own hugely speculative investments.

COVID was like a switch flipped, and certain companies that have historically been good businesses were adversely affected. Suddenly sports arenas couldn't open up, because sports teams weren't playing games. So otherwise great businesses suddenly had no cash flow or had negative cash flow. Similarly, relatively lower quality businesses historically, like supermarkets, did incredible business as people stayed home and avoided restaurants and going out.

COVID was a game-changer for the psychology of investing. It tested the limits for investors who were overcommitted or overexposed. The COVID selloff in March of 2020 only lasted several weeks but did create huge dislocations. Our firm, always looking across asset classes, found a few things to do very quickly in distressed debt, in mortgage securities, and in the equity markets. But the real buying opportunity was very limited. The markets were down but the fundamentals were also down. The economy was in the worst tailspin in, perhaps, close to a century, and not everything that went down in price was bargain-priced. But picking through the set of opportunities, we found there were some good places to place capital.

DR: We mentioned *Margin of Safety* and you've mentioned Benjamin Graham's famous book. What other books would you recommend a value investor should read?

SK: I would recommend a number of books, not all of which are officially investment books. I love Graham's more accessible book *The Intelligent Investor*. I would encourage people to read Daniel Kahneman. *Thinking, Fast and Slow* is about the two parts of our brain and how our brains work, which I think everybody should be interested in. How do we make decisions? What are our behavioral biases? His latest book, *Noise*, is also about the decision-making process.

I'd recommend anything by Michael Lewis. *Moneyball* is really a value-investing book. It's about finding value in athletes, in baseball players, but those principles apply across areas. Lewis is often writing about the contrarian or the divergent thinker who's able to add a lot of value. I'd also recommend anything Roger Lowenstein wrote. He wrote a great biography of Warren Buffett. And I'm always fond of Jim Grant's contrary thinking. He wrote a book about credit called *Money of the Mind*. It's incredibly important, almost an exposé of the psychological aspects of credit. All investors should be aware of that line of thinking.

DR: If somebody can't invest with you and your fund, what do you recommend they do if they want to be a value investor? Do they find some other value-investing organizations, or they learn the skills themselves?

SK: It's tough for the little guy to become a full-time value investor if they have a day job. If they are really passionate about it, people have successfully taught themselves the principles of value investing. I have a friend who does some research and comes up with really interesting ideas. But by and large, most people are going to prefer to find a value-based mutual fund or some other professional investor who does it for them.

DR: Are there other investors that you admire? Other than Warren Buffett.

SK: Warren and Charlie Munger [vice chairman of Berkshire Hathaway] have taught the whole investment world a huge amount. One of my former colleagues, David Abrams, is exemplary. David's a great thinker. He's a great writer. He runs a hedge fund in Boston, has been doing it for a couple of decades with great success and with very good downside protection.

DR: Do you teach value investing anywhere?

SK: I do. I often appear as a guest speaker in classes at Harvard Business School, Columbia Business School, Yale undergrad, a number of others like Penn. I like speaking to kids, to young people. It keeps me fresh, and I feel like it's an important part of giving back to the field.

DR: Where did your interest in politics come from? What impact do you hope to have through your political giving?

SK: I'm appalled when I look at the state of our government. We deserve good government, and we also need to demonstrate that a democratic government works for the people. I don't think we have been able to count on that lately.

I always yearn for the time when you can have an election and where you'd be indifferent about who won, because they're both great candidates. So many times we see the opposite. I'm interested in good governance. I'm interested in ensuring democracy, and I support people who will support democratic principles, and who will put the interest of the country ahead of party and ahead of self-interest. It's much rarer than you'd like to see.

DR: When you are not investing or preparing to invest, what do you do with your time?

SK: I read a lot. I have diverse reading interests—biography, history, politics, sociology. I'm interested in and curious about the world around me. I do read fiction. Sometimes you learn more from fiction than you do from nonfiction. I love theater. I love spectator sports, and am also very involved in my family foundation.

DR: How important is philanthropy to you? What particular areas?

SK: My philanthropy is very meaningful to me. If you ask me the thing I'm proudest of, I'm proud of the firm I've helped to build up, Baupost, and our investment record over time that served our clients. But I'm even prouder of the ability and commitment to giving back that my wife and I have typically achieved through grants from our family foundation. We support people in the greatest need in the Boston area and beyond in Massachusetts, and elsewhere in the world from time to time. We're focused on medical and science research, and may be one of the largest funders in the country of eating-disorder research.

Probably the largest single area is bolstering and improving American democracy, which is a major area of focus for our family foundation. Protecting democracy to make sure that my kids and grandkids have the same blessings that you and I have had to live in a democratic America.

DR: You and I are both from Baltimore, but you've been living in Boston most of your life. Do you still root for the Orioles or do you now root for the Red Sox?

SK: I realized in the early 1980s, when I made the decision to stay in Boston, that I had to choose. They play each other 18 times a year. I was drawn to the sustained misery of Boston's losing streak, of having not won a World Series in over 80 years, since 1918. I think that was what let me make the switch. That and realizing that I was going to be seeing Boston play a lot more than I saw Baltimore play. But in my heart, I still hold significant affection for Baltimore, and if the Red Sox aren't playing, I'll root for Baltimore.

RAY DALIO

Founder, co-chief investment officer, and board member,
Bridgewater Associates

> *"You have to be an independent thinker, because you can't make money in the markets betting with the consensus because the consensus is built into the price."*

The first hedge fund—actually then called a "hedged" fund—was created in 1949 by Alfred W. Jones. By "hedging" his investments, he was using investment techniques, like shorting a stock, that would protect his overall returns in the event that the stock market declined, dragging down the values of some of his "long" investments.

Since that time, an incalculable number of funds have been created to hedge against market declines. A variety of trading techniques are used to protect against the downside.

The appeal of such funds is the downside protection. Traditional mutual funds or "long" investment funds are limited by law and regulation in their use of downside protection techniques and are thus more vulnerable to market corrections and declines.

With hedge funds, which typically invest in liquid or readily tradable assets and securities, there is no requirement that their investments be hedged, and in fact a great many hedge funds do not actually hedge their investments in the traditional sense. For that reason, the application of the term "hedge fund" is probably a misnomer in many instances.

Jones had another novelty in his "hedged" fund. He charged a fee of 20 percent of the profits—far above the fee traditional mutual funds or long-only funds charged.

Jones's progeny have continued to charge an equivalent (or greater) fee. That fee has clearly attracted many highly intelligent, highly motivated investment professionals. And they, by and large (with obvious exceptions in difficult market periods), have achieved impressive returns from time to time. However, Warren Buffett has successfully wagered that stock market index funds, with lower fees and volatility, will outperform a cross section of hedge funds over a 10-year period.

So why do investors invest in such funds?

Buffett notwithstanding, a fair number of investors have thought they could select very strong hedge funds to invest in and have thus kept the hedge fund industry heavily capitalized during much of the past several decades. For many of the leading hedge funds, the results have generally been positive over extended periods. And their managers have become quite wealthy. If a hedge fund manages $40 billion and achieves a 20 percent return in a particular year ($8 billion profit), 20 percent (or $1.6 billion) of that profit is earned by the hedge fund for its professionals for that year's work. And this can lead to senior hedge fund professionals (particularly the founders) having extraordinarily large current incomes, even by the rarified standards of the investment world.

To be sure, there are thousands of hedge funds operating in major markets at any given time, and many of these hedge funds are not that successful and tend to come and go. It is not difficult to start a hedge fund, though those doing so typically have some trading experience at another hedge fund or at an investment bank. And there surely are a few hedge funds that are very successful for several years—maybe even a decade or longer—but generally a bad year or two can effectively end a hedge fund as investors withdraw their capital (though that may take some time—months or even years). With some obvious exceptions, the leaders of hedge funds have found it hard to be consistent in their performance, year in and out, through up markets and down markets.

This reality makes all the more remarkable what one organization, Bridgewater Associates, has done: it has been around for 47 years (founded in 1975); has produced more net gains since inception than any other hedge fund; and now manages more than $150 billion, making it the world's largest such fund.

What enabled Bridgewater to do what no other hedge fund organization has been able to do—endure for nearly a half century and scale to a size that no other fund can match?

The simple answer is Ray Dalio, Bridgewater's founder, and for most of its history its CEO and CIO. In recent years, at an age when most other founders are focusing on matters other than the financial markets, Ray is still a co-CIO, a member of the firm's board, and a guiding presence behind the firm.

This result might not have been predicted early in Ray's career: he was a commodities trader; he was fired from one job after punching a boss in the face; and he once lost all of his net worth (then modest) with some bad trades (forcing Ray to borrow from his father to support his young family and make ends meet).

But Ray persevered. He learned from his mistakes. He began to develop a set of principles for his investment activities, as well as for his life. He applied these well-defined and rigorous principles to everything Bridgewater did. While that could mean vigorous self-reflection and analysis for Ray and all of the Bridgewater employees, the principles obviously worked. And the returns tended to be not only consistent but also above so many peers for so many years.

But that was not enough for Ray. He was interested in more than attaining market-leading returns for his fund. He was quite interested as well in explaining to others the principles that drove his success, and he published them in 2017 in *Principles*, a number one *New York Times* best-selling book. In addition, in recent years he has been interested in educating the public about his concerns on a variety of fiscal and economic issues—like excessive government debt or artificially low interest rates—and has done so through articles and public appearances. In 2021, he published another best-selling book, *The Changing World Order,* to explain his observations of historical societal cycles and suggestions for navigating them in the future.

As an investor, and as an author and public educator, it is clear that Ray Dalio has what might be described as a "beautiful mind"— analytical, logical, thoughtful, well reasoned. I saw all of those qualities when I first met Ray at a Giving Pledge* session and have seen them time and again as I have interviewed him on various occasions.

Like other extraordinarily successful investors, Ray is also committed deeply to philanthropy, and is devoted to providing his resources and time to projects relating to the environment, wellness, and education. In these efforts he invariably brings his considerable intellect and passion. The term "Renaissance man" is perhaps overused when applied to some in modern society, but not when it is applied to Ray Dalio. I interviewed him virtually on July 7, 2021.

DAVID M. RUBENSTEIN (DR): You built the world's largest hedge fund and are still involved deeply in its investment decisions. Did you aspire to be an investor when you were young, growing up on Long Island?

RAY DALIO (RD): No more so than somebody aspires to play video games. I caddied, and people I caddied for were into investing. I took my caddying money and invested it in the stock market, $50 at a time. The first stock I bought was the only company I heard of that was less than $5 a share. I figured I could buy more shares, so if that went up, I'd make more money. That was dumb. The company was on the brink of bankruptcy.

But by luck it tripled in price because it was acquired—I was hooked on the game. I didn't think of it as a career. I just thought of it as a fun and money-making game to play and if I did it right, I'd make a lot of money. I didn't even think about the losing money part. I was too naive. I learned about that later.

DR: Your perspectives on investing are widely followed around the world. Your book *Principles: Life & Work* has been a global bestseller. Were you surprised that such a serious, reflective book could sell millions of copies, including in countries like China?

---

* Established in 2010 by Warren Buffett, Melinda French Gates, and Bill Gates, the Giving Pledge is a commitment by very wealthy individuals and families to give at least half of their net worth to philanthropic causes or projects during their lifetime or upon their death.

RD: I was pleasantly surprised.

DR: You have become financially very successful and could easily turn over the investing reins at Bridgewater. Is the pleasure of investing compelling you to stay in the game and make regular investment decisions for your hedge fund?

RD: Yes. I love the game of trying to figure out what's going on in the world, what's going to happen, and betting on it. I also love being a mentor to those I've passed the lead responsibilities to.

DR: How do you compare the pleasure of investing with the pleasure of giving away your money, which you are actively doing through your philanthropic programs?

RD: I love them both, though they are very different. Philanthropy is harder to judge my performance in because it doesn't give me clear feedback. In investing, I can measure my performance objectively to three decimal points, which I like better because it helps me learn and be better. However, I find that philanthropy is a much more direct linkage to helping people and the environment. While I intellectually know that when I do investing I'm helping people to have better lives, which includes people who don't have much money such as those benefiting from public pension funds and the like—still, the connection between the investing activity and seeing the social benefit of it is much less clear. Philanthropy is much more personal to provide help. But I like doing both. I'm essentially running two companies that are very different but both rewarding.

DR: There are many different investment approaches—macro, value, distressed, long, short, and so forth. What would you say has been your main approach, the approach that enabled your hedge fund to become the biggest in the world?

RD: I'm a global macro investor. That means that I look at the whole world and the interconnectedness of it, try to figure out how it works, then I bet on what will happen, and then it gives me clear feedback. I love that. It keeps my views of how things work and my theories of what's going to happen practical. We are in every liquid market in the world—all stock, bond, currency, and commodity markets, and any country where there's good liquidity. If the Federal Reserve or other central banks make moves, where are the growth rates, where is the productivity? How will politics or international relations affect the markets? Those are the sorts of questions I wrestle with and bet on.

DR: You attended high school on Long Island and, by your own admission, you were not valedictorian of your class, right?

RD: Quite the opposite. I was a C+ student. I didn't like high school. I barely got into college. But I loved college because I could pick my own courses and study what interested me.

DR: When you were in college you were working as well. You then got into Harvard Business School. Were you surprised to get in? Why did you apply to Harvard?

RD: I did very well in college. I didn't take it for granted that I would get into Harvard Business School, but I wasn't surprised. I was excited, because this was a place where people came from all over the world, a mixture of students from all different countries—and the smartest students. To be able to be in that kind of environment—I was not ever in an environment like that before.

I was very excited the first day I was there and excited all the way through. I loved the way they taught the case-study method, which was not to sit there, remember what you're told, and then regurgitate it back for a test. It was real thinking, dropping us into real cases and debating "How would you approach that?" That was a great education—a big, wide, eye-opening experience.

DR: Why did you not join a large investment firm after graduating?

RD: When I was a kid, I traded in different markets. Then, when I was in college, I decided I wanted to trade commodities, because there were low margin requirements [i.e., very little equity had to be invested relative to the value of the commodity being purchased; the brokers provided the debt or leverage needed to pay the difference between the equity invested and the commodity price].

By using a great deal of leverage provided by the broker, it was possible to make outsized profits if you bought the right commodities at the right price. So, I started to trade commodities. That was my game. I traded stocks before that.

I graduated in 1973. The summer of '72, I went to the director of commodities at Merrill Lynch. I was the first person ever from Harvard Business School to do that, because the commodity area was not an interesting area, but I had the background. He gave me a job, and I thought it was great. Then, when I graduated, the commodity area was hot. There was a big oil shock, the first oil shock, and commodities were hot, and stocks were not.

I was offered the job of director of commodities at Dominick & Dominick, a brokerage house that went on to have some financial problems. I was basically thrown in the middle of the world's hottest market at that time, because there was the oil shock, commodity shock. Stocks were going down. I grabbed that opportunity. My job after that was director of institutional commodities at another brokerage firm. That didn't last very long, because I got into a fight with my boss, and in 1975, I set up Bridgewater.

DR: How did you capitalize Bridgewater?

RD: I didn't capitalize it. I didn't even think of it as a company. I was just the guy institutional investors would pay some money to give them advice, and then I traded my own account. I had a two-bedroom apartment I shared with a guy I went to business school with. He moved out; the other bedroom became the office. I got a couple of people to help me—a guy I played rugby with, and an assistant. There was no capitalization. There was just me doing that and getting paid.

DR: When and why did you start Bridgewater?

RD: Nineteen seventy-five. I wasn't a classic good employee. I was kind of rebellious. I was my own guy, got in a fight with my boss, who's a good guy, but we got in a fight. In '75, on New Year's Eve, we both got a bit drunk and I punched him. Not working for someone else and doing my own thing suited me.

DR: You've written a book on principles that govern your investment career and your life. What are the principles that enabled you to build Bridgewater into the largest hedge fund in the world?

RD: My most important principle that helped me build Bridgewater is "pain plus reflection equals progress." I learned the hard way that pain was a teacher. That lesson was hammered into me when I made a big, painful mistake that cost me a lot and taught me a lot in 1982. I had started Bridgewater in '75. We had Paul Volcker becoming head of the Fed in 1979. In 1980, we had inflation. We had "Whip Inflation Now" and very tight money policies. I had calculated that America and banks had lent a lot more money to foreign countries than those countries were going to be able to pay back, and that we were going to have a big debt crisis.

It was a controversial point of view at the time. It got a lot of attention, and it turned out to be right. Mexico defaulted in August 1982 and a lot of other countries followed, and I thought the world was going to go into a depression-like economy because of this debt crisis.

I couldn't have been more wrong. August 18, 1982, was the exact bottom of the stock market, because the Fed eased a lot, interest rates plunged, and everything went up.

That mistake cost me a lot of money. I had to let everybody in the company go. I was so broke, I had to borrow $4,000 from my dad to help pay family bills. The reason I say that was one of the best things that happened to me is because it gave me a fear of being wrong that I needed to balance my audacity. I wanted the big upside but couldn't take the big downside, which led me to reflect on what to do about that.

At the time, I felt like I was on the safe side of a dangerous jungle and I had a choice. I could stay on the safe side and have a safe but mediocre life, or I could try to cross through the risky jungle to have a great life if I could get to the other side. I didn't want to have just a safe, mediocre life, so I had to figure out how to safely cross the jungle.

That painful mistake changed my whole approach to decision-making. The two most important things I learned were to find the smartest people I could who disagreed with me so I could stress-test my thinking, and to learn how to diversify well so that I could keep the high returns while reducing the risk.

What people don't realize is that diversification has nothing to do with return reduction. If you have equally good bets and you diversify, you have the same average return of those bets, but you have much less risk. That's not just true in investing; that's what life's about. Thinking. It had a big effect on how I ran Bridgewater and how I approached life.

I realized that to do that I needed to go through it with people who were on the same mission as me and could help me by seeing things I couldn't see, and I could help them by seeing things they couldn't see. We would look out for each other as we crossed that jungle. That was the approach. It was so rewarding and enjoyable that I didn't want to, and still don't want to, leave that risky jungle and live in a land of success. That very painful mistake taught me that knowing how to deal well with not knowing was more important than anything I know. It also led me to have, and to see how great it is to have, meaningful work and meaningful relationships operating in this idea-meritocratic way. From then until now we had great upside with limited downside, and meaningful work and meaningful relationships.

All of that came from reflecting a lot on my painful mistake. Most importantly it changed how I look at painful mistakes. I learned to look at my painful mistakes like puzzles that will give me gems if I can solve them. The gems are principles that I can use to handle these situations better in the future. Every time one of those would happen I wrote the principles down, which helped me think more deeply about them, communicate them to others, and refer to them in the future. I also learned how to turn them into computerized decision rules that I could back-test and use to make investment decisions.

DR: Normally hedge fund guys give up after a couple of years, maybe five years. They just can't be that consistent over a long period of time. You have been consistent over 40-plus years and built the biggest fund that has ever existed in the hedge fund world. What do you think is the central reason you were able to do that? Consistency in following your principles? Hiring smart people? What was it that enabled you to build the biggest one?

RD: First, knowing how to create great upside with limited downside, which I just explained. Second, converting my written-out principles into algorithmic decision rules that I could back-test to see how they would've worked in the past. These decision rules produced track records that I call return streams. Then I had these criteria programmed into a computer and put their return streams together into a well-engineered portfolio of bets that balanced each other. That process of writing down my principles and putting them into algorithms gave me the ability to test and modify my criteria to see how they would have worked in different time frames in different countries. To be able to put them together in that way worked well for me and Bridgewater.

Third, the company's culture was key. Having a culture in which there's thoughtful disagreement and meritocratic decision making, so the best ideas win out, was a big thing. It was a culture in which we would challenge each other's ideas and hold each other to high standards.

DR: If somebody says, "What do you think it takes to be a good investor?" would you say hard work, vision, brilliance, luck, a good team?

RD: High-quality independent thinking, humility, working well with others, and resilience. You *have* to be an independent thinker because you can't make money in the markets betting with the consensus, because the consensus is built into the price. You have to have humility to have the healthy fear of being wrong that pushes you to do things that raise your chances of being right. You have to work well with others because they bring you what you don't have and they stress-test you. And you have to have resilience because you will have losses which will hurt sometimes, which is OK if you limit them to acceptable losses.

DR: What's the greatest pleasure in being an investor?

RD: There are different types of investors who derive different kinds of pleasures, so I can't answer what's the greatest pleasure for investing in general. But I can tell you what my greatest pleasure is in being a global macro investor. It is being on a mission with others to figure out how the world works and to successfully bet on it.

DR: As you look back on your investing career, any regrets? What gives you the greatest pride?

RD: All the regrets I have, I wouldn't have wanted to do without. While I made lots of painful mistakes, I wouldn't want to have not made them. Do I regret that in 1982 I went broke, essentially? No, because it gave me a painful gift that changed my perspective. I like the learning process, which is that painful mistakes lead to reflections that produce progress. So I don't have any regrets. I'm just so very grateful for the life that I've had, including the painful mistakes.

DR: What are you the most proud of? Building the largest hedge fund in the world?

RD: The two things I wanted most in life, and am most proud of, were having and giving others meaningful work and meaningful relationships. I think that's important, and I think I did a pretty good job of that in my company, my philanthropy, and my family.

Also, I wanted to evolve well personally and contribute to evolution. As I see it, everything is about evolution and contributing to it. One is born with one's DNA and environment, interacts with reality, grows and acquires knowledge and physical possessions, and passes that along before, or upon, death. I feel that I've done that pretty well.

DR: Are there new worlds, within the investing world or outside investing, that you would like to conquer at this point in your life?

RD: I'm excited about too many areas, so I have a breadth versus depth challenge. The world is going through revolutionary change in many areas, which is exciting to try to understand in and of itself. I remain excited to do that, both as an investor and in my philanthropy. I'm particularly excited about trying to have a big impact on ocean exploration and helping people who are struggling the most have more equal opportunities. And I am especially excited about spending quality time with my family, especially my grandchildren.

DR: You have become a believer in Transcendental Meditation. What are the benefits? Does it help you be a better investor?

RD: Whatever success I have had has been more due to Transcendental Meditation than anything else. That's because it gives me the equanimity to think clearly and to think imaginatively. It also makes me healthier because it reduces stress. I've done it since 1969, so for a long time. I was inspired by the Beatles, who had gone to India and experienced Transcendental Meditation there.

I'll explain how it works. There's a mantra, which is a sound in the form of a word that has no meaning. When you repeat it silently in your head, you can't have other thoughts, so they go away. Then the mantra disappears, and you go into a subconscious state. That is where peacefulness and a lot of creativity come from. So meditation brings you into that state. It's a physiological exercise that is relaxing rather than stressful. It's not a religious thing. You carry the effects with you even when you're not meditating. When various challenges come at me, I can approach them with much more equanimity and creativity than if I didn't meditate.

DR: More than some great investors, you've been willing to talk and write about your perspectives and principles. Do you view your position in the investing world as having some educational or teaching responsibility as well?

RD: Yes. I believe that I and you and others at our stages of life should pass along the valuable things that we've learned. I think it's a mistake to just do things and then stop doing them without passing along those things we've learned that could be valuable to others. We should instead put our learnings out there for others to take or leave as they like.

DR: In recent years, you've been a strong believer in the value of investing in China. What prompted that interest, and are you concerned about the Chinese economy overheating or the government imposing too many constraints? Anything else that worries you about the Chinese economy?

RD: I started to go to China in 1984. Deng Xiaoping came to power in 1978, and they developed an open-door reform policy. I was invited there by CITIC, which was the only window company—the only company allowed to deal with the outside world. They invited me to teach them about world financial markets. I was curious to go behind the wall, and I found that I loved the people there. I went there repeatedly, for no financial purposes, because there was no money in China.

Since then I've had amazing, wonderfully close contact. Over 37 years, I've been able to see up close and, in my small way, contribute to the greatest economic miracle of all time. In those years, per capita income for over a billion people has increased by 26 times, the poverty rate (as measured by people being hungry) fell from 88 percent to less than 1 percent, and the life expectancy increased by 10 years. My intimacy of contact gave me an understanding of and also a great admiration for what has been accomplished.

Over my lifetime, I've also gotten to live the American Dream. So

I'm grateful to and love the United States. What frustrates and saddens me is that there's not a mutual understanding between the countries, and rather than producing a win-win relationship, both sides are increasingly producing a lose-lose relationship, which could be disastrous. I try my best to help increase mutual understanding, but it's not easy.

DR: As you look at the US economy, are you worried about the artificially low interest rates and the rise of federal debt we've been incurring over the last 10, 20, 30 years?

RD: Yes. I'm like a mechanic, so I'd like to explain the mechanics behind my concerns. The price of something is equal to the total amount spent on it divided by the quantity sold. I look at how debt and money are produced and how they are passed through the system relative to the quantity of goods and services sold. I know that one person's debts are another person's assets, and that balancing inflation against growth is more difficult when there are lots of debt and financial assets outstanding. And I see how big they are and how fast they are growing. The way the economy and the Fed work is that whenever the economy is too weak, the Fed wants to stimulate it, so it gives the economy a shot by creating a lot of money and credit to stimulate spending. After it gives that shot, there is more spending on goods, services, and financial assets, and everybody's happy. By seeing the amount of money and credit, I can estimate inflation. Now, the Fed is faced with high inflation because of the enormous amounts of debt and money it created, so it's trying to put on the brakes while deficits and debt creation are still large at the same time, which is a formula for stagflation. The Fed's balancing act will be very difficult, because an acceptable interest rate for the debtor to service their debts will probably be too low of an interest rate for the creditor to compensate for inflation. I think that's where we are. The fact that the US can print the only reserve currency in the world gives the US enormous advantages and economic strength, but the current set of circumstances makes it challenging to maintain that exorbitant privilege.

DR: What do you think of cryptocurrencies?

RD: Cryptocurrencies are remarkable accomplishments in structure and acceptance. Those, like Bitcoin, that help as store holds of wealth, are accepted globally, and are limited in supply, are like digital gold. They are interesting as such, but I doubt they will replace gold because I don't expect them to be held as central bank reserves. Their ownership and movements are also traceable, and if they are really successful and become competitive with fiat currencies, I suspect governments will outlaw them. On the other hand, they are evolving quickly to take different forms that might create alternative digital assets that work better. The one thing I am pretty sure of is that money as we know it will become less valuable and less used relative to alternative forms of money that will compete to be the currency of choice. That's because money, which is a debt asset, has to be a good storehold of wealth as well as a medium of exchange, and these fiat currencies, which are debt assets, won't be good storeholds of wealth without being unacceptably high burdens on debtors. In the future, you and I will probably hold a few different types of currency, if our governments allow us, because it won't be clear which one is best.

STAN DRUCKENMILLER

Investor and philanthropist; former chairman and
president, Duquesne Capital Management;
former lead portfolio manager, Soros Quantum Fund

> *"Making money, that's not the big motivator, but I do love
> winning."*

O ver the past three decades, there have been few investment deci-
sions that caused as much global attention as the decision by Stan
Druckenmiller (then principally managing George Soros's Quantum
Fund) to short the British pound, believing it was clearly overvalued.
When the Bank of England did devalue it, the result was a profit for the
Soros fund in excess of $1 billion—a then unheard-of amount for one
trade.

Stan had previously been an investor known only to investment
cognoscenti, and that was due to both his success in leading Duquesne
Capital Management and to having been selected to lead the
high-profile Soros Quantum Fund. After the Bank of England trade,
everyone in the world seemed to know him—and wanted to hear his
views on markets.

Stan's investment style defies description a bit. Overall, he is focused on liquid investments. In the liquid area, he is part macro investor
(investing in ways designed to capture macroeconomic or geopolitical trends he foresees), part public equity investor (investing in stocks
that he believes are likely, in a meaningful way, to grow or recede in
value), and part an investor who takes positions based on his views and

research (or the views of others he respects) but is willing to reexamine those views constantly.

Stan did not grow up with an obsession to invest or to make large sums of money. Rather, he was intent on getting a PhD in economics (from the University of Michigan), but opted out of that career path and began working at Pittsburgh National Bank. In time, he drifted into investments while at the bank, and then started his own hedge fund in 1981 to pursue his eclectic approach—that is, some macro-trend investing, some "value" stock picking, some distressed-securities investing. That fund's success attracted George Soros to hire Stan, who insisted on being able to continue managing his own fund. When Stan left the Quantum Fund in 2000, he resumed running Duquesne full-time, to the delight of its investors.

But in 2010, he decided to return investors' capital and manage only his own funds. As a result, his investment performance is private, but the investment world has no doubt that he is continuing to find creative ways to significantly outperform the markets through insightful macro-economic bets and careful selection of public securities.

For many years, the EF Hutton brokerage firm had an advertising slogan: "When EF Hutton talks, people listen." The same can be said of Stan Druckenmiller, for he commands universal respect in the financial markets.

That can be attributed to the historic British pound investment. But that occurred decades ago. The respect today is due to the enviable track record he compiled for decades for Duquesne's investors when he was running the fund. And the respect is no doubt due as well to Stan's low-key, non–master of the universe style, and to his willingness to admit mistakes and share the credit when appropriate.

As a man of few words, Stan does not seek public forums to provide his views or discuss his successes. Rather, he is content to make his investment decisions, implement them, realize the profits, and not talk about what he has done.

At this stage in his career, he still enjoys the investment game of outwitting the markets, but much of his activity now is designed to enhance the capital for his extensive philanthropic commitments to education, medical research, and community-based antipoverty efforts.

I have come to know Stan by serving with him on the investment committee of the Memorial Sloan Kettering Cancer Center. He chairs the committee, and his leadership has provided extraordinary returns. Watching him lead the committee is a master class in the art of investing—asking the right questions, focusing on the relevant information, and mentoring the investment staff. And he does all of this with his trademark laconic, low-key, and humble manner. I interviewed Stan virtually on June 30, 2021.

DAVID M. RUBENSTEIN (DR): You left the PhD program in economics at the University of Michigan to take an analyst position at Pittsburgh National Bank, and the result was one of the most successful investment careers over the past 40-plus years. Have you ever thought about how your life would have been different had you obtained the PhD? Any regrets about the way things turned out? No sorrow about not winning a Nobel Prize in economics?

STAN DRUCKENMILLER (SD): I have no regrets. I was an English major at Bowdoin. My junior year, I took a course in economics, so I could read the paper and have some sense of what might be going on in the world. Undergraduate economics was like I had seen the light. I loved the "invisible hand," comparative advantage, marginal costs, all that stuff.

I like to teach. I went to Michigan thinking I was going to be a professor of economics, but graduate economics is basically trying to jam the world into a math formula, believing that economics is a hard science. I didn't think it worked. I wasn't particularly good at it. I actually left to take a short-term construction job in Vermont, but that ended when I was ultimately given an offer by Pittsburgh National Bank to join its investment operation as a research analyst.

DR: So you might have been a construction magnate?

SD: I would have been a failure in construction. Probably would have failed at everything else. My mother-in-law says I'm an idiot savant, and I agree with her. I have one talent and was lucky enough to end up in that area.

DR: How did you happen to come to Bowdoin? It's a great school, but it's out of the way from where you grew up.

SD: I was in Richmond, Virginia, in high school. I had gone to public school through the eighth grade, at not very good schools. My verbal SATs were a disaster, even though my math SATs were fine. Bowdoin was the best school out there that didn't rely heavily on SAT scores. They had no requirements. That all sounded good to an 18-year-old who didn't know anything better. I'm glad I went there, because it turned out to be a great experience.

DR: It worked out for you and for Bowdoin.

No matter how well you do in the rest of your life, you're going to always be remembered for the famous trade betting against the British pound when you were working with George Soros. Were you worried that could end your career if it didn't work out? Do you get upset when people talk about this bet as if that's the only thing you've done in your life?

SD: I wasn't at all worried about it. That was the whole reason we went so big in that trade. It's because there was no worry.

My explanation there is simple. The deutsche mark and the British pound were linked. They were trading at an agreed-upon fixed exchange rate. You had the German economy booming because of the reunification with East Germany. I knew the Bundesbank was obsessed by inflation. All Germans are because of their experience in the Weimar Republic. Those high interest rates were affecting the British economy, which was suffering from the expensive value of the pound.

Frankly, I didn't think they were going to devalue the pound when I put the trade on. I just thought the most I could lose was about half a percent. There was no way I could lose more than half a percent, but I could make 20 percent, so it was more of a risk/reward bet.

I put it on in August of '92. I only did a billion on the pound. I think the Quantum Fund was $7 billion. Then the day before they broke, the head of the Bundesbank had written an article in the *Financial Times,* which basically said that they didn't want to be linked to the pound anymore. It was said in more subtle language than that, but not very subtle, and at that point I realized this thing actually might work out.

We tried to bet $15 billion on a pound devaluation. That was our target. That was more George's influence. I went in and told him that I was going to take the fund to 100 percent of its value (or $7 billion), and he had sort of this puzzled, condescending look on his face. I thought he didn't agree with my thesis. What he didn't agree with was 100 percent. He wanted to go to 200 percent, because he said it was a once-a-generation deal where you couldn't lose any money. You might make a lot.

I don't mind that people talk about it. I know where I made my money. The irony is that I made a lot more money on the aftereffects of the pound devaluation than I did on the pound itself. Buying British stocks, buying gilts, buying European bonds. That trade really benefited the fund for almost two years because of the concentric circles of politics.

DR: George Soros may have said, "Put in more," but you had the original idea. Is that fair?

SD: Yes, it was completely mine. That's not a knock on George. He was doing philanthropy at the time, and he definitely influenced the size we wanted to do. The irony is, we only got to $7 billion invested anyway, because the news of the devaluation broke that night. In fact, the market became dysfunctional overnight.

DR: Everyone seems to follow your words of advice or thoughts about the investment world. Do you feel a special responsibility to be careful about your public comments? When you have an investment idea or thesis to invest on, do you work hard to not tip off what you're doing?

SD: I do feel a responsibility. Unlike Warren Buffett, who holds a position for 10 or 20 years, I can have total conviction in an idea and, if the circumstances change, have total conviction the other way in two weeks. My performance is more a matter of having an open mind or a thesis and taking the losses than it is on being right a greater percentage of time. So, whenever I give public comments on a position, I always say, "I could change my mind in two or three weeks. This is the way I operate. You really shouldn't be listening to anything I'd say in terms of short term because my views could change."

DR: When you put a position on something, do you try very hard to keep it secret for a while?

SD: Yes, I have to be extra cautious about that.

DR: What is the joy of investing all about for you? Is it using your gray matter to analyze an opportunity, outwitting the markets, making money, having more money to give away?

SD: First and foremost, it's the intellectual stimulation. Every event in the world affects some security somewhere, so it keeps me sharp. I don't think it's a coincidence that a lot of people in retirement invest for fun and invest for a living. I like trying to envision the world 18 months from now versus today and where security prices might be. Making money, that's not the big motivator, but I do love winning. It's a bit of a disease, but it is what it is, and I have to deal with it. So yes, I like to win. You get your grades in the paper every day. There's no hiding when your investments are going bad. It's right there in the newspaper to show you.

DR: Years ago you stopped managing money for others and are now essentially investing your own money. Is that less pressure or more pressure, and why did you make the decision to stop managing other people's money?

SD: I've never felt I was particularly effective with managing funds over $10 billion. My style is that I need to be able to move and change my mind. My positions are held for more like a year to 18 months. Sometimes they don't even last that long. Over $10 billion I would kind of freeze up and not put on the kind of leverage I would at $2 or $3 billion. I thought I was less effective. So in '93, Duquesne started returning all appreciated capital to the investor, to try and keep the fund size down.

It's one of the primary reasons I left Soros seven years later. Even though I was paying all profits back to investors, because my own money just kept compounding, I had gotten too big, and I realized that if I continued to be successful, size would become an increasing problem.

The biggest disappointment has been the answer to your other question about whether it's less rather than more pressure. My clients were always great. They never complained. But I still thought not having clients would be a benefit. It hasn't benefited me at all in terms of pressure. For whatever reason, my desire to win, I still feel the same pressure I always felt.

DR: You're seen as one of the deans or giants of macro investing. What precisely is macro investing, and what is so challenging about doing that kind of investing?

SD: I started off as a banking chemical analyst at Pittsburgh National. Being a bank analyst, I learned about liquidity and the Fed and all that stuff. I used to use interest rate forecasts and currency forecasts to figure out where to invest in the equity market, and it dawned on me, "Why don't I also invest in the bond futures themselves, or in the currencies?" They were more predictable than equities. They responded to true economic forces rather than being a fashion show.

My investment philosophy became one of having a quiver of arrows: equities, bonds, currencies, commodities. You didn't always feel the need to play in a certain area, so it gave you discipline. If you couldn't figure out the equity market, there was something else out there you could deal in.

The term "macro investing" is used generally more about funds that make bets on a top-down basis only, so they're making most of their money in bonds and currencies, and they use equity futures. Because of how I started investing, I've always used bottom-up investing. In fact, my economic forecasts don't come from unemployment rates and stuff like that. They come from information I get on companies from the ground up. I'm sort of a hybrid. I guess the term would be "multi-asset manager."

DR: You do make concentrated bets on certain companies or certain industries. What you're saying is those often lead to your making macro bets?

SD: That's correct.

DR: Did you invest as a child or as a college student? What were your interests?

SD: No, I never invested. I thought I was going to be an English professor. I did play a lot of poker and other games that I enjoyed.

DR: Warren Buffett was investing when he was in fourth grade or something, but that's not you?

SD: I don't think I ever made an investment before I went to Pittsburgh National.

DR: When you did go to Pittsburgh National? Is that when you started doing your investing, when you were there at the bank?

SD: Not technically. In my personal account, yes. I had an incredible mentor there, and he made me director of research. I was 25 years old, with a bunch of 35- and 40-year-olds reporting to me. I was director of research, which at the bank meant that I provided a list and portfolio managers could only buy something with quotes on that list. To that extent, I might have been investing, but I didn't start investing real, live money until I left the bank and started Duquesne.

DR: When you started Duquesne, who were your initial investors? How did it perform? I was surprised that the name Duquesne was available.

SD: I thought it was cool and sexy. I don't know why I thought that but I did, and it definitely had a big Pittsburgh flavor around it. I went to New York and talked about gold at some meeting and I met this guy, Joe Ossorio, who ran a firm called Drysdale Securities. He asked me what in the world I was doing at a bank. I said, "What else am I going to do?" I was making $43,000 a year as head now of the entire investment department. He said, "I'll pay you $10,000 a month just to talk to you, and you can start an investment firm." Those were the original funds behind Duquesne.

DR: Were you living in New York or Pittsburgh?

SD: Two days a week in New York and five days, including the weekends, in Pittsburgh, back and forth.

DR: How did you get connected with George Soros initially, and were you still managing Duquesne when you were working for him?

SD: I was managing Duquesne when I worked for him. I figured he would fire me within a year because I was his ninth successor in something like three or four years.

DR: How did you first get connected with him?

SD: I read his book *The Alchemy of Finance* and there was a chapter in there that really caught my eye called "The Imperial Circle," which was how he thought about currencies. There was a sell-side guy from Merrill

Lynch I talked to about the book and he said, "Would you like to meet him? My wife works there." So I called Soros up because I wanted to talk about this currency thing, and that's how we got connected.

DR: If you read that book and understood it, you're one of the few. I couldn't figure it out.

SD: I only understood the fourth chapter. The rest of it was a little rough, except that you realize, once you get to the experiment part, that he doesn't employ any of the theories you hear that he espouses.

DR: What would you say are the qualities of great investors? Are there certain qualities they have in common?

SD: My original mentor was a guy in Pittsburgh named Speros Drelles and I'd say I learned most of what I know about the business from him. What I learned from George was very simple. It was about sizing positions. Not whether you're right or wrong, but how much you make when you're right and how much will you lose when you're wrong, and that if you have conviction on something, you have to go big and take big positions.

If you think about it, whether it's Warren Buffett, Carl Icahn, or George Soros, almost every great investor is a big concentrator above what they would ever teach in business school. It was sizing of positions that I learned from George.

DR: Inflation is beginning to rear its head in the US. Do you see this being a problem for some time? Given the large stimulus we have and the borrowing now occurring, are you worried about the value of the dollar?

SD: The answer on inflation is I don't know. I think it's remarkable that the Fed at least projects the confidence they have. Per our earlier discussion, this is something I could change my mind on. But when you have monetary and fiscal stimulus five to 10 times what it was back in the guns-and-butter period, and you have the Fed saying something that people are already talking about as transitory, it's been my experience, looking at Latin America and other economies, that once people start talking about inflation, it's too late. I'm very worried about inflation, but I'm open to being wrong. We'll see how it plays out.

The deficits terrify me. I ran around the country giving speeches about entitlements 10 years ago. Every metric I talked about is worse than I projected, with the exception of interest rates. I used interest rates of 4 percent, which I thought were quite reasonable at the time. Interest rates have been at historic lows. If, in fact, interest rates ever normalize, we're not going to be able to service the debt. For the life of me I can't understand why the Fed is rooting for inflation.

DR: Climate change and its impact on humanity and on economies is an important issue, but do you consider it being too removed from your day-to-day investment decisions? In other words, when you're making investment decisions, are you worried about the impact of climate change on your positions, or is it just too removed from what you're worried about?

SD: Like I said earlier, every world event affects the price of something. Climate change has a big impact on metal prices. You can't make a solar panel without silver. The whole grid that's being redone because of climate change is very bullish for copper.

The irony is that, in the immediate term, it's also very bullish for energy prices, because you need energy to redo the world's infrastructure. Climate change will also affect the fiscal situation. It affects everything. Obviously, it's very important for the world, but it also affects my investment strategy over the intermediate and now longer term.

DR: As you look for potential investments, do you rely on your reading, discussions with others in the investment community, research by your staff, or friends you run into somewhere? How important is detailed research for you when you're making a decision that might be based on your gut or your intuition?

SD: All of the above. I would say reading. I also use a lot of charts, because sometimes the charts or graphs about how markets are trending seem to demonstrate things I honestly don't know, and it will make me work harder on a thesis if I'm long on an investment and the markets are not acting in a way that would be helpful to my investments. Or if something's acting great and the news is terrible, that will catch my eye. Research inside the firm is extremely important. But particularly in today's fast-moving world, if I have an idea and I think it's right to put a position on, then do the research and it doesn't confirm what I thought, I'm very willing to take the position off. I will move ahead of research, but I will never keep a position if the research doesn't confirm it.

DR: When you make a decision and it doesn't appear to be working, how long before you say you were wrong and you take off the position? Is that a week, a month? Do you or some people hold their position for a year or more?

SD: I've held positions for years, and I've held positions I thought I was going to hold for years for 10 days. If the world changes, the thesis behind a position I put on, I'm out. I've never used a stop/loss in 40 years. I think it's the dumbest concept ever, selling something because the price went down, but I will sell at a loss immediately if the reason I own something has changed.*

DR: Do you have a view on the desirability of cryptocurrencies as an investment?

SD: I'm the last person you should be talking to about cryptocurrencies. There's people with a lot more knowledge of the situation than me. My guess is that blockchain technology will be important for some payment system that probably hasn't even been discovered yet. It's probably more of an area for private equity, finding some 25-year-old who left Stanford or MIT.

DR: Do you have a view on SPACs [special purpose acquisition companies]?

SD: I have a view that they're just part of this orgy of money that's chasing all asset prices. SPACs in and of themselves I don't have a problem with, but what they've become with the [Federal Reserve chairman Jerome] Powell free-money regime, they're not great investments.

---

* A stop/loss order requires a broker to buy or sell a client's position in a stock as soon as the stock achieves a certain price — regardless of the reason. These orders are generally used to prevent further losses if a stock is going down or to lock in a profit if a stock is going up.

DR: Do you think a high degree of intelligence or a high work ethic is more common in great investors?

SD: I think you need an IQ probably of 120. Everything over that is somewhat unnecessary. Work ethic really matters. Passion matters, and it affects your work ethic, because people who are in this business tend to love it, and if someone loves a business and you don't, they're going to outwork you.

DR: What about a willingness to persist against the conventional wisdom? Is that important?

SD: That's huge. Also being willing to persist against your own emotions. In my business, the higher something goes, the more you want to buy it, and the lower it goes, the more you want to sell it. So you're constantly fighting your own emotion and conventional wisdom.

DR: What are your principal philanthropic interests, and how much time do you have to devote to them?

SD: I love America, and the reason I love it is the American Dream, but there's a stain or a patch on it. There are communities all across the country where there are kids that don't have a shot at that American Dream. That was my thinking behind backing Geoff Canada when he dreamed up the Harlem Children's Zone. Blue Meridian is sort of like Harlem Children's Zone 10.0, so that's a big area. Health is a big area for my wife, Fiona, and me, mainly through NYU and Sloan Kettering in the cancer arena, and then the environment. I've been a board member forever of EDF [the Environmental Defense Fund]. The one thing I would say is it's not dissimilar from my other investment philosophy, which is "Bet big." You've got to find great management, a great leader in an area you care about, and back them to the hilt.

DR: Any other outside interests, hobbies, or sports? You're a golfer or a tennis player?

SD: I'm pretty passionate about golf and not particularly good at it. I exercise six to seven days a week. I like watching the Pittsburgh Steelers. My main outside interest is my family. I'm somewhat antisocial.

DR: Do you enjoy overseeing nonprofit investment committees, like those at your alma mater Bowdoin or at Memorial Sloan Kettering? Is that enjoyable or a lot of pressure?

SD: There's some pressure. Committees can't invest the way I do. I'm wrong a lot, and when I'm wrong, I take a position off. I feel dangerous if I'm recommending something and the committee's not going to meet for another quarter. The main thing is to find a great CIO and let them pick the managements as opposed to me, but there's pressure. It's more obligation. I don't know whether I enjoy it, but I feel it's something I should do. So I do it.

JIM SIMONS

Founder, Renaissance Technologies;
mathematician and philanthropist

> *"The way I've really succeeded is by surrounding myself with
> great people."*

G reat investors have traditionally relied on their intuition in making major investment decisions, though that intuition has typically
been applied after a review of some type of information or data. The
theory had always been that no type of machine-made decision could
possibly be better than a human decision.

That is probably still true in most areas of investing. But in some
areas—publicly traded securities, commodities, and currencies—the
advent of sophisticated computers, using the best possible data, has
spawned an approach known as quantitative investing. In this type of
investing, complex computer-spawned algorithms are developed to take
advantage of market inefficiencies, even if the inefficiencies exist for
very brief periods. The result can be rapid computer-driven market sales
or purchases, with potentially very high returns.

The undisputed master of this type of investing for the past three-
plus decades has been Jim Simons, whose Renaissance Technologies
hedge fund has achieved investment returns thought to be all but impossible. For his flagship Medallion fund (now available only to employees), average annual net returns have apparently exceeded 40 percent
for more than 30 years.

As is often the case in the investment world, Jim's spectacular returns attracted many others to use their math and quantitative expertise to build similar investment firms. And while all of these firms, including Jim's, have complex algorithms that were developed by humans, the notion took hold that computers—properly programmed by humans—could make investment decisions and act on them better and more quickly than a human. This was revolutionary in the investment world, though the idea that machines can outperform humans in certain areas of investing is now largely the accepted wisdom.

Jim came to the investment world relatively late in a career that had earlier been focused on his real passion—mathematics. In that area, he was a world-class mathematician, leading the math department at the State University of New York at Stony Brook (from the age of 30) and developing award-winning math theorems. But he left his math career behind him—a rare occurrence in the math world—to develop a way in which his expertise could be applied to the trading world. The result changed the investment world forever.

Jim's firm helped launch an industry where math and science skills are the coin of the realm in developing trading programs. Many others have followed him into the varied world of quant investing, but no one has exceeded his multiyear track record, and it seems no one is likely to do so anytime soon.

Jim's success has enhanced his philanthropic efforts, many of which are focused—not surprisingly—on advancing research in math and science.

I have known Jim for many years, initially introduced by friends who had invested with him. I foolishly did not do so. In recent years, I have served with him on the board of trustees of the Institute for Advanced Study, where he—not surprisingly—used his investment genius to produce outstanding results for the Institute's endowment fund. We were also original signers of the Giving Pledge, and I have spent time with him at the early meetings.

No doubt math brilliance has been a key to Jim's success. But I have thought it might also be his refusal to ever wear socks—even for a black-tie dinner. (I interviewed Jim when this clothing pattern became apparent—it was at an Institute dinner where he was receiving the Albert Einstein Prize. You know someone is brilliant when he is a recipient of a prize named after the Institute's most famous professor and the symbol of genius-hood.)

This interview occurred in Jim's foundation office in New York City; he of course had no socks. I was tempted to follow suit, but was not sure that my investment acumen would really increase as a result, and thus was conventionally dressed around the ankles. But who knows? Maybe no socks is part of the genius pattern. Einstein also did not wear socks — apparently he thought they were an unnecessary adornment. He may have been right.

I interviewed Jim in person on June 18, 2021.

DAVID M. RUBENSTEIN (DR): Many great investors had an interest when they were young in some aspect of investing or business. You were focused principally on math, but not as it related to investing?

JIM SIMONS (JS): Totally correct.

DR: Sometimes those who are gifted at math had a good deal of parental pushing or coaching in that direction. That was not true with you. But you recognized relatively early that you were good at math?

JS: I always liked math, from being a little boy on.

DR: Did you find the math at MIT, where you got your undergraduate degree, and at Berkeley, where you got your PhD, very challenging? How long did it take you to earn each of those degrees?

JS: I moved fast through MIT. I graduated in three years, stayed a year as a graduate student, and then they sent me out to Berkeley to work with a guy named Shiing-Shen Chern. He was on sabbatical, but I worked with someone else. The second year I was there, Chern appeared. He was a great geometer of his day — differential geometry. We became friends in my second year. In six years out of high school I got a PhD.

DR: Your area of expertise in the math world is probably not something I can really understand, but what is the essence of your specialty?

JS: The field I was in is called differential geometry. I worked in an area called minimal surfaces of higher-dimensional things.

I studied that area, and after five years produced a paper that solves a lot of problems in the area. That paper still gets citations after almost 60 years. It's had 1,750 academic citations, which is a lot of citations. That was a terrific paper, and that was why I won a prize a few years later called the Veblen Prize [the Oswald Veblen Prize in Geometry]. But I'd also done some work with Chern that is now extremely famous.

DR: You pursued a career in math and in teaching math, with a side tour to help the US government with some code-breaking. Was that career exciting and fulfilling, especially when you were building a great math department at SUNY Stony Brook? What led you to switch careers and go into the investing world?

JS: My first investment was when I was very young, and it ultimately worked out very well. When I was at MIT, I had two very good friends from Colombia, and they were smart guys. They were good friends, and I always thought they should start a company together. After I graduated from MIT, one of the two and I took a motor-scooter trip. We were going to go from Boston to Buenos Aires, but we only got as far as Bogotá. That was quite a trip.

After I got my PhD at Berkeley, I came back to teach at MIT. That winter, I went down to Colombia and told these two, "I'm not leaving until you guys found a company together." I knew that they were very smart, that they could be good businessmen, and they could start a good company. So we found one while I was there, and I invested some money in it. I managed to invest 10 percent. One of their fathers-in-law put up 50 percent. They were richer than I was and they covered the rest, but I had 10 percent. I had borrowed money from relatives, and I wanted to pay them back.

I was at MIT and then at Harvard for three years, teaching and working on this business that I started in Colombia. There was a job that I was aware of in Princeton at the Institute for Defense Analyses, which did code-cracking. I didn't know what they did, but they hired mathematicians, and it paid a lot. I applied for that job and I took it, primarily because it paid a lot so I could begin paying back the debts I had incurred with the company in Colombia, which got off to not as fast a start as I had hoped.

The work at the institute was code-cracking, People know that now, but I couldn't even tell my wife what I did. "How was your day?" "Fine." That was as much as I could tell. But you could use up to half your time doing your own work, in my case working on this geometry problem. The other half had to be on their work, which was code-cracking, and I acquitted myself well.

I finished the paper I mentioned while I was there, and I solved a long-standing problem in the code-cracking field. The National Security Agency, which was the parent of the Institute for Defense Analyses, made a special purpose computer to implement this algorithm I had come up with. As far as I know, as of about 10 years ago, that equipment was still running. So a better algorithm has not been created. Do you remember the name Maxwell Taylor?

DR: Famous general.

JS: General Maxwell Taylor, who headed my organization, wrote a cover story in the *New York Times Magazine* about how well we were doing in Vietnam, that we had to stay the course and so on and so forth. I had a different opinion. I thought the whole thing was totally stupid. I wrote a letter to the editor—which was immediately published because of where I was—saying, "Not everyone who works with General Taylor agrees with his views," and then I gave my views—that this was the dumbest thing we could ever have done and we should get out of there as soon as possible.

No one said a word, but a few months later a guy came along and said, "I'm a stringer for *Newsweek* magazine, and I'm doing interviews of people who work for the Defense Department who are against the war, and I'm really having trouble finding anyone. Could I interview you?" I was 29 years old. No one had interviewed me before. So I said "sure."

He said, "What do you do?" I said, "We're supposed to spend at least half the time on their stuff, and up to half our time on our own stuff. So for the time being, I'm spending all my time on my stuff, and when the war is over, I'll spend all my time on their stuff to make up for it."

Then I did the only intelligent thing I did that day. I told my local boss that I gave this interview. He said, "I've got to call Taylor." He went into his office, called Taylor. Five minutes later, he came out and said, "You're fired." I said, "You can't fire me, because my title is 'permanent member.'" He said, "You know the difference between a permanent member and a temporary member? A temporary member has a contract, but a permanent member does not have a contract."

So I was fired, but I wasn't worried at all. I had a family, three kids, and a wife, but I knew that because of the paper that I just mentioned, I would easily get an academic job, and I was offered several. Stony Brook came along and offered me the job of chairman of the math department. They were having a hard time finding a chairman of the department, which was a weak department. The physics department was very strong at that time, and I thought that would be real fun. So I took the job. The provost who interviewed me said, "You're the first person I interviewed for this job who actually wants it." But I said, "I really want it because most mathematicians don't want to be chair. It's a pain in the ass, but I thought it would be fun."

I was 30 years old. I came to Stony Brook. They had a lot of money because Nelson D. Rockefeller was the governor at that time and he loved the state university. We built them a very good math department. I recruited a lot of great people, and I realized I loved recruiting.

While I was there, in the early years, I worked on the stuff which is now called the Chern-Simons theory. I came up with what I thought was a beautiful result in three dimensions, and I showed it to Chern. He said, "We could do this in all dimensions." I said, "Let's work together and do that," and we did. We worked together and we did it, and it came out as a paper.

It was a very good piece of mathematics, but five or six years later the physicists started taking it up, for one reason or another. Now it applies to almost every branch of physics, which was totally amazing to me, because I don't know any physics. It's used in string theory, condensed-matter physics. It's used in making quantum computers. Now there's something called Chern-Simons gravity. It's worked with astrophysics. That's the most amazing thing that ever happened to me.

DR: You're at the top of the profession. You've got a famous paper. Why did you not just stay in that world?

JS: The Colombian business finally paid off, and I had some money. The father-in-law of one of the founders was so pleased about the whole outcome that he made a Bermuda trust with my family as the beneficiary, because I had sort of generated the idea, and he created this trust with $100,000 in it.* That was very nice.

Very shortly after that, my Colombian friends came to me and said, "We have all this money. We want you to help invest it." "What do I know about investing?" "Well, figure it out."

I knew a mathematician who had taken up commodity trading. He was doing pretty well, and I went to visit him and said, "We have some money. We'd like to invest with you." The trust put in $100,000. The other guys put in quite a lot of money.

There was no fixed fee, but he had 10 percent of the profits or something like that. I said, "But if we lose too much money, you have to stop." He says, "What's too much?" I said, "If you're down 30 percent, you have to stop." Just as I was walking out the door, I said, "Oh, and if we make too much money, you have to stop." "What do you mean?" "Well, if you make us 10 times our money after fees, you have to stop." So we could sort of think a little bit. He couldn't object to that. Within nine months, he had multiplied the capital by a factor of 10.

He stayed in the business. He made some money, he lost some money, but never anything like that. So now instead of $100,000, there was a million dollars in the trust, and it got me interested in trading.

DR: You were still teaching at Stony Brook?

JS: I was still at Stony Brook, and I started to fiddle around with trading currencies. I slowed down doing math and got into this trading business. It wasn't based on mathematics at all. It was just based on hard thinking, but it worked okay.

DR: Did you say you might go full-time in investing then?

---

* A Bermuda trust is a legal structure that separates the legal ownership of an asset from the beneficiary of the trust; this is typically done to ensure the beneficiary of the trust receives the intended benefits regardless of the legal status (e.g., death or divorce) of the trust's legal owner.

JS: I spent a year at the University of Geneva, but I was already trading currencies at a low level. When I came back, I left the department. I was part-time for a year, then I just got into the business.

DR: You decided to start an investment company called Renaissance at some point?

JS: It was first called Limroy. It was a Bermuda company, but Americans or anyone could invest in it. I was running this company, and I had a small team. We did trading, but we also did some investment in venture capital. The trading went very well. Some of the venture capital went well, some of it didn't go so well, but at a certain point, the board felt that "this venture capital stuff, we don't want to see that, we just want to see the trading." I closed down Limroy and we started something called the Medallion Fund. In the previous few years, we had been working on statistical studies and so on. We got into math and started a fund we call Medallion.

DR: When you started that, you had left Stony Brook?

JS: I was already gone. I left the university several years earlier. I was still living at Stony Brook. So we started the Medallion Fund, based on some things that we had learned over the previous couple of years. It was run by a fellow named Jim Ax. He wanted to move the operation to California, and I said, "Okay," because I was still involved in some other things.

He was running that fund, and it went okay for about six months, and then it started losing money and losing money. I said, "I have to understand the system you're using." He says, "It's very complicated." "Just boil it down to three dimensions, let's say."

What I realized is that what he was really doing, aside from all the bells and whistles, was trend-following. Years ago, trend-following in commodities would have been great, but people had caught on that there are trends in commodities and currencies, too. So everyone was jumping into that, and it just didn't do well. I insisted he stop. He didn't want to. I was the boss. A guy named Henry Laufer, who was terrific and had discovered a short-term system that Ax wasn't using, came back to work for me. We worked together and came up with a good system, a fast trading system.

DR: Commodities still?

JS: All commodities, currencies, no stocks at all. With Medallion, I told all the investors, "We're going to stop. We're going to do a study period. You can even get your money back if you want." Almost everyone stayed. It took six months. We developed Henry Laufer's system—I call it Henry Laufer's but I was part of the development—and we put it in place and never looked back.

DR: I'm not a math person, but I understand what you did. Your idea was to look at how, let's say, stocks or other things go, and look at anomalies in the market. If there's an anomaly, you can move in and take advantage of that trade before the anomaly is no longer an anomaly. In other words, you see an inefficiency. You go trade against the inefficiency, and then when it becomes efficient, you get out?

JS: Yes. Sometimes those anomalies last for a very long time. Sometimes they never go away. They're all small, but you pile up a bunch of anomalies together and it's wonderful.

DR: Being a math wizard helped you figure this out?

JS: Totally.

DR: Somebody who didn't know math wouldn't be able to have done this?

JS: I think that's right.

DR: When you started doing this, did you get deeply involved every day in looking for the anomalies? Or the math models showed you what the anomalies were and you didn't have to exercise discretion? Are anomalies apparent from looking at the computer models, or you say, "I'm not sure I like what the models are showing me"?

JS: We had all this data. We finally had ticker data, and we would just search, or someone would come up with an idea: "If this happens and that happens, I'll tell you, test it out, see if it works." The chain grew and grew and grew, with the help of very good scientists we hired who were always looking for anomalies.

DR: You hired mathematicians and scientific people?

JS: Scientific people who weren't necessarily mathematicians. They'd be physicists. We had a couple of astronomers hired. But in this first period, it was still futures we focused on. We hadn't gotten to stocks, which was clearly a bigger market but we didn't know how to do it. We had an idea of how to do it, and while we were working on it, two guys came to work for me, Bob Mercer and Peter Brown.

I had their name from Nick Patterson, whom I had hired a few years earlier. He had been at the Institute for Defense Analyses. He was terrific and helped us a lot. He said, "This guy Bob Mercer, you ought to work with him. He's very good." I interviewed Bob and offered him the job. He said, "I always work with Peter Brown, who's younger. You have to hire him, too." I said, "Okay, fine."

One of them I put into the futures area and the other I put into our new public stock area. A few months went by and they said, "We really like to work together. We want to do one thing or the other." I said, "Okay, make the equity system work." We were trading at a very low level, but it was not working very well. They worked for maybe two years on this. I finally said, "Look, I'm going to give you another six months, but if you can't make it work after that, you have to let it go." Within two or three months, it started to work. They had discovered this, that, and the other thing that started to work. Equities is a major part of Medallion.

DR: Were they mathematicians as well?

JS: Computer scientists.

DR: You began to become a big investor in the stock market. Did you get out of the currency world, or you were doing both?

JS: Still doing both.

DR: When it became apparent that you were achieving annualized numbers that were better than anybody else's, did you realize that you were becoming one of the great investors in the world, or you didn't really see it that way?

JS: I wasn't thinking, "Am I a great investor?" I was thinking, "I'm making a lot of money." Medallion had outside investors, of course, but it was growing and growing because everyone left his money in. It was compounding at a great rate, but there was a limit to how big the fund could be, because it is cash trading. If you have a huge fund, and you want to do a fast trade, you're going to move the market too much. So the fund couldn't be all that big.

We realized that, but the employees were all invested. We decided we just had to throw out the outsiders. That took, I think, two or three years, but by 2005, the fund was 100 percent employee-owned.

DR: Later you began to take outside investors for other funds?

JS: Yes, we did. Medallion was still only employees.

DR: Medallion has been reported to have spectacular returns, 40-plus percent returns or something like that, for many years.

JS: Higher than that. Higher than 40 percent.

DR: It had very high returns. You became wealthy. Now you're putting a lot of your energies into philanthropy. You were an original signer of the Giving Pledge?

JS: I was, although I did it very early on. I thought I would just do it to show the flag. It never occurred to me that I was joining something. When we started having the Giving Pledge meetings, I didn't want to join a club. My son and my daughter have signed. Marilyn, my wife, likes to go to those meetings, because it's social. I'm not social. I get pleasure out of the philanthropy.

DR: You're focused on math and science and things like that?

JS: The foundation was formed in '94. We were already giving a fair amount of money away, and Marilyn thought maybe we should start a foundation. I liked the idea because I could put money in and get a tax break, but it didn't have to come out of the foundation. She worked out of her dressing room for a year, writing checks and so on. Then she got a little office, hired two people, and I kept throwing money into the foundation as I was making a fortune. It worked out.

In 2010, I decided to stop being at Renaissance and put my full time into the foundation. By that time, we had focused more or less 100 percent on supporting math and science. Then I was chair of the board of Renaissance, but I wasn't involved at all in their work. It continued well, and I gave all my time to the foundation.

DR: If you were to give somebody advice about how to be a great investor, what would you say? Specialize in something or know what you're doing or pray for luck? What would you say it takes to be a great investor?

JS: You do need a little luck. I have frequently given talks, and occasionally I use the following title: "Mathematics, Common Sense, and Good Luck."

DR: Those are the key things?

JS: The way I've really succeeded is by surrounding myself with great people. I like recruiting. I still like recruiting. With the Medallion Fund, I surrounded myself with the smartest people I could find.

DR: You're not afraid of hiring somebody that thinks they're smarter than you?

JS: If someone's smarter than me, all the better. I'm sure we have some people who at least think they're smarter than me, and they probably are. My secret to success was finding good people.

DR: It's a very impressive story. Did your parents live to see your enormous success?

JS: They did. My father died of Alzheimer's, but he knew I was doing very well. I was supporting them. My mother lived longer, but they lived long enough to see their son flourish.

JOHN PAULSON

Founder, Paulson & Co.

> *"The most important thing is to concentrate on a particular area that you know better than other people. That's what gives you an advantage."*

The Great Recession of 2007–09 was caused by a number of factors, but none more significant than the implosion of the housing market, large parts of which had been financed by subprime mortgages. Those mortgages were ones in which the borrower did not have to meet normal credit standards for a mortgage and typically did not have to make any down payment. But prior to the implosion, the investment community loved buying these mortgages (often in bundled, securitized form), for they paid higher interest rates than the typical home mortgage.

Before the subprime mortgage crash, which occurred when many of the borrowers could not sustain the higher interest charges (amid a severe decline in home prices), many investors who focused on high-yielding investments feasted on subprime mortgages. When the economy slowed, there were certainly some in the investment community who warned about a possible crash. Perhaps there were more than a few who also shorted the subprime mortgage market, anticipating a decline if not a crash.

But there was one individual, a theretofore relatively low-profile hedge fund manager in New York named John Paulson, who not only anticipated the decline (if not crash) but also followed his instinct with a massive bet—the largest in his career, which had been one of specializing in risk arbitrage (betting on the successful completion of announced mergers of publicly traded companies). Paulson bet correctly, so much so that his trades betting on the mortgage market decline apparently reaped $20 billion in profits—without doubt the most successful and profitable single bet in Wall Street history by any one investor.

That ended John's low-profile status. He instantly became one of the world's most famous hedge fund investors, and his thoughts on the investment world became eagerly sought—as was his philanthropic support for many projects in his spheres of interest.

Despite the fame and enhanced wealth (and the publicity from some enormous gifts to the Central Park Conservancy and Harvard University), John remained his low-key self—the product of a public school education in New York City, a valedictorian at New York University's undergraduate business school, and a Baker Scholar at Harvard Business School.

I came to know and respect John from various business and social connections in New York, but spent the most time with him when he joined the board of the Council on Foreign Relations, where his thoughts on the investment environment and the economy were given extraordinary weight. Perhaps everyone was waiting to hear about the next subprime mortgage-like opportunity—I know I was. But on those kind of matters, John wisely kept his counsel, and reserved that type of information for his day job. I interviewed him in person on August 12, 2021.

DAVID M. RUBENSTEIN (DR): You made one of the most famous investments in Wall Street history. Over a period of time, around 2006 or so, you put a short on the mortgage market. That trade, it is reported, made roughly $20 billion for you and your investors. Nobody has reported anything more profitable than that on essentially one trade in the last couple of decades. Did you have any doubt that this trade was going to work?

JOHN PAULSON (JP): We were pretty convinced that segments of the mortgage market were overvalued and were likely to implode. We took a concentrated position in these securities, and what we expected to happen happened.

DR: I assume you wanted secrecy. You didn't want everybody to know what you were doing. How did you keep it secret, and where did you get the instruments that enabled you to do this kind of short?

JP: We were running a merger arbitrage firm and had gotten to about $6 billion under management, which was large. But in 1986–87 we made it to the 50–75th place range, in terms of ranking of hedge funds, and we were looking for ways to leap to the top of the industry, but it was very competitive.

We were looking for some type of asymmetrical investment that could get us there. I had developed a specialty back in the late '80s, at the time of Drexel imploding, of shorting, or betting on the decline in value of, investment-grade corporate bonds. That is an investment that is structured to have relatively little downside but substantial upside. However, the probability of an investment grade bond defaulting is very rare.

But we found an area where it does happen, primarily with financial companies, as these companies are highly leveraged and a small decline in their assets could wipe out the equity. And if they do fail, many times the unsecured bonds issued by these companies will go to zero. We had shorted bonds of financial companies at the time of Drexel and had some success there. Later, we shorted the bonds of some insurance companies, like Conseco, that ultimately failed. I was always looking for mispriced credit securities.

We finally found that in subprime mortgage-backed securities. They have a unique structure where the mortgages were bundled into a security and the security was divided into about 18 tranches ranging from "B" to "AAA." We focused on the "BBB" tranche, which was structured in a way where a loss of 7 percent in the pool would wipe out the BBB tranche.

We thought that the housing market was overvalued, that mortgage securities were in a bubble, and that it was likely that the losses in these pools would exceed 7 percent and probably be as high as 20 percent. We did a lot of research in the area. We were tracking the mortgage market very closely, tracking the performance of the underlying securities, and they kept deteriorating.

Then we started shorting them en masse. But we couldn't hide the trade, because in total we shorted in excess of $25 billion of these securities. We were active with every major bank on Wall Street. They had limits on how much they could do. No bank went above $5 billion of exposure. We were interacting with the trading desks of all the banks, and thus it became hard, if not impossible, to keep what we were doing a secret.

DR: It was reported at the time that Goldman Sachs in particular had been an advisor to you. Is that true?

JP: They were not an advisor. They were a counterparty. They were actively trading, and in order to sell securities, they had to buy them from someone. We would short them to Goldman and they'd resell them to someone else, like all the other trading desks.

DR: If you made $20 billion, how much did you have at risk? Was there a chance that whatever you put up could have gone to zero?

JP: Yes. We were managing, at the time, around $6 billion. We told our investors, "We'd like to take a hedge and we'd like to pay 2 percent in premiums to buy protection on these mortgage-backed securities." For 2 percent of cost per year, we could short bonds with a notional value of 200 percent of our assets under management. Then we said, "If these securities defaulted, we could make 100 percent if the bonds fell to 50 and 200 percent if they fell to 0." Our funds at the time were making 10–12 percent a year. I said, "On the downside scenario, in our main funds, if the securities don't default and we lose 2 percent, we'd still make 8–10 percent."*

---

* Stated differently, if a bond has a face value of $1,000, and a 1 percent fee (or $10) is paid for a hedge that will ensure the bond can be purchased in the future at $1,000, the cost of the hedge if the bond does not decline in value is $10. Since the hedge fund is earning 10 percent a year, the cost of the hedge would decrease the return of the fund's overall performance by the cost of the hedge, meaning the fund would yield 9 percent, still an acceptable return. If the bond defaults and is worthless, the party who provided the hedge—to get the 1 percent fee—is obligated to pay the hedge fund the entire value of the bond, or $1,000. That can produce staggering profits relative to the cost of the investment in the hedge.

All the investors said, "If you believe in that, go ahead. We're not putting our capital at risk. It seems like a good risk return tradeoff."

But the way these securities work was asymmetric. You essentially risk 1 percent to make 100 percent.

DR: It can't be that easy, because nobody else quite did what you did. Did you have any sleepless nights, saying, "I might be wrong and maybe I'll lose a lot of money," or you didn't worry about that so much?

JP: Again, the downside was very limited. I think the reason other people hadn't done it is because there had never been a default of investment-grade mortgage-backed securities. They were viewed as the safest securities next to Treasuries. That was essentially true, up until that point. What others missed was that the underwriting quality of securities had never been as poor as it had been in that period. The fact that they hadn't defaulted in the past had nothing to do with whether or not the securities being issued would default in the future.

DR: The idea for doing this came to you one day when just reading the newspapers or watching Bloomberg on TV? Where did the idea come from?

JP: We developed a specialty that very few people had in shorting credit (or debt) securities. The difficulty in shorting credit securities is you have to actually borrow the securities and you have a negative carry. Credit securities are typically held for the long term, trade infrequently, and are hard to borrow. Plus, if the securities do not default, the cost of the negative carry can be quite high. Thus, profiting from the short credit strategy is quite challenging and is not an easy task. For these reasons, very few people short credit.

But, because of the asymmetry of this short, I never gave up on looking for large amounts of credit securities that could be borrowed, that could be shorted, and that could default. Finally, in 2006, we found the mother of all credit shorts in the mortgage-backed securities market, a market that at the time was larger than the Treasury market. But because of the credit default swaps [a form of insurance against the default of a security], you didn't have to borrow these securities to short them. You could just buy a credit default swap on the securities and benefit just like a short if the securities declined.

We were shorting $100 million of mortgage-backed securities at a clip, $500 million a day, and in some cases a billion dollars a day. There was massive liquidity to set up these short positions.

DR: It was reported in the press that, after the investment's success, you had to write a check at one point to the IRS for over $1 billion. Does it feel nice to write a check over a billion dollars to the IRS, or is it a little bit painful?

JP: We were big supporters of not only the US Treasury but also New York State and New York City, and we paid a fair amount of taxes.

DR: Do you have in your office a check that says a billion-plus to the US government? You don't keep that check?

JP: I didn't keep the check, but I did keep both the state tax returns and the federal returns.

DR: People must be coming to you all the time and saying, "I have a great idea." Has anybody ever come up with an idea as good as that one? That was more than 10 years ago.

JP: It's very hard. I haven't found anything that is as asymmetrical as this particular trade—asymmetrical meaning that you could lose a little bit on the downside but make 100 times on the upside, so you can potentially make a lot of money without risking a lot of money. Most trades are symmetrical. You could make a lot, but you also risk a lot, and if you're wrong, it hurts.

DR: You've always said, if you have something good, you'd let me know. You haven't had anything as good as that yet?

JP: I would say not as good. The area that's most mispriced today is credit. The 10-year Treasury bond is about 1.3 percent, and the 30-year Treasury bond is about 2 percent. We're coming into an inflationary period. You have current inflation well in excess of long-term yields. There's a perception in the market that this inflation is transitory. I think the market bought the Federal Reserve line that it's just transitory due to the restart of the economy and that it's eventually going to subside. However, if it doesn't subside, or it subsides at a level that's above the 2 percent that the Fed is targeting, or it stays in the 3–5 percent range, then I think ultimately interest rates will catch up and bonds will fall. In that scenario, there are various option strategies related to bonds and interest rates that could offer very high returns if interest rates do move up to those higher levels.

DR: When you've had a life-changing event or an unbelievable success, as you did with that trade, is there a temptation to say, "I don't want to tempt fate and try it again," or you want to prove that you can do it again and you're looking for another deal just as good as that one?

JP: We do look. But you have to be realistic. We have put on some trades at a smaller scale that have potential returns of 25x to one, related to both interest rates and gold prices. Our viewpoint is that the market currently is not expecting much inflation, but that if inflation does prove to be higher than the market currently expects, that will result in both higher gold prices and higher interest rates. If you get those two happening at the same time, which admittedly is challenging, we have set up positions that could result in 25x to one.

DR: After you made your famous trade, you put on a trade where you bought a lot of gold or gold futures. You were what some called a gold bug. You were a big believer in gold. Gold is now about $1,700 an ounce or so. Do you believe that gold is now a good investment at this price?

JP: Yes, we do. We believe that gold does very well in times of inflation. We saw what happened the last time gold went parabolic [i.e., prices rose sharply in a short period]. It was in the '70s when we had two years of double-digit inflation. The reason why gold goes parabolic is that basically there's a limited amount of investable gold—I think it's on the order of several trillion dollars' worth—while the total amount of financial assets is closer to $200 trillion.

If you own long-term Treasury bonds that are yielding 2 percent and interest rates move up to 5 percent, those bonds fall materially in value. Likewise, if you have cash sitting in a bank that you're earning 0 percent on and inflation's 4 percent, you're gradually eroding the value of your money. As inflation picks up, people try and get out of fixed income. They try and get out of cash. The logical place to go is gold, especially if it starts to rise in inflationary times. But because the amount of money to move out of cash and fixed income dwarfs the amount of investable gold, the supply-and-demand imbalance causes the value of gold to rise. And the rise feeds on itself.

DR: When you did your famous trade, you became world-famous. How did that change your life? All of a sudden, people are calling you all the time? High school friends are saying they always knew you were going to be successful and they're calling you for contributions? How did your life change?

JP: I remember one of our investors called me in February '07. He said, "John, I just got the monthly results. I think there was a mistake. It said 66 percent. You meant 6.6 percent." And I said, "No, it was 66 percent." He goes, "That's impossible. I've invested with Soros, with Paul Tudor Jones, with everyone. No one's been up 66 percent in a year. How can you be up 66 percent in a month?"

Shortly after that, all our investors got these results and it leaked out to the press and then became the cover story in the *Wall Street Journal,* which was picked up globally. That performance continued throughout the year. The credit funds wound up close to 800 percent net for the year. This performance became kind of a global phenomenon. We became very well known. And it did change my life, in a positive sense. We became one of the top five hedge funds with assets under management at that time. It opened up a lot of doors.

DR: You had this big hedge fund, then you decided to do what many people have done who've been successful on Wall Street. They put their money into a family office. Why did you do that?

JP: People go one of two ways. Certain people like the business and develop an infrastructure to raise more money, expand the partnership, and create something that could survive beyond themselves. That creates separate value.

Personally, I never really liked the business side of the business. I was never fond of raising money or going to meet investors. I found that stressful. I did like the investing side. That's what I found interesting. That's what I got excited about. Once we achieved a certain success, we started to deemphasize the fundraising aspects. And as investors naturally moved on, we didn't replace them or seek to raise more capital.

Over time, my capital in the fund became a larger and larger portion of the assets under management. Eventually we got to the point where the amount of people I had who were managing the business was probably 75–80 percent of the people in the firm, versus the 20–25 percent of people involved with actual investing.

I was handling compliance, money-raising, investor reporting, legal, HR. Ultimately I decided that I was spending too much time on managing the business—over half my time, which really wasn't producing incremental returns over the cost, and I decided to just focus on investing. In June 2020, we returned the outside capital to the investors and became a family office.

DR: Let's talk about for a moment where you think the economy's going. You've mentioned inflation. When I worked in the White House under President Carter, I was responsible, I like to say, for the double-digit inflation. Obviously, others were involved as well. Are you worried about inflation? Is that your principal concern right now in terms of the economy?

JP: I wouldn't say I'm worried about it, because we have zero fixed income. We do believe we will get more inflation than the market is currently expecting, so we've positioned our portfolio to benefit if we do get more inflation. If inflation does become embedded at higher levels than anticipated, that will benefit a good portion of our portfolio.

DR: Do you think the Fed has kept interest rates artificially low for too long?

JP: Have they kept it artificially low? Yes. Have they kept it artificially low too long? I don't think so. We went through probably the worst financial crisis imaginable with COVID, in which the entire economy shut down. If it wasn't for the aggressive policies of the Fed and the Treasury, we could have dived into a deep recession. By providing all the monetary and fiscal stimulus that they did, they minimized the downturn, which resulted in a rapid recovery, allowing the economy to have a minimal GDP contraction and a sharp GDP upward correction.

DR: Are you worried about the size of the debt and the deficit in the United States?

JP: Absolutely. We did borrow a lot of money in order to stabilize the economy. But at some point that money either has to be paid back or monetized via higher rates of inflation. Paying back is very confiscatory and would likely result in a long period of slow growth.

The easier alternative is to monetize the debt via inflation. The way that works with inflation, GDP grows more rapidly on a nominal basis. And since debt's expressed in nominal terms, the debt-to-GDP ratio can come down with inflation. I think we will have a choice, and inflation will be the more desirable outcome.

DR: People are always looking for bubbles to burst. You actually picked up one of the most prominent bubbles that burst—the mortgage-backed security bubble. What about the SPAC market? You think that's a bubble waiting to burst?

JP: I don't think it's quite a bubble, but it shows evidence of a frothy market. There's just too much liquidity. I would say the SPAC market is overvalued—for people who invest in SPACs, on average, it will be a losing proposition.

DR: Are you a believer in cryptocurrencies?

JP: I'm not a believer in cryptocurrencies. I would say that cryptocurrencies are a bubble. I would describe cryptocurrencies as a limited supply of nothing. There's no intrinsic value to any of the cryptocurrencies except that there's a limited amount.

DR: Based on what you've just said, why would you not put a big short of some type on cryptocurrencies? Or maybe you have, but you think that's a good short?

JP: The reason why we shorted the subprime market in size is because it was asymmetrical. Shorting a bond at par that has a limited duration that trades at a 1 percent spread over Treasuries, you can't lose more than the spread times the duration, but if it defaults, you could make the par amount. In crypto, there's unlimited downside. Even though I could be right over the long term, in the short term—as with Bitcoin, which went from $5,000 to $45,000—I'd be wiped out on a short side. It's just too volatile to short.

DR: Let's talk about how you got into this business. You were born in New York, and your parents came from two different countries.

JP: My father was from Ecuador. My mother was from New York City, but her grandparents were from Eastern Europe, from Russia and Ukraine. My parents met at UCLA. My father studied business. My mom was a psychologist. Then they came back to New York. And I was born in New York.

DR: You went to high school here in New York?

JP: Yes. We were a solid upper-middle-class family, but we couldn't afford private school, so I went to New York City public schools K–12. At the time, the schools were fairly high quality. I had a great public school education. After high school, I went to NYU, and after NYU, to Harvard Business School.

DR: At NYU, you were in the School of Business. And you were valedictorian?

JP: Yes.

DR: Your parents must have been impressed you were valedictorian. You went where after college? What did you do?

JP: I loved school. I was excited about it. I started some businesses while I was in college, so I was enthusiastic about studying business. But what happened is that the longtime chairman of Goldman Sachs, Gustave Levy, was a graduate of NYU. He taught a course called the Distinguished Adjunct Professor Seminar in Investment Banking, and I was invited to take that course. Only 12 students took it. And he brought in the heads of all four principal areas at Goldman Sachs. One of them, risk arbitrage, was run by Bob Rubin. Risk arbitrage historically was the most profitable area of Goldman Sachs. I decided I wanted to go into risk arbitrage. They said, "If you want to do that, first you have to go to Harvard Business School. Then you have to work in M&A. And then, if you're really good, you could work in risk arbitrage."

I followed that path. I went to Harvard, then worked in M&A at Bear Stearns. And after becoming a partner in M&A at Bear Stearns,

I went to work in risk arbitrage for one of the largest boutiques at the time, which was called Gruss Partners. After four years there, 12 years after graduating business school, I started Paulson & Co. in 1994.

DR: You graduated from Harvard Business School as a Baker Scholar, which means you were in the top 5 percent of your class. Did you consider going to Goldman Sachs and working for Bob Rubin?

JP: I did but I got slightly sidetracked. I graduated in 1980, when the prime rate hit 20 percent and Volcker [Paul Volcker, then chairman of the Federal Reserve] was trying to kill inflation, so the stock market was depressed. We were in a little bit of a recession. There wasn't a lot of recruiting by investment banking. At the same time, consulting firms were sprouting like mushrooms, and they were the most attractive place to work. They paid double the starting salaries the investment banks were paying at the time. I was seduced into consulting. My first job after graduating from Harvard was working for the Boston Consulting Group. After two years, I realized that wasn't really what I wanted to do. I did want to work on Wall Street. But when I looked at Wall Street, there were always two sides. One was called the agency side, where you work in investment banking, represent clients, and earn fees. The other was the principal side, where you earn money by investing your capital. The really wealthy people worked on the principal side. My dream was to work there.

DR: For people who don't know, what is risk arbitrage?

JP: It's investing in mergers. Let's say a stock's trading for $30 and someone's offering to buy it for $50, and after the merger's announced, the stock goes to $48. There's a $2 spread. It doesn't seem like a lot of money. But $2 on $50 is 4 percent. If the deal closes in four months, if you do that three times a year, three times four would be a 12 percent rate of return. If you can have a portfolio of these deals and they all earn about the same thing, you can make a steady return.

DR: But your focus was typically on announced deals.

JP: Yes. Risk arbitrage is announced deals. You can try and anticipate. You're in a sector that's consolidating. You see which companies are being bought. You may feel strongly that this company seems like it's ripe for a takeover. You can buy it prior to the takeover, and you could be right. But that becomes more of an event-arbitrage situation than a risk-arbitrage one.

DR: You started your company in 1994. Did people rush to give you money? How much money did you start with?

JP: No, it was a very difficult time. Raising capital was a challenge. I started the firm with the limited savings that I had and painstakingly, over time, raised money. As my track record became longer and I showed an ability to minimize downside and maximize upside, we raised more and more money.

DR: What are the qualities to be a good investor? Is it hard work? Luck? Good contacts?

JP: Before you start investing, you need a lot of experience. The type of experience depends on the type of investing. For someone in risk arbitrage or private equity, probably the best place to start is mergers and acquisitions, where you become familiar with valuations and merger agreements and takeover laws. You could apply that later on to purchasing companies on your own behalf or trading in the securities of companies undergoing mergers.

DR: What are you looking for when you hire? High IQ? Hard work ethic? Good schooling?

JP: All of the above. Schools are a funnel to select the best people, so we go to the best schools and look for the brightest people. You also need people who have an agreeable personality that won't be disruptive to the organization.

DR: You know some of the world's best investors. Are there certain qualities they have that you admire? Is it hard work? Research? Diligence? High IQ?

JP: It's all of the above. It's organization, ethical conduct, discipline, and focus.

DR: Are you looking to keep investing? You're not interested in going into government, I assume.

JP: I intend to keep investing, and I am not interested in a role in government. I've tried to make my life simpler so I can work less and enjoy other aspects of life. Returning outside capital was a big move in that direction. Now I don't have to write investor reports or travel to meet with investors or worry about balancing funds or other people's tax issues. I still concentrate on investing, which I like but requires less time than I previously committed.

DR: Do people come up to you all the time and say, "You have any good ideas for me?"

JP: Sometimes. But the worst thing is to give someone an idea casually and then it turns out the wrong way. You feel terrible. I prefer not to give investment advice.

DR: What's the best investment advice you've ever received?

JP: The best thing is to invest in areas that you know well. Anyone can be lucky in a particular investment, but that's not a long-term strategy. If you invest in areas that you don't know, ultimately you're not going to do well. The most important thing is to concentrate on a particular area that you know better than other people. That's what gives you an advantage to succeed in investing.

DR: What is the most common mistake investors make?

JP: They look for get-rich-quick schemes and they buy based on stories. They chase investments that are going up, and ultimately those investments deflate. Then they lose money.

DR: If somebody came to you and said, "I just got $100,000 my father gave me. I got it for my bar mitzvah, or a wedding gift. What should I do with $100,000?" What would you tell them?

JP: I always say the best investment for an average individual is to buy their own home. If you took that $100,000, put 10 percent down, get a $900,000 mortgage, you can buy a home for a million dollars. It was just reported that home prices were up 20 percent in the last month over the prior year. If you bought a home last year for a million dollars with $100,000 down, and the home was up 20 percent, that's $200,000 on a $100,000 investment. You'd be up 200 percent. Over time, essentially, that's what's going to happen. The longer you wait, the more the house is going to appreciate and the greater return you'll have on your equity investment. The single best investment for anyone with that type of money would be to buy their own house or apartment.

DR: What would you tell people not to invest in?

JP: A lot of people disagree with this, but I think you shouldn't invest in cryptocurrencies. I think cryptocurrencies, regardless of where they're trading today, whether they go up from here or down, will eventually prove to be worthless. There is no value to them. It's just a question of supply and demand, and once the exuberance wears off, or liquidity dries up, these will go to zero. I wouldn't recommend anyone invest in cryptocurrencies.

DR: Any regrets in your career?

JP: No.

DR: And you hope your children get into the investing world at some point?

JP: I always say you should do what you're passionate about. From a very young age, I happened to have found investing to be fun. I like buying things, selling things. I like making money, and the independence that earning money gives me allows me to have a lifestyle. That's what I like. But you can't force that upon someone. The most important thing is to pursue your passion. You can be successful in anything. You can be successful in music, dance, medicine, physics, math. The important thing is that you pursue a career in what you're naturally passionate about. That will improve your odds of achieving success.

Private Equity
and Buyouts

SANDRA HORBACH

Managing director and co-head of US Buyout
and Growth, The Carlyle Group

> *"Complacency will destroy an organization. . . . You need to continually innovate and raise the bar in terms of your team and the capabilities that you build to support investments."*

Carlyle's success over the past 35 years was due to the skills of a number of highly talented investment professionals, and more than a few of them would merit inclusion in a book like this. But to bring as much objectivity as possible to the interviews, I decided not to include any of my partners—with the exception of a truly unique individual, Sandra Horbach.

A native of Bellevue, Washington, Sandra had an early interest in international diplomacy, and learned Chinese in college as a way to jump-start a career in that area. But there was little demand for Chinese speakers in the United States in the 1980s; so Sandra decided a career in finance might be more productive.

As a result, after graduating Phi Beta Kappa from Wellesley College, Sandra pursued the financial world at Morgan Stanley in New York. After several years there, she went to the Stanford Graduate School of Business for her MBA, after which she joined in 1987 what was then one of the country's leading buyout firms, Forstmann Little. At the time there were hardly any women at any level in the buyout world.

As she rose to partner in 1993, Sandra became an extraordinarily respected buyout professional, helping to lead some of her firm's most successful investments. When a problem arose in a buyout, she was often given the assignment of fixing it, as was the case with Gulfstream. It was seemingly an investment loss when she got involved but, after her efforts, the investment became one of the firm's biggest successes ever.

When buyout pioneer Ted Forstmann decided to slow down Forstmann Little's activities, Sandra was pursued by all of the major buyout firms, and Carlyle was fortunate that she decided to join our firm. She successfully led Carlyle's foray into consumer and retail investments and rose to her current position as co-head of the firm's largest business, its US buyout and growth activities.

In her current position, Sandra is one of the most senior and experienced women in the entire buyout world. She is also one of the leading women in the financial services world, helping to encourage young women to join the profession, as well as mentoring those who do so.

I thought an interview with her would provide some unique perspectives on both the earlier days of the buyout world (when enormous amounts of leverage was the coin of the realm) as well as insights on how that world is operating today. She brings the perspective of someone who has done buyouts directly for a good many years and the perspective of someone who now oversees a large team of investment professionals who are doing the investing directly. I also thought a conversation with Sandra about her investment career in a male-dominated profession would show some of the challenges that she faced and might also encourage other women, as she is regularly doing, to join the profession and experience its pleasures and opportunities. I interviewed Sandra virtually on June 14, 2021.

DAVID M. RUBENSTEIN (DR): You are no doubt one of the most experienced and successful women in the world doing buyouts. When you first started several decades ago, were there many other women doing buyouts? Were there any role models for you?

SANDRA HORBACH (SH): There weren't other women doing buyouts when I first started out in the business, so there were no female role models. I was fortunate to work with a number of great investors—all men—who served as role models.

DR: Did the men treat you with the respect due to an investment professional with an MBA from Stanford, or was that not the case many years ago?

SH: Some did, but some were clearly skeptical about my abilities. Over time, I tried to prove myself, and usually ended up with very positive working relationships.

DR: Today the large private equity firms are major interviewers at the leading business schools. Was that the case when you graduated? How did you get into the buyout world?

SH: There were no private equity firms interviewing at business schools when I was in school. These PE firms were all very small at the time. They weren't recruiting anywhere, let alone at business school. Generally, you had to know someone to get in the door. I didn't really know anyone in private equity, so I did an independent job search networking with Stanford and Morgan Stanley alumni, and somehow found my way into the private equity world. I banged on a lot of doors and fortunately talked my way into a role that didn't exist at Forstmann Little.

DR: How big was Forstmann Little when you joined, in terms of individuals and capital under management?

SH: There were five partners, so I was the sixth investment professional and only woman. Forstmann Little had over $1 billion in capital when I joined in 1987. It was one of two firms of that size at the time.

DR: Who taught you the buyout business in the early days of Forstmann Little? Was it one person, or did you teach yourself? How did it work?

SH: It's an apprentice business, so I certainly learned at the heels of some great investors. In my early days at Forstmann Little, I worked primarily with Brian Little, one of the founders, and John Sprague, another partner at the firm. After a few years, I transitioned to working directly with Ted Forstmann, and I believe I learned the most from working together with him. He was a pioneer in the industry and a great investor.

DR: In those days, the transactions were much more highly leveraged than today. How much leverage did the firms typically have? I realize that Forstmann Little had a different situation than most, but the deals were leveraged at 90 percent leverage or something like that?

SH: That's correct. Most firms used 90 percent debt and 10 percent equity. As you mentioned, Forstmann Little had its own committed sub-debt fund, which allowed for safer and more creative capital structures. That was, at the time, a real competitive advantage. So we used less bank debt financing than most of the other leveraged buyout firms.*

DR: Was your job initially to analyze the opportunities and to arrange the financing? What was your job as a young professional?

SH: I was responsible for identifying potential attractive investment opportunities, conducting diligence and arranging for financing, and then helping oversee the portfolio company until it was sold or taken public (typically four to seven years after the investment was made).

DR: Was it that competitive in those days to win a transaction, or were there just a very few real competitors?

SH: At the time it always seemed competitive, but in retrospect, there was much less competition than today.

DR: Was price the principal deciding factor in winning a transaction, or was the certainty of closing also a key factor?

SH: It was both. You had to hit a certain threshold on price, but certainty was also very important, because at the time you couldn't readily get

---

* During Forstmann Little's heyday in the 1980s, it was somewhat unique in having a subordinated debt fund that it could commit to its buyout transactions. Other firms had to typically go into the financing markets to raise the subordinated debt often needed to provide the funds for a buyout investment. Like all other buyout firms, Forstmann Little had to go into the financing markets to raise the senior debt needed for a buyout transaction. But having the subordinated debt already in hand from its own fund, Forstmann Little had a bit of an advantage. The other firms would typically secure their subordinated debt in the high-yield market, and the cost was usually higher and with more terms than what Forstmann Little committed to the investors in its subordinated debt fund.

committed underwritten financing for the whole transaction, which is why our sub-debt fund was such a competitive advantage.

DR: What did your firm or others do to add value? Were there that many operating partners, former CEOs, involved to help add value, or that wasn't part of the business then?

SH: We didn't have the tools we have today to drive value creation, but we did assemble strong boards of directors and leverage their industry or operational expertise to advise management teams. For example, our Gulfstream board of directors included George Shultz, Bob Strauss, Bob Dole, Henry Kissinger, Don Rumsfeld, and Colin Powell.

DR: Pretty impressive. Was fundraising a major part of the business then, or were funds raised less frequently and at much smaller sizes than today?

SH: Fundraising from our limited partners was always important, and we raised a new fund about every four to five years. We were fortunate, we had great relationships with our limited partners and they were very loyal investors; so we had a lot of repeat investors who would invest with us in fund after fund. But they were certainly smaller funds.*

---

* In the buyout world, like the venture world, the equity capital to make investments typically comes from a fund that a buyout or venture firm will raise from institutional or individual investors. Raising these funds can be time-consuming, for an enormous amount of due diligence is typically done by investors on the capabilities and track record of the fund being raised. Because investors are now all over the world, raising a large buyout fund of $10–20 billion can take as much as a year, and maybe even two years. With COVID, fundraising was made a bit easier because presentations to investors could be done through virtual means, without the need to travel. The capital for a buyout fund, like a venture fund, is committed by the investor to the fund, and is only actually provided, or funded, by the investor when the buyout, or venture, fund has a transaction ready to proceed. Investors then fund their pro rata share of the investment. Management fees are typically paid annually by the investor on the total amount the investor committed to the fund. So a $1 billion fund making an investment of $100 million would entail the investors' funding 10 percent of the committed capital to the investment. Thus, an investor who committed $50 million to the fund would

DR: What were some of the major transactions on which you worked?

SH: I mentioned Gulfstream Aerospace, which I spent a lot of my time working on for about eight years. We were a small firm with fewer than 10 investment professionals, so I worked on most of the deals we did, including Community Health Systems, General Instruments, Yankee Candle, Topps (the baseball cards and Bazooka gum business), Stanadyne (a conglomerate where the crown jewel of the business was Moen Faucets, which later we sold to American Brands), Citadel Communications and then XO Communications, Aldila, and Department 56. Not all name-brand companies.

DR: You bought Gulfstream from Chrysler. It had some problems after you purchased it. How did you and your colleagues deal with those problems and turn around the company, so it was successfully sold to General Dynamics?

SH: I had not been involved in the oversight of Gulfstream after the acquisition. When we started to see issues at the business, Ted Forstmann asked me to go to Savannah [the headquarters] to determine if the problems were solvable. He instructed me to look at it like it was a new investment and to come back with a recommendation to the partners about a path forward.

After spending several months at the company, I believed that the problems were fixable, and laid out my suggested turnaround plan. Fortunately, the partners were supportive, and together we came up with a plan that we took to our limited partners (LPs), who agreed to support it. As I mentioned, we had our own subordinate debt funds, so we convinced the LPs to convert all their sub debt into equity.

In essence, we bought ourselves time by shoring up the capital structure to fix the company's problems. First we replaced the entire management team and then went about taking costs out and redesigning

---

fund 10 percent of that commitment for an investment of $100 million, or $5 million. Each year, the investor would pay a management fee, typically between 1 to 2 percent of the committed amount, or $500,000 to $1 million a year in this example.

a flawed Gulfstream 500 development program. We found partners to help support the increased cost of the new G5 development program through revenue-sharing agreements with Rolls-Royce and Vought, which at the time was, ironically, a Carlyle portfolio company, and we assembled the world-class board of directors I mentioned earlier, who became the best airplane salesmen one could ask for.

DR: Why do you enjoy the buyout business? I presume you do.

SH: I certainly do. I've been doing it for a long time. I love learning about new businesses and understanding what drives a company's success. I also really enjoy working with management teams to support them and realize a company's potential.

DR: What are the most important lessons you've learned?

SH: I've learned a lot of lessons over the years. Humility is key. Diversity of opinions results in better investment decisions. I've learned how the right leaders can totally change the direction of a company, and that it's better to pay up for a great business than to buy a mediocre business for a low multiple.*

And lastly, I've learned that complacency will destroy an organization. You can't rely on your past success. You need to continually innovate and raise the bar in terms of your team and the capabilities that you build to support investments.

DR: What are the key attributes, in your view, for a good buyout professional?

SH: Intellectual honesty. You don't want to talk yourself into a deal by only seeing the positives. Curiosity is also very important. You need to be humble but decisive and possess excellent interpersonal skills. You need to be able to read people well and interact with all different types

---

* Buyout investments are typically bought on a multiple of a company's EBITDA. The EBITDA number is seen as the real earnings of a company, and thus is seen as the best proxy for a company's ability to generate profits. Buyouts are typically bought as a multiple of EBITDA. A low-growth, industrial-manufacturing company might be bought at 6–8x EBITDA. A high-tech company, with greater earnings growth potential, might be bought at 15–20x its EBITDA.

of people. And you have to be willing to work hard. It's a competitive field and, in order to win, you need to be driven. I would also say be forward-looking and recognize the importance of pattern recognition, but also understand that the past does not dictate the future.

Lastly, you have to be able to accept failure and move beyond it. If you're in the private equity business long enough, you will have a deal that does not go well, and you will lose investors' money, which is a horrible experience. But we're in the business of taking risks. You have to be able to handle that responsibility.

DR: After Teddy Forstmann decided to wind down the firm, you left and joined Carlyle as the head of its consumer and retail buyout business. You had many offers to join other buyout firms. What was it about the buyout business that made you want to stay in it? Why not become a CEO or CFO or something else in finance? What is it about buyouts that you found so enjoyable and rewarding?

SH: I enjoy working with many different types of companies and management teams and therefore constantly learning and being exposed to new things. So, while I did have some other opportunities come my way, I never seriously considered doing anything other than private equity. The question for me was really which firm, and I didn't realize how different and special Forstmann Little was until I left and started meeting with those firms. Fortunately, Carlyle turned out to be a great home for me, so thank you for hiring me.

DR: You're now co-heading Carlyle's US buyout and growth business. How has the buyout business changed from when you began in it?

SH: I would ask the question "How hasn't the business changed?" When I started in the industry back in 1987, it wasn't even considered an industry. It was just a handful of small firms doing this new type of investing called leveraged buyouts. Now private equity is an established global asset class with trillions of dollars under management and thousands of firms investing all over the world. As the industry has grown and evolved, firms like Carlyle have added significant resources and capabilities to drive value creation. Intense competition, high valuations, and increasingly large fund sizes mean PE firms have to keep raising the bar on how we identify great investment opportunities and add value to drive great outcomes.

DR: Are the transactions today safer because there's less leverage? Is there more value added by the buyout firms, or the price is much higher because there is more competition?

SH: The prices are definitely higher, but at the same time we're putting much more equity into the capital structure than in early days, where we saw 90 percent debt to 10 percent equity. The competition continues to get tougher and tougher, and that's why we have to be so vigilant about adding value-creation capabilities to the team and also being very selective in the types of companies that we buy.

DR: Can you take us through how a typical buyout process works from the time a prospective deal arrives at the firm to the time you decide to try to buy it, and then, if that effort is successful, what happens post-acquisition?

SH: Our process starts annually with reviews of each of our six industry sector leads, where we align on the subsectors they will prioritize for investment opportunities. Carlyle is very industry focused. Once we have alignment, the sector teams will go about sourcing actionable and attractive investment opportunities. When they identify an opportunity that they believe meets our investment criteria, they'll bring it to the fund heads for a review, which we call a "heads-up." It's a high-level overview where we discuss the merits of the investment.

If we give the green light to proceed at the heads-up meeting, the teams will then engage in rigorous diligence and we'll do a series of successive deep dives on the business. We pass on many deals during this part of the process if the diligence proves disappointing. Finally, if the deal team recommends proceeding with an acquisition, and diligence has checked out, and we (the fund heads) approve the deal, we will recommend it to the investment committee, which ultimately gives final approval (or not) to the deal.

DR: How many deals are considered in a typical year by your group and how many are typically done?

SH: We look at a lot of deals. We have a large funnel and we will consider hundreds of deals every year, but most of those are not pursued because they don't meet our investment criteria. As I mentioned, we have six industry verticals, and each one will actively review between 10 to 20 deals per year. That's roughly a hundred companies in a year that will get a very thorough review. From that we might move forward on six to 12 companies in any given year.

DR: How does the firm try to add value once a company is purchased? How involved do the Carlyle investment professionals get in overseeing the company once it is purchased?

SH: Carlyle investment professionals are very involved in the portfolio companies, serving on boards and helping oversee the execution of the value-creation plan and ultimately the exit. In addition, we have a team of 30-plus functional experts in our global investment resources team who oversee talent and organizational performance, digital transformation, technology and cybersecurity, procurement, revenue growth opportunities, as well as ESG and government affairs. We have a large team and they're focused on driving results at the portfolio companies.

DR: How important is ESG these days when you're looking at a prospective investment? What about after an investment is made? Was ESG a factor when you first got into the buyout business?

SH: ESG was not a factor back in the early days, and it's become much more important in today's marketplace. Our LPs care a lot about the type of companies we invest in and how we drive ESG initiatives across the portfolio. So we integrate ESG analysis in every transaction and the diligence that we do, and we provide market-leading ESG reporting to our LPs. We generate significant value creation through sustainability initiatives such as operational efficiencies, ESG-linked financings, sustainability-oriented brands, and workforce engagement, as well as productivity and diversity.

DR: How has gender diversity changed the profession since you first joined the buyout world? Are there many women at buyout firms today?

SH: The industry has made progress improving diversity since I joined the buyout business, but most of it has taken place over the last 10 years. This is another area that LPs care a lot about, but we still have a long way to go. There still, sadly, are very few women in leadership positions in the industry. I've often been referred to as a "unicorn," which is not a good thing. There needs to be more diversity in our business. I am proud to say that Carlyle leads the way here. Today 50 percent of my investment team is diverse, and over half of our assets under management are managed by women.

DR: When you and your team are looking at doing a buyout, what are the most important factors in assessing the desirability of the investment? Price, management, competition, ability to add value? What is the most important thing in the end, or is there no one thing?

SH: It's all of the above. It starts with the profile of the business: the historical performance and projected outlook, market position, sustainable competitive advantages, barriers to entry, etc. The management team is critically important. We have a systematic way of assessing every management team before we make an investment, so we're really bringing the science and data to the art of CEO and C-suite assessment. Price matters, but even more important is the value-creation plan.

DR: In your experience, what is the key to making a buyout work? How soon into the ownership phase of a buyout do you typically know whether that buyout is going to work well or not?

SH: It starts with selecting the right company and right management team up front and having alignment with the board and the management on the value-creation plan from day one. Now, obviously, there are factors outside of our control, for example a pandemic, that can derail a deal. But if you've made the right investment decision and have the right team running the company and have put in place a proven capital structure, you should be able to navigate most circumstances.

DR: How often do you need to replace the CEO?

SH: Forty to 50 percent of the time. Oftentimes bringing in a new CEO and team is part of the value-creation plan our teams identify. I can't overstate the importance of the right team and making sure they are aligned with the value-creation plan.

DR: Can you tell relatively soon into the process that something is not working as it was supposed to, or does it take a lot longer than the first year or so?

SH: It varies depending on circumstances. For example, if there is a fundamental issue with the company's operations or business model, that usually comes out in the first year or two. Other times, a company can be impacted several years into an investment if something in the market-place has changed—if there's some disruption to the business.

DR: How hard is it to turn around the company once it becomes clear that there is a problem of significance?

SH: It's never easy, but I could give you a lot of examples where compa-nies have been successfully turned around. In most of these situations it's because we've been able to bring in a new management team to effect that turnaround.

DR: How long does a firm like Carlyle typically hold on to its buyout investments?

SH: In today's market, we typically hold our portfolio companies for four to seven years, because it does take time to implement the value-creation plan.

DR: When you get ready to sell, do you simultaneously look at sales to "strategics"—companies already operating in the relevant area—sales to private equity firms, and IPOs? What is the determining factor in deciding which way to proceed?

SH: Even before we've closed on a new investment, we're thinking about what the right exit will be for a company—an IPO, strategic sale, or sale to a private equity firm. Most of the time we're focused on the first two as preferred options. It's usually pretty clear to us if there will be stra-tegic interest, and that's the preferred exit for us, given that you can monetize the investment all at once. There are some companies where there is no strategic option or where it's too big, so the only option for exit is an IPO. In this case, we sell our holdings over a number of years. Carlyle has taken many companies public over the years. We've taken four companies public during the pandemic—which is something none of us expected, going into COVID.

DR: For investors who want to invest in buyout funds, what is the advice you would give them? What are the key factors in assessing the attrac-tiveness of a particular buyout fund?

SH: I believe it's all about the team and the industry-sector expertise, their track record, and value-creation capabilities. In today's competitive environment, private equity firms with scale and resources to drive long-term value creation, I believe, will be the winners in the long run.

DR: What would you say are the principal changes in the buyout business since you first entered it?

SH: Principal changes would include the scale and global nature of the industry, the enhanced capabilities and sophistication of private equity firms, and the depth of resources they bring to drive value creation at the portfolio companies. Importantly, many of the most successful firms have now been around for decades, with senior leaders such as yourself and other founders who established the industry and who offer great insights and investment judgment. The industry will continue to change and evolve, but with the benefit of decades of experience and perspective.

DR: Has the investor base changed all that much over the years? Are there more sovereign wealth funds and individual investors than there were when you first got into the business?*

SH: It's grown more than it's changed. Today there is a real mix of pension funds, sovereign wealth funds, corporate pension funds, high-net-worth individuals, and family offices. Historically, it was much more weighted toward pension funds and sovereign wealth funds.

---

* Sovereign wealth funds are gigantic pools of capital that are invested on behalf of a country and its citizens. The first of these is generally thought to be the Kuwait Investment Authority, created in the early 1950s to enable Kuwait to invest its oil revenue in stocks and bonds, to diversify the country's assets. Today the largest sovereign wealth fund is thought to be the Government Pension Fund Global of Norway, with about $1.3 trillion in assets. Other large sovereign wealth funds include the China Investment Corporation (CIC), the Abu Dhabi Investment Authority (ADIA), the Public Investment Fund (PIF) of Saudi Arabia, and the Government of Singapore Investment Corporation (GIC).

DR: As you look back on your career and doing buyouts, what do you find most satisfying?

SH: Working with my teams and helping lead young investors. As I said earlier, it's an apprentice business, so it's satisfying to see people learn and develop, and it's also been gratifying for me to be able to sponsor and mentor so many women in the industry and help bring them along to be part of the leadership for the future.

DR: To succeed in the buyout world, what are the skill sets that you think are most helpful? Intelligence, hard work, networking, personality? What skills or personality traits might not be so helpful?

SH: You need humility, intellectual honesty, intelligence, curiosity, decisiveness, and strong interpersonal skills. You have to work hard and be driven and forward-looking in terms of where the businesses are heading. You can't rely on the past to dictate future success. Unhelpful skills, to me, would include arrogance, lack of integrity, laziness, lack of rigor in evaluating companies, and then having weak interpersonal skills or low EQ [emotional intelligence].

DR: How do you expect the buyout world will evolve over the next few years? More competition, more women and minorities, more specialized funds? How do you see change occurring in the buyout world?

SH: I think the larger private equity firms will continue to take share, given their superior capabilities and resources to drive value creation. I hope that we will see more diversity, especially at the senior level, across all PE firms.

DR: Would you recommend the profession to younger men and women?

SH: Absolutely. I feel so lucky to have stumbled into this profession. You will never be bored; you'll always learn new things, and you'll be lucky to work with really talented people. It's been quite an adventure.

DR: Any wish you had pursued a different profession?

SH: Absolutely not.

DR: You didn't want to be a doctor? You didn't want to be a lawyer?

SH: When I was really young, I thought I would be a lawyer. Then, when I was working in investment banking and I saw what lawyers really do, I changed my mind and pivoted to business.

DR: So did I, and I am a lawyer.

SH: I know and am glad you did.

DR: How hard has it been to do buyouts over the last year and a half? Your team has been largely working, as many professionals have been, from home. How do you do buyouts remotely?

SH: It surprised me how productive our teams have been throughout the pandemic. Our industry focus and the fact that our sector teams have tremendous networks within their industries allowed us to continue to do deals, since our teams already knew many of the CEOs running the companies they were targeting. We were able to do a lot of diligence over Zoom, and in cases where we had already met the management team, we would proceed by doing it all remotely.

To the extent that we did not know the management team, we found a safe, appropriate way to meet, because we do believe you have to be able to sit across from management, face-to-face, to determine whether you have alignment in terms of what to do with the business and what the partnership will be like going forward. So we did insist on in-person meetings, and we were able to do that safely, with appropriate social distancing.

We were also successful in taking the first technology company public entirely virtually during the pandemic. ZoomInfo (a software company unrelated to Zoom) was 100 percent virtual. It's really going to change the way people are thinking about managing businesses and the travel that we all have historically done to raise money, to find deals, to do IPOs and exits. There's a lot of learning that will come out of COVID.

ORLANDO BRAVO

Founder and managing partner, Thoma Bravo

> *"At the end of the day, the combination of a deep analytical approach to business problems with a deep understanding of people and how to inspire them is our secret sauce."*

The leveraged buyout boom of the 1980s—symbolized for some in the epic buyout battle in 1988 over RJR Nabisco (memorialized in the book *Barbarians at the Gate*)—was a disruption to the way corporate acquisitions had heretofore been done.

The buyouts of that era were often led by relatively small investment firms, though they had access to large amounts of capital; the capital structure for the buyout might have 90–95 percent debt, so they were clearly "leveraged" buyouts; a fair number of the transactions were "unfriendly" (i.e., the target company did not really want to be bought, or at least not by a leveraged buyout firm); many of the assets of the target company might be quickly sold upon completion of the acquisition, reducing employment in the company, among other concerns; and concern about ESG factors was not really a focus.

The focus was on maximizing the leverage to minimize the equity, thereby improving the ultimate investment returns for the equity when the resale of the company or its assets occurred.

These early-generation buyout transactions, with a few exceptions, were typically led by former investment bankers; they tended to have little industry specialization or expertise; and they focused often on selling assets or cutting costs rather than adding value through techniques designed to grow revenue and earnings or through additional synergistic acquisitions. And they tended not to spend time on ESG concerns.

In recent years, a new generation of buyout leaders has emerged. While they have built on many of the approaches and techniques developed by the buyout pioneers, the new generation has developed its own approaches: less leverage; greater ESG focus; more growth in the revenue of the underlying company. Perhaps most important, the new generation tends to be highly specialized in one sector, and as a result is able to add enormous amounts of industry experience immediately to the purchased company.

One of the most successful investors of this new generation has a last name that surely reflects the views of his abundantly pleased investors—Orlando Bravo. His enormous success in the modern buyout world might not have been predicted in Orlando's youth. A native of Puerto Rico, he was a tennis prodigy (who roomed with Jim Courier and practiced with Andre Agassi at the famous Nick Bollettieri Tennis Academy), and his youthful ambition was to be a professional tennis player.

But Orlando ultimately decided to skip a try at professional tennis and instead pursue an education at Brown (where he did play tennis), and then Stanford law and business schools. During this time, he became fascinated with the art of buyouts and the growing importance of enterprise software (computer software designed to enable a company to operate more effectively and efficiently), and he built a buyout business second to none in enterprise software at a firm now known as Thoma Bravo.

Orlando's success has been due to many factors—a single-minded focus on buyouts in an area that many buyout firms did not fully understand until recently; a "secret sauce" of principles, metrics, and processes to enhance the value of the companies he and his colleagues bought (at prices that once seemed high and later, after his firm's efforts, seemed cheap); and a competitive spirit that even the best of professional tennis players would admire.

The success of Orlando's approach was evident to many in the buyout world when, during the pandemic in 2020–21, he was able to raise three new funds in excess of $22 billion without having to meet investors in person. The fundraising was done virtually, and he was massively oversubscribed even at that level. Regularly returning investors' money at multiples of invested capital helps a great deal.

Orlando has not forgotten his roots. He has now begun to turn his attention to philanthropy and in particular to helping Puerto Rico, first in a massive way after its hurricane damage in 2017, and now on a regular basis to help education, entrepreneurship, and other social needs in the country.

A few years ago, a mutual friend introduced me to him—we had not met on the private equity conference circuit—and I found him to be an extraordinarily engaging, modest, and focused person who was quite easy to like instantly. I could readily see how he became so successful at a relatively young age, and how he seems likely to be one of the buyout industry's superstars for quite some time. I interviewed Orlando virtually on June 25, 2021.

DAVID M. RUBENSTEIN (DR): You and your firm have become global leaders in enterprise software buyouts, compiling over the past two decades an almost unmatched track record for any buyout firm in any industry during this period. What exactly is enterprise software, and why has it been such an amazing and attractive area in which to invest?

ORLANDO BRAVO (OB): Enterprise software is basically all the intellectual property written in code in the software that a company, the intellectual property holder, sells to a corporation—it could be a small business or it could be a Global 2000 company—to do three things for that company. It could be to help them run business processes, like how to send invoices, how to do their accounting, how to do their online marketing. That's one piece—running their business right for the user. The second piece is all that code that runs your IT department, makes sure you get data in, data out, that all the machines communicate with one another, and that now, in the cloud environment, you communicate with the outside world and use and analyze data. The third piece, which is super popular now, is cybersecurity—every piece of code that protects all that IT environment around you so that your data and your process can be safe.

It has become, aside from asset management, in our opinion the best business in the world, because you make a product once and you can resell it over and over and over again. That product produces usually 90 percent gross margins, and you get paid before you deliver the service, almost like private equity. We're getting a management fee before we invest the money.

These software companies sell you that piece of software and they get paid before installing it or providing the service, which is truly amazing. The benefit that it has is that a buyer of these companies can create a lot of improvements. These companies are undermanaged, typically, from a bottom-line standpoint, and some of us in the industry have brought this category to the world of institutional investors by making them fundamental investments.

DR: Beyond the inherent attractiveness of the industry over the past two decades, what has your firm done to add value to your investments? Has there been a so-called secret sauce that you and your colleagues have applied?

OB: We feel our secret sauce is that we look to accomplish big positive changes in the companies we buy and seek to do it with the existing management teams. What that allows you to do is invest in the most innovative software spaces, because you don't want to break that innovation curve by replacing people that they need. We are then able to inspire them with an analytical approach to decision-making, to run their businesses differently. That's our secret sauce.

People can copy our metrics, our processes, from doing all these deals, and some of these things are well-known. But they can't copy that style and culture we bring into the equation. At the end of the day, the combination of a deep analytical approach to business problems with a deep understanding of people and how to inspire them is our secret sauce.

DR: Do you fear that something will come along in the tech area that will replace enterprise software as the great growth engine for so much of the tech world and the economy?

OB: Blockchain. If you don't consider blockchain enterprise software, yes, I fear that. If you consider it part of the software industry, then I really don't see anything else.

DR: Do you invest in blockchain?

OB: Personally I do. I'm a big believer in it.

DR: But your firm has not yet done that?

OB: We're thinking of doing that. We haven't yet figured it out.

DR: In the early days of the buyout world, in the 1970s and 1980s in particular, buyouts got a bad name for being overleveraged, financial-engineering efforts by former investment bankers, resulting in times of economic distress and a large number of bankruptcies, not to mention job cutbacks and a lack of concern for ESG factors. Is that still the case? Why should the general public think that buyouts are good for society in any industry?

OB: That is definitely not the case anymore, and it's an area of frustration for me. I'm a student of private equity and I learned from the pioneers of the industry. Some of the things that were being done in the '80s and '90s were actually good, even though in retrospect they look bad, because they were breaking up poor corporate practices being done by management and inefficient ways of doing business. That's no longer the buyout world, because at these high prices, you make no money using that strategy.

In terms of why it's good for society, it's always great to have assets move to the person that can produce the most value. If we ended up with fewer employees at the beginning of a deal, that's okay, because those employees will be empowered in a much bigger way, and the people who are not there anymore, in this economy, can find other great jobs. For the young people we work with, we also teach them a style of doing business in a way that makes them better leaders for the future.

DR: As you were building your track record in the buyout world and trying to gain credibility and experience, was it a bigger challenge being from Puerto Rico, or being Latino, or being a former star tennis player, or was there no bias against you?

OB: I love that question. They counterbalance each other. Being Puerto Rican was a challenge, but things are getting better now. When I was lucky enough to get job offers, whether it was in investment banking or the few jobs that were in private equity in the '90s, it was always to be in the Latin America group, which was popular at the time for firms. It may have given me an angle, but it was an angle I didn't want. I wanted to go where the money was, which was up north, not south. So being Puerto Rican was a bit of a challenge, but I used tennis to counterbalance that. The way I would try to get jobs, summer jobs in business school or whatever, is to go play tennis with somebody at the firm or the head of the firm, and that was great.

DR: Since you're such a good tennis player, I assume you'd have to let them win, right?

OB: No. I would not do that, because then they wouldn't think I was good enough.

DR: But who was going to be good enough to play with you?

OB: I was intense. Edge matters, you know? There were some good players, but I did okay.

DR: Where did you grow up? How did you become a child tennis star? Why did you go to Brown to play NCAA tennis rather than play in the Pro Tour?

OB: I grew up in Mayagüez, Puerto Rico. Small town, isolated place. There were two tennis courts at a local Hilton hotel and two tennis courts in the local college. When I was nine years old, my mom—her family's an immigrant family from Cuba, always moving around and looking for bigger things and better things—she took me to this tennis tournament in San Juan, an exhibition match with Vitas Gerulaitis. That was kind of it for me. She put me in tennis lessons with a local person, playing every day, and little by little I started going to San Juan. I loved going to the main city. Then somebody took me under their wing there.

The first time I went to the US was in Miami, where I got to the finals and I lost to Jim Courier. That was a 12-and-under tournament. Then we became friends, and the rest went from there, but it was my avenue, or maybe my mom's plan for me, to have something broader than my local place.

I went to Nick Bollettieri's tennis academy for about two years during high school. My roommate there was Jim Courier. I was the same age as Andre Agassi. Same age as Pete Sampras. Same age as Michael Chang. We're all playing these tournaments. But they were always top 10 in the country. I was kind of number 40 in the country. When they turned 17, you could really see the difference in athletic ability. So going pro wasn't realistic. The sport of tennis is punishing that way, in that many people at my level did go pro. You really struggle through that. It's just brutal. I used tennis as a way to get to an Ivy League school.

DR: I assume you were the star of the Brown tennis team?

OB: We had a really good team. We were in the top 15 in the country at the time. I was really good in doubles, I was one of the top, and in singles, I was three or four. Then the world started opening up and I wanted to do less tennis and more school and jobs.

DR: What prompted you to go to Stanford Law School and Stanford Business School?

OB: I was going to go to Harvard Law School. That was like the dream, right? This is Harvard. I got in and that year, a friend of mine who was really this worldly kid—that's one of the benefits of these great schools—told me, "You've got to interview for these investment banks. They're in town."

I didn't know what investment banking was. I said, "Wait a minute, I get to work on Wall Street, and they pay me $35,000 a year, and I get to be like people in the movies?" And he said, "Yes, it's kind of like that. The only thing you need to do is wear a tie, and you've got to buy some wingtip shoes. That's what they wear." We went to a secondhand store, I bought some wingtip shoes, and I interviewed. They gave me a job, and I'm like, "I want to do this."

I called Harvard and Stanford and I asked them—because I got into Stanford Law School as well—"Can you let me defer for a couple years so I can do this?" Harvard said, "No way, you're going to have to reapply." Stanford said, "You're welcome to come here anytime. We'll defer you as long as you want."

Once I started working at Morgan Stanley, we would have these groups called the little group meetings. I was in the Latin America group, but the other little group was the tech group of people thinking about going to open up an office in Silicon Valley. I was always intrigued by that group. I'm like, "That's where I want to be."

DR: How did you wind up in the buyout world?

OB: What I intended to do upon graduation was a cop-out—going to law school because I didn't know what I was going to do. A big moment for me and buyouts happened in investment banking in the middle of my first year at Morgan Stanley. The company I was working on representing was the largest supermarket in Puerto Rico, which was a billion-dollar deal. They put me in that deal because I'm Puerto Rican, and they let me participate in most of the meetings with the buyers. Two of the buyers were private equity firms, but I didn't know what that was. I asked the associate on the deal, "Who are these guys? They don't have a company. They don't have a corporation. These are two guys with an office and a phone and they combined are a multinational, billion-dollar company?" He said, "Yes, that's kind of the way it works."

They were smarter, more entrepreneurial. They seemed better negotiators. They moved faster. I said, "That sounds really cool. I want to do that." And little by little, I started getting more into it.

DR: What led you to specialize in enterprise software? Was it hard to convince your firm's investors that was a viable buyout category in the early years? Was it hard to convince software entrepreneurs that a buyout firm could help in growing the value of the company?

OB: It was hard first to convince some of the partners at Thoma Cressey, my predecessor firm, because I made my share of mistakes in venture deals while I was in the firm's office in San Francisco. Carl Thoma gave me a bunch of responsibility and authority early on. I almost got fired over that, because that was the 2000 dot-com bust, and it was also stuff I didn't know anything about. He gave me a second chance in sticking through it and being in the middle of tech.

The firm liked buying companies with recurring revenue, things like contractual processing and outdoor advertising and media. We came up with this theory that recurring-revenue software was really good, and it was cheaper at the time than any other recurring-revenue category. We came up with a quasi-solution to the fact that these companies weren't making money by saying, "Look at their gross margins, maybe we can get an operator that can make them really profitable." Given the size of the firm at the time, which was a $450 million fund—it was small—Carl Thoma let me do it. He gave me another chance, and he actually believed in it.

DR: His firm was based in Chicago, was it not?

OB: He set up an office in Chicago, which was the main office, and a little one in San Francisco, where I was, and a small one in Denver. Now, over two funds, we quickly became a software firm, because about 50 percent of the deals in the first fund were software and about 60 percent of the deals in the second fund were software. We decided, "Let's just do software only."

Still, it was nearly impossible to convince investors to do this. We went out to raise $1.2 billion and we ended up with $822.5 million, but I know that if two accounts hadn't come in, that would have been dream over. That's been the best one we've ever had, but it was hard.

DR: What were some of the types of deals you did that made it clear you could do this very well? Were there some early deals that are memorable to you?

OB: All of them. The first one was a take-private of a software company that did exactly what I explained before. They ran the entire business of a distributor—HVAC, tile, equipment, any kind of fasteners, you name it. I remember telling Carl Thoma at the time, "Look at this thing. Why would anybody buy a distributor when you can buy the software company that runs all their business?" In that deal, we were able to partner with the person who became chairman of our operating committee, who's my mentor, now in his mid-80s, Marcel Bernard. With existing management, he was able to get them from a negative margin right to acquisitions and things they hadn't done before. We made around five times the money in three years on that deal.

That deal was important for me personally. When we were assigned to sell the company, the CEO called me and said, "You remember that time we had dinner and you described roughly how much was in it for management and the investor if things worked out?" I said, "I vaguely do." He said, "That night, I went over to my wife, and I said, 'All private equity guys are full of it.'" But later he realized that we could help a bit, and by doing so the company would improve, and the customers and employees would benefit. He later appreciated what we could do to help improve to such an extent that he became an investor with us.

We did another deal with an existing manager where we sold the company for about three times what we paid for it. Then we did another deal that we sold for 17 times what we paid. Then we did a $250 million deal that was huge for us at the time—that was Datatel—with existing management that was sold for about 4 times what we paid for it. These numbers were happening, but for investors at the time, software was little, it was new, and they had better choices.

I see their point. They could invest in people like Carlyle and Blackstone that had a long track record. Why take the risk?

DR: Has your approach changed in assessing and adding value to buyouts since you started? Do you do things differently than you did years ago?

OB: The philosophy's the same, but the tactics are totally different. The industry has changed. For example, going back to 20 years ago, you could cut some costs and make money in software because it was cheap enough. Now you can't do that.

But the philosophy of taking a complex problem and dividing it into its component parts, putting up P&L (profit and loss statements) for those managers and giving them responsibility, accountability, and authority to make decisions, and reporting on a monthly basis and not changing our mind as an investor on what the mission is, both operationally and strategically. That has remained the same.

DR: Do you typically serve on the boards of the companies in which you invest?

OB: Yes, we do.

DR: How often do you change the CEO of a company you invest in?

OB: We go in and we try to work with existing management. Of course, sometimes that's not possible, they may not want to do it or we're not seeing positive progress and it's better to change, but that's been the exception and not the rule.

DR: What is the average period in which you hold your investments?

OB: Generally about 3.3 years.

DR: Where do investment opportunities typically come from? Investment bankers? Your own contacts?

OB: Relationships, our own contacts, but they're all banks. They're investment bankers, ultimately, but they really come through the industry.

DR: How long does the due-diligence process typically take before you decide, "Yes, I'm going to do this" or "No, I'm not going to do it"?

OB: It used to take three months. Now it takes three weeks. But we have a history of knowing the company, hopefully for years and maybe even a decade or more.

DR: What percentage of deals that you review do you actually do?

OB: The ones that we do due diligence on, 75 percent. The ones that we review, 25 percent.

DR: Does a decision have to be unanimous within your investment committee to go forward?

OB: In practice, yes. We look for that unanimity. If somebody is really upset about it, we try not to do the deal.

DR: Have you had regrets about deals you've passed on?

OB: My biggest regret is that we did not have enough money to pursue almost every deal we seriously reviewed. They have almost all gone up in value. Enterprise software has been booming in recent years. So I wish we have been able to do more deals.

DR: How long before you decide you need to move drastically on a deal when it's not working? Do you wait a year to replace a CEO or do something different?

OB: We have waited too long, typically. Part of that is our culture of trying to work with existing management. We've gotten better at that over time. Sometimes it would take us two years, which is way too long. Now? Maybe nine months.

DR: How important are ESG factors if you're looking at a potential acquisition? Do you have the capability to add ESG resources and assistance?

OB: Yes and yes. Sometimes we might like a company's basic product, but the company is not really very innovative or able to attract creative young people—keys to a strong company. We can help that type of company, and we do. We can add ESG capabilities, for instance.

DR: During COVID, you raised nearly $23 billion in new capital across three funds. How hard was it to raise that much capital during COVID? Did you have to physically meet anybody?

OB: We didn't physically meet a single person, and it was surprisingly easy. The numbers were good, the existing relationships are good, and that's what drove it. But what surprised me the most, at the beginning of COVID, the way LPs behaved even at the riskiest time was unbelievable. A lot of them learned their lesson from the financial crisis. They did their best work ever, because they were more precise. They really dug in, but they did the work. They didn't panic, and they can get through.

DR: Was it difficult to operate the firm during COVID?

OB: Not at all. That's the part that I'm the most proud of. Thinking through how we go back to work now, it's not a black-and-white world, in my view. It's just a better world.

A couple of factors play to our advantage. One is that we have a relatively small investment team of about 40 people, and we have kept it that way, on purpose, for a host of reasons. Leadership could call in the same time zone, in the same city. We didn't have a Miami office then. We would go on walks in the afternoon at 6 p.m., and I was able to talk to every single associate in an hour walk, see how they were doing, so that part was good.

The second part is that our culture is good and we have good people. There's no personal agenda. People knew what they needed to do.

The third thing is the way we're organized. We are organized, even in the flagship fund, into discrete deal teams in each software category. We have a team that does real estate software, automotive software, cybersecurity, infrastructure. That meant that every person knew exactly what they needed to do. We don't need to direct traffic. People could just be so productive immediately.

It was our most productive year of returning money back, a record year and a record year of new investments. In the past 12 months, we invested $8 billion in a great number of new transactions. Why? Because people weren't on planes going everywhere and sitting in meetings that were not helpful. So we could get more done.

DR: How has the buyout world changed since you began in it?

OB: It's so much better now. It's bigger, it's more competitive. It's showing its great relative performance versus other types of ownership. It's innovating, with long-dated funds, core funds, SPVs [special purpose vehicles] to keep companies longer. It's a reflection of the innovation that's happening to cope with innovations in tech, new ways of doing deals. If you step out of the deal business for six months, you're really behind because you missed the new innovations of how deal participants behave on a transaction.

DR: What changes will we likely see in the future?

OB: I think you'll see people creating or approaching what I call whitespace—areas that are not touched by buyouts now, areas in which we are not currently investing—and crushing it. We have a whitespace we're trying to develop, which is the really large software buyout. We're almost there. In the last nine months, we've been doing that, in companies like Proofpoint that we bought for $12 billion, RealPage that we bought for $10 billion. Those deals are much more of a negotiated transaction. If you extrapolate four years from now, if those software companies are growing 20 percent per year and purchase-price multiples don't go down, these companies are going to be twice the size and value they are today. Where's the capital in the world to be able to do that? People want to push that. It's going to be fascinating how these whitespaces get captured by our entrepreneurial community.

DR: If someone wants to become a buyout investment professional, what's the best training and educational background, in your view?

OB: I'm a huge fan of a liberal arts educational background. In general, I think it makes individuals broader, more thoughtful, more worldly.

DR: What did you major in?

OB: I did political science and I added economics. I started in history. It just makes you a more interesting, thoughtful person. It makes you think a little deeper. I enjoyed my law school background because of that. I still read Supreme Court opinions, and they're fascinating to me.

At the same time, you've got to learn how to read financial statements. You need to get trained on accounting somehow to be able to track the flows of money and deals in a company and make a judgment.

DR: What are the skills that a top-notch buyout professional possesses?

OB: Salesmanship and the power of persuasion. I think that's why we see quite a bit of people with law school backgrounds in the industry. The rest of the stuff isn't that hard.

DR: What are the qualities that will not be helpful in the buyout world?

OB: While buyout is a control business, in this world we're living in, trying to control is not doable. You're going to get super frustrated. You can't control people. You can own a lot of the company, but it doesn't work like that anymore, especially now. People who want things to be completely organized and process-oriented, it's hard for them, because this is such an unstructured business, and deals are a messy, unstructured world.

DR: If someone wants to invest in buyouts, how would you recommend that they select one or more firms? What should they be careful to avoid?

OB: It's been said so much, but you have to go with the best culture that's a good fit for you. If you're working with good people, where you feel at home and you feel comfortable, that would be my number one thing. I would avoid firms that are not performing. It is a momentum business. Once you start not performing, the firm doesn't work for anybody. I would look at performance and culture.

DR: With your success, you have become actively involved in the philanthropic world, and started your own foundation. What are the areas of your greatest passion in philanthropy?

OB: I was involved in philanthropy on personal causes before, but once Hurricane Maria happened we started a relief mission on day two of the hurricane to small towns around Mayagüez, where I'm from. The catalyst for getting involved was a town called Lajas. The mayor told a reporter, then it got back to me, that he had a shelter with 35 people that had a day-and-a-half supply of food and water. I knew that the government of Puerto Rico wasn't going to get there. FEMA was going to get there ultimately, but not in a day. I told the reporter, "Let him know that we're going to be at this airport in a day and a half." We loaded up a plane with a bunch of food and water and IVs and other things, hydration, formula, whatever, to just keep them going for that time. When we landed in that place, I said, "I've never done this before. I wonder what I'm going to see. I wonder how many other groups are here. There's got to be something." There was nobody there, and I was like, "Wow."

My learning from that was not to assume someone will step in. If you care about a cause or issue you need to do something about it, because no one else is going to do anything about it.

There were a bunch of other local heroes that were doing work and helping people, and then we started relief missions to Puerto Rico out of Fort Lauderdale until more institutionalized help came. Once I was there, I encountered a bunch of young people, particularly in sales, and they would approach me: "I have a new baby. I'm a salesperson, I went to school here, and I can't do business because the communications are down. I can't make any money." There's a lot of hardworking, honest people there. I remembered them. I got in touch with my high school friends. I said, "I'm going to stay here from the philanthropy side." We formed the Bravo Family Foundation, mainly focused on Puerto Rico.

Puerto Rico is one of the most unequal places in the world in terms of wealth. It's a place that doesn't work, partly because of that. We provide meaningful opportunities for young adults for both personal and professional growth.

DR: Have you relocated to Florida from California to be closer to Puerto Rico?

OB: I am an East Coast person at heart. I feel a lot more at home here, and it's close to Puerto Rico. It's a new thing. We're trying to do things differently as well at Thoma Bravo.

DR: Any regrets as you look back on your career? Any regrets about not pursuing a professional tennis career?

OB: Man, how can I have any regrets? Look at the luck. Software and private equity over the last 25 years, you couldn't be in a better place. I met so many good people, got to travel around the world, want to do it even more.

On the professional tennis career, I would have loved, now that I look back on it, to have made it into the qualifying rounds. I would have never made it into the main draw, but to make it into the qualifiers of Wimbledon or the US Open, now that I'm old, I would have loved that.

I was at Wimbledon three years ago, and I was in the players' area, and I have a friend who's a coach of one of the players. He said, "Do you have your rackets here with you?" I said no. He had a racket. He goes, "I got you these grass court shoes. We're going to go hit on the court during the tournament," and I stepped onto one of those grass courts. It was the first time I hit at Wimbledon. I remember I texted my mom. I was like, "I made it. I made it in a different way, but I'm here. I'm touching the holy grass. I did it."

DR: Now the players who are better than you, they're all coming to you for jobs?

OB: The ones who were really good have a lot of money, but yes, we can help with that.

Distressed Debt

BRUCE KARSH

Co-founder and co-chairman, Oaktree Capital Management

> *"To be a successful distressed-debt investor, you have to be unemotional and contrarian, because your job is to buy at the height of fear and panic."*

In the late 1970s, a few investors began buying companies using a great deal of debt. The early investments of this type—known as leveraged buyouts—would typically have just 1–5 percent of the purchase price be the "at-risk" capital, or equity. The 95–99 percent of the purchase price that was borrowed was debt, secured typically (and legally) by the company's assets.

The novelty of leveraged buyouts, or LBOs, was that the lenders of the debt—typically banks or insurance companies—knew that the intrinsic value of the assets might not be worth enough to repay the loan, but the cash flow or profits from the company would, by contrast, be enough to repay the loan in time, assuming the company did not go bankrupt.

Most of these early buyouts worked quite well, and the returns on the equity were enormous, for the equity component was quite small and the leverage was quite high. However, some of these early buyouts did not work out—perhaps because the economy turned down or the business stopped growing, and the cash flow thus could not support the debt.

To avoid those challenges, after a good many highly leveraged buyouts did not work in the late 1980s and early 1990s, lenders to buyout investments required much more equity to be invested. Today a buyout might have 30–60 percent of the purchase price in one type or another of equity (or truly "at-risk" capital).

One of the lessons of failed buyouts was that those investors (few in number at first) with the courage to buy the defaulted (or anticipated-to-default) debt at a discount actually made attractive returns as the "failed" buyout turned around, and the debt became worth much more than had been the case at the time of the bankruptcy.

And so grew a whole new investment category—distressed debt.

This is the category where investors purchase debt (typically but not always in buyout transactions)—ranging from the most secure, senior debt to the least secure, junior debt—in anticipation that the underlying equity will at some point be impaired, if not eliminated. If that occurs, the debt owners will have an opportunity to own part or all of the failed company, for their debt will be swapped for equity in the restructured company in a bankruptcy court proceeding or out-of-court restructuring process. Senior debt is the most secure debt in a buyout—debt that must be paid before any other debt or any equity is paid from available proceeds; it is usually thought at the outset of an investment that, in the event of a business problem or restructuring, there will be sufficient assets to repay the entire senior debt from the company's assets. Junior debt is paid after the senior debt is paid, and it is at greater risk of not being fully repaid.

The reason why this type of investing—investing in a company's "distressed" debt—has grown so large is that 1) there are now an enormous number of buyout transactions; 2) a portion of these transactions—even with larger equity components—will not work as originally intended, meaning the equity and debt will be worth less than was anticipated at the inception of the buyout; and 3) the owners of this kind of debt have proven in recent decades that outsized returns can be achieved by a) exchanging their debt for equity and then helping the restructured company, often with new management in place, grow in value as the original equity investors had expected to do; or b) selling when the market for the distressed debt recovers.

Investors in this area generally buy debt at deeply discounted prices, and they may buy even more if the price continues to go down. Their view is that the debt—which can be bought and sold in public and private markets quite readily—will in time be exchanged for equity in a restructured company, and that equity will in time exceed the cost of the debt that was purchased. In some cases, the discounted debt will simply recover in price and trade back to par.

Over the past few years, with generally robust economies and debt markets, distressed-debt opportunities have not been as plentiful as during the Great Recession. But these opportunities will inevitably return in due course as interest rates increase, economic growth slows, and easy-money policies are reversed. That phenomenon began in 2022, and more distressed-debt investing can be expected in the foreseeable future.

This is clearly not an investment area for the inexperienced or unsophisticated, for it is highly technical and governed by often arcane rules and practices. For that reason, a knowledge of the intricacies of buyouts, debt, bankruptcy, and out-of-court settlements is required to be successful. And those who invest in this area generally have to be prepared for contentious negotiations, extensive litigation, and some adverse publicity, as the various parties often argue their cases in public settings (like courts). But the rewards (in the form of attractive returns) can be quite high.

To put distressed-debt investing into context, consider this example:

Acme Manufacturing is purchased in a buyout for $100 million, with $40 million in equity. A bank has provided senior bank debt of $30 million. This debt is secured by the buildings and manufacturing machinery, and any intellectual property or other tangible assets of Acme, which are thought to be worth $30 million. If Acme went bankrupt, the bankruptcy court would require the senior bank debt to be paid in connection with a restructuring of the company or the assets would be sold in liquidation, with the proceeds used to repay the bank.

The buyout is also financed with $30 million of high-yield bonds, but the assets of Acme are only worth $30 million, all of which would go to the bank to pay off its loan in the event of a bankruptcy. So the high-yield debt is not certain to be repaid in a bankruptcy proceeding, unless the value of the company's assets increases substantially. For that reason, the bonds will offer their purchasers a higher interest rate than the bank will get on its loan, but with less certainty of being repaid.

If Acme does poorly as a buyout, and the company's ability to survive as an ongoing entity is in question, the high-yield bonds will no doubt trade below their initial price of par.

If the bonds trade below their initial value — $30 million — distressed-debt investors may well buy the bonds. If, for example, they trade at $15 million of value (or half the face amount), a distressed-debt buyer may conclude that 1) the company will turn around and the bonds will ultimately return to their par value of $30 million (in which case the purchase will have been at half the bonds' ultimate value); or 2) the company will go bankrupt in time, and in a bankruptcy the $30 million of bonds might be exchanged for a significant portion (and perhaps 100 percent) of the equity in a restructured company. The distressed-debt investor may be pleased with this result, having concluded that such a possibility will yield an attractive return (well above the amount invested) as the restructured company moves forward with a balance sheet less burdened by debt and perhaps a new and better management team. The result for the distressed-debt investor may well be an even higher return than would have been received had the high-yield bonds been repaid at par.

This is an oversimplification of the distressed-debt investor perspective.

Over the past quarter century, one of the leading firms in the distressed-debt area has been Oaktree Capital Management, a Los Angeles–based firm founded in 1995 by Howard Marks and Bruce Karsh. Together they have been a remarkable team. Bruce is the chief investment officer and has overseen the extraordinarily successful distressed-debt investment activity; Howard has been the face of the firm, dealing with investors and media, and responsible for overall investment philosophy and firm culture.

As the face of Oaktree, and as the author of legendary memos to the firm's investors and highly respected books on investing, Howard is no doubt the better known of this unique duo. He is nearly 10 years Bruce's senior and was the person who hired Bruce at Trust Company of the West (TCW) in 1987 and then suggested to Bruce that they leave TCW and start Oaktree (now part of a larger publicly traded investment firm, the Toronto-based Brookfield). I have interviewed Howard on a number of occasions, and I have always finished each interview realizing how little I really know about the investment world compared to him.

But I thought it would be interesting to interview Bruce for this book, for he has rarely given a public interview, and he is someone I have come to know and greatly respect over the past two decades. Bruce and I served for about a decade together on the Duke University Board of Trustees, and our family investment offices have worked together on a number of projects.

Bruce is also one of the most self-effacing great investors I have ever met. He does not really like to talk about what he has achieved or to focus any attention on himself. But his record is unmatched, and he is a true legend in the arcane area of distressed-debt investing—and in many ways a real pioneer in that world. Bruce does more than distressed-debt investing, but that is where I wanted to focus our discussion, for that is the area he helped to build into an investment category. I interviewed Bruce virtually on June 16, 2021.

DAVID M. RUBENSTEIN (DR): You are widely considered to be one of the most successful and respected investors in distressed debt, among other areas. What exactly is distressed debt?

BRUCE KARSH (BK): The term "distressed debt" refers to the debt or other obligations (for example, trade claims) of a company that has either failed to pay interest or principal when due or that investors expect to default in the future. The holder of that debt or obligation often is highly motivated to sell.

That's the narrow definition. Over the years, we've broadened the definition of distressed opportunities well beyond that to encompass other kinds of investments, including purchases of real assets at distressed prices or from financially distressed sellers.

DR: What exactly does a distressed-debt investor do? Does it buy the debt of a company at a discount and sell when the value increases? Wait for a court or out-of-court restructuring, when a debt becomes the equity? Get involved with the restructuring itself? Do you just sit there and wait or do you get involved in negotiating?

BK: Different distressed-debt investors do different things. Since we started our first fund in 1988, we were among the largest investors in distressed debt and very quickly became the largest in the business. When you're that sizable, you tend to have the largest debt positions and therefore you don't really think about trading.

There are hedge funds out there that do trade actively in distressed debt, but our strategy was very simple. We wanted to become the largest creditor, and we wanted to become actively involved in the bankruptcy process. We wanted to influence what the plan of reorganization ultimately looked like. In some cases we would create big equity stakes for our investors and stay involved with the company. In a subset of those cases, we would also put in new management teams. It of course depends on the situation, but our favorite investments were those where we took large equity stakes and became actively involved.

There were other situations where the debt we bought at a discount was exchanged for a package of cash, restructured debt instruments, and/or equity securities. In many of those cases, we would simply sell the restructured securities in a relatively short period of time after the reorganization or bankruptcy ended.

If you look at our history of investments—and we've made over a thousand investments since 1988—the ones that have produced the largest profits, the highest internal rates of return (IRR), and the highest multiples of invested capital (MOIC), would be those where we've created the largest equity stakes.*

DR: How long does a distressed-debt investor typically need to hold on to an investment, and what type of returns are you typically seeking?

BK: A distressed-debt investor can hold on to something for 30 days or up to 10 years. It depends on the nature of the investor and how the company performs. Our base case is to be involved through the reorganization process. It generally takes about two to three years from the time we start buying the debt securities until the end of the bankruptcy or reorganization. When we receive large equity stakes in a restructured company, however, we have at times held those stakes for five years or even longer.

DR: The type of return you're typically seeking is what?

---

* In the world of private investments, there are typically two basic ways to measure an investment's success. The IRR is the annual percentage by which the investment's value increases; an investment of $1 on January 1, 2022, that is worth $2 on January 1, 2023, would be a 100 percent IRR. In that example, the MOIC would be 2x the invested equity.

BK: It has changed dramatically over the course of my career. During the years I invested at TCW, from 1988 to 1995, we generated a gross IRR of over 31 percent on all 160 investments we made. And our gross multiple of invested capital (MOIC) was approximately 2.3 times the $1.7 billion of capital deployed. Gross realized profits were $2.5 billion versus less than $0.3 billion of realized losses. Those were the halcyon days. There were plenty of great opportunities and little in the way of competition. Interest rates were considerably higher in those days, and the distressed-debt area was much more inefficient then.

Today interest rates are near zero. Due to the outsized returns we and others garnered over the years, there's considerably more competition and the area is much better known and understood. Sellers today aren't as unsophisticated as they used to be. As a result, we'll gladly accept a 15-20 percent gross return these days if we think the risk is low, but we generally hope for 20-plus percent.

DR: In recent years, with the economy being relatively strong in the US for some time, has there been much distressed debt? If not, what do distressed-debt investors do during this time? If there is a fair amount of this type of debt, is it typically from buyouts that did not work out?

BK: Let me first give you some historical perspective. I started investing in 1988, and the first downturn was 1990–92. That was a time when we were buying in large part the defaulted debt of failed buyouts. That was the prime era for doing so, because so many buyouts had been done in the 1980s that were highly leveraged and ill advised.

In the early '90s, real estate values also took a plunge. S&Ls [savings-and-loan associations] were taken over by the RTC [the Resolution Trust Corporation], while the FDIC took over failed banks. Both institutions proceeded to sell off real estate–related assets. When that opportunity arose, we began purchasing mortgages at deep discounts, often buying from the RTC or FDIC. And in some of those cases, we ended up foreclosing on the underlying collateral and owning the real estate, creating the assets at a substantial discount to their real worth.

Those were the types of investments we were making until the recovery took hold in the mid-1990s and up until the next great buying opportunity, which was in 1997-98. During that latter period, there was an Asian currency crisis and the default of one of the country's largest hedge funds, Long-Term Capital Management. These events created significant dislocations in the capital markets, leading to attractive opportunities for distressed-debt buyers.

During the Asian crisis, we focused on buying so-called Yankee bonds—bonds issued by Asian companies that were denominated in dollars. We were able to purchase the debt of financially solvent Asian companies at deep discounts without assuming any foreign currency risk. I recall buying a Samsung Electronics bond back in 1998 at a 20 percent yield to maturity. Even back then, Samsung was one of the most dominant companies in Korea, and their dollar-denominated bonds were yielding 20 percent. The bonds of other Asian companies were even cheaper. But in 1997–98, that was the golden opportunity.

Another outsized opportunity set for us was the tech, media, and telecom (TMT) meltdown during 2000–02. When the tech bubble burst, the valuations of equities in TMT tumbled, and the prices of many TMT bonds traded at deep discounts. That was also the period of corporate scandal—Enron, WorldCom, and Adelphia. There was intense skepticism about whether managements were reporting financial results correctly, particularly in the wake of the Enron bankruptcy.

Given all that, and given the plethora of defaults and bankruptcies and the fear of many more on the way, there were terrific opportunities for distressed-debt investors. I remember that period fondly because we were able to buy a huge amount of public debt at 40 to 50 cents on the dollar. In some cases, the issuers of the bonds were actually rated investment grade [companies that have strong credit ratings and are generally considered to be safe investments] or had recently been downgraded from that status.

At that time, investment-grade bondholders were very unsophisticated and, if there were downgrades (or even the fear of one), they were likely to sell the bonds. But there were precious few buyers of downgraded TMT bonds and therefore a significant imbalance between supply and demand created exceptional buying opportunities.

We believed the bonds we purchased during that time period would never default, and we were right. In retrospect, it was like shooting fish in a barrel for those distressed-debt investors brave enough to step up and buy those bonds.

During the early 2000–02 period, there were a few buyouts that went awry, and the opportunities were mostly in the affected industries, telecom in particular. Once again, our investment record from that period will show that the largest profits and the highest MOICs were derived from investments in the debt of buyouts that didn't work out well.

Then, in the latter part of 2008, the Global Financial Crisis devastated the markets. That was mind-boggling in terms of all the distressed-debt opportunities that surfaced. In the last 15 weeks of 2008 alone, we invested approximately $400 million per week in all types of distressed debt, including of course buyouts that seemed overwhelmingly likely to fail. Values recovered quickly, however, in 2009, once the markets realized that most banks and other financial institutions weren't going to fail, causing investor psychology to recover.

So from the beginning of my career, you can see that we've invested in buyouts gone bad whenever available, but also in other kinds of distressed-debt opportunities that the times and unique circumstances presented. However, I always favored investing in buyout debt, whether already defaulted or trading at levels that implied a default was inevitable.

Typically, we would focus on companies owned by the best buyout firms, like Carlyle, KKR, Blackstone, and others. The top PE firms generally know what they're doing, pick good companies, and either have good management teams in place or make a change and put good managers in to run their companies. If these buyouts go bad, it's generally because there's too much debt on the company or some other short-term problem that came out of the blue. But typically the value of these companies recovers well, and thus these have historically been my preferred distressed-debt investment opportunity.

DR: The most recent economy has been pretty good. What are you doing now?

BK: In March 2020, when the markets realized that the pandemic would have a dramatic impact on economies around the world, there was a bear market in equities that lasted for 34 days, and then a recession for three months. We were extraordinarily active, and fortunate to have significant capital on hand for distressed-debt investing when the pandemic hit, and we were able to raise the biggest distressed-debt fund in history—$16 billion—immediately afterward. My group—we call it the

Global Opportunities Group—deployed a total of $14 billion in 2020, with $3.6 billion of that invested during March through June, the height of the pandemic panic. That was the most our group had deployed in any 12-month period, surpassing the previous record set during the Global Financial Crisis in 2008–09, when we invested over $11 billion in the 12 months after Lehman Brothers filed for bankruptcy.

Ever since the S&P [Standard & Poor's 500 index] bottomed at the end of March 2020, the equity markets have essentially gone straight up, with very minor corrections along the way. The US economy is firing on almost all cylinders, fueled by the substantial fiscal and monetary stimulus that's been unleashed over the past year and a half. Needless to say, defaults in the leveraged loan and high yield bond markets are at historically low levels, and so is the incidence of distress in this country. So what is there to do? The answer is that there are always US industries and companies needing capital for one reason or another. The other outlet for capital deployment is outside the US, and we have teams dedicated to finding opportunities in Asia and Europe, which they have done.

We're searching the globe for distressed-debt opportunities that can yield attractive returns but that also provide the downside protection we demand in all our investments. The Opportunities Group has had a very productive team based in London for over fifteen years that sources opportunities mostly in western Europe. Europe has historically operated on a bit of a different economic cycle than the US from a timing perspective, as it tends to lag our country both in terms of the economic recovery and the distressed-debt opportunity. In the last five years, Oaktree has also built out a strong group in Asia, and that team has been very active helping us find attractive investments in China and India over the past 12–18 months.

The other thing that we've done is in essence expand the definition of distressed debt to include opportunistic direct loans. For example, we've made loans at high rates of return to companies that need capital to grow. The borrowers are not "distressed"—they're not over-leveraged or facing imminent defaults—but they may be technology companies or startup entities where their equity cost of capital is higher than the rate at which we would lend them capital.

DR: When you buy distressed debt, are you typically buying a company's senior debt, which has a better chance of being repaid, or the company's junior debt, which is not secured by assets and is thus a bit riskier?

BK: There are different ways to play it. When I started out in 1988, the idea was that we would buy high-yield bonds (i.e., junior debt) that went bad. About a year or two later, when banks were forced to sell loans at discounts, our funds at TCW were among the first and ultimately the biggest buyer of those bank loans (i.e., senior debt) in the country. I think it's fair to say that we pioneered that.

As a lawyer, I believed it was a competitive advantage to understand and feel comfortable in a legal process when others might not, particularly in the early days of my career in distressed-debt investing. Owning senior secured debt provided creditors with a commanding position in the bankruptcy, so I actually favored those as our preferred investment. But there were certain times, particularly at the height of a panic or sell-off, and usually at the nadir of an economic cycle, where I felt it made sense to wade deeper down in the capital structure and buy more junior or subordinated debt.

At a time like this, where distressed-debt investors with return expectations like ours generally can't buy senior secured debt because the yields are too low, there is no choice but to focus on more junior debt. Either that or find ways to originate senior loans in situations that don't fit the classic definition of distressed debt but still provide acceptable returns with the risks well under control.

DR: Do you sometimes find yourself owning so much of the debt that it gets exchanged for control of the equity of the restructured company? Did that not happen with the Tribune Company when it went bankrupt about 14 years ago? Do you then run the company yourself, or do you try to sell your position as quickly as possible?

BK: There are times when we would run the company ourselves, and in those cases, like PE firms, we would be actively involved on the board of directors and select management teams. The Tribune buyout and subsequent bankruptcy worked out well for us, principally because we bought the debt so cheaply and therefore created our equity stake at such a low cost basis. Once we took control of the company and I became chairman of the board of directors, we quickly decided to spin off the newspapers (the *Chicago Tribune* and the *Los Angeles Times*, among others) into a separate public entity, which turned out to be a good decision. We kept the local TV stations and digital assets until the newly renamed company, Tribune Media, was bought by Nexstar Media Group in 2019. Tribune was a case where we held onto our equity stake for nearly 10 years but still managed to generate a respectable IRR in excess of 15 percent and made close to $1 billion in profits on the investment.

A deal I'm even more proud of than Tribune is Charter Communications, a large US cable company. In that situation, we specifically targeted junior debt with the intent to create a large equity stake in the restructured company, which is exactly what occurred. Like Tribune, I joined the board of directors.

When our Oaktree funds sold the last of our equity position in 2014, the Charter investment produced the largest profit the Global Opportunities Group had realized on a single company up to that point—a little over a billion dollars. We were very proud of the management team that the Charter board had recruited and placed in charge of running the company—a world-class CEO and CFO who are still in place. In the case of Charter, we held our stock for approximately five years.

There are limits to what we will do. I'm perfectly happy having Oaktree funds hold equity for a long time, perfectly happy with Oaktree professionals joining boards of directors, and okay with changing management teams when needed, but we're not going to send Oaktree people in to actually run companies.

DR: Many would say that those who do distressed debt are tough, mean people who are yelling and screaming at everybody. You're a laid-back, easygoing guy. How did you get into this business, and how can you be so nice about things?

BK: When I worked in the mid-1980s for Eli Broad [a leading Los Angeles–based businessman], I was exposed to the distressed-debt area and thought, given my background as a lawyer, I would be the perfect person to lead an effort like this. I also saw craziness happening in the LBO [leveraged buyout] market in 1986–87, and that's when I approached Howard Marks at TCW and suggested that he hire me to develop and run this area for him.

I wanted to do it at TCW, even though Eli offered me the opportunity to do it at his insurance companies, because I wanted to have a premier money management firm sponsor and help me develop the business. I always had an eye on growing this business, and I always thought there would be a great opportunity to do so.

And, importantly, I felt that Howard would be a great partner and a huge help in growing the business if the investment returns were as attractive as I thought they could be. Needless to say, Howard has far exceeded my expectations both as a savvy business partner but even more so as a terrific person with whom to work.

The first fund, organized in 1988, was just shy of $100 million. The second fund and related accounts were established in 1990 and aggregated over $400 million in committed capital. Instantly our group at TCW became the 800-pound gorilla in distressed debt, and it just snowballed from there.

I had a long-term vision to grow this investment area, and I always thought it would be better to keep a low profile if I wanted to have large pension plans as clients and keep buying bad loans from banks. Pension plans are generally conservative organizations that don't want to read about messy bankruptcies, and banks certainly didn't want to read about outsized successes achieved at their expense when the "bad loans" they sold turned into profitable investments. And, as you know, this approach dovetailed nicely with my personality, as my nature is to maintain a low profile and not boast about personal or professional successes.

You're right that years ago the people doing bankruptcy investing were tough, blustery people who enjoyed yelling and screaming. I never yelled, ever. Back in the day, I would attend reorganization meetings of creditors, most of whom were work-out professionals at commercial banks, because that's who the largest creditors were then. It would do me no good to bluster and yell. I was focused on building relationships with them so that I could influence everyone involved to agree with me on what an attractive reorganization should look like. My mode was to do what came naturally to me, which was to be friendly and try to forge relationships. That helped with advancing the reorganizations and also helped me in the future, as the large creditors tended to be represented by the same people from the same financial institutions.

DR: You went to the University of Virginia Law School and then you went to practice law at O'Melveny & Myers in LA?

BK: Yes, and I met my wife of 42 years at UVA Law School, Martha Lubin Karsh, who was in the class below me. After graduating from UVA Law School in 1980, I first clerked for Justice Anthony M. Kennedy, when he served on the Ninth Circuit Court of Appeals, and then I joined O'Melveny & Myers in the fall of 1981. I practiced law at O'Melveny for approximately three and a half years.

DR: How did you happen to go to work for Eli Broad?

BK: It was a serendipitous set of events, really. Richard Riordan, who had been mayor of Los Angeles back in the 1980s, was a very successful and well-known venture capitalist, buyout professional, and head of an eponymous law firm called Riordan & McKinzie. Dick tried to hire me away from O'Melveny to join his law firm but I turned him down. Unbeknownst to me, he happened to be best friends with Eli Broad and mentioned my name to Eli as a bright young lawyer. Eli then called me and made me an offer to be assistant to the chairman of his company, Kaufman and Broad, which at the time owned a few large insurance companies (SunAmerica being the most prominent) and the largest homebuilder in California, KB Homes. The opportunity to work directly with Eli and to expand my horizons well beyond the practice of law was too good to pass up.

DR: You worked for Eli for how many years?

BK: I worked for Eli for two and a half years, and I remember that time fondly. Eli was a brilliant investor and businessman from whom I learned a great deal. I feel like, in essence, I earned my master's degree in business just by watching Eli in action and being by his side almost every day during that period of time.

DR: And then you decided to make a career out of distressed debt?

BK: Yes, it was during the time I worked for Eli that I came across the very first distressed-debt fund ever raised. It was sponsored by two true pioneers in the distressed-debt field, both of whom worked at Bear Stearns at the time—Randy Smith and Basil Vasiliou. They were attempting to raise a $50 million fund, I believe, and Eli asked me to look at it for his portfolio. I was already familiar with distressed debt and had helped Eli's insurance companies evaluate the debt and equity of Johns Manville, a premier building materials company that filed for bankruptcy due to massive asbestos litigation. I recall looking at Smith and Vasiliou's fund and thinking it was an unusual and innovative investment activity.

So I recommended it to Eli but he opted to pass on it for various reasons. However, I kept thinking about that fund, particularly as the leveraged buyout mania of the 1980s got crazier and crazier. I thought a recession would one day surface and create a flood of defaults and bankruptcies and an exceptional investment opportunity in distressed debt. That's when I decided to approach Howard to help me establish a distressed-debt fund at TCW. Howard liked the idea, as well as my pedigree and background, and hired me to do it.

DR: That was about doing a fund at TCW to buy distressed debt? You did that from 1987 until 1995?

BK: Yes. I joined TCW in 1987, initially helping the High Yield group under Howard's wing with their "homegrown" problem credits. It took us about a year to raise the first distressed-debt fund in 1988, and once that fund was formed, I spent 100 percent of my time working on that fund and then successor funds at TCW. I did that until April of 1995, when we started Oaktree Capital Management.

A key element in forming Oaktree was an agreement by TCW to continue to allow the $2.6 billion in distressed-debt funds that we had established there to be sub-advised and managed by us while we worked at our new company, Oaktree.

DR: Your initial capital to build Oaktree came in from the commitment you had from TCW to fund part of your business?

BK: In a way, yes—indirectly. We capitalized Oaktree with $10 million of our own money, and that first year our new company was cash-flow positive, in no small measure because of the credibility we had as the largest distressed-debt manager in the world owing to those TCW assets.

DR: When you started Oaktree, how many firms specialized in distressed-debt investing?

BK: When I started in '88, it was a cottage industry. There were only a few. The recession in 1990–92 and the incredible returns we were able to achieve brought in other players. By '95 when we started Oaktree there were maybe 10-20 firms of any real consequence.

DR: When a buyout is announced, do you look at it and say, "Maybe I should be ready to buy the bonds when they start sinking"? Or do you wait until they start sinking before you do something?

BK: The latter. We start focusing on the buyouts when there appears to be a real prospect of a default and/or bankruptcy. Sinking trading prices of the bonds give that signal.

DR: Is it disconcerting that your investment thesis depends on somebody else failing? Is it hard to be friendly with people in the buyout world when you're going to buy their debt at a discount?

BK: I never want to crow about someone's mistake or talk in the press about our returns at the expense of any buyout firm. As you know, a buyout firm can have a failed investment or two and still produce a solid overall fund result for their investors. My philosophy is that it's a long ball game, and I try hard to maintain good relations with my friends in the buyout business.

DR: Speaking of that, you are not as well-known as your partner, who is very visible. Why have you decided not to be that visible?

BK: First, let me emphasize that I've got a partner who's incredibly gifted in terms of his communication skills, both written and verbal, as you know well. It makes perfect sense for Howard to be very visible, and it helps Oaktree enormously.

Second, I never wanted a lot of publicity. It suits my personality to stay out of the limelight. And I feel fortunate to have a partner who's great with the press and on TV, and is happy to do so, which obviates the need for me to be visible.

And, as I mentioned before, the initial reason I kept a very low profile was business-related. When I started at TCW, distressed-debt investing was a new area, with some controversy attached to it. I wanted mainstream investors to endorse the field, and I knew they wouldn't do so if there were very public fights, litigation or, worst of all, liquidations. We've always tried to avoid company liquidations. What Howard and I would tell the mainstream institutions is, "We didn't create the problem—we're going to solve the problem. We're going to take debt that should not have been debt and turn it back into equity and restore jobs and restore companies to viability." That's a good pitch, and it really helped in the early days to bring the state and corporate pension plans into our funds as LPs.

DR: Does it help in this business to be known to be willing to be litigious?

BK: In my view it hurts you. There's precious little litigation we've ever been involved in. I always wanted our company to be known as the folks who would get people to settle, because I thought it was good for returns and good for the development and growth of the business. There are a few players who specialize in litigation. It may work for them, but it's not a great business model, in my opinion.

DR: What is the skill set that you think is helpful to being a successful distressed-debt investor? Intelligence, hard work, research skills, finance skills?

BK: I think you need all that, because at bottom we're value investors. To be a successful distressed-debt investor, you have to be unemotional and contrarian, because your job is to buy at the height of fear and panic. My antennae are always up and on the lookout for those times when fear and panic are present. It's almost always the optimal time to buy, and those are the periods I enjoy the most—deploying capital when I sense few other investors are buying and most are selling. After the Global Financial Crisis hit in 2008, it felt like the world was ending. An investor could say, "I'm going to wait, because things look too uncertain. It looks like the financial system is falling apart." At Oaktree we saw massive panic selling and instead bought well over $5 billion of distressed debt during the 14 weeks between the Lehman Brothers bankruptcy filing and year-end 2008. This was clearly our time—we just don't get that many great buying opportunities. Needless to say, when the markets recovered in 2009, it was a banner year for Oaktree and our Opportunities funds.

DR: As you look back on some of your best deals, which ones are you most proud of having done?

BK: I can't really pick out one or two deals that I'm most proud of from the thousand-plus investments we've made, so instead of individual deals, I would say I'm most proud of the fact that we picked the right time in the economic and distressed-debt cycles to raise our largest funds. Since we invested the largest funds in times when the supply of distressed debt was most plentiful, those funds sport the highest IRRs and MOICs among all of our funds. I don't think many other investment firms can make that claim.

Over the past 34 years, there have been several periods when the supply of distressed debt was not robust. The key is to try to have less capital at those times but also to make sure to have plenty of dry powder when the great buying opportunities appear, and they may only surface every five years or so. I'm proud that we've sized our funds well to fit the opportunity set.

And because we've done a superior job at sizing our funds, it's certainly had a positive impact on our overall track record. After 34 years of investing, our gross IRR is 22 percent per year, and that's mostly without help from leverage. Another source of pride is what we call our "batting average." As of year-end 2021, we had invested $53.4 billion in capital and generated $42.3 billion in gains, $33.6 billion of which was fully realized. At the same time, losses on that capital stood at only $4.5 billion, with only $2.7 billion of that realized.

DR: Nobody in the investment world makes every deal work out. You must have had one or two that did not work out. As you look back on those, what was the mistake you made, in hindsight?

BK: Of course I've made my fair share of mistakes during the past 34 years. I'd say the industry group that contributed the most to our losses is dry bulk shipping. Investing in the dry bulk shipping sector at a time I thought was perfect—in 2012–13 as day rates were bottoming out in the shipping world. Everything seemed right, as the global economy was recovering from the Global Financial Crisis and historically depressed day rates were rising strongly. We began buying boats at historically cheap levels and teamed up with a very successful Greek operator who invested alongside us.

Then, in 2015, China decided to throttle back on their purchases of iron ore and coal. China, being the biggest customer in dry bulk transport, had a huge impact on the market. When they started pulling back, rates just collapsed. I thought that the building of new boats would also collapse and the area would soon return to balance in terms of supply and demand.

What I didn't realize is that the entities that make ships are basically state-controlled, and they don't care what the rates are. They're making boats in large measure to create jobs, and so they just kept making boats, which elongated the down part of the cycle. That was something of a learning experience, and we're more careful today to think about the potential impact of governments on industries with significant governmental involvement.

It's only now, after six years, that we're starting to finally get an imbalance of demand over supply. As global demand has recovered from the pandemic and supply chains have restarted, dry bulk ships are in great demand. We've turned around a great deal of the unrealized losses recently because the economy is red hot and day rates have risen significantly, but we still have a way to go to break even.

DR: How do you disguise it when you're buying debt, if you do, to keep the market price from going up until you complete your buy?

BK: Over the years, we've developed incredibly strong relationships with certain Wall Street firms, and they are hesitant to give us up. We are one of the biggest fee-payers to many Wall Street trading desks, because we do so much trading in Oaktree overall. We've never really had problems getting our fair share of anything we want to get. Do other investors eventually hear what we're buying and sometimes ride along? Yes. It's part of the game.

DR: Do you see a wave of distressed-debt opportunities coming along in the next year or so as the economy slows down and the stimulus wears off?

BK: There's a huge amount of below-investment-grade corporate debt out there. The high-yield bond and leveraged loan markets are at the highest levels they've ever been, and private debt has skyrocketed in terms of volumes and popularity. At Oaktree we call that stacking the logs. They're all stacked and they're stacked really high.

The problem is seeing a spark that will begin the bonfire. I don't see it. The economy is way too strong. I don't see defaults being anywhere near levels that would be interesting for the next year or two.

I'm not expecting great things on the corporate-debt side in the US, unless there's some exogenous thing that comes out of the blue. I didn't predict the pandemic, but that created a terrific buying opportunity for us. And, of course, there's always a chance that the US Federal Reserve will become concerned enough about the growing inflationary threat that they tighten financial conditions to a level that will bring on the next downturn—and distressed debt buying opportunity.

DR: Do you recommend this area of investing to young professionals? What's the great pleasure of distressed-debt investing?

BK: Five or 10 years ago, children of friends of mine came to me and said they wanted to go to Wall Street. They asked me about distressed debt and other areas, and I said, "I would pass on Wall Street and go to Silicon Valley." That's where all the exciting things are happening, and if you've got the skill set, that's where you should be. If you want to be on Wall Street, I would point to private equity. Distressed debt is intellectually challenging and exciting, but it's highly cyclical, and there are times when you just have to be patient and try not to do stupid things, and that's not easy for everybody.

Venture Capital

MARC ANDREESSEN

Co-founder and general partner, Andreessen Horowitz;
co-creator of the Mosaic internet browser;
co-founder of Netscape

> *"It's fundamentally a game of outliers. The money is made on the aberrations."*

Today it is quite common for investors to provide funds for new companies whose founders might have a new concept or technology. The investors who provide funds at the outset of a company's start (before there are offices, customers, or many employees) are often called "angel investors." The investors who provide funds when a company has had something more than a concept in an entrepreneur's mind are often called "venture investors" or "venture capital investors."

In recent years, as the technology boom has transformed our lives, entrepreneurs like Bill Gates, Steve Jobs, Jeff Bezos, Larry Page and Sergey Brin, Mark Zuckerberg, and Elon Musk have become household names. Their products and services are ubiquitous and life-changing. The angel and venture capital investors have also become—in the investment community and beyond—household names, in part because of their sagacity in seeing value in startups and in seeing them through to IPOs, and in part because of their extraordinary wealth as well. (Venture capital investing has proven so profitable for the leading venture capitalists—who typically get a profit share, or carried interest, of 20 to 30 percent—that they now populate the Forbes 400 list alongside the leading entrepreneurs.)

That was not always the case. In the infancy of venture capital in the 1950s and 1960s, the concept of funding new companies—startups—from scratch was thought to be too risky, and there were few investors even willing to consider the concept.

In the 1990s, James Clark, the founder of Silicon Graphics, and a legend in the tech world, came to Carlyle's office seeking venture capital for a company he was planning to launch with Marc Andreessen, a recent college graduate. Apparently, while in college, Marc had helped to develop a way to navigate the internet, and the new company was going to commercialize this method in some ways that were not yet clear to my partners and me.

As I recall, we first wanted to understand what the internet was, and then we proceeded to ask why anyone would want to navigate it. When we got past that, we focused on our greater area of expertise—the cost of participating. The valuation for this new company with no revenues was to be over $100 million.

Being the brilliant investors that we were, we naturally said that was a ridiculous valuation for a completely new startup. So we passed. (We also passed when they returned with a below $100 million valuation.)

That company was Netscape. It was later sold to AOL for $4.2 billion, and Marc became the chief technology officer of AOL. I wish I had known at our first meeting precisely how much of a tech wizard Marc really was—or how much of a venture-investing wizard he would turn out to be.

After leaving AOL, Marc created, with Ben Horowitz, another technology company, Opsware, and later it sold to Hewlett-Packard for $1.6 billion. He then became a very active angel investor in Silicon Valley, investing in such companies as Twitter and LinkedIn. In 2009, Marc formed Andreessen Horowitz to enhance his venture capital investing and give investors a chance to invest alongside him and his partner. (Having learned from our earlier mistake, I told Marc at the outset that Carlyle would be pleased to buy a small minority stake in his firm, but he politely told us that he already had more than enough capital to get the firm going. It would have been a great investment.)

The firm has emerged in recent years as one of the leading venture capital firms in the country, with enormous successes in such companies as Lyft, Airbnb, Stripe, Groupon, and Zynga, and has been particularly prescient in its early investments in blockchain technology and cryptocurrencies. Coinbase was an enormously successful investment for the firm at the IPO valuation—perhaps on paper its most profitable investment. (The value of Coinbase and other crypto-related companies saw a large decrease in value in the tech correction of mid-2022.)

Beyond investment successes, Marc has also become a leader in the venture world as a commentator on and writer about technology and its benefits for society. Indeed, through his writings and speeches, he is a much more public figure than many of the other leading venture capital investors, certainly in the Silicon Valley area. As a result, he is one of the most influential and impactful individuals in the entire venture world.

I interviewed Marc for my *Bloomberg Wealth* show in person on June 22, 2021, at his offices in Menlo Park, California. We covered the venture landscape, and it was easy to see—again and up close—why he has become such a force in venture capital and technology.

DAVID M. RUBENSTEIN (DR): The venture capital world has been booming. I've never seen anything like this. Are venture capitalists smarter than they used to be? Why are such incredible profits being realized by venture capitalists now?

MARC ANDREESSEN (MA): One possibility is we've all gotten carried away again, the way we did in the late '90s, and things are too hot.

The other possibility is our society is going through a real technological transformation. It was already going through a transformation before COVID, and there's a good argument that the pandemic has accelerated that transformation. A lot of digital businesses have accelerated through COVID, and it feels like the world is going to change in some pretty fundamental ways coming out of COVID. In that case, you have these new tech companies driving this change and realizing the benefits.

DR: In the old days, venture capitalists would make money on maybe 10 percent of their deals and lose money on 90 percent. Now you seem to make money on everything. Does anything ever fail anymore?

MA: We made a commitment to our investors when we first raised our fund. I said, "Look, we're trying to get to the moon. Every once in a while, we're going to have rockets blow up on the launchpad and put a big crater in the ground."

The statistical layout of top-end venture capital, if you look at the 50-year history of it, is about a 50/50 success rate. Basically 50 percent of the companies make money, 50 percent of the companies lose money.

DR: It used to be the case that in a very successful deal, the venture capitalists might make four, 10, 15 times their money. Now you seem to make 500 times your money in some cases. For example, a deal that your firm did, Coinbase, seems to be one of the most successful venture deals of all time. [Coinbase went public on April 14, 2021, and rose that day to a value of over $100 billion; it has since gone to $15 billion as of June 1, 2022.] Was that obvious to you when you made the initial investment?

MA: We are 100 percent confident every time we make the investment that it's going to be a big company. We are wrong a lot of the time. There's a lot of twists and turns along the way. A huge part of it is the competence and capabilities of the founders and the CEO of the company. They deserve 99 percent of the credit when it works out.

DR: What is a Series A investment?

MA: Series A typically means first institutional money. It's like the first step towards being a serious business with a serious lead investor, with a serious board of directors, with a serious amount of money. There's a real commitment being made by everybody around the table that they're going to devote a lot of time and effort to making this thing work.

DR: When a firm like yours does a Series A round, you expect to do a Series B and then a Series C, and then typically you go public?

MA: Our goal whenever we back these companies is that we want them to become long-lived, enduring, independent, stand-alone institutions. That usually results in their going public at some point. Sometimes they go public after two rounds of financing or three rounds of financing. Sometimes these days they'll stay private for longer and raise five or six or seven rounds of private financing. The returns have gotten bigger. The wins have gotten bigger. The markets have gotten bigger. You've got 5 billion people on the planet now with smartphones that are networked together. You get one of these companies that has mass appeal, they can get really big.

It takes a long time to get that big. It takes a lot of money to get that big. But we have tech companies now that are worth more than

$1 trillion, which was inconceivable when I started in the industry. Some of these companies just end up raising a lot more money than the historical norms would suggest, and they stay private for longer.

DR: It seems as if all the big deals are coming out of Silicon Valley. What about Austin, Boston, New York City? Is Silicon Valley so far ahead that nobody can catch up?

MA: Pre-COVID, Silicon Valley had a powerful lock, in particular on the talent. Where is the newly minted MIT or Stanford or Berkeley grad who wants to be a part of the action and wants to be at the best companies, around the best people, going to go? Historically, most of those graduates would come to Silicon Valley. Just like if you want to be a filmmaker, you come to LA, or if you want to be a hedge fund manager, you go to New York. It's this superstar-city concept.

In the post-COVID world, that looks like it's changing pretty dramatically, because we've all gotten so much more used to this idea of remote work and distributed companies. So you see a lot more activity happening outside the Valley.

It's possible that there's a new Silicon Valley in Austin or Miami or whatever. It's also possible Silicon Valley just moves to the cloud. It's possible these companies shift to running online. Maybe they run without a central location. Coinbase just went public without a headquarters address.

DR: Has COVID changed the way people look at venture capital deals because you can do so many things remotely?

MA: We're at the beginning of a grand experiment, seeing how far we can push this whole idea of remote work. CEOs have lots of different views on how well remote work works. You've got CEOs like Reed Hastings and Tim Cook who are dismissive of it and think everybody should get back in the office. You have many other CEOs, especially young ones, who are like, "No, this is great. Let's not require everybody to come to San Francisco. Let's take advantage of all this talent all over the world and have these companies run virtually."

We have all these tools. We have videoconferencing and Slack and we have all these amazing capabilities now. We built the internet. Maybe it's time for business to move online.

DR: What about China and India? Are they great potential rivals of Silicon Valley, or they're not really going to be able to compete with what you do?

MA: China's been very impressive for the last 20 years or so. Like anybody, they have their own challenges. They don't have a perfect system, either. India has a bunch of companies that are doing really well or scaling. Both of those countries have vibrant ecosystems with a lot of very talented people.

DR: Do you invest there?

MA: We don't invest as much there. This is another pre-COVID/post-COVID thing. We, historically, view venture capital as sort of a craft business where you're hands-on with people whom you get to know well and you partner with for a long time.

In the past, we were worried about trying to do that remotely. In this new world, we have to revisit that assumption, because maybe remote is the default. That's one of the big open questions for how this whole industry's going to work.

DR: Let's suppose an entrepreneur says, "I've read about Andreessen Horowitz. I'd like them to back my company." How do they get you to back their company? Do they call you up? Do they knock on the door? They send you an email?

MA: It's a people business. It's a deep personal-connection business. A venture capital investment is the closest thing to a marriage that's not a marriage, because it's a 10- or 15- or 20-year relationship. Are we the kind of people they'll want to be in partnership with for a decade, and vice versa?

Typically, that starts with a warm introduction. It starts with a way to establish a personal connection where you have people vouching for each other.

DR: Suppose somebody is a terrific entrepreneur on paper, but they've never done this before. What's the likelihood that you would back somebody who has never done a deal before?

MA: If they've never founded a company before and they just have a plan, it's unlikely that they will raise top-end venture capital. However, once in a while, you get somebody who's not done it before but they've already built the product. The classic example of this would be Face-book. Mark Zuckerberg had already built Facebook at Harvard by the time he started the company. I had already built the Mosaic browser by the time I started Netscape. The Google guys had built the Google search engine at Stanford.

If you've already built the product, you have a calling card to be able to raise money, because you already have something that's real. The best thing to do as a first-time founder is build a product. Now, there's a chicken-and-egg thing there. You might need the money to build the product, and that's where people get stuck.

DR: You compete with a lot of other well-established firms in Silicon Valley. Do you say, "I don't want to go in if Sequoia's going in"? Or you don't mind being in bed with competitors?

MA: We end up cooperating a lot more than we end up competing. We love competing. We really like the fight. But you end up cooperating, because it's really up to the founders. The good founders choose their investors. They might choose us for one round. They might choose another venture firm for another round. You end up around the same table a lot of the time, working together.

DR: How do you assess what kind of profitability you want in order to decide how much you're going to put in and when you're going to do it?

MA: We do some quantitative modeling, especially later-stage. Is this the kernel of something that could grow into being something very important and very large? Almost every time that happens, you end up making a lot of money.

We focus a lot on this concept of importance. Are people going to find it inconceivable to live without this product? If we have that, then it's easy to build the spreadsheet. If we don't have that, then we would not do that deal.

DR: Let's suppose somebody comes in and they make a presentation and you, the founder of the firm, like it a good deal. Can you get out-voted by your colleagues or not?

MA: We run what we call a single trigger-puller system. Each general partner in our firm—we have about 22 right now—has an investment budget. And each of those general partners can make an investment decision without a vote. A lot of the best startup ideas don't fit in existing boxes. If you have a committee discussion process, you'll end up talking yourself out of some of the best deals.

DR: If somebody says, "I want you to do this," and you say, "I don't want to do that," can they forum-shop by going to your partners and saying, "Marc didn't like it but you might"?

MA: Yes, they can do that. Our basic model is that the GP, the general partner who's the closest to the domain, who understands the most about that market sector, should make that decision. That said, sometimes one partner doesn't like it, another partner likes it, they pick it up and do it. We do talk a lot. Every once in a while, entrepreneurs try to work around us.

DR: It's like a child with a parent. They forum-shop.

MA: Every once in a while. We tend to pick up on it when that happens.

DR: Let's suppose a proposal comes in and you see the fingerprints of another firm on it. Do you say, "You've been turned down by somebody else. We're not interested"?

MA: Not necessarily. Each top-end venture firm has its own bar. It has its own set of criteria for whether it thinks a deal should be done or not. The top-tier venture firms, as a group, have kind of a collective bar. Is a top-tier venture firm going to fund this company or not?

After you've been in the business for a while, you tend to have a sense of, "Okay, this is going to get funded by a top-end venture capital firm" or it's not.

If it is going to get funded by a top-end venture capital firm, and if my firm doesn't think it's a good idea, you do wonder who's right. The other firms are quite smart. This is one of the regular discussions we have. If another one of these top-end firms is interested in it, that might be a positive, substantive signal. If the other top-end firms have looked at it and all passed, that might be a substantive negative signal. That said, some of the best deals in history have been passed on by a large number of people. Uber was passed on by a very large number of venture capital firms.

Every once in a while, you get these outliers. It's fundamentally a game of outliers. The money is made on the aberrations. You want to be generally open-minded and humble about your conclusions about what all these different signals mean.

DR: For those who aren't experts, what is an angel venture capital investor?

MA: An angel typically means an individual with their own personal checkbook, as compared to a classic venture capital institutional investor that raises money from outside investors.

DR: You do angel investing at the firm, and you also do growth capital. Can you explain what growth capital is?

MA: Growth capital is funding the companies in their later stages of development, where the product's working, the business is working, and now the job of the company is to scale. Usually that means a big go-to-market expansion. It means hiring a big sales force, doing big marketing campaigns, or expanding international operations where you know you have a business that works. Growth capital substitutes for what used to be early IPOs.

DR: The theory used to be that after a Series A, Series B, maybe Series C, you go public. That was the Holy Grail. But now, some companies don't want to go public for many years. Some companies like Stripe are still not public. It has a $95 billion private market value (in the last venture rounds) but it is still not public. Why do some people not want to go public?

MA: The public market is complex, and it can be a hostile environment. Over time, the public market has gotten shorter- and shorter-term in nature. The marginal investor in the public market is interested in short-term performance. So you can end up with this tightly compressed time frame as a public company, where people are on you about what you're doing for them this quarter or this year. Some of these more aggressive entrepreneurs that have a 10- or 20-year vision want more flexibility in how they build their business.

DR: How do you and your partners keep in the deal flow?

MA: A lot of it is personal relationships, this extended network of people who are in this world, people we've known for a long time.

We have a big media operation at our firm. We just launched a new site called Future, which basically is devoted to all these ideas. We do a lot of interviews. We do a lot of podcasts. We do a lot of video. We put out a positive and constructive vision of the future of the tech industry and how entrepreneurship fits into that, and that tends to attract entrepreneurs.

DR: You wrote an article recently about how technology is something that we should be more thankful for, and that, at least in Washington, we beat up on tech companies. Your article's saying, "Look at all the wonderful things that happened in technology during COVID, including the vaccine." Can you elaborate?

MA: COVID was extraordinarily challenging and traumatic for a very large number of people. COVID's a bad-news story, and I'm not pretending otherwise.

That said, the expectation was that this was going to be a five-year slog. There was going to be profound economic damage, potentially another Great Depression.

Here we sit, 18 months later, and we're coming through it. A huge part of that is the vaccines. The most widely deployed vaccine in the US is the vaccine from Moderna. Moderna is a classic American biotech startup, with a new technology called mRNA, a breakthrough technology. It usually takes five years or 10 years or 20 years to develop a new vaccine, and they were able to do it in two days. That's an example of the kind of breakthrough innovation that's now coming out of this ecosystem we have in the US.

I also point to the role the internet played. Imagine going through COVID without the internet. Imagine going through it without Zoom and without Slack and WhatsApp and all of these new technologies. The experience of going through COVID, while it's been bad, it hasn't been nearly as bad as it would have been without modern technology.

DR: A famous economist, Herb Stein, once said, "If something cannot go on forever, it will stop." Do you worry that because the economy might soften at some point if interest rates are raised, or just because of the business cycle, the wonderful world of venture capital will slow down?

MA: It's a cyclical business. It has a history of boom/bust cycles, just like any other sector of the economy. That said, we do not have a great track record in our industry of predicting these cycles.

Most of how we either perform or fail to perform is micro, not macro, which is to say it's based on the success or failure of individual companies. If you look at the history of venture capital and startups, many of the best companies have been formed during the hot periods. But many of the companies have also been formed during the cold periods.

It's possible there's another cyclical boom-and-bust cycle coming. Our plan for that cycle would be to keep working with our existing companies, keep investing in new companies all the way through, and bet on these micro-level, fundamental, technological and economic changes that continue to happen.

DR: Sometimes people say that Silicon Valley venture capitalists have big egos and that they think they're masters of the universe. You haven't observed that?

MA: Not even a trace. I have no idea what they're referring to.

DR: Let's talk about your own background. You didn't come from the West Coast or the East Coast. You came from the middle of the country?

MA: Right. In my later years, I discovered I'm an archetype. Philo Farnsworth, the inventor of television, was a guy like me, grew up in the Midwest. We're tinkerers who end up coming to the coast. Robert Noyce, who was the founder of Intel and the father of the semiconductor industry, was another one of these. I encourage people to read about Bob Noyce and how he grew up in the cornfields in Iowa, tinkering with tractors, and then brought that ethos to what ended up becoming semiconductors. So I'm an example of that.

DR: You were a gamer? Did you produce any video games? What did you do as a young boy?

MA: I was a kid right when the personal computer was first coming out. In those days, you'd have the expensive personal computer, like the IBM PC, that we couldn't afford. But you did have these consumer PCs.

Remember the company Radio Shack? They had these computers that cost $200 or $300 at the time. They were real computers. You could program them and you could make games. They were powerful enough to build software, but they were also simple enough you could understand the entire machine. That was a key moment in the history of the industry, and I happened to hit that exactly right.

DR: Sometimes leading venture capitalists or tech people go to Stanford or MIT or Harvard or equivalent universities. You went to a very good university that wasn't as famous as those. But it had a great technology area in computers. Is that right? The University of Illinois.

MA: It had something very special. It was one of four universities at the time that were called National Supercomputer Centers. The National Science Foundation had basically decided to fund four major universities in the US with state-of-the-art computers. That also meant state-of-the-art networks. In those days, what's now known as the internet was known as the NSF Net. This is in the '80s and '90s. Illinois was one of the hubs of the NSF Net, which made it one of the hubs of the internet. So it turned out to be a great place for the kind of work that I do.

DR: You developed something called Mosaic. It was a way to navigate the internet. I remember you came to my office as a young man, and you were trying to convince us to invest in something that would commercially take advantage of the Mosaic system. Netscape was the company you were starting. You said it would help people navigate the internet. I remember our saying, "What is the internet? And why do we need to navigate it, anyway?" We chose not to invest. That was our big mistake. How did you hook up with Jim Clark [a Stanford computer scientist and entrepreneur] and how did you build Netscape?

MA: In those days, it was a given that there's no money to be made on the internet. Up until 1993, because it was taxpayer-funded, it was actually illegal to do business online. The crazy idea at the time was that there was a possibility here to be able to build businesses online. That was a new and radical idea when we first started doing it. Jim was a legendary founder in Silicon Valley. He founded what at the time was considered the best Silicon Valley company, called Silicon Graphics. They did the graphics technology that created movies like *Jurassic Park* and *Terminator 2*.

He had left his company and, in the time-honored tradition of Silicon Valley, decided to start a new company. He knew all these incredibly smart people but he had a nonsolicit agreement with his previous company. He quite literally needed fresh bodies to start a company with. A guy he worked with knew that I had just moved out to the Valley, and put the two of us together.

DR: Netscape boomed, and it ultimately was bought for $4.2 billion by AOL. You became the chief technology officer of AOL and moved to Washington, DC. Ultimately you came back to the West Coast to build a company called Opsware. Why did you leave AOL after the company you started was sold to them? And why did you come back to Silicon Valley?

MA: It's the entrepreneurial bug. Big companies are fantastic. Big companies do most of the big things in the world. They provide most of the products and services people use. But for the entrepreneurial personality, there is this tendency to say, "What's the next new idea?" A group of colleagues and I decided it was time to try something new.

DR: You came back. You started this company called Opsware with Ben Horowitz. And you ultimately sold it to Hewlett-Packard for $1.6 billion. Then you said, "Why don't I take some of the money and just do angel investing"?

MA: That's right.

DR: Some of the companies you angel-invested were things like Facebook?

MA: With Facebook I became involved as a director. But LinkedIn, Twitter, the whole series of those, yes.

DR: Were you just sitting at a Starbucks and somebody would come in and you'd say, "Okay, I'll give you $50,000, $100,000"? How did you decide which of these angel-invested companies you wanted to do?

MA: It was basically working through the network of all the people we knew. In those days, there weren't that many angel investors. There were maybe a half dozen of us at the time. It was not that large a universe. Tech was very out of fashion. This was 2003–07 or so.

DR: In the end, you decided to make more of a business out of this, and you started this firm called Andreessen Horowitz. Who is Mr. Horowitz?

MA: A longtime friend and partner. He was basically our best young executive at Netscape. Had Netscape stayed independent, I think he ultimately would have been the CEO.

DR: You started this firm in what year?

MA: Two thousand nine.

DR: How much money do you manage now?

MA: About $18 billion today.

DR: And how many professionals do you have looking for deals or doing deals?

MA: The deal team is probably 60 people or so in total.

DR: When people can approve a deal, after they approve one, do they tell you they've done it?

MA: Everything gets discussed. We have different vertical teams that go out and work in all these different categories. Ben and I are on each of the vertical teams, so we're in the middle of everything.

DR: Did Silicon Valley really need another venture capital firm? What were you going to do that was different?

MA: We thought the Valley did, based on our experience as entrepreneurs. We had worked with some of these great VCs. What we were always missing was "Who are the people we can work with who have done this before? Who has actually founded and run a company? Who really understands the full nature of that entrepreneurial journey?"

There are many great venture firms. Generally they were founded in the '60s or '70s or '80s by former entrepreneurs or operators, but over the years they transitioned to being run almost like investment banks. We thought it was time to go back to the well and build a firm with founders who understood the process more deeply.

DR: Today, when you're doing deals, do you have more confidence in your ability to assess what's going to work than you did 10 years ago?

MA: We have greater confidence in our ability to construct the portfolio. I have a lot of confidence now in our ability to put together a portfolio of 20 or 30 or 40 companies that, together, represent what top-tier venture capital looks like in this era.

Which of those companies will be the ones that work? Don't know. What will the cycle be? Is this going to be an up cycle or down cycle? I don't know that, either. There is a lot that's unknown in the process. I don't think that ever goes away.

DR: How do you know what a good venture firm is, and how do you get into one as an investor?

MA: Generally, they're the ones you can't get into. The venture capital firms that are open for outside money are generally the ones you don't want to invest in.

There is a platform worth looking at for people who want to learn more. You can't invest in us through this, so this is just an industry observation. It's a platform called AngelList, where angel investors are able to take money from people who want to follow their deals.

People should go in cautiously. This is a very speculative area.

DR: What should somebody look for in a venture fund they're going to invest in?

MA: It's the reverse of how most investment markets work. The best entrepreneurs get to select which venture capital firm invests. That ends up being the big hinge in the market.

DR: The standard way venture firms work is you commit capital, let's say over a five-year investment period, and then the fund typically lasts maybe 10 years or so?

MA: Fifteen. These days, longer. Often the tail extends out to 20 years, because these companies take a long time to develop.

DR: Somebody who invests in a venture fund today should be trying to get rates of return of 20 percent or more?

MA: Top-end venture is 3x net of fees. You're hoping for more than that. You're hoping for 5x or more. You're illiquid the entire time, so you would hope to get paid for the illiquidity. Twenty to 40 percent if things go well is sort of baseline.

DR: What are the skill sets for good venture capitalists? A high degree of intelligence? Hard work? A lot of luck? Dress the part? Don't wear a tie?

MA: There's the classic route, which is business school and becoming trained up as an investor, maybe working at an investment bank. Some lawyers have become VCs. I didn't do any of that. The other approach is to get really good at building and running tech companies. Be an engineer or be a product manager and help products get built, and then, at some point, become part of the management team or become a founder yourself, and then leverage those skills across into the investment side.

The highly successful VCs, historically, are idiosyncratic people from very different backgrounds. You have people with very different backgrounds and experiences.

DR: What's the pleasure of being a successful venture capitalist? You enjoy building a company from scratch or helping somebody build it?

MA: You get to be part of the team. It's tremendous when these things really change the world. The downside is you don't get to run the companies. You're a backseat driver.

The advantage is you do get to see all the new things. You get a front-row seat at this amazing show of all these incredible people with all these new ideas.

DR: Many people think that cryptocurrencies are not a real thing and not a great asset category. But you are a big investor in Coinbase, among other crypto-related things. What is it about cryptocurrency that you think makes it an enduring investment proposition?

MA: Fundamentally, it's a technological transformation. There's a fundamental technological breakthrough that has happened. It's an area of computer science called distributed consensus. It's the ability for a lot of people and software on the internet to be able to form trust relationships in an untrusted environment.

Money is one application of being able to have distributed consensus. There are many other things that people are going to be able to do with this technology. Many of the smartest people in computer science are going into this field, and they're pushing it forward at a rapid rate. To us, it looks like it's the eighth or ninth fundamental architecture change, a breakthrough technological transformation happening in the tech industry. We take it very seriously because of that.

DR: So your view is not whether Bitcoin is good or not or worth X or Y. It's that the whole technology underlying Bitcoin is going to transform the world?

MA: Bitcoin is an internet computer that's spread out across hundreds of thousands of physical computers all over the world. It's a transaction-processing system that runs without any sort of central location. It's like a giant distributed mainframe. It processes transactions, and out of that transaction processing comes the ability to exchange money. Out of that process comes this token, the Bitcoin, that's a representation of value of the underlying system. It's a new kind of financial system.

DR: Another area people are very interested in is biotech. You're doing a lot in that area as well. Why are you interested in that area?

MA: We think biotech and computer science or engineering are basically merging. What you have now with a lot of biotech entrepreneurs is you have people who understand biology but they also understand engineering and they understand software. They understand data and they understand AI, and they're basically slamming these disciplines together and building a new kind of biotech.

Moderna, by the way, is a great example of that. The reason they could develop that vaccine in two days is because it's an engineering vaccine. It was implemented with computer code, which is a completely new way of developing a vaccine. We're seeing a lot more biotech entrepreneurs who have this kind of engineering-centric mentality. That plays to what Silicon Valley does well.

DR: What about quantum computing? Is that an area you're interested in?

MA: Yes, we are. That one is a longer road. But in the long run, it looks very promising.

DR: Let me ask you a few lightning-round questions. What's the best investment advice you've ever received?

MA: From Warren Buffett, probably: Put all your eggs in one basket and watch that basket. Deeply understand the nature of what you're investing in.

DR: What's the most common investment mistake that you observe?

MA: People read about something in the paper, see it on TV, and take a flyer without deeply understanding it.

DR: If I gave you $100,000 tomorrow, what would you do with it?

MA: Put it in an S&P 500 index fund. Don't get fancy.

DR: What mistake in the investment world have you made that in hindsight you wish you hadn't made?

MA: For most forms of investing, the mistakes are the investments you make where you lose money. In our world, it's the investments you don't make.

DR: If somebody wants to be a venture capital investor, what would you like them to know most about the art of venture capital investing?

MA: It's an alchemy of understanding people, understanding technology, understanding markets. It's quite literally a liberal art. It encompasses all these dimensions. It makes sense to try to go deep in understanding the nature of how these new products get built and how these companies get built and try to get as deep into the substance as possible.

MICHAEL MORITZ

Partner at Sequoia Capital; author and former journalist

> *"The pleasure of the venture business is proving that the impossible is possible."*

Over the past three decades, probably the most consistently successful of the Silicon Valley venture firms has been Sequoia Capital. It made highly prescient and profitable investments in companies such as Google, Yahoo, Cisco, PayPal, YouTube, Zappos, LinkedIn, Stripe, Zoom, and WhatsApp—and those are just the US investments. Its Sequoia China arm, Sequoia Heritage (its family office), and its public market fund have also been extraordinarily successful.

Sequoia began in 1972 and was led for many years by its founder, Don Valentine. The firm was successful from the beginning, but its success since the mid-1990s has produced levels of profit for its partners and investors that could never have been imagined in the wildest dreams of anyone at Sequoia's (or any venture firm's) beginning.

The firm's success is due to many individuals—as President Kennedy famously said, "victory has a hundred fathers and defeat is an orphan." But other than the firm's founder, probably the most impactful of the Sequoia partners has been the principal architect of its expansion into multiple lines of business, Michael Moritz (now officially Sir Michael Moritz).

Such a role might not have been readily predicted from Michael's background. He grew up in Wales—not the home of many world-class venture capitalists—the son of refugees from Nazi Germany, and immigrated to the United States after getting a degree at Oxford. While he also got a degree at Wharton once in the States, his ambition was to be a journalist and author.

He joined *Time* magazine and became quite adept at covering the emerging tech industry in Silicon Valley. He came to know Steve Jobs very well (though Jobs was upset that the 1983 Man of the Year article on him was transformed by *Time*'s editors into a Machine of the Year story celebrating the personal computer). Ultimately, Michael used his knowledge of Apple to write the then-definitive book on the company, *The Little Kingdom: The Private Story of Apple Computer.*

Michael went on to join Sequoia, and quickly learned the venture investing world. In addition to his knowledge of Silicon Valley and his razor-sharp mind, he had a journalist's ability to get to the heart of a company's essence and to articulate that story succinctly and in easily understood terms—helpful skills in convincing your partners to support your deal and also in convincing entrepreneurs that having you in their corner would be a real plus.

When Michael was, in time, selected as Sequoia's managing partner, he did so well in that role that in 2006 and 2007 he was recognized as the world's top venture capitalist by *Forbes*. A few years ago, for health reasons, he stepped back from the managing partner role, though he is still actively involved in the investment process at Sequoia. He is also actively involved in philanthropic pursuits, particularly in the San Francisco Bay area, and in one area overlapping with my own interests, the University of Chicago (where his wife went to college).

I have really not known Michael well, but have greatly admired the successes he has had at Sequoia. And those successes were apparent to me year after year from the various nonprofit investment committees on which I served, for Sequoia regularly delivered eye-popping returns. I interviewed him virtually on June 9, 2021.

DAVID M. RUBENSTEIN (DR): There are many unlikely stories in Silicon Valley. Of all the ones I've heard, yours is the most unlikely. You are from Wales. You are a journalist. You don't have a Stanford degree. You are not somebody who was an operating executive. How did you get out of the journalism world and get into the venture world? It seems like an unlikely pattern.

MICHAEL MORITZ (MM): It was because of the founder of Sequoia Don Valentine's willingness to go in directions that others were not prepared to go. I applied to five venture firms. The other four turned me down.

DR: How did you go from being a journalist to being a Silicon Valley venture capital investor without doing the normal things you have to do? How did you come to Sequoia?

MM: I had a history degree and not a double-E [electrical engineering] degree. I had been a journalist. I hadn't worked at Intel. I had not run anything and therefore I was not somebody that most firms in the venture business wanted.

Don Valentine felt that people were too straitjacketed by their thinking about what made successful venture investors. He pointed to several people he knew who didn't have the typical Silicon Valley background such as Arthur Rock, who was the first investor in both Intel and Apple. There are plenty of examples of people in the venture business with great technical and operating knowledge who have been remarkable failures.

DR: I don't know a lot of Jewish people from Wales.

MM: My parents were refugees from Nazi Germany. My father got a job in Wales, which is where my parents eventually settled and lived, and I was born there.

DR: I have been almost everywhere, and I know the Jewish community in lots of different places. Is there a Jewish community of any size in Wales?

MM: It is small. When I was there—this was a long time ago, and it has dwindled further—there were probably about 800 families.

DR: When you were beginning your career in the United States, you got an MBA from Wharton?

MM: I don't admit to that.

DR: I thought I read that.

MM: No, it's true. I have one. The best thing about Wharton for me was taking English classes with Philip Roth.

DR: How did you go into journalism? Did you say, "I really don't want to use my MBA for anything. I want to be a journalist"? Did you just join *Time* magazine and work your way up?

MM: I had been interested in journalism when I was at Oxford. I'd done the normal things somebody who's interested in journalism does. I worked on the student magazine and had edited it. I always had a hankering to be an ink-stained wretch.

Part of the reason that I came to America originally was that trade union rules, at the time, restricted the major newspapers in Britain like the *Times,* the *Guardian, Daily Telegraph,* and the *Financial Times* from hiring graduates straight from undergraduate college.

I didn't want to go and work at Goldman Sachs or McKinsey or any of the other obvious places, or a huge industrial company or an accounting firm or wherever most people wound up. I just had no interest. So, not unlike applying to the venture business, I'd written to a bunch of American newspapers and magazines, and *Time* magazine made me an offer. I joined *Time* at the end of the 1970s.

DR: You famously wrote an article on Steve Jobs. It was one that he didn't like that much, and your relationship with him ended. Is that apocryphal?

MM: No. That's true. I think neither of us liked the article, but for different reasons.

Steve took rightful umbrage that it was a grotesque portrayal of him. And I agreed with that. I didn't feel it was fair. I also felt that the editing that had been done on the piece in New York was insensitive. Shortly after that event I left *Time*. That was a big part of the reason I left.

DR: Then you wrote a book on Apple?

MM: I had been working on it when that *Time* article appeared. The first book about Apple was my book *The Little Kingdom*. Most people would say that, unlike the *Time* article, my book was a fair and balanced portrait of Steve and the early years of Apple.

DR: You write with a great pithy style, which is direct and not with a lot of excess verbiage. Does that style enable you to cut to the quick in the venture world? Do you think your ability to write so precisely has helped you to communicate what you think about companies, to understand companies?

MM: The direct answer is yes. It's about listening intently and communicating clearly and distilling everything to its raw essence, which is something that you learn as a journalist. In journalism, you frequently deal with the unfamiliar. You have to come to grips with murkiness and obscurity. You're confronted with imperfect information, and you have to try and arrive at an objective conclusion that you distill into a story. The process of figuring out an investment has a lot of similarities to that.

DR: When you joined Sequoia as a young person, you were mentored by somebody. Eventually you worked on a number of deals that became very famous. Two of the most famous are Google and Yahoo. Did you find those deals? They came into the firm and you worked on them? How did you get connected to those?

MM: Like almost everything at Sequoia it was the result of teamwork. With Yahoo, Doug Leone [a senior partner at Sequoia who later became the firm's senior managing partner] and I were pecking around trying to figure out where to invest in the internet. We called a friend and went to see him, because we were scouting. We were trying to get educated about the internet. He mentioned that he'd just come across this directory of sites on the internet called Yahoo—this was late '94 and early '95—and that he'd found it useful. Our ears perked up, and we asked for an introduction. Shortly afterwards, I went over and met these two fellows, Jerry Yang and David Filo, in a trailer in Stanford. We eventually wound up investing in Yahoo. It opened our eyes to what was possible on the internet.

DR: They tell a story in the venture world that you and Kleiner Perkins invested $25 million in Google. They were supposed to get a CEO, and after a year or two, when they didn't have one, you guys asked for your money back. Is that apocryphal?

MM: It's largely apocryphal. Today people forget because of everything that's happened since, but Google, for the first 14 or 15 months after the investment, was not in the search business that we think of it being in today. It was in the search licensing business, trying to sell its technology to internet providers and also large companies. And it had burned through quite a lot of money. So there was a real urgency about getting the management installed and helping them. It was a way of heightening the sense of urgency around the recruitment of management. I don't think there's any investment where Sequoia has ever requested its money back.

DR: Many people passed on Google because search engines weren't exactly novel at the time. What was it that you saw in the two founders that was worth your investing in it?

MM: Many people had also passed on Cisco Systems, which was an investment we made in 1987, shortly after I joined Sequoia. Many people passed on Elon Musk and X.com, which became PayPal. In large market areas, we've always thought it's rarely ever too late. With Google, the technology was distinctly better. It led to a far better consumer experience. The searches were more accurate. They were faster. They had all the attributes that consumers by the billions later flocked to.

DR: When you are looking at a deal, what is it that you're most looking at? Is it the management, the quality of the entrepreneur, the quality of the idea?

MM: It's a happy balance between the three legs of a tripod: the quality of the founders, the market opportunity, and the distinctiveness of the product.

DR: I assume you and Sequoia look at maybe 1,000 deals a year, and you might ultimately decide to do 10 or something like that—a very small percentage?

MM: The numbers have got larger over the years. The deal flow today is probably tens of thousands over the course of a year, largely because of the internet and how easy it is to send business plans and ideas to us. We do everything from very small multi-hundred-thousand-dollar seed investments to much larger growth equity investments. The deal numbers are larger than they used to be, but they're still very small in the great scheme of things.

DR: How does somebody get a presentation to you? You can't have enough people to review everything. Is it referrals by well-respected people? How does somebody get into your consciousness?

MM: We actually look at everything. Let's say we each get 25 emails a day from various entrepreneurs from all over the world. It doesn't take long to go through them and sift them. Chances are there won't be anything in particular that catches our eye.

It's certainly true that we pay particular attention to referrals from people we know or people we've been in business with, or if it comes with a warm endorsement. But we encourage people from anywhere, if they have an idea they think is of merit, to not stand on ceremony and send it to us.

DR: When people make presentations, are you looking at the same things you just mentioned? Are you looking at their presentation skills? What is it that, when you see the whites of their eyes, you're looking for?

MM: It's trying to imagine, can we be a shareholder in this business for 20 years? I know that sounds ridiculous and most people think that's pie-in-the-sky thinking. But those are the hallmarks of our great investments. Can we be a shareholder for 20 years if things go right? We know that lots of things can go wrong along the way and there's no certainty and the chances of failure are fairly high, particularly if you're investing very early on—but, each year, only one or two of the very best seed investments will be major companies in 2040.

DR: When Mark Zuckerberg was in college, my now son-in-law told me about Facebook. He wanted me to invest and I said, "That one wouldn't get anywhere." Then I had shares in Amazon at the beginning, and I sold them right away. So I have made my mistakes. I look back on them all the time and kick myself. When you make a mistake by passing on something and then it works out, does that give you heartburn, or you just go on to the next thing?

MM: You learn from it. We passed when Reed Hastings of Netflix came to see us in 1998 or 1999. Maybe it was because of the hurricane of the dot-com boom, but I just hadn't understood the business properly. Now this was when Netflix was in the DVD business, not the streaming business. I hadn't understood the consumer pain around Blockbuster and all the rest of it. There are all sorts of companies we've passed on, and you could build a great portfolio from the investments where our judgment was wrong. We learn from the past but don't dwell on it. The future is where the business is.

DR: Let's suppose you do a deal and it doesn't look like it's such a great deal after you did it. Do you tell the CEO entrepreneur, "This isn't working out and you've got to go"? Or "We're just not going to fund you anymore"? How long does it take before you realize you may have made a mistake?

MM: The mistakes vary. The mistakes are higher at the very early seed stage, when there's just a few hundred thousand dollars at stake. We make far fewer mistakes as the sums of capital increase, just because there's more data to go on before you make the investment. We're not up for participating in a long campaign that will be a fruitless campaign because the market dynamic has changed or the product has been eclipsed by a competitor. That doesn't make any sense.

When that does happen, I say to the entrepreneurs, "Look, these are painful conversations, but you don't want to fritter away the most precious years of your life if we can't collectively pursue something that we can win and where you can flourish." But if we think there's a chance of winning, we are unstinting in our efforts to try to support that company and the people in it.

In large part, with all of our best investments there have been bleak and dark times where we thought, "The investment is in jeopardy." But as you know, just as well as I do, there are inevitably very painful encounters or painful chapters along the way for every successful company. I cannot think of a single investment we have made where things didn't go wrong before they started to go right.

DR: When you have an investment committee, is unanimity required to go forward? Or can one partner say, "Sorry you don't like it but I'm going to do it"? How does it work?

MM: We try not to use the word *committee*. We try to use the word *team*. And we try to keep the teams in the various areas pretty small. But we require unanimity. It's been frustrating at times over the years, but on the whole it's served us well.

DR: Suppose there's not unanimity, but a partner who likes the deal says, "Can I invest in it personally?" Or that's not allowed?

MM: It's not allowed.

DR: Very often in Silicon Valley the entrepreneurs who have built these companies tend to be white males. Is there more diversity now? Or was it never just white males building these kinds of companies we all read about?

MM: You're right to say that it was predominantly male and white. If you look at the history of Silicon Valley, that's certainly true. The venture business has mirrored society. It's been an evolution. If you go back to the late '30s, with David Packard and Bill Hewlett, through probably the mid to late '70s, the business was predominantly white and predominantly male. One of the things I did very early on when I joined Sequoia in the mid '80s, when I realized what was happening, was we started focusing on the immigrant community, people in particular from India, from Europe, and also from China. The makeup of our investments began to change as there was more of an influx of immigrants from outside of Europe. There'd been a lot of European immigrants to Silicon Valley, but then there were more immigrants whose roots were from outside of Europe.

Also in the '80s, for the first time there were female entrepreneurs. The first female entrepreneur we backed as a CEO was probably in 1986–87. I think we backed two of them that particular year. One of the nice things about what's happened in the last 25 years is that there's been an increasing number of women entrepreneurs that we've backed, and that's a reflection of the increased intake in university computer science departments over the past twenty years. You see it in the composition of our partnership as well. That has changed over the years. It began with a couple of white males. It became much more of an immigrant-centered partnership. And today there's a big composition of both sexes and people of color.

DR: I assume you get even more resumes than you get deal opportunities. How do you discern who you're going to hire? Is there a screening process? What is the best way to get into Sequoia as an employee?

MM: Hunger.

DR: Just be hungry? You must have a lot of people who go to Stanford Business School. You can't hire everybody. You're looking for people who have been entrepreneurs themselves? People who have been operating executives? People who are unusual, maybe they're quirky, but they have a different mindset about how to look at things?

MM: It's all of the above. But the most important attribute isn't any of that. It's hunger.

DR: Carlyle made an investment years ago in a company that was the Expedia of China. It was called Ctrip. We thought we were geniuses, because we more than tripled our money, and then we didn't pay much attention to what happened. One of the founders is a guy named Neil Shen, and we let him get away. Some smart firm in Silicon Valley hired him and let him build their China business. Was it happenstance that Sequoia found him?

MM: It wasn't happenstance at all. When people ask me about my favorite investment, my glib answer is always Sequoia, because that's been the best investment of all time. If you look at the Sequoia of the early 1990s compared to the Sequoia that existed 10 years ago and continues today, it was completely transformed, not because we were geniuses, but because the world around us changed. We recognized that there were huge business opportunities outside of the United States, as technology spread for a variety of reasons in different places, one of them being China.

And so we decided to almost 20 years ago build a business in China at a time when it was considered a ridiculous thing or a hazardous thing to do. In the process we uncovered Neil. We decided together that we would build a business in China. Over the course of the last 15 years, thanks to Neil and lots of others, it has become a very important part of our overall business.

It was difficult at the beginning to raise money for China from skeptical limited partners. We decided early on we were not going to franchise the Sequoia name. If we were putting our name on anything, it was going to be something we were going to be really proud of. Obviously, this business has blossomed. But it's just one of several businesses that we've built inside of Sequoia.

DR: I talked to Neil about this. He told me that he told you guys he had to make the final investment decision. He couldn't be going back to an investment committee in Silicon Valley. Carlyle basically always has a centralized investment committee of one type or another. So, while our international arms have to be part of a centralized investment committee that ultimately goes back to the United States, you had the foresight not to do that.

MM: I've always thought that was a big flaw of the way that other people think about it. It reminds me of the histories of World War I, where the generals are making the decisions from comfortable dining rooms 30 miles behind the lines. It doesn't work. You've got to be on the front line. It would be like asking the China team to make a decision about something in Silicon Valley. It's very difficult to do.

You have to understand what you don't know. We understood a fair amount about the investment business. We didn't understand anything about the intricacies of China.

DR: Recently you've announced you're opening up in Europe, but you're doing it out of your main fund. You're not going to do a kind of China model. You're going to not have a separate Europe fund.

MM: Several of us grew up in Europe, so Europe has always been a lot more comfortable for us than China and India and, remember, most of the European companies wind up doing a lot of business in the US. We're much more versed in Europe than we were when we went to China. We've made investments there over the last 15 years or so, and because of the increased number of opportunities, we decided to open a London office fairly recently. We talked about opening something in Europe as long ago as 20 years ago, but the market had never been rich enough. Recently it has become rich enough.

DR: Historically, Sequoia's business model, as I understand it, was to go into Series A and maybe Series B round venture investing. You've mentioned that you now do seed investing and, in effect, growth capital. But your business model originally was Series A and Series B?

MM: Largely. Things have evolved. We've found today that we're now able to invest at any stage, but our favorite activity is to be the first investor in a business—whether it is at the seed, venture, or even growth stage. There's a company I've been involved with for maybe 12 or 13 years now, Stripe. Our first investment was as a seed. That was 12 years ago, when it was five or six people. We've invested, I think, in every round of Stripe since then. We invested at the seed stage. We invested in the first round of the Series B stage. And we've invested all the way up to fairly recently, when the valuation was around $95 billion.

DR: Amazing. Historically, people in Silicon Valley were looking to make 10 times their money or even 20 times their money, but they recognized that maybe 90 percent of the deals historically don't work out. Maybe ten percent would. You still make a lot of money, because those 10 percent would make 10 to 20 times your money. What is it that you're looking for in a deal in terms of your multiple and your invested equity compared to what it might have been years ago?

MM: My little shorthand is "twenty, twenty." Do we think we can be an investor in a new company for twenty years and compound at more than twenty percent for twenty years? It doesn't get any more complicated than that.

DR: The venture world when you first joined it was a pretty good business. The people that were running the venture firms were pretty successful. But they weren't in the Forbes 400 themselves. Now that the founders or the senior people are multibillionaires, does it change the motivation to work as hard?

MM: It varies, and depends on the individual. Some people slow down and become complacent and don't want to work as hard, which is fine. The lifestyle I've chosen for myself, where I'm involved with more successful Sequoia companies today than I've ever been involved with in my entire life, some people might say that's a sickness. I happen to enjoy it. If somebody wants to punch out after they made a lot of money, that's fine, but they can't stay at Sequoia. We only want the hungry. It doesn't matter what the age is.

DR: Is the culture in your firm one where everybody has an office, or nobody has an office? Everybody is dressing casually? Is it kind of a loose culture compared to what you see on the East Coast and people like me who are private equity guys wearing suits and ties all the time?

MM: Appearances are deceptive. You can go to any of the successful Silicon Valley companies and you might see people walking around in sandals and shorts, but that's the veneer. That doesn't tell you how hard-driving or how competitive or how fast-moving the company is.

I think the same is true in the venture business. Any successful business is not a loosey-goosey business. And our business is the successful Silicon Valley companies. Yes, the weather's better. We don't have to wear coats. We are not hung up on formalities that don't mean a whole lot. We just want to be effective.

DR: In the earlier days of venture capital, maybe 20 years ago, the funds were roughly $100 million, $200 million. They were small. Then Silicon Valley went to gigantic funds for a while. Now they've gone to smaller funds. Your fund sizes are still below $1 billion typically?

MM: The venture funds certainly are well below a billion.

DR: When the buyout people, the private equity people, go to raise a fund, we have to go out and knock on doors. It takes a while to raise the funds. You raise your funds in a day or so? Just tell people it's available and it's done?

MM: Yes. We try to give people advance notice so it's not a big surprise. But the sums of capital we're going after aren't vast compared to your world. And we have a certain track record. So it doesn't tend to involve a lot of complications when we raise a fund, and now three of our businesses have evergreen vehicles, which means we aren't tied to any fund life.

DR: If somebody wants to invest their money in venture capital and cannot get into the best firms—let's say your firm—do you recommend they not invest in venture capital? Or that they just find some newer firm?

MM: Investing in venture capital funds, because of the skewed nature of the return, on the whole it's a fool's errand. Those investors would be much better off just buying a basket of the best technology companies in the public market.

DR: Like many people who've been extremely successful, you're now involved in philanthropy. Is that an important part of your life?

MM: It sure is. But the majority of my time is working on Sequoia and Sequoia-related investments. The philanthropic stuff is very interesting, but it is not the main part of my life.

DR: Do your friends call you Sir Michael?

MM: They're shot on sight if they do.

DR: Were you surprised when you were knighted?

MM: Yes. It was somewhat amusing. I hadn't expected it.

DR: You may be the only person in the Silicon Valley venture world who has been knighted.

Today it appears that everything that Silicon Valley touches is turning to gold. We're reading about the great deals. Is it the case that people today are more successful doing venture investing than they were 25 years ago? Is it a higher hit rate today, for whatever reason?

MM: What people miss is that there are many more opportunities, and our world has expanded massively. It's expanded for two reasons. One, it's expanded geographically. "Silicon Valley" today is a shorthand for technology investing around the world, whether it's in China, India, Southeast Asia, Latin America, or Europe or wherever else. So that's one thing—a huge geographic explosion that has changed the whole dynamics of the world of technology investing.

The second thing is that the world of computing has changed massively. When you and I were young, you could measure the number of computers. At the beginning of our respective careers, I'd imagine there were fewer than 1 million around. Today, obviously, they're in the billions, and at very low cost. That has opened up the market opportunities available to us.

When I joined Sequoia, it was largely semiconductors and hardware-related investments. We would never have thought we'd be investors in financial services companies or advertising companies or entertainment companies or media companies or merchant retailing kinds of companies. Those were investments that we would have thought would have been way beyond the purview.

There are many more places where venture capital firms show up now. There are many more opportunities to be successful. There are a lot more venture capital investments being made in a lot more industry segments. But I don't know what the hit rate is compared to 30 years ago.

DR: People like you are the rock stars of the venture world. If you go to a restaurant, do people come up to you with deals or opportunities or resumes all the time?

MM: In San Francisco it's a small world. Every now and again at a restaurant there will be somebody who comes over. I have a buddy who used to coach the Manchester United soccer club. Whenever he walks down the street—even though he's been retired for a decade—he's asked to pose for a selfie or sign an autograph. He's mobbed everywhere he goes. All he wants to do is go for a peaceful walk.

DR: To keep conversant with new technologies, new opportunities, do you do a lot of reading? Or you just read the investment memos? How do you keep in shape to be ready to assess deals and outcomes?

MM: A bit of both. We cover such a waterfront of investments that it's impossible to be an expert in everything. You have to understand where your strengths and weaknesses lie. We also have a team bench that's been pretty carefully designed. We want people who have opinions about everything, realizing that all of us are stronger at some things than we are at others. We have complementary strengths, so that we often rely on the judgments of different partners at Sequoia in particular industry areas where they may have more expertise.

DR: In my world, the private equity world, when a deal comes to an investment committee, the memo can be 100–200 pages. I tell people who prepare them that the quality of the deal does not vary directly with the size of the memo, but they don't get the point. Sometimes they have these long memos. Do you have long memos before you approve things? Or it's a very short memo or just an oral presentation by the partner in charge?

MM: The shorter the memo, the better. I'm a big fan of the way they conduct the meetings at Amazon, without PowerPoints and with just a five- or six-page description.

People tend to overcomplicate these things. For our early-stage investments we know that any financial prediction is going to be wrong, we just don't know how wrong. So huge spreadsheets are useless and worthless. Even with the Stripe investment, which isn't, in the grand scheme of things, that long ago, the original memo that we put together was probably no more than three or four pages. If you can express yourself clearly and you have a strong opinion, you don't need a lot of paper.

DR: The pleasure of what you do is finding companies and helping them get to a state where they're important?

MM: The pleasure of the venture business is proving that the impossible is possible.

DR: And the biggest frustration is missing a deal? Or getting it wrong on a deal?

MM: No. I think the biggest frustration is people not understanding that Sequoia is the longest-term investor on the face of the earth.

PART THREE

Cutting Edge Investments

The investment world never lacks for new areas to pursue. The idea that something "cutting edge" will grow in value is always certain to attract capital ready to achieve a seemingly "outsized" profit.

Also, the amount of such capital can seem limitless at times, given the increasingly global nature of the investment world and the ease with which capital can be raised these days.

In this book, there was not enough space to cover every new cutting-edge investment category that has arisen in recent years. But I have selected great investors to discuss their area of focus in a number of the most interesting (and at times controversial) areas that are comparatively new—they have arisen and grown dramatically over the past decade or so (and become quite prominent).

These areas include cryptocurrencies, SPACs (special purpose acquisition companies), infrastructure, and ESG (environmental, social, governance). Of course, infrastructure—bridges, roads, airports, and tunnels, among many other large-scale projects—has been around for centuries. Only relatively recently has this area—traditionally the province of government finance, construction, and oversight—become an area of strong private-sector investment appeal.

Perhaps the most written about of these new areas is cryptocurrencies. They have become extremely valuable in many cases (certainly compared to their underlying value—generally zero) and have attracted investors, often young, from all over the world, though the "correction" in mid-2022 may significantly reduce the interest in this area.

I have not invested—yet—in cryptocurrencies directly. But through my family investment office, I have invested in several companies that service and provide infrastructure for the crypto-currency world. So I am not an unbiased person on the principal controversy surrounding the crypto world—i.e., many leading investors and professionals in finance believe there is typically no inherent value underlying these currencies, and thus they may ultimately be worthless.

My own view is that there is now so much interest around the world that I believe it will be too difficult for Western governments to eliminate or measurably restrain these currencies. Too many individuals and investors seem to feel that government-issued currencies are increasingly being devalued and are not as readily transferrable around the world—without government intelligence or knowledge—as cryptocurrencies. And that is appealing to many individuals and investors. I suspect the effort of the US and other NATO governments to seize Russian oligarch assets during the Russia-Ukraine war will accelerate the appetite of wealthy individuals to have non-traceable assets. But time will tell. The decline in crypto values in mid-2022 certainly does give one some pause for reflection and renewed analysis; the losses for many investors in cryptocurrencies in mid-2022 may well douse the crypto flame for a while.

For far different reasons (including reduced controversy), I believe ESG will continue to be a growing factor in the investment world, and investors insensitive to ESG factors will not be particularly successful in the future.

Carlyle has been an industry leader in this area, with a dynamic leader, Meg Starr, overseeing our efforts to ensure all of our portfolio companies are implementing strong ESG programs and policies. The only problem is that this talented ESG leader was in my youngest daughter's college class. You know you are getting a bit old when your child's classmate is emerging as a leader in a firm you started several decades ago. But this phenomenon does keep one young—I hope.

Cryptocurrencies

MIKE NOVOGRATZ

Founder and CEO, Galaxy Digital; former president, Fortress Investment Group; former partner, Goldman Sachs

> *"We have this convergence between the metaverse of stuff that's built in the digital world and the real world, which is happening at lightning speed as blockchains become more and more important."*

O ver the last decade or so, one of the most volatile, controversial, and (for some) wealth-creating investment areas has involved the numerous types of cryptocurrencies that have been created virtually and often anonymously. While there had long been a variety of academic discussions about the potential simplicity of digital currencies, no viable digital currency had come into existence. That changed in 2009, when Bitcoin was created by Satoshi Nakamoto, apparently a pseudonym for one or more individuals whose identity has still defied detection.

Bitcoin is a currency that uses a decentralized software technology known as blockchain as a way to record ownership in a tamper-proof manner. Blockchain had been developed in concept by a number of cryptographers in the 1980s and '90s, but its use was not widespread or linked to currencies. But after the Great Recession of 2007–09, when distrust of government and its form of currency—conventional money—increased, there was evident interest in finding a currency that was not linked to government. When Bitcoin surfaced and took hold, it played that role.

Whatever one may think about the merits of Bitcoin or other cryptocurrencies that were subsequently developed, there seems to be little dispute that blockchain technology has considerable value. As a result, separate from cryptocurrencies, blockchain-technology-focused companies have become of great interest to venture capital investors, for the application of blockchain technologies can no doubt ease record-keeping. But with respect to currencies, at some point, if large-population governments themselves authorize their own digital currencies—which seems quite likely, in the not-too-distant future—they may well utilize some form of blockchain technology. (A "block" is a group of encoded information; when that group has the requisite information and is full, another group is created. These groups of "blocks" become a "chain" as more and more blocks are created to hold new information.)

Unlike traditional government currencies, such as the dollar or euro, Bitcoin—or any cryptocurrency—has no government backing or centralized administration. Indeed, the value behind the cryptocurrency is generally (with a few exceptions) nothing of traditional substance or value, and administration (really, the recording of who owns how much of the digital currency) is done virtually through a blockchain.

Since Bitcoin's creation, more than 19,000 other cryptocurrencies have been created, representing a total market value of approximately $1.2 trillion as of June 1, 2022. Bitcoin remains the most valuable of the cryptocurrencies, with a market value as of that same date of $565 billion. (These values change rapidly; this is probably due to the fact that these cryptocurrencies have attracted hordes of speculators who frequently trade in and out of cryptocurrency and also use a fair bit of leverage, giving these currencies unusual volatility. This became quite apparent in May 2022, when cryptocurrencies lost enormous value almost overnight.)

Beyond cryptocurrencies' volatility, there are many other concerns associated with cryptocurrency. Its critics feel that 1) many cryptocurrencies have no substance behind them, and thus will ultimately collapse and hurt investors; 2) those investing in crypto are often nonprofessional investors seeking quick, unsustainable profits who may not understand the risks; 3) the anonymity of crypto generally helps the transfer of wealth by those who are seeking to hide wealth that might be ill-gotten (such as through some type of criminal activity, like ransomware); 4) crypto devalues legitimate currencies, and thus lessens the ability of governments to affect economies in ways that benefit citizens; and 5) a great deal of electricity is used by those trying to "mine" some cryptocurrencies like Bitcoin. ("Mining" is the complicated process of using computer hardware to facilitate the blockchain process and be rewarded in effect by gaining Bitcoins for one's own account. This process can be complicated, time-consuming, and thus energy-intensive, given the electricity needed to power the computers used in the process.)

These concerns have clearly not deterred millions of investors from avidly buying and selling the enormous number of different cryptocurrencies now in the market. They may be attracted to the fact that the best known of these cryptocurrencies, Bitcoin, has risen from a few cents per Bitcoin to values, at times, over $60,000 per Bitcoin (though it has at times lost half its value almost overnight). Almost inexplicably, the volatility of cryptocurrencies seems to attract investors more than deter them—perhaps in part out of a belief that there will be much more volatility on the upside, as cryptocurrencies have become a part of life.

Indeed, many investors feel that they are on the ground floor of a technological and financial revolution—the ultimate replacement of paper currency with digital currency and, at some point, the likely seamless coexistence of government-backed digital currency with cryptocurrency. In the view of those investors, being on the ground floor of a revolution along these lines can be quite profitable, as many of the early investors in personal computers, the internet, e-commerce, and smartphones learned.

In this regard, it might be noted that governments did not always issue and control currency. Banks or other financial institutions often did this in Europe and the United States in the 1700s and 1800s, and there was no central arbiter of value or legitimacy. Some cryptocurrency enthusiasts see a future where the equivalent could happen. Tech companies could well lead that decentralized effort, as some have considered doing. (Facebook has abandoned its effort to create a digital currency, but other tech companies could pursue one in the future.)

One of the most vocal and visible supporters of cryptocurrency as a legitimate asset class, and therefore as a valid way to make profits, has been Mike Novogratz, a former Goldman Sachs partner and president of Fortress, the first of the private equity firms to go public. At Goldman and at Fortress, Mike's expertise was in trading, often in new and esoteric areas.

While at Fortress, he was intrigued by Bitcoin, became an early investor (and reportedly is now one of its largest individual holders), and after leaving Fortress started and runs as CEO a now-public company, Galaxy Digital, in order to pursue investments in cryptocurrencies and related companies and technologies. Galaxy Digital invests in digital currencies and companies involved in the whole general area of crypto assets and blockchain technologies. From this platform, and with his years of credibility as an investor-trader, Mike has also become one of the most visible and articulate proselytizers of the crypto world.

Throughout his career, Mike has shown a strong interest in fighting the conventional wisdom about what is an attractive investment, showing no fear of pursuing often novel and uncharted waters. This trait as a fighter may well come from his background as a Virginia state high school wrestler and as an All-Ivy wrestler at Princeton. Mike's passion for the whole subject of crypto is infectious, and has surely been one of the many factors underlying the growth of crypto as an asset likely to survive and prosper for some time.

I have not worked directly with Mike, though we share some philanthropic interests (such as those relating to the importance of preserving and enhancing democracy). I interviewed him virtually on December 20, 2021, before the May 2022 large decline in crypto values.

DAVID M. RUBENSTEIN (DR): You are one of the country's—if not the world's—leading proponents of the value of cryptocurrencies as both a way of transforming global finance and as a way to make an appealing investment. When did you initially come to this conclusion? Have your views strengthened over time?

MIKE NOVOGRATZ (MN): I originally stumbled into Bitcoin in 2013 and looked at it as a really interesting speculative asset. This was coming on the heels of the second financial crisis. We had the global financial crisis in '08, then the European financial crises. Central banks, at that point, were printing lots of money. We had QE2 [Quantitative Easing 2].* Bitcoin, the first of the cryptocurrencies, was originally designed as a peer-to-peer system of digital money—the first ever—or digital gold. The unique innovation of Bitcoin was that it was the first digital signature you couldn't counterfeit. Up until then, on the computer you could only control+copy+paste [which meant that "hackers" could corrupt the system and keep it from being foolproof].

The innovation that Satoshi [the pseudonymous creator of Bitcoin] gave us was authenticity on the blockchain. When you could have authenticity, you could have scarcity, and that intrigued me. I bet on it as a speculative bet, and I was right. I became semipublic, because I made some comments about it. I didn't know the press was there. Next thing I knew, I was always asked about it.

DR: Why do you think so many well-established figures in the financial world like Jamie Dimon have been so negative for so long on the value of cryptocurrencies? I assumed the views of the financial world's establishment is not a deterrent to you?

MN: No. Some might ask how something that is six years, eight years, 10 years, now 13 years old (in other words, Bitcoin), how could it have value? What I think Jamie Dimon missed, and lots of older people missed, was that there was a generational movement here. The Baby Boomers have been in charge of our country for 30-odd years, since Bill Clinton. Since then, the ratio of debt to GDP [gross domestic product] has gone from 40 percent to 130 percent. Inequality has gone up. The planet has become less stable.

There was a real longing on the part of younger people—Gen Z, millennials—to have their own thing. To say, "You guys have been horrific stewards of the economy. It's time for you to step down." And none of them will step down. Young people are looking at this calcified system and saying, "We can rebuild something better."

---

* QE2 was the second effort of the Federal Reserve to keep interest rates low and the economy vibrant during the Great Recession; this was accomplished by the Fed's buying massive amounts of longer-term government securities.

The energy of crypto comes from the youth. I noticed that early on by visiting the people who got engaged with it. It was hard for older people to understand because they weren't spending enough time with young people.

DR: Are you now one of the largest owners of Bitcoin? Or is it hard to know who owns how much and thus it is impossible to know who else owns how much?

MN: The interesting thing about the blockchain is it's all public. You know what is in each wallet [the anonymous account of a cryptocurrency owner]. And people move (i.e., trade) these currencies around a decent bit. Like all assets in society, there's still a skew towards the few owning a lot more than the many. I read a statistic recently that the top 1 percent of wallets own 40 percent of the Bitcoin. That's a little better than it is in the equity market, but it's still pretty similar. My company owns a bunch of Bitcoin. We own a bunch of other cryptocurrencies as well, but we're not at the top in those.

DR: Are you worried that the US government will come along and regulate cryptocurrencies in a way that will essentially destroy their value or make their use more complicated and challenging?

MN: I don't think so. These communities can mobilize quickly, and they are a lot of voters. The tone is already shifting. There are 60 million Americans who own crypto. A lot of them are single-issue voters. I think it's very difficult to be too anti-crypto as a politician now.

DR: What do you think is the principal reason that currencies that have no inherent value or government backing are so appealing to so many people? Is it concern about the value of current government currency? Or is it the opportunity to maintain secrecy as to ownership?

MN: Look at what happened in Turkey this year. The Turkish lira is down about 80 percent over three years. They have a crappy leader, who threw any kind of prudent monetary and fiscal policies aside to push his agenda. And when you have bad stewardship of an economy, the currency devalues. People have bought Bitcoin in emerging markets almost as an essential place to store their value. You've got hardworking people who are trying to save money. But when you depreciate a currency 76 percent in three years, it's really difficult.

In the West, in places like the US and Europe, Bitcoin is a report card. It's a report card on how Chairman Powell and [Secretary of the Treasury] Janet Yellen are doing. If they can get our economy back on track, and get the deficit heading down and inflation stabilized, there'll be less need for people to put money into hard assets. But until then, people are buying crypto as a hedge against the debasement of fiat currencies.

DR: Is the appeal to some of cryptocurrency that it is hard to trace ownership and thus can be used for illicit transactions like ransomware?

MN: It's used, like lots of things, for some illicit purposes, but that's a tiny fraction. It becomes a story that people are nervous about and focus a lot of energy on, but the reality is it's a nonstory.

DR: Was Bitcoin the first of the cryptocurrencies? Who created it? Is it a surprise to you that the creators are still anonymous? Why would they choose not to take some of their large amount of Bitcoin and use them for some other purpose? So far, I think, their wallets are untouched.

MN: Satoshi Nakamoto—he or she or they—created it, and probably never expected it to grow to a multitrillion-dollar asset. It's now just under a trillion dollars. I expect it will go over $10 trillion, to replace gold. My hunch is that the creator probably died and with him/her went his/her keys to opening the wallet containing his/her Bitcoins. Either that or a group of people created Bitcoin, and one died and the other guys lost their half of the keys. The mystery around how Bitcoin got created, who created it, gives it some sense of magic.*

How do you create a store of value? It's a story. It's a narrative.

This mystery of who Satoshi was gave Bitcoin some of its brand and appeal. Again, we could take that same technology, we could fork it [meaning take the basic source code for Bitcoin and use it to create

---

* Because of the encoded way in which Bitcoin was created, and the fact that no one has ever proven ownership of the Bitcoins initially allotted to the creator(s), it is possible the creator(s) died, or perhaps lost the encoded means to claim those Bitcoins.

a new cryptocurrency], call it David Rubenstein coin, and it would be worth something, but probably a lot less than a trillion dollars.

DR: With that name, the value would no doubt be a great deal less. What is it about the process of buying or selling Bitcoin that can dramatically impact the use of electricity and thereby impact global warming?

MN: That's another one of these stories that's not a real story that we have to address. Total Bitcoin consumption of energy is about 0.55 percent of the world's energy consumption. We spend more electricity on Christmas lights than we do on Bitcoin. YouTube uses seven times as much electricity as Bitcoin does. Because it became a story, the Bitcoin and crypto community has to address it.

Eighty percent of our mining is sustainable and green. Bitcoin uses a system to prove authenticity that's computer-generated, and computers thus use lots of electricity. As the Bitcoin community grows, the problems that these computers need to solve are more complex and use more electricity. Bitcoin will continue to use electricity, it will continue to use more electricity, but the absolute number is much smaller than people expect it is.

DR: You are familiar with the famous tulip-bulb craze in the Netherlands in the 1630s. Why is that analogy not apt for Bitcoin?

MN: Cryptocurrencies aren't just Bitcoin. I would break them into two buckets. There's Bitcoin, which is digital gold. Then there's Ethereum and the Ethereum-like coins, which really are building new technology infrastructure.

There's a utility to building on top of a shared database. A blockchain is a globally shared distributed database where no one owns all the data. And we're seeing, with NFTs [nonfungible tokens], organizations like the NBA [National Basketball Association] making $100 million of extra revenue because they're selling digital goods on a blockchain.

I think seeing what happened to NFTs got people excited this year, as they saw real-world companies [such as sports merchandise companies] entering the blockchain space. As we have this convergence between the metaverse of stuff that's built in the digital world and the real world, which is happening at lightning speed, blockchains become more and more important.

DR: Where did you grow up, and what were you interested in doing as a youth? I assume it was not Bitcoin.

MN: I was a military brat. I grew up mostly in Alexandria, Virginia. My dad was a 30-year army officer, and I was a wrestler. I spent a lot of my free time training and in wrestling.

DR: You were a star high school wrestler and the star of the Princeton wrestling team, right?

MN: I was a good high school and college wrestler. *Star* is probably an exaggeration.

DR: But aren't you in the Wrestling Hall of Fame or something like that?

MN: As my son said, "If you get rich enough, they'll put you in the Hall of Fame." I do a lot for the wrestling community. It's an important part of my life. Wrestling is a sport that creates leaders. It's a tough sport, and so I support it.

DR: Why did you pick Princeton? And what were your nonwrestling interests at Princeton?

MN: I picked Princeton partly because I went there to visit and it was beautiful. It was the same year Brooke Shields was going, and it had been in the movie with Tom Cruise — *Risky Business* — and it just seemed to be in the zeitgeist at the time.

I studied economics. I wrote my thesis on how race affects the level of disposable income. This idea of fairness in America has always been important to me. And I think this is reflected in my interest in cryptocurrencies — they are readily available to everyone and have no inherent biases.

DR: How did you get involved with the investment world? And how did you become a trader at Goldman Sachs? What was your specialty?

MN: I originally thought I would go work in DC and politics. I was interviewing with an ex-Princeton guy who had been the assistant secretary of the Army, and he told me, "You've got nothing to add in DC at 24 years old. So why don't you go to Wall Street, make some money, and come back when you're 40." So I went. Lived on my friend's couch. I got a job at Goldman because I ran into another guy who got me an interview. I started as a salesman. I switched to trading, partly because traders made a lot more money than the salesmen. And making money was important to me at the time.

DR: How did you come to join Fortress? What was the reason for its early success and the decision to become the first private equity firm to go public?

MN: One of my partners at Goldman, Pete Briger, and I decided we'd try to work together. He already knew the person who became the third Fortress founder, Wes Edens. And we all had the same idea that one plus one plus one can equal 10, that you could create a conglomerate of alternative asset management businesses and try to sell trust that we're going to do what we say we do. And we thought that if we put those three things together, there would be diversity of earnings and scale to platform and we could take that public. We put Fortress together with the idea that it could be the first public alternative asset manager, and we actually did that.

DR: When you left Fortress, is that when you first started getting serious about cryptocurrency?

MN: I had bought crypto at Fortress, and it had gone up and then it came back down. When I left Fortress, I visited an ex–college roommate of mine, Joe Lubin, at his office in Brooklyn. He was one of the founders of the Ethereum project. It was then I realized this whole group of people was plotting out a revolution to disrupt almost every industry—to make things in a much more egalitarian, transparent way. I've always seen crypto as a progressive move even though lots of libertarians love it. Crypto at its core goes after the rent-takers. It goes after banks and insurance companies. All your classic business functions of rent-taking are in the crosshairs for crypto.

DR: What did your friends say when you said you were going to be investing in this area? Or did you not tell anyone?

MN: No, I was very public. I have friends who are like, "Dude, you should have told me about it," because they all feel like they missed out on a great investment opportunity. I was like, "I was on TV every week telling you about it." Originally, I think people were bemused, and they were a little skeptical.

We bought it at $100 per Bitcoin and it went to $1,000 per Bitcoin. Everyone who didn't buy at $100 really felt bad. And then when you bought it at $1,000 and it went to $10,000, they felt bad. It's been this ensuing cycle of when's the right time to buy.

DR: When did you start Galaxy Digital? What does it do?

MN: I started Galaxy Digital [which invests in cryptocurrencies and companies that facilitate the crypto world] at the beginning of 2018, right before the market collapsed. I used to call it the Goldman Sachs of crypto, then I called it the Drexel Burnham of crypto, and people looked at me like, "Didn't Drexel go bankrupt?" I was like, "Yes, but Mike Milken became a credentializer, a person who was so central to the development and use of junk bonds and high-yield financing that he gave credibility to the whole area." We thought we could play that role, bring lessons learned from the traditional financial community to the crypto community and translate what was going on in crypto to traditional finance. And that's what we've been doing. We are simply trying to be a credentializer for cryptocurrencies.

DR: It's a public company, and thus there is a fair amount of disclosure. Is that a problem when you're investing in cryptocurrencies?

MN: No. Part of what we brought is this idea of let's do things the right way, and convincing people in crypto that, yes, this is a revolution, but you can't live outside of the government. Governments have real roles to play in people's lives and are going to be around. Let's take the best of what crypto can be and figure out how to integrate it into society.

DR: What would you estimate has been the return of Galaxy Digital to date in investing in cryptocurrencies?

MN: A lot. I have billions of dollars of net worth that I've made through being a crypto investor, and that probably comes from less than an $8 million investment.

DR: Why didn't you tell me about this then?

MN: I get that a lot.

DR: Do you view your role as both an investor in and a proselytizer for crypto?

MN: I do. I learned this early on from a guy named Alex Marcos. He had donated one Bitcoin to every student at MIT. He was funding a lot of the Bitcoin core developers. I was like, "Alex, you're a real philanthropist in this space." And he said, "Dude, I own a whole bunch of Bitcoin. I want us to build the greatest ecosystem. This is investing in my ecosystem."

I always figured I have my role to play. It was trying to take a complicated thing and make it simple, so people understood it. But I own enough Bitcoin that having it go up in value made prophesizing worth something.

DR: As an aside, I interviewed a legendary investor named Bill Miller, who used to be at Legg Mason. He bought a lot of Bitcoin, I think.

MN: I love Bill. Yes, he did. And Bill taught me something. When I was talking about Bitcoin, I said, "I think it could go to this price." Bill's the largest investor in Amazon whose last name is not Bezos. And he was like, "If you take that analogy, Bitcoin will go to 5 percent of gold, then 10 percent of gold, then 30 and then 80 and then 150." And he said, "Each time you're resetting the story, but it's the same story." When you have a unique asset—the leading cryptocurrency or the leading e-commerce company—its value will keep going up. So do not sell. That's how he allowed himself to stay in Amazon the entire time.

DR: You now regard cryptocurrency as an asset category, like equities or bonds or private equity. Is that right?

MN: I do. That wouldn't have been true two years ago. But what we've seen is that almost every major hedge fund now is participating in crypto. We've seen family offices and the wealth channels start investing in crypto. Now we've got all the college endowments and pension funds just starting, sovereign wealth funds are just starting to invest in it. Almost every major investing group is participating.

DR: Do you see any way that this category of investment can be eliminated by market forces or government fiat?

MN: I don't. I think the blockchain-based financial system—we call it DeFi [decentralized finance, meaning that there is no central arbiter of value or administrator]—will win over time because it's better. It's a better product. It settles trades atomically, which means it's same-day settlement. It's transparent. We wouldn't have had the mortgage crises if we had all of Bear Stearns and Merrill Lynch's balance sheets on-line. It's composable, which means you can build on top of what exists. So you see this amazing amount of innovation. I think it's a better system.

DR: Are you worried that when the next big market correction occurs, or we go into a recession, the values of these cryptocurrencies will drop dramatically?

MN: I'm not unrealistic. All asset prices in the world have gone up with this really cheap money that we've seen. I think of Tesla all the time. I own two Teslas. I think it's a world-class company. If you told me it was worth $400 billion, I might think that's expensive, and then it's worth a trillion dollars.

Valuation in general is a question for all of us to ponder. If the valuation of all assets in the world goes down, I would assume crypto assets come down, too. I think, relative to other asset classes, crypto is going to get more and more market share.

DR: Is it hard to sell a cryptocurrency? Or is that as easy as selling any security?

MN: It's become just as easy as selling any security. It used to be hard. But we've got all the infrastructure now that these markets trade billions of dollars a day.

DR: Have you considered investing in various companies that service the industry, or that are not likely to fluctuate in value in quite the way that a cryptocurrency might fluctuate? I should disclose that my family office led an investment round in Paxos, a company that services the crypto industry. We were the lead investor setting the terms for additional capital being invested by a number of investors. You may be familiar with Paxos?

MN: I know them well. It's a great company. We have investments in over 150 companies in the space.

Part of the thesis was that I was going to use my own money and then the company's money to understand what's happening, then take the lessons we learned from being an investor and bring them to all our clients.

DR: You are investing in lots of different companies, then?

MN: Yes, over 150.

DR: For the average person who is not as wealthy or as savvy as you are, how would you recommend that such a person participate in cryptocurrency investing? Are there limits to how much you would recommend an average investor should invest in cryptocurrency?

MN: It is still an 80 to 120 vol or volatility asset, which, to put it in English terms for non–market junkies, is five to 10 times as much risk per dollar as an average public stock investment. For most people, I tell them put 5 percent in. I used to say 2 percent to 3 percent, but I think there's a lot less risk in the asset class than there used to be. That seems paradoxical, because the prices are higher. But I'm so much more convinced this is an asset class than I used to be. So I would say 5 percent, and I would split that between one-third Bitcoin, one-third Ethereum, and then one-third Galaxy shares.

DR: Do you expect the next several years to be as attractive for cryptocurrencies and crypto investors as the last several years have been?

MN: I think that on a risk-adjusted basis, it'll be more attractive. On an absolute basis, it's probably hard to have the kind of returns we've had.

DR: Do you expect the whole concept of decentralized finance [DeFi] to continue to grow? Do you see this area, as opposed to cryptocurrencies themselves, to be attractive and likely disrupt existing financial institutions in a meaningful way?

MN: I do. That probably will start in 2023, when, as a portfolio manager, you'll start thinking, "I'm invested in Jeff Sprecher's ICE [Intercontinental Exchange], which owns all these exchanges around the world (including the New York Stock Exchange), and they're going to start losing market share to a decentralized version of themselves." What's stopping mass adoption of DeFi is the KYC/AML [know your customer/anti-money-laundering] issue.*

You've got to know your customer. That requirement is going to be solved technologically this year, is my prediction.

DR: What about NFTs as an asset class? Do you see that growing as well?

MN: There are two basic themes going on with NFTs. One is the metaverse—people spending more and more time in a virtual world. You're going to see monster advances in how we participate with NFTs with AR [augmented reality] glasses and VR [virtual reality] worlds in screens. When I talk to people my age, they're like, "Visit the metaverse as an amusement park." When I talk to people my kids' age, they're like, "We live in it."

And then NFTs in general are unique objects. Unique objects are going to be more and more valuable, placed in the metaverse. So I think it's a monster bull market. Visa told me they expect the average Visa holder to go from using their card 0.9 times a day to 10 times a day, because they're going to be buying digital goods. So Visa's big push into crypto and the metaverse is because they think you're going see more and more people buy digital shirts and digital sports memorabilia and digital jewelry.

DR: Wow.

MN: Visa is a half-a-trillion-dollar company.

DR: What comes after cryptocurrencies and NFTs as the next new type of investment category? Is it best to be on the ground floor of these new categories if possible, or wait until there's been some settling-down period?

---

* Those in the investment world who take money from others for investment purposes are required under US laws and regulations to know whose money they are investing and to take precautions to ensure the money is not being laundered as a way to hide how the money being invested came into the customer's possession.

MN: It's about risk adjustment. I have spent my life with this thesis that I'd rather look foolish than be foolish, and so I've invested in a lot of fringy frontier things.

I was early in psychedelics as a healing mechanism. If you were a psychedelic investor four years ago, today you feel smart. On a risk-adjusted basis, psychedelics is a better investment today than it was then. It's pretty clear to me that it will go through the FDA approval process. We'll use psychedelics in three to four years to heal mental health issues like depression and anxiety. With any portfolio, you should take some portion of it and go for the real risky stuff, but it should be a small portion of it.

DR: What are the skills that you think make one adept in investing in the whole area of crypto and NFTs?

MN: Passion is one of them. I always tell friends I meet, "Buy Bitcoin, Ethereum, and give someone some money for venture and leave it at that, unless it becomes a life passion of yours." There's a whole group of what they call crypto degens [inveterate gamblers in cryptocurrencies who often invest without much detailed knowledge] who spend their whole life trying to understand all the nuances of what's changing and how fast this ecosystem is evolving. It is morphing, evolving faster than anything I've ever seen, and therefore to be a casual investor in it is very dangerous other than making the macro bet.

DR: Does a more conventional trading background help with your being an investor in this area or it doesn't make a difference?

MN: It's some weird combination of macro and venture. The whole story is a macroeconomic story, but it's now really becoming a tech play. It was the macro story that got all the air into the sails, but now we're really rebuilding technology.

DR: For those who want to become professionals investing in these areas, what preparation would you recommend, other than being a wrestler?

MN: It's the same preparation that investors have always had. And it's something that I feel strongly about. We hear this phrase "the democratization of finance" a lot. I don't think everybody should actually be an investor. When I go to the doctor, I want them to have gone to a good med school, and I always check the diploma on the wall to see what med school it was. If I'm giving someone my money to invest, I want them to have studied what it takes to be an investor. Here I hire a mix of people who have done three years of Goldman Sachs or some great trading experience or venture experience, people who have a real passion for it.

DR: When you are not investing, what outside interests do you have?

MN: I love throwing parties. That's my fun outside interest. I probably have more parties and events at my house than just about anyone you'll ever meet. But I spend a lot of my time on criminal justice reform. It's one of the blights on American society. Half of my time, my free time, is spent trying to sort that issue out.

DR: Any interest in ever serving in government?

MN: I, as a macro investor, am a policy and politics wonk, and I would never rule it out completely. I've lived a pretty unconventional life in terms of following rules and breaking rules, and I really do think that people who take elected leadership positions should follow the rules of the land. I always told myself, if I go 10 years without breaking one of the rules, then I'd think about running. But my kids always yell at me for speeding.

DR: Do you enjoy investing in crypto as much as anything else you have done in your professional career?

MN: This has been one of the great chapters of my career, mostly because of all the young energy. It's an idealistic, mission-driven business.

DR: How many other cryptocurrencies are there now? How does one start a cryptocurrency? Have you started one? And will you?

MN: I haven't started one. Listen, crypto is an amazing technology for creating community. These are communities. If you want to think about an NFT, it's a nonfungible token, which means it's a diverse token. But the NFT ecosystems are like cryptos. We now have this capacity for any artist in the world to make a living as long as they can find 500 or 600 people around the world who connect to their art. That's an unbelievable shift from where we were five years ago. There are thousands of cryptocurrencies. And if you add NFTs, there are tens of thousands. Not all serve the same purpose. It's a disservice that we call everything that's a digital token a cryptocurrency. There are probably 10 separate buckets that they should go in.

DR: If the US government comes up with a digital currency, will that affect the crypto world adversely or positively?

MN: It's a huge positive, assuming that the government makes the smart decision and allows private companies to run a US digital crypto, which is the direction we're going in now, opposite of what China's doing. It's the same infrastructure that everyone's going to need. Your bank account becomes a wallet on your phone. It's the same wallet that's going to own your Ethereum and your Bitcoin and your opera tickets and your health care records. With great certainty, within 10 years your health care records will be NFTs.

DR: The Chinese government has outlawed cryptocurrencies for its citizens. Why did they do that? And why has that not impacted the price of Bitcoin, as an example?

MN: The Chinese government believes strongly in controlling their citizens. And Xi Jinping, the president of China, more so than the last few leaders, has been clear and straightforward that anything that puts the stability of him or the Communist Party at risk he's going to smash down. They've created a centrally run crypto, which is completely the opposite of the ethos of the crypto spirit, because they get complete information and complete control over people's spending. The difference between a digital currency, shifting money around on Venmo, and cryptocurrencies is programmable money. If Xi wants to cut off Uighur money, he can hit one button, he knows exactly who the Uighurs are, by what they buy and sell and where their transactions are. If he wants to cut off gay money, he knows who's gay just by what their shopping preferences are, because the government has complete transparency into what everyone buys. To me, that's a totalitarian dystopian world that I want no part of. That's the downside of a real centralized system. And that's what they're going for.

BETSY COHEN

Chairman, FinTech Masala

> *"Thinking about things differently is the key to success."*

Traditionally, when private companies with growing revenue or earnings seek to raise equity—for their internal needs or for the benefit of their existing investors—they take the company public through an initial public offering (IPO). Doing so requires engaging law and investment banking firms, getting approval of a prospectus from the SEC, and presenting the opportunity to purchase stock during a "road-show" with prospective investors. This process can be expensive and time-consuming—at least six months or so.

Over the past half-dozen years or so, a less-time consuming and less expensive process has taken hold: a special purpose acquisition company (SPAC) is formed with investors' funds; the SPAC files to go public with the SEC; since the SPAC has only cash, the SEC clearance is comparatively quick and inexpensive; the SPAC subsequently purchases a private company; and that company becomes a public company. The SPAC typically is given 18–24 months to find a real company to buy; the shareholders in the SPAC typically get to approve the purchase; and the SPAC creator or sponsor is rewarded by receiving a healthy amount of stock (and also warrants to buy additional stock on favorable terms) in the new public company.

As the SPAC process developed, investors in a SPAC would benefit if the price at which the SPAC's shares traded increased from the price that they had initially paid for the shares (though that did not actually occur as frequently or to the degree expected by the SPAC sponsors).

In recent years, it has been evident that the bloom has been off the rose more than a bit on SPACs. The share prices (post the announcement of the company being purchased) have not consistently gone up, and investors have become wary of many SPAC investments. Indeed, a majority of SPACs completed after 2015 are trading today below the initial typical $10 initial public share price.

At this point, it is unclear how the SPAC world will further develop. In 2020, 53 percent of the companies that went public in the United States did so through a SPAC. In 2021, that number increased to 59 percent. That percentage may well decline, but SPACs are likely to be part of the investment world for many years into the future. They provide a way for a company to get public much more quickly (and less expensively) than through the conventional IPO process.

One sponsor who has fairly consistently made money for her investors and has become a leader in SPAC creation and investing is Betsy Cohen, an experienced former law professor, lawyer, and banker who has specialized in SPACs in the financial services industry.

No doubt a large part of Betsy's success is due to the fact that she has a career-long background in financial services and her SPAC transactions are focused on the financial services industry. So when she sponsors a SPAC, the market generally feels quite comfortable that due diligence on the target company has been appropriately done.

I have served on the Brookings Institution board of directors with Betsy for a number of years, and have always admired her insights and eloquence. But I had not realized until relatively recently that she had, in addition to the accomplishments of her earlier careers, also mastered the SPAC world. I interviewed Betsy virtually on September 2, 2021.

DAVID M. RUBENSTEIN (DR): I'm going to start with a basic question. What exactly is a SPAC?

BETSY COHEN (BC): A SPAC is a deceptively simple legal structure in which a public company that has raised cash in the marketplace—done an IPO—looks for a private company with which to merge. That's the pathway the private company takes to become public. It's a reverse merger.

DR: And "SPAC" stands for what?

BC: Special purpose acquisition company. It means that, in raising the funds to capitalize the SPAC, no company in which those funds will be invested has been identified. It's a mandate from the investors to the sponsors of the fund to find a company that they think will perform well on the public markets.

DR: When was the SPAC first conceived?

BC: I'd say it was in the mid-'90s. A SPAC is a response to the need for capital. It's not always the same kind of company that needs capital. So, when it was devised, we were coming out of a recession and there were large private companies which needed access to capital that couldn't find that capital, except through a public vehicle. This was the vehicle that was devised. It's gone on to solve other capital-raising issues — most recently, the identification of the need for capital for companies that are growing quickly, not only in the fintech area, but growing quickly in life sciences, growing quickly in pure technology. These companies benefit enormously from being able to access this capital and, most important, to also have conversations with investors about what the company has already accomplished and what it might accomplish during the next couple of years.*

DR: Why have SPACs become so popular in recent years?

BC: There was a bias among investors for companies that were growing quickly. Those companies needed access to more than private equity money. I'm sorry to say they needed independence from the private equity funding sources in order to grow and to scale the companies. They were at an inflection point in growth where they needed to have substantial capital, and maybe at a valuation that reflected where they were in their growth cycle as opposed to where they might have been several years previously.

---

* Typically, these companies believe there is a benefit to being public rather than continuing to rely on the generally more expensive route of venture or growth capital. That type of capital seeks higher returns than public investors generally do.

DR: Can you explain how a SPAC is put together? Who organizes it? Does that person have to invest money? How does a SPAC organizer or sponsor get compensated or incentive?

BC: Generally—and this is prior to 2021 or the latter part of 2020—sponsors were people who knew a particular field, or who thought that they were excellent operators from their prior experiences, and who wanted on behalf of investors to find a company that required a change in management in order to meet its greatest potential. People who either had the management experience—prior CEOs of large companies or small companies—or were simply investors organized these companies. They were the sponsors.

Initially, the cost of carrying out the investigation and evaluation, and the capital-raising for the IPO, were done primarily by the sponsor alone. But as the field matured, there were many investors in that sponsor group to contribute to a fund to meet expenses, from inception to the closing of the transaction. A sponsor also gets paid in founder shares. Those shares are meant to have no value at the beginning of the process, but if the sponsor chooses wisely, they'll have a great value at the end of the process.

DR: Who are the typical SPAC investors? What is the appeal of investing in a SPAC when you don't know where it is going to invest?

BC: It's more or less the parallel of a private equity fund, but in a public context. They're looking to invest with people they think will do work on their behalf and find excellent companies that will have good returns. The additional element that grew up in this SPAC area was to compensate early investors, because there's a period of time between the raising of the IPO funds and the actual culmination of the transaction, which is the opportunity cost, and that opportunity cost was paid for by virtue of a warrant or incentive provided to the investors in the SPAC.

DR: As we say in private equity funds, they're investing in blind pools, so the investors don't know who the private equity GP is going to buy. It's also true here. The investors in the SPAC don't know who their SPAC sponsor is going to buy. But one of the appeals of SPACs to investors, over private equity funds is that the investors' capital isn't locked up for 10 years. Is that correct?

BC: Ninety days after a SPAC transaction is completed, the warrant to buy more shares can be exercised, enabling the sponsors and investors to liquify part of their investment. There are people who do that. Early on, there were lots of investors who were arbitraging this relationship. We try not to include those arbitrageurs in our initial SPAC IPO but rather to look for fundamental investors who are actually interested in owning a company we might identify.

DR: How long does a SPAC sponsor have to find a company to purchase before the SPAC investor says, "I don't want to give you any more time"? How long do you have before the money goes back to the investor?

BC: Eighteen to 24 months is the normal period.

DR: So in that 18 to 24 months, you as a SPAC sponsor would have the right to find some company. When you find a company, you then go to the investors and say, "Do you approve of this investment, and can I get your permission to go forward with this?" Is that how it works?

BC: Yes. Somewhere along the continuum the appropriate public document is filed with the SEC. That document works its way through the SEC until disclosure is deemed adequate. Then a meeting of the holders of record of the public company is held, and there is a vote on whether to proceed with the proposed investment.

DR: Does it have to be unanimous? Suppose you don't approve?

BC: It varies with the state of incorporation of the SPAC entity. The traditional state is Delaware. There 50 percent of the outstanding shares need to vote, and a majority of that 50 percent need to approve.

DR: If a majority of the SPAC investors approve, you've got the consent to proceed as you want? You already have the cash, because when somebody invests in your SPAC they give you the cash up front. Is that right?

BC: Yes, and it's then placed with a trustee and invested in cash instruments or Treasuries or some cash equivalent.

DR: Here's a part of the SPAC world that is unclear to some investors. If you raise, for example, a $100 million SPAC, you might buy something for more than $100 million. Suppose you want to buy something for $200 million. You're $100 million short. What happens? You go out and you raise money not from SPAC investors but from a separate group of PIPE [private investment in public equity] investors. Is that right?

BC: Yes and no. Generally, the SPAC is buying a minority interest. It's not buying 100 percent of the company. One of the important points for the investors in the SPAC is that the sponsors be very careful about the ongoing management of the company that they're buying, because that will be the ongoing management of the entity. Going back to your example, you might raise $100 million in the SPAC and $100 million in a PIPE. So, the company would have $200 million in capital that it could use. The SPAC investors made an earlier investment and tend to get better terms, but their capital might be locked up for two years. The PIPE investor knows the target company, and has capital committed for a shorter period. But knowing the target company is appealing to PIPE investors, and they are willing to forgo some upside.

DR: Was it ever the case that you raised in a SPAC exactly the amount of money you wanted to spend? In other words, you've raised $100 million because you wanted to spend $100 million, or did you always want to invest more than $100 million? Was the PIPE always part of this process, or just recently?

BC: I'd say over the last five years it has been part of the process. If I were to date the new, modern SPAC, it might be from 2014–15. Initially, SPACs raised 100 percent of the money that was required. As the companies that were available for acquisition became larger and more complex, and their needs became more complex, the addition of the PIPE gave them access to more capital.

DR: Let's suppose I'm a person who has some money to invest. I like you and I think you're a good SPAC sponsor, because you've obviously done well in the SPAC-sponsoring business. What is my reason to put money in the SPAC versus putting money in the PIPE? Is there an advantage to being in the SPAC or is it better to be in the PIPE?

BC: It depends on the individual investor and what that investor is seeking. The SPAC investor may have its money locked up for two years or so before a company is identified. But the SPAC investor will probably receive warrants to make the overall investment more attractive, and thus better than the terms available to the public market investor once the target company has been identified and the stock market prices that transaction (presumably at a higher price than the SPAC investor paid). Warrants to the SPAC investor make the investment even more attractive.

However, for an investor who wants to have capital tied up for a shorter period and would like to know the name of the target company before committing to invest, the PIPE investment will have those attractions. Too, the PIPE investor will generally be able to sell its public shares in the company before the SPAC investor.

DR: Through my family office I have invested in PIPEs. The reason we've done so is, not surprisingly, that we believe the PIPE price is lower than the price will be once everything is completed. In other words, I think it's going to be good. People are buying it because they think the stock is going to go up, not because it will stay at the same price.

What about our friends at the SEC? How deeply do they get involved in the approval process?

BC: There are two points at which they get involved. The first is when they're looking at the blank-check company as a blank-check company. There their involvement is on the level of disclosure of conflicts and things of that sort. Beyond that, remember that the holders of this stock have the right to vote on the acquisition and have the right to sell. That is a lighter load for the SEC.

The second SEC involvement comes with the identification of the company. It's a process, not unlike the process in an IPO, in which the SEC is concerned about proper disclosure and the other usual things in terms of a company going to the public market.

DR: In recent months, it appears that sometimes it's been harder to raise the PIPE than people initially thought it was going to be. In some cases I've been asked if I want to invest in a PIPE, and while my team and I are looking at it, I'm told that they abandoned the deal because they couldn't raise the PIPE. Is raising the PIPE a challenge these days or am I seeing the wrong deals?

BC: You're not seeing the wrong deals. One, it's a capital-flow issue. Two, it's the perception of investors in terms of which way the market is going for a particular class of stock. I don't think that one conclusion applies to all SPACs. It has become apparent to PIPE investors that they ought to look at the sponsor and see 1) who the sponsor is—whether they think that the sponsor has performed the kind of due diligence that would be appropriate for the investment; 2) whether they think that this particular sector, because there's sector rotation in the public markets, is in favor or out of favor; and thus 3) how they think it'll trade on the public market, etc.

DR: If a person is investing in a PIPE, they're doing so because they presume that, once everything is effectuated, the stock price will go up. Do PIPEs show an increase of 5 percent, 10 percent, 15 percent? Is there a history of PIPEs actually going up rather than down?

BC: It's very sponsor-sensitive. Some PIPEs go up. We've had the good fortune of having good returns on our PIPEs, but it's not true across the board. It's true potentially to a greater extent in sectors of the market that are currently in favor, such as biotech.

DR: I'm talking to you, in large part, because you are one of the leaders of the SPAC market, maybe the leader. You've done extremely well. Can we talk about how you got into that market? Did you just wake up one day and say, "I really want to be in the SPAC market," or did it happen by serendipity?

BC: I've been the founder and CEO of eight public companies, and so I always have an idea. One of the companies I started was an internet bank, The Bancorp. It began in 2000. That bank facilitated the growth of the nonbank fintech industry, by providing banking services for it, and I saw that as an opportunity. Over the 15 years that I was the CEO, I had contact with 1,600 fintech companies, and could follow them. I had a real petri dish there. I decided to step back from that role as CEO at the end of 2014. But I'm not very good at retirement. I spent the next week thinking about how I could build on the knowledge that I've gained. How could I use the knowledge I had to take the next step and to shift my view from being a founder and an operator to being an investor? The SPAC was, for me, the natural place to land. I decided to pursue this as a possibility, and I've been doing it since the beginning of 2015.

DR: You are originally from Philadelphia. Did you go to school in Philadelphia? Were you trained in the financial world?

BC: I went to Bryn Mawr College, where I was not trained in the financial world, then went to the Penn Law School. After clerking I taught in the fields of banking and insurance—anything that had numbers in it—and then moved on, because teaching wasn't for me. I formed a law firm with my husband, whom I met in law school. We practiced commercial law for a couple of years, but I was sort of an itchy person. I thought I would have more fun being the client than being a lawyer. In the early '70s, we founded our first entrepreneurial entry point by forming a leasing company, then a leasing company in Brazil, and found holes in the market. It's my way to find holes in the market and try to fill them. I did that over the course of the next many years, forming banks and real estate companies.

DR: When you went to University of Pennsylvania Law School, were there a lot of women in your class?

BC: There were six women out of a class of 200. There were three of us who were on the law review, so it was a little bit self-selected. I was the articles editor of the law review.

DR: In other words, 50 percent of the women were on the law review, but not 50 percent of the men?

BC: Right.

DR: What about in the financial services world? When you were getting into financial services, were there a lot of women then doing that?

BC: There were no women when I started. When I applied for a charter in Pennsylvania for a traditional bank in 1973, I was the first woman to apply for a bank charter, probably in the country.

DR: Back to the SPAC world. When you do a SPAC now, do you have a set of investors that you typically go to and that presumably like you because you've made money for them? Do you go always looking for new investors? Are your SPAC investors different than your PIPE investors?

BC: The answer is yes and yes and yes. I do look for fundamental investors in the IPO of the SPAC. We try to have 70 percent of the investors be those who are actually interested in being in the whole thing over a period of time. Often, they are repeat investors because they have made money with us. Some have been making money with me for 50 years, but we always are looking for new investors. On the PIPE side, some of the businesses that we do are more appealing to one group than to another. So we're perhaps a bit more discriminating in terms of investors that we might approach for a particular PIPE transaction.

DR: What kind of rate of return do you think a SPAC investor should expect to get or is seeking to get? Are they seeking 6 percent rates of return, which are a traditional public equity return? Are they seeking double-digit rates of return? What kind of returns are they seeking? What kind of returns are they actually getting?

BC: I don't have in front of me the information for the industry as a whole. If you look at the years 2015 through 2020, they were getting pretty good returns, above 6 percent. During the course of this year, 2021, they're probably not getting those returns, except on a sporadic basis and with what are deemed to be good sponsors.

DR: Presumably a SPAC investor and a PIPE investor are seeking returns that will be better than you can get on the S&P 500 index?

BC: Absolutely. That's a hard bogey to reach during these past couple of years.

DR: How many SPAC deals have you now led?

BC: A lot. Twelve.

DR: Do you tend to be in the financial service industry only?

BC: I am because I try to do what I know.

DR: So you've done a dozen of them. Some people have invested in all dozen of your SPACs, I presume. You invest personally in those as well?

BC: Absolutely.

DR: If somebody had been lucky enough to invest with you from the beginning and they've stayed in, they would probably have at least a double-digit rate of return?

BC: I would say so. The first transaction we did with the company was sold a year later at a 50 percent premium. The second one is trading at 90 percent above its issuance price. Those are the mature ones here.

DR: Some people tell me they think the SPAC market has plateaued and maybe is receding a bit. Do you think that the SPAC market will be here in five years or so? Do you think there's always going to be some kind of SPAC market?

BC: The SPAC market is not an independent market; it's like the IPO market. There are times when it's good for companies to issue stock in the IPO market, and there are times when it's not. I think the same will be true of the SPAC market. It's just another path to the public market for companies that need to talk to investors about what they're going to do over the next two to three years rather than what they've accomplished to date.

DR: I assume you normally do a lot of due diligence on the SPAC. You do it in person? You go meet the SPAC CEO, among other things? During COVID, what have you been doing?

BC: During COVID, we have been relying on Zoom, in terms of meetings, and we've been finding people in the local area. We have a large network that can do in-person due diligence.

DR: Any regrets about anything you've done in the SPAC market, or you're pretty happy with everything? If you had to do it all over again, you would be in SPACs?

BC: Companies, like people, are not linear in terms of growth. Of course there are those we're happier with than others. But we do believe that we've made good decisions. They can't be 100 percent perfect, but that we've made good decisions for differentiated financial technology companies that, over time, will have good returns.

DR: Like me, you went to law school, and like me, you wound up in the business world. Do you think you'd have been better off if you got an MBA from Wharton as well? As a JD, I always wonder whether I'd be better off.

BC: I really don't think so. One of the things law school did for me was to give me a fount of knowledge. Like being a general practitioner as a physician, you see a lot of different things. You learn from that. I think — and this is a personal view — that business school turns out people who specialize in groupthink. They learn a way to do something, and they think that is the way. I'm less of a fan of business school than some people in my field, because I think that thinking about things differently is the key to success.

DR: When you're doing SPACs these days, is there a beauty contest where somebody who has a private company and is thinking of going through a SPAC says to everyone interested in being their SPAC sponsor, "Come and do a beauty contest"? Does that happen?

BC: More so over the last two to three years, when there were more SPAC sponsors in the market. Since the market has become soft, it's harder to do, because in order to execute on a SPAC appropriately, you need deep knowledge of the capital markets. You need lots of skills that are not always all present in a sponsor.

You're not going to always be able to close deals. We've seen it. There will be sponsors who are not doing the proper due diligence. There's much more concern about the quality of the sponsor today than there was when the market was frothy, maybe a year ago. The thought that you hold the beauty contest and the best person wins — that's much less so today.

DR: When you do due diligence, you have a whole team of people that does that with you?

BC: I do. I have about 15 people in my organization.

DR: Is there one SPAC deal that you're particularly proud of? Is there one deal that you think shows the kind of things you're capable of doing, that set a good standard for the SPAC market?

BC: It seems like a long time that we've been doing this, but the first company that we closed, we closed in 2016, and the next one in 2018. I would look to those two that have had the opportunity to be through a series of market cycles, have had the opportunity to use the capital that we've raised for them effectively. As with everything else, it's not day-to-day. An investment should not be looked at each and every day but over time. Those are the two that have had the most time to come to maturity, and they've done very nicely.

DR: Can you explain why somebody would want to do a SPAC deal rather than an IPO, because IPOs are readily available as well? What is the advantage of doing a SPAC deal for a company over an IPO?

BC: I would disagree with you that IPOs are available to anybody who wants them. They're not necessarily. A SPAC might be better because of company size. A SPAC might be better if the target company has not yet scaled sufficiently to have past financial performance to warrant an IPO. One of the great opportunities with a SPAC is that you're able to talk to investors about what you will accomplish over the next couple of years, instead of only what you have accomplished. That's a real differentiator.

Infrastructure

ADEBAYO OGUNLESI

Chairman and managing partner, Global Infrastructure
Partners; former executive vice chairman and
head of global investment banking, Credit Suisse

> *"The thesis, at least the way we invest, is that we think we can do
> a better job of running these assets than the government can."*

O ne of the cutting-edge investment asset classes to develop over
the past two decades has, perhaps surprisingly, been basic civic
infrastructure. Before that, certainly in the United States, infrastructure
was seen as the province of government-led financing, construction, and
operation. The general view, certainly since the end of World War II in
the United States, was that roads, bridges, tunnels, airports, seaports, and
the like were the responsibility of the government, for the private sector
would not find these areas to be sufficiently rewarding to attract investor interest.

That view began to change in the early part of this century, after
a number of Australian banks and investors (led by Macquarie Bank)
bought infrastructure assets in that country, and then to some extent in
Europe and the United States, and showed quite attractive returns on
these investments. As these results became better known, large institutional investors—especially the US and Canadian pension funds and
the global sovereign wealth funds—found real appeal in this area.

Indeed, the area has grown so significantly that now almost every
institutional investor is investing in infrastructure. And the concept of

infrastructure has expanded to include large-scale energy and water-related projects. Currently nearly \$1 trillion is invested in, or committed to be invested in, unlisted (non publicly traded) infrastructure assets being managed by investment firms that focus solely on this area, or by investment firms that also invest in other areas (like private equity). In 2000, only about \$7 billion was invested in these types of infrastructure or committed to these types of infrastructure or investment firms.

The appeal of infrastructure investing is due to several factors: these kinds of assets have long durations; very predictable cash flows with comparatively little volatility; monopoly-like holds on a market (how many toll roads or airports are there going to be in a market?); and lower management fees and "carried interest" (profit share) than private equity or venture capital. The fact that society would clearly benefit from better infrastructure was perhaps a factor for investors investing in their own countries, but most investors in this category seem principally motivated by the long-term, relatively predictable returns.

Not surprisingly, banks, investment banks, and private equity firms also noticed the appeal of this asset class to their investors and clients, and they began to develop funds or other vehicles to build new infrastructure assets ("greenfield projects") or to buy and rehabilitate existing infrastructure projects ("brownfield projects"). To be sure, these funds, especially in the United States, did not initially find greenfield or brownfield projects easy to secure and complete—state and local governments were often worried that these new investors would supplant government and union workers; would make cost cutting a priority, impairing safety or other essential public needs; and would be less worried about environmental or other governmental priorities. For these reasons, it could take years to put all of the pieces together to identify, secure, and close an infrastructure investment of any meaningful size.

Despite these real concerns, the appeal of infrastructure investing has become apparent in recent decades to investors throughout the world.

The appeal of decades-long, relatively predictable returns has simply triumphed over the various challenges that this asset class poses for investors.

I recognized the appeal of infrastructure investing, but also saw its

challenges—including finding experienced investment professionals—
in trying to build an infrastructure business in my own firm. My principal
mistake, in hindsight, was not earlier trying to recruit Adebayo ("Bayo")
Ogunlesi, a brilliant Nigerian-born and Oxford- and Harvard-educated
investment banker, to lead our infrastructure effort.

I had heard that Bayo, whom I had known for many years, was preparing to start a new infrastructure business. He was negotiating to build
an infrastructure business with the support of his longtime employer,
Credit Suisse (where he had been head of investment banking and was
then executive vice chairman). He told me that his effort—involving
large capital support from Credit Suisse and General Electric—might
not happen. If it did not, he would get back to me.

But it did happen, and the rest is infrastructure history. Bayo went
on to build the world's largest independent infrastructure-investing firm,
Global Infrastructure Partners (GIP). Bayo's firm had quick success
with investments in several London airports, and is currently the largest
independent infrastructure-investing firm in the world, now managing
$81 billion in infrastructure assets, and achieving private equity-like re-
turns for its many pleased investors from the firm's start in 2006. If only
I had called him a few months earlier. I interviewed Bayo virtually on
January 18, 2021.

DAVID M. RUBENSTEIN (DR): Historically, at least in the United States,
bridges, airports, seaports, tunnels, roads, and toll roads were thought
to be the province of the federal government or state and local governments. What changed to make these kinds of facilities, now often
collectively called infrastructure, the kind of facilities in which private
investors want to invest?

ADEBAYO OGUNLESI (AO): In some respects, the US is both ahead and
also behind other countries. Most infrastructure in the US is actually in
private hands. Telecoms, that's infrastructure, that's all privately held.
Electricity generation, with the exception of TVA [the Tennessee Valley
Authority], and the municipal utilities in California, for example, are all
privately owned. The one area that continues to be in the public sector
is transport infrastructure: airports, ports, and roads. The rail systems,
mostly freight railroads, are all private, although Amtrak is quasi-public.

What happened is that in the '80s—part of it was ideological, part of it was also capital driven—a number of governments decided to privatize their infrastructure assets. Margaret Thatcher probably started this in the UK. British Telecom used to be government-owned. British Petroleum was government-controlled. The airports were all government-owned. The utilities were all government-owned. Thatcher went on this spree of privatization, largely by floating shares in all of these companies. What she did was make it possible for everybody who lived in the UK to have the opportunity to buy shares in whatever companies were being privatized.

The reason why Margaret Thatcher did more was probably mostly ideological. She thought the government in the UK was too big. It was a reaction to the direction that successive Labour governments had taken. Following on that, Australia privatized their airports. The prime minister at that time did it because he thought these things would be better run in private hands. Since then, if you look around the world, the US is one of the few places in the developed world where transport assets continue to be owned by governments. Frankfurt Airport is a publicly traded company. Zurich Airport is publicly traded. Even Beijing Airport is a listed company.

The US is one of the few places where all of these assets are in public hands. That was a function of federal government policy in the aftermath of the First World War and then the Second World War. Basically the government transferred some military airfields to public-sector owners and also started providing capital for modernizing airports. The condition was that they had to be publicly owned. That's when you have the transition to all the airports in the US, with the exception of Puerto Rico, being owned by states or by municipalities, with Reagan National and Dulles being owned by the federal government.

DR: Was the Australian firm Macquarie an early leader in investing in these types of assets? Was Australia different from the United States in allowing private investors to invest in these types of projects decades ago?

AO: Macquarie was, I think, the first real infrastructure fund manager that existed. They built the business. As I said earlier, what happened in Australia was they decided they were going to privatize all the airports. Every single airport in Australia today is in private hands. Sydney Airport, which is the biggest airport in Australia, was a publicly traded company. Macquarie took it public, and now we're in the process of buying it, together with some other investors. [The deal closed in March 2022.]

DR: Has the idea in recent years been to buy existing infrastructure projects and operate them more efficiently, or to build new projects in a more efficient way?

AO: The answer is both. If you look at the transactions being done in developed markets, most of them are people buying publicly owned existing infrastructure assets—airports, toll roads, ports. There are a lot of people buying existing infrastructure assets. The thesis, at least the way we invest, is that we think we can do a better job of running these assets than the government can.

I'll give you one example. Gatwick Airport has a single runway, and we bought it from a private owner, the same company that owns Heathrow Airport. Gatwick was doing 50 movements—takeoffs or landings—an hour. We set a team of business improvement specialists at our firm to do some analytical work. They concluded that we could go from 50 to 55 movements. I remember the management of Gatwick saying, "It can't be done. It's already the busiest single runway at a commercial airport in the world." But pre-COVID, we had gotten up to as many as 58 movements an hour. We did that by figuring out what is the best way to sequence aircraft through a runway. Is it landing, landing, takeoff? Is it takeoff, landing, then takeoff, landing, landing? Our team did some simulations and worked with air traffic control. The net result is that we increased the number of movements, which is good for the airlines, because they can run more flights at peak times. It's good for passengers, because they can also have more flights at peak times.

It's simple things like that. I'll give you another example. When we bought Gatwick, they were processing about 150 people an hour through security lines. In 2019, we were up 600 people an hour through security lines. The reason we were able to do that was one of our team members figured out that one of the biggest impediments to how quickly you get people through the security line is the size of the screening tray. The machine that does the scanning can only do so many trays per second. If you fly into Heathrow or Gatwick, they have these giant trays that allow you to put everything you have into one tray. You can get people through security lines much faster. It's good for passengers because when they get through security lines, they're not stressed. They have time to spare before their flight, so they go and they spend money. They buy things in the duty-free shop. They buy a coffee, buy books. They buy newspapers, and of course that's good for us. It's good for everybody.

DR: What is it about infrastructure investments that make them so appealing to investors? Is it the high rate of return or the predictability of the rate of return or the duration of the rate of return?

AO: There are three things. One is that infrastructure properly invested in are not really correlated to other asset classes. Absent a major financial dislocation, infrastructure assets behave differently from the stock market or private equity or anything else. That's one thing the investors like about it.

The second thing they like about it is that it has fairly steady cash yields. Across the four funds that we've raised, the average annual cash yield is between 10 percent and 12 percent. If you're a pension fund, being able to count on high single-digit cash yield, year after year, is a good thing.

The third reason people like infrastructure is that it's like any real asset. In the last 15 years, nobody worried about inflation. But as inflation starts to rear its ugly head, one of the things that many infrastructure assets do is that they give you inflation protection, because in many of them, their revenue structure is specifically inflation-linked. So if you're worried about inflation, you invest in infrastructure.

DR: Will the new infrastructure bill passed by Congress increase or decrease the need for private-sector infrastructure investors?

AO: The new spending in this bill is $550 billion spread out over 10 years. Every other year, the American Society of Civil Engineers (ASCE) rates the quality of American infrastructure. They rate bridges, they rate sewer systems, they rate roads, they rate airports. I think the last overall grade was like a C-minus. If your child showed up with a report card that looked like that, you would ground them and take away their iPad and iPhone because it was all Ds and C-minuses.

The ASCE estimates that the funding gap for US infrastructure runs into the trillions of dollars a year. So, quite frankly, any new money spent on infrastructure in the US is good. This is certainly the largest amount that the US has authorized for a very long period. But I think it's somewhat irrelevant.

Here's the fundamental, bigger point. The traditional model for funding infrastructure has been that the public sector would do it. That model is broken, and it cannot be fixed. Even pre-pandemic, governments had to spend money on defense, health care, education. In places like Europe, they had to spend money on aging populations. When you go through that panoply of needs, it's not a surprise that infrastructure in the US is at a developing-world level. If you fly from Dubai or Singapore to New York, judging just by the quality of the airports, you'd think that the US was the developing country. There needs to be a new paradigm about how you fund infrastructure, because the governments simply are not going to be able to afford it. All the spending they had to do in the pandemic is simply going to make it worse.

They're going to have to figure out ways to get private capital to come in, because there's a lot of private capital that wants to come in, and the private sector does it better. It's more efficient, it's more effective. In the longer term, that's the real strategy that needs to be put in place.

DR: Who's investing in infrastructure? Where's the money coming from?

AO: Most of the money is coming from pension funds, sovereign wealth funds, and other institutional investors. We have something like 400 different investors. Very few family offices invest with us. There are some high-net-worth individuals, but very few. Most of the money comes from the same institutional investors who invest in private equity. All of you guys should stay in your lane. You're now straying into our lane. You've got Carlyle raising infrastructure funds. Blackstone's done it. KKR has done it. Brookfield has done it. On a serious note, we think it is a good thing that more alternative asset managers are doing it, given the magnitude of the need.

DR: We're very small compared to you. What now constitutes an infrastructure investment? Does the investment have to revolve around a project that used to be a government-only project?

AO: It is fair to say that people are playing fast and loose with the definition. We think of infrastructure as a business that provides a critical or essential service in an economy. It does not have to be government-owned. We've made something like 40 investments in our flagship funds. Half of them have been situations where we've gone to energy companies and transport companies who have infrastructure assets buried within their portfolios, and we've bought them or partnered with the companies to own those assets.

So, for example, Hess Oil is an oil-and-gas company. But it owns a series of pipelines, gathering systems, and processing plants. I went to John Hess, the CEO, and said, "If you sell me a 50 percent interest in this business, I will pay you 10 or 12 times the multiple on this business, and the day you announce the transaction, your stock price will go up." That's exactly what happened, and John and his company have been outstanding partners to us. One of the things we have done at GIP is focus on how can we take infrastructure assets that are buried within larger companies and help them monetize.

DR: Do infrastructure investments always involve the investor having control to be able to effectuate change or improvements? In other words, will you make a passive investment in infrastructure if you're not really able to effectuate changes?

AO: We like situations where we can control the asset and make changes, because we think that's where you can drive things like focusing on customer service and operational efficiency, improving how they spend capital and capital discipline. But we've also made some investments where we are essentially a passive investor. So, for example, we did a transaction with Abu Dhabi National Oil Company where we bought, with a group of other investors, an interest in the gas infrastructure assets they have. It was done as a lease; they continue to run the asset. They pay us a fee, and at the end of 20 years, the ownership reverts back to them. If we like the risk profile, we will do it.

DR: Is it harder or easier to get approvals for brownfield or greenfield infrastructure investments?

AO: Much, much easier for brownfield. One of the problems with the US today is that getting approval for greenfield investments is incredibly difficult. I remember when Trump was president and he had the "Infrastructure Week," he had that long list of approvals you needed to build something new. It's just a nightmare. The federal government needs to streamline the processes for getting approvals, which is making it very hard for people to build new and desperately needed infrastructure.

DR: What parts of the world are the most difficult in which to make these kinds of infrastructure investments? The developing world, the developed world, the US?

AO: In certain areas, the US is the most difficult. It is almost impossible to own any airport in the US. The FAA has a pilot program where state and city municipalities can privatize the airports. This program has been in operation for 25 years or something like that. Only two significant transactions have ever been done through it: Puerto Rico's airport and Westchester County's. That tells you that there is something that doesn't make sense about the process when you compare the success other countries have had.

In emerging markets, you've got to worry about political risk. You worry about currency risk. You've got to worry about all manner of other issues. But in China, do they really need infrastructure investment from third parties when they have more money than anybody else? Not really. But in other countries with greater need for third-party capital, there are always challenges in securing and operating infrastructure investments.

DR: Is the rate of return typically less than a private equity or venture capital kind of investment or is it the same?

AO: It varies. It should be lower than venture, because venture capital is a marginal high risk. For our flagship fund, we target gross returns of 15 percent to 20 percent. In our first two funds, which are the most mature, we actually delivered higher returns than that—in the low 20s. The net returns are 17, 18, 19 percent, something like that. Most infrastructure fund managers are looking for mid-teens returns, which is obviously a little bit lower than private equity. But we think our returns are competitive.

DR: Are unions often concerned about what happens when a government-built and -operated facility becomes privatized? Is it difficult to get investments made when there are unions involved?

AO: That is usually the excuse that governments give, in the US at least, when they don't want to go the extra mile of privatizing their assets. They say, "People are going to come in and fire everybody." When we bought Gatwick Airport, they had fewer than 30 million passengers. By 2019, we had increased that to almost 50 million passengers. When you're growing like that, you're not firing people, you're hiring people. The UK is as unionized a country as the US is, and we never had a problem with the labor unions at Gatwick Airport. So I think it is a myth that is out there. But if governments really want to protect employment, they can certainly do it in the terms at which they privatize. For example, when we bought a port in Australia, one of the explicit requirements was that we couldn't fire people, unless it was done by voluntary attrition. We lived with it. It's possible to manage.

DR: Is the competition to buy or invest in infrastructure assets greater than it was 10 or 20 years ago?

AO: For sure. Ten years ago, there were probably three infrastructure fund managers, maybe four, who had funds in the $5 to $10 billion range. Today, there are probably 10 in that range. We raised one that was $22 billion. Brookfield raised $20 billion. In the next couple of years there will be probably half a dozen firms who raise $20 billion funds.

DR: Is infrastructure now a well-recognized asset class? Do you see it growing? Will more assets be privatized and more investors want to invest in this area?

AO: It is certainly a recognized asset class now. When we raised our first fund, many of the institutions we talked to weren't quite sure where to put it. Some of them put it in their fixed-income buckets. Some of them put it in their real estate bucket. Today, just about every major institution has a separate infrastructure asset class. It could be within real assets, which would include real estate and timber and things of that sort.

Is there going to be growth? The answer is, undoubtedly, yes. Every year, they do these surveys of where investors want to put money. Infrastructure is either number one or number two. It's always between infrastructure and private credit. Regrettably, from your point of view, private equity is no longer number one; growth equity is no longer number one. It's either private credit or infrastructure. With inflation starting to rear its head, I think that's going to expand even more.

DR: How can small investors, individual investors, participate in this type of investment?

AO: I think the only place where they can, at least as a matter of structure, is Australia. Of course, they participate indirectly through their pension funds and other asset managers.

DR: Did you grow up in Nigeria saying you wanted to be a global infrastructure investor? Was that your ambition as a child?

AO: I couldn't even tell you what a global infrastructure investor was growing up. I thought I wanted to be a lawyer.

DR: You grew up in Lagos?

AO: I grew up in Ibadan, which is a university town, but went to boarding school in Lagos.

DR: How did you decide to go to Oxford for college? What did you study?

AO: It was not unusual for people to go to university in England or in the US back then. Even though there were universities in Nigeria, my going to Oxford was a function of the fact my parents had gone to university in England. The year that I went, there were four or five of us from my boarding school who went to Oxford. I studied politics, philosophy, and economics.

DR: How did you go to Harvard Law School, and what led you also to go to Harvard Business School?

AO: I decided I wanted to be a lawyer, but I wanted to be a corporate lawyer. I'd spent some time in the US, and I decided that the best corporate lawyers were actually American-trained lawyers. So I applied to Harvard Law School. At the time I applied, it wasn't clear that Harvard Law School actually admitted into the regular JD program people who were not either Americans or Canadians or in a US university. Why they let me in, I still don't know. I have a theory. This was in 1975. I think Harvard, in its farsighted way, said, "This kid from Nigeria, we'll let him into the law school and he'll go back to his country and become rich, and then he'll endow buildings at the law school."

Why did I go to business school? I'd grown up with an aversion to numbers. I dropped math as soon as I could in boarding school. So when I got to the law school, I said, "Maybe I should face my fear of numbers by applying to the business school, and all of these people who are my classmates will end up being CEOs of major companies. Then I can tell them, 'I did better than you in business school, so you have to hire me as your corporate lawyer.'" I applied to business school and the joint JD-MBA program, and as they say, the rest is history.

DR: You went to practice law at the firm of Cravath, Swaine & Moore, where I had been a summer associate. Why did you pick Cravath?

AO: Right after law school, I spent two years in Washington. First I clerked for Judge Skelly Wright of the US Court of Appeals for the DC Circuit, then for Justice Thurgood Marshall on the Supreme Court.

DR: That's pretty impressive. Were you impressed with Thurgood Marshall?

AO: It's still the best job I've ever had. He was of course a legal giant, a great storyteller, a wonderful man. It was a lot of fun.

Going back to Cravath—I thought I wanted to teach corporate law. I said, "You should at least practice it for a couple years before you show up in school to teach it." Cravath had a pretty good reputation as a corporate law firm. That's why I picked it.

I taught part-time at Harvard Law School for five years or so. Then I taught part-time at the Yale Law School, then at the Yale School of Management.

DR: What prompted you to leave the law and go into investment banking?

AO: I got a call from one of my closest friends. We grew up together, went to boarding school together, went to Oxford together, and then he came to Harvard as well. But he then went back to Nigeria, and at the age of 24 or 25, he was a special assistant to the minister of petroleum and energy. He called me up one day, and he says, "The Nigerian government is looking for advisors on this big liquefied natural gas project they want to do. Cravath will be the legal advisor. Who do you recommend as an investment banker?" I gave them the usual suspects—Goldman, Morgan Stanley, First Boston.

First Boston got hired, and then it turned out that Cravath had a conflict, because the government's partner in the project was Shell, and Cravath did a lot of work for Shell. So they couldn't do it. Somehow the people at First Boston found out that their client had this good friend working at Cravath, so they called up the firm and said, "We understand you have this lawyer called 'Bayo.' Why don't you ask him if he'll take a leave of absence and spend three months with us as a consultant?"

I had a parade of senior people come to my office and say, "We have this request from First Boston, an important client. You already have an MBA, so people are suspicious about whether you really want to be a lawyer or not. If you do this, when partnership time comes, it won't be a good thing for you." I said, "I'll go, I'll get to know the First Boston people much better, and when I come back, they'll be my clients."

I got to First Boston and they discovered that I have an MBA. They started campaigning. "Would you rather be a banker than a lawyer?" I'd like to say that the reason why First Boston was so insistent was because they thought I had brilliant skills of some sort. I imagine their reckoning was, "Our client's best friend is working for us. We'll get hired for the second phase of the project." They were correct. We got hired, but that did not matter. They had not reckoned with the political risk in Nigeria.

Three months after I started, there was a coup. The government got tossed out, the project got cancelled, and the people at First Boston were looking at me. They said, "What do you want to do?" I said, "I want to do international projects." They said, "Here's a business card. Here's a credit card. Why don't you go around the world and see if you get us hired to bid on international projects?" And that's just what I did.

DR: How many years were you at First Boston?

AO: I was there for 23 years.

DR: And you rose up to be the head of investment banking?

AO: Correct.

DR: I remember one time I called you and said I was going to start some infrastructure fund at Carlyle, and you said, "I've gotten Credit Suisse and GE to agree to do something. If it doesn't happen, I'll call you." Who came up with the idea of Credit Suisse and General Electric doing this together? Was that you?

AO: Yes. At the time, I had what I thought was the best job at Credit Suisse (as First Boston came to be known). I was the chief client officer. I could hang out with clients and I had no management responsibilities. Then I decided I wanted to do something different. So myself and a couple of colleagues said, "What can we do that's different that we would enjoy? Why don't we start an infrastructure fund management business?" I went to the CEO of Credit Suisse and I said, "I want to start this business and I want you to commit a billion dollars." To his credit, he said, "Fine." Then he wanted us to do it inside Credit Suisse, which I didn't want to do. Fortunately, we got a call from GE. Jeff Immelt, the CEO, had decided that they wanted to raise an infrastructure fund. I told him, "I'm going to be leaving Credit Suisse to start a fund, and if you give us a billion dollars, we'll cut you in on the action." He gave us half a billion dollars, and because it was a joint venture, it had to be outside of Credit Suisse. So that's what we did.

DR: What year was that?

AO: Two thousand six.

DR: Now you manage $100 billion or more?

AO: It's $81 billion.

DR: Eighty-one billion dollars. You are the largest infrastructure firm in the world?

AO: Macquarie is probably still the largest. We are the largest independent one.

DR: How many employees do you have now?

AO: We have about 350 employees, of whom about 150 are investment professionals. Then we have almost 40 people in what we call our Business Improvement Team. These are men and women who worked in industrial companies, and they are not infrastructure experts. They worked at companies like GE, BP, Honeywell. Our thesis when we started GIP was that if we could apply industrial tools and techniques to infrastructure businesses, we would be able to generate outsized returns, and that has proven to be the case.

DR: Can you give an example of one of your best-known investments, one you're really proud of?

AO: We invested in Gatwick in 2009. We sold a 50 percent interest in it to a French company called Vinci in 2019. We made above 10 times our initial investment. So that worked out very well.

DR: Did you ever lose any money on anything?

AO: We have two investments that turned into goose eggs. One was an investment of roughly $600 million in an industrial waste company in the UK called Biffa. What they did was they picked up industrial waste, which they disposed of in landfills. There was a transition going on in Europe, when the UK was still part of the European Union. Under EU regulations they had to move away from disposing of garbage by putting it in landfills, so they had to replace them with energy from waste plants and anaerobic digestion plants. Our thesis was that we'd use that industrial waste as feedstock to build those two kinds of plants, which we did. What we did not reckon with was the financial crisis. When it happened, the two biggest types of customers Biffa had were restaurants and construction businesses. After the financial crisis, all of that waste supply evaporated, and ultimately the company went bust.

DR: Is the skill set that it takes to be a good infrastructure investor different than being a good private equity investor? What are the attributes you look for when you're hiring somebody?

AO: It's the same skill set with regard to being a good investor. One, you need to have some domain knowledge about whatever it is you're investing in. So we try to invest in sectors where we actually know something about the industry. Two, you have to be intellectually honest in recognizing what the risks of a transaction are. Three, you have to understand that infrastructure investment is different from private equity.

If your target returns are IRRs of 15 to 20 percent, which means you make two or three times your money on an investment, you really can't afford to have a major investment that's a dud. One of the things that's critical about infrastructure investing is you have to focus on protecting your downside. When we have investment committee meetings, we don't spend a lot of time looking at the upside case. Most of the time we spend on the base case and then the downside case, because our thesis is that if you're underwriting an investment at 15 percent and you end up at 12 percent, big problems aren't going to happen.

DR: You were an investment banker for 23 years. What is the skill set that is different between investment banking and private equity or infrastructure investing? What different skill set do you have to employ?

AO: I will answer that obliquely by saying that when I decided to start GIP I went to see Henry Kravis [co-founder of KKR] to ask him for advice. He said, "I'll give you two pieces of advice. One of them you will accept, the other one you probably won't believe, but five years from now, come back and see me." He said, "The first one is, just remember, any fool can buy a business, you just have to pay more than the next guy. It's not when you buy a business that you celebrate. It's when you sell it at a profit." That's fine, I remember thinking. Then he said, "The second thing that you should understand is that no matter how smart you are, or how smart you think you are, there really is no substitute for experience in the investment business."

I remember at the time thinking, "We've raised billions of dollars of funds to get this firm started. I've worked as a banker with some of the most astute investors, Berkshire Hathaway's energy business. How hard can this be?"

Five years later, I did go see Henry. I said, "Henry, you were right, because when I think about how we used to look at investments when we first started GIP and how we look at investments today, it's night and day." The difference is that in investment banking, you're always trying to get to yes. You're always trying to advise your client to do something, buy a business, don't buy a business, sell a business, don't sell a business. That is a very different skill.

In investing, you're not selling. In fact, when we hire new people from investment banking, we can always tell at the very first investment committee, because they are the ones who are emphasizing everything that's good about the investment. They don't spend any time on what could go wrong, and they're always optimistic. Whereas experienced people say, "Here's what could go wrong. Here's all the bad things that you need to know. You make the decision."

DR: Any regrets about the way your career turned out? You don't regret not being a law professor, I assume.

AO: No regrets. I've had fun in every single thing I've done. I didn't think I would spend 23 years in investment banking. I did. I had a blast. I didn't think that investing would be even more fun than investment banking, but it has been, so I have no regrets.

DR: Do you have any outside interests? You can't work 24 hours a day, seven days a week. Do you have any hobbies or sports? Are you a great athlete or great anything else? Any philanthropies you're interested in?

AO: In my youth I was quite athletic. I played field hockey. I think almost nobody in America thinks men play field hockey. I remember when I got to Harvard, I said I wanted to play hockey. They said, "There's the ice rink." And I said, "No, I want to play field hockey." They said, "Where's your skirt?" Because apparently in the US, only young ladies play field hockey. Then I played an even more obscure sport—cricket—which nobody in America understands. Then I decided to take up golf because I thought golf would be easy, and I found out that golf is very hard. I love to read. I read something like 100 books a year. In philanthropy, we tend to focus on education, give a scholarship to go to Harvard, to Oxford, things like that. But we also set up a family foundation and we're getting our two sons involved in figuring out what it is that they want to support with philanthropy.

DR: Do your children want to be infrastructure investors?

AO: No. We have two sons. They are 36 and 32. Both of them are in the music business. So my wife and I are convinced that we must have committed some big crime or something in a prior life.

DR: Are you a big music person?

AO: Not particularly. I like music but my sons are much more into it than I am.

DR: A final question. To run the biggest independent infrastructure firm in the world, the qualification is you need to be from Nigeria, have a JD and an MBA from Harvard, and be an investment banker first. Those are the things that are required, right?

AO: No, the only thing required is you have to be lucky, because we raised money at a time when people were giving money to people who are not experienced. I'd hate to think what reception we'd have gotten if we tried to do it today. So a) you need to be lucky, and b) you need to surround yourself with the smartest people, just like you did, David. Clear obstacles out of their way. Then you ride the coattails of their success.

ESG [Environmental, Social, and Governance]

DAVID BLOOD

Senior partner, Generation Investment Management

> *"Today, in many places in the world, if you do not consider ESG, you are not fulfilling your fiduciary duty."*

For much of the history of investing, the principal focus for investors was on achieving the highest rate of return (in a legal and norm-consistent way). There honestly was relatively little to no concern about the effects on the environment, the overall social impact, or the manner in which the profits were achieved. Concerns about a diverse board, workforce, or supplier base were also just not part of the ecosystem of investing (or business).

For some, that kind of approach essentially meant that investing was simply not as socially acceptable an activity as might be desired: capital was being placed in companies or industries or geographic areas inimical to socially responsible outcomes.

Over the past few decades, though, and particularly over the past few years, a new investment consideration has emerged—ESG, an acronym that stands for environmental, social, and governance. These three factors are ones on which investors are increasingly focusing their attention. Environmental—will the investment impact the environment in some hopefully favorable way? Social—will the investment address appropriately social issues like equity, diversity, and inclusion? Governance—will the investment be in a company that is governed in a way to reflect all stakeholder interests rather than just shareholder (or executive) interests?

When some in the investment community began a few decades ago to focus on ESG factors in assessing investments' desirability, it was a small minority. The vast majority of investors still wanted to focus on the traditional criteria of profitability (and ultimately rate of return). There was a view that a concern about ESG on the part of a company would detract from a focus on profitability, and thus produce lower rates of return.

Over the past decade, and especially in the last few years, this traditional perspective has changed in two respects. First, investors are much more focused on the ESG qualities of their investments, out of a greater concern for the societal impact of their investments. Second, investors increasingly believe that companies with strong ESG metrics will actually outperform investments without such metrics (in part because customers are more attuned to these concerns; desirable employees are similarly focused on working at such places; and other investors are likely to be more interested in supporting such companies).

These views may not now be held universally in the investment world. And even among those who do believe ESG factors are increasingly important and relevant, there is some resistance to the desire of some very ardent ESG advocates to keep certain nonprofit organizations, like university endowments, from having any investments in oil and gas companies. There is also some resistance in the investment community as well to having public companies address in detail how they are addressing climate change in their operations.

But clearly the movement toward ESG-related investment is now a component of the investment world, and likely to become increasingly more important.

Of the investment firms making ESG the driving force in all their investment decisions, perhaps the best known is Generation Investment Management, which was started in 2004 by seven founders including former vice president Al Gore and former Goldman Sachs partner David Blood (producing the inevitable nickname "Blood and Gore"). A committed environmentalist and outdoorsman, Blood had led Goldman's asset management arm before retiring at a relatively early age not long after the firm went public (over his objections).

From its inception, Generation was focused only on investing where strong ESG performance was a key part of the companies in which investments were made (initially only public companies). Generation's startup capital primarily came from the founders and some family and friends. For the reasons mentioned earlier, outside investors were a bit skeptical that the returns would be all that attractive.

The founders' view was that a focus on ESG would produce better returns—returns that outperformed general market indices. They turned out to be right. Since Generation was formed, the company's flagship Global Equity fund has outperformed its comparable public market index by about 500 basis points—a noteworthy difference in the world of public stock performance.*

Also, the company's founders remain resolute in keeping Generation a private company, one not subject to the pressures placed on a public company—pressures that may clash at times with a focus on ESG. I interviewed David, who had once been a ski area neighbor of mine, on a Zoom call on September 30, 2021, when he was in the company's headquarters in London.

DAVID M. RUBENSTEIN (DR): Why has ESG become such an important part of the investment world in recent years?

DAVID BLOOD (DB): It has become more and more mainstream over the course of the last five or 10 years. First, the issues around sustainability have become very clear. People recognize that they're driving economies and therefore matter. Second, the mechanics of and the academic research around what ESG really means to businesses, and by extension to investors, have become more clear. The business case for sustainability, and certain investors' track records, have credentialized ESG to the point where it's no longer a fringe activity. It's no longer considered trading value for values. It's considered a much more rigorous approach to investing.

---

* Data as of December 31, 2021, sourced from MercerInsight, a database of Mercer Investment Consultants. Data is gross of fees since inception of Generation's Global Equity fund on May 1, 2005.

DR: The long-held presumption in the investment world was that if one invested with a focus on ESG, one would get a lower rate of return. Is that a fair summary of conventional wisdom?

DB: Yes, it is due to the sense that any time you limit your opportunities you're going to, by extension, make your investment challenge greater. That was the conventional wisdom 20 years ago, when we got started—that ESG was really about exclusion. You would exclude the oil companies or you'd exclude tobacco companies or whatever. A lot of the research around that was pretty categorical. If you reduce your opportunity set, it's going to result in a penalty.

But as time has gone on, and people began to realize that environmental, social, and governance factors are tools to help you understand what a company does and how a company does it, that attitude began to change. People began to realize that ESG would provide differentiated insights in understanding businesses and management teams.

At the same time, unfortunately, particularly in the United States, the notion of ESG has become a political issue. Oftentimes people think of sustainability or ESG as someone trying to impose values on the portfolio, or as a left or left-of-center initiative. It's manifested in the acrimony that we see in the US.

We've tried from the very beginning to say, "No, the investment framework that we talk about, which is long-term investing, is best practice." Sustainability—broadly defined to include things like climate change, health, inequality, water challenges, the whole array of large issues that are increasingly interlinked and driving economies—plus ESG are tools or a framework to help you understand economies, businesses, and management teams and ultimately deploy capital in a more effective, risk-adjusted way.

DR: Do people now believe that ESG can actually increase returns? Is that conventional wisdom today?

DB: Increasingly so. When we first started, there was a question as to whether considering ESG was permitted from a fiduciary duty perspective. Today, in many places in the world, if you do not consider ESG, you are not fulfilling your fiduciary duty. Investors want ESG to be part of what is considered as part of the assessment of a possible investment.

Investors do not want their investment to harm the world; they want their investments to help the world.

DR: Are there people who still believe that ESG will not increase returns? Or is it universally accepted today that attention to ESG will increase returns?

DB: It is increasingly universally accepted. When Larry Fink says that sustainability and ESG are mainstream, I think it kind of is.

DR: Why is it the case that attention to ESG will, in your view, produce better returns? Is this true in public markets, which have been your main focus, or in private markets as well, in which you are now also investing?

DB: We've been investing in private markets for 12 or 13 years, so for a long time, but we believe that sustainability and ESG are relevant to all asset classes. We started with the public equity markets because that's what people focus on. When you turn on CNBC, you're going to hear about the public equity markets, mostly, versus the private markets or the fixed-income markets. Because our goal as a firm is to produce both outstanding investment results and to promote sustainability in the capital markets, we wanted to go and focus on the area that was most popular. But yes, sustainability and ESG matters to all asset classes.

DR: How does an investor measure a company's ESG performance or record? Is there a standard measurement tool that everyone agrees upon, or to some extent is it in the eye of the beholder? Will there be a standard metric at some point if there isn't yet?

DB: That happens to be one of the most important questions around these days. The issue with sustainability and ESG is that, as you said, those terms are often used and explained sort of in the eye of the beholder. That becomes a challenge, because what ESG means to you or what it means to me might mean something else to someone else. We've tried hard to help set this framework and make it clear, but there are initiatives now that are helping to drive some conformity in sustainability-related disclosure for investors. The IFRS [the International Financial Reporting Standards Foundation] recently consolidated the leading investor-focused sustainability disclosure efforts to create the new International Sustainability Standards Board, which will function alongside and connect to the board that sets international accounting standards. This will bring some major standardization to sustainability-related disclosure for investors, including bringing transparency to the assumption behind companies' sustainability-related targets, and will make it part of general purpose financial reporting.

DR: Are the three components of ESG equally important, or is one more likely to indicate greater potential value to a company?

DB: It depends on when you ask that question. We think of it consistently across all of our businesses. It's true that, with some companies, the focus will be greater around governance or around the environment or social challenges. On balance, they're all indicators of understanding business quality and management quality. In certain cases—for example, the transition to net zero [carbon emissions] and the energy transition that we're embarking on—if you're a business that is focused on that, the environmental footprint and what you're doing to help transition to net zero will be the most important aspect of your business agenda.

DR: Can you explain the difference between investing with a focus on ESG and "impact investing"?

DB: This is also an important question, because it confuses folks. The first thing we would tell you is that all investing has impact. To pretend that some businesses have impact and others do not is a little misguided. What people tend to mean by impact investing is that you are trading impact for return. There's some kind of concession. That's really an extension of philanthropy.

We do feel that impact is a critical component to capital allocation and will be increasingly so. We believe that impact will be part of the risk-and-return calculation going forward. That's particularly important as we make the transition to net zero.

DR: Let's talk for a moment about how you came to the investment world and ultimately to co-found Generation Investment Management. Were you always interested in the investment world as a youth?

DB: I've been in the investing business now for 25 years, and have been in finance for 40 years. I went to Hamilton College to be a teacher or forest ranger. I did not dream of being an investor when I was growing up. I dreamed of something very different. My mom was a teacher and I had lots of mentors who were teachers, and that's what I wanted to do.

When I went to Hamilton, in my sophomore year they discontinued the education department, so I had to look around for a major. The closest thing to education was psychology, in particular child psychology, which, as you know from running firms, is a good discipline to know in order to manage investment bankers and managers.

I couldn't get a job as a psychologist, so my dad said—this was in the spring of 1981—"Look, you've got to get a job, and you should apply to banks because they hire people like you." I applied to 70 banks in the United States and was rejected by 69 of them. Got one yes, at Bankers Trust, started my career in finance there and found out that I was pretty good with numbers, then went on to Harvard Business School and on to Goldman Sachs. I certainly did not aspire to be an investment banker when I was a senior in university.

DR: What did you do at Goldman, and what prompted you to leave to do something else?

DB: I had a somewhat unusual career at Goldman Sachs. I was in just about every division of the firm. I started in 1985 in investment banking, spent some time on the fixed-income trading floor, spent some time on the equity trading floor, ultimately was treasurer of Goldman Sachs for a while, then moved to the asset management business in 1996. I found that I enjoyed the investment business, but what I really did at Goldman Sachs was help build businesses. I considered myself, within Goldman Sachs, an entrepreneur.

I was also one of the partners who voted to stay private when Goldman Sachs considered going public and then went public. I made that vote because I felt that it would change the culture of the firm, and I didn't think that was a good idea. So, when Goldman Sachs went public, it became very clear to me that it was going to be just a few years before I would go do something different, and that was true. I left four or five years after the IPO.

As I was realizing I was going to leave, I began to think about what I wanted to do. I said, "I am interested in social justice, I am interested in poverty. Perhaps I can bring together my interest in investing with my interest in poverty and the environment and maybe we can develop a business on that basis." I had already become familiar with sustainable investing through one of my partners, Mark Ferguson, who worked with me at Goldman Sachs. It's almost 18 years to the day since we wrote our first business plan. Then I met with Vice President Gore at Harvard. We talked about what we were trying to do and he talked about what he was trying to do, and we realized that while his interest was the environment and my interest was in poverty and social justice, it was really the same coin, but different sides. That's how we came together as a team.

DR: How did you first meet Al Gore?

DB: I was introduced to him by Phil Murphy, who was my boss at the time. Phil is now governor of New Jersey. Al had approached Goldman Sachs about representing him to make an acquisition of a company called Sustainable Asset Management. One of the senior people at Sustainable Asset Management, Colin le Duc, was another co-founder of Generation. Colin, Mark, and I wrote the Generation business plan, and Phil asked me to go to Boston to meet Al and I did, because it's not every day you get to meet the vice president of the United States. I brought our business plan, not because I wanted to convince him. I was there to try to teach him the difference between buying a company and starting one. That conversation led to the idea that perhaps we should do it together. The old joke of "Blood and Gore" was too easy. That's how it all came together.

DR: What was the initial investment thesis, and was it hard to raise money at the outset?

DB: Our original business plan had four boxes: public equity, private equity, credit, and our foundation. We started with public equity, because that's what two of our seven founders knew best, and they are great at it.

Our investment proposition was long-term investing, sustainability as a driver of economies, and ESG as a tool to understand business quality and management quality, and that was what we put to the broader investor community. I had run Goldman Sachs's asset management, so I knew a lot of folks in the industry. We began to develop our business.

We started our firm in October 2003. We did not take third-party money until October 2005. We started with our own money, then broadened it out to institutional investors. In the public market, you really don't get traction until you have a three-year track record. I think we might have had $500 million at the three-year track-record mark, but our three-year track record was pretty good. It was in the middle of a global financial crisis, where people were wondering about long-termism and sustainability. That's what led to the rapid growth of our assets under management.

DR: How much is now being managed, and how has performance been? Has the performance been better than a standard stock market index, reflecting the value of your approach?

DB: The public information on our assets under management today is $36 billion.

DR: I read that the rate of return, since you started, was 12 percent or something like that?

DB: Since inception, we're the second-best global equity manager in the world.* We compete against mainstream managers. We also have done well in our private equity funds.

From the very beginning, we knew that if we did not deliver strong investment results, our mission to promote sustainability would fall on deaf ears. We knew we had to be excellent investors, and we're competitive people. Everything we do is driven by the desire to be excellent in investing. Our framework, our commitment to sustainability and ESG, is about excellence in investing, but we're mission-driven to promote sustainability. Each reinforces the other. We know that if we don't deliver strong investment results, our advocacy around sustainability is uninteresting.

DR: What surprised you the most about your firm as it grew and performed and attracted others in the ESG world over the years?

DB: Two things. The first is that when we founded the firm, I had helped build five or six different businesses within Goldman Sachs, so it never

---

* Data as of December 31, 2021, sourced from MercerInsight, a database of Mercer Investment Consultants. Data is gross of fees since inception of Generation's Global Equity fund on May 1, 2005.

occurred to me that starting an investment firm would be tricky or hard. We collectively, the seven founders, went into it with high confidence. After three or four years, we realized how lucky we had been. A number of things went our way, including performance. Even great investors in the public market can have difficult years. That wasn't true for us. We're a much humbler group today than we were, because building businesses, as you know personally, is not straightforward.

Second, we underestimated how important mission is. That has become, particularly as the years have gone by, the most critical factor in terms of how we attract and retain people, and also how we attract and retain entrepreneurs and how we build our broader stakeholder community, including with our public companies. Initially we thought mission was important. We underestimated how important it is.

DR: As you look at this type of investment focus, ESG, what are the criteria that make one a good investor? Is it a high IQ, intensive research, belief in the mission, or a combination of all those?

DB: A combination of all those. To be a strong sustainability or ESG investor is no different than being a strong whatever kind of other investor there is. We don't recognize the difference between what we're doing and what you're doing.

DR: Is it harder or easier to invest with an ESG focus in the public markets or the private markets?

DB: It is harder to identify impact in the public markets than in the private markets, because the private businesses, particularly at the growth stage that we invest in, are typically focused on a specific industry or objective. In the public market, the companies are much larger, and can have multiple business objectives. Nevertheless, we believe you can invest effectively in the public markets, which we've done for all these years, and in the private markets as well. When you're driving for maximum impact, the private markets are a pretty good place to do that.

DR: For someone who wants to invest in this area, do you recommend investing in funds as opposed to trying to do ESG investing oneself? What criteria should be used to determine whether a fund is not only good at investing but also good at applying ESG principles?

DB: The problem of "greenwashing" is a big deal, particularly for retail investors but even for some institutional investors. A number of firms are now claiming sustainability and ESG as credentials or as an approach, and there are many examples of that simply not being true. That is unfortunately causing a great deal of confusion in the marketplace. We see the SEC looking at it. We see the European Commission looking at it. It's an issue that's going to have to be addressed.

Ultimately, understanding sustainability and ESG is hard. It is not a checklist exercise. The reason why we think being a qualitative manager and a concentrated manager is a better approach is that this allows us to spend more time on understanding businesses and on the sustainability and ESG drivers of those businesses. You need both. To be an outstanding sustainability and ESG investor means you're an outstanding investor, and you need to be able to demonstrate both the rigor of your sustainability and ESG work as well as your investment results.

DR: What is greenwashing, for those who may not be familiar with the term?

DB: It means that you're, in effect, claiming to be sustainable or committed to ESG, but it's a label as opposed to action.

DR: What type of excess return do you think one should reasonably expect from investing with an ESG focus in public equities? Should somebody expect to get 100 basis points, 200 basis points, 300 basis points over a non-ESG-related kind of public equity firm, or there's no way to measure what the excess return would be?

DB: It's hard to measure what an excess return might be, and there are plenty of examples of sustainability or ESG managers who underperform. We configure the question a bit differently to say, "What is your return expectation in the public equity markets?" We do not recognize or accept that there is a difference between sustainability and ESG and mainstream investing. We think it's one and the same. In fact, we would say, on any of the investment committees I sit on, that if you're not considering ESG and sustainability, you're making a mistake.

DR: Do you do ESG-related investments in the public debt area as well?

DB: We do not. We decided to stop after our first fund, principally because to do debt business right, you need to be a much more sizable firm, and we like being about 125 people.

DR: What have you learned through this whole process? In hindsight, would you do anything differently with your firm?

DB: We feel like we're very fortunate. We've had a number of positive things happen to us, and so we're a humbler lot. We feel like we were at the right place at the right time in terms of thinking about sustainability and ESG. We've been fortunate to be in a position to promote this philosophy.

DR: Is it easy to recruit employees with an ESG focus?

DB: It's easy for us. We are looking for people who bring both the passion and rigor of a traditional investor but who have the passion for and understanding of the importance of sustainability and ESG. I will say to someone, "If you do not believe that sustainability and ESG will make you a better investor, do not come here," because that's what we believe. We think it makes you a better investor. We find it relatively easy to find great people who have that philosophy. If we were trying to hire a million people, that might be trickier. But we don't find it a challenge.

DR: Very often, when good investors make some money, they get involved in philanthropy. Is there any particular area of philanthropy that is appealing to you?

DB: The Generation Foundation was established when we started the firm. Five percent of the partners' distributable profits of Generation go to the foundation. It is focused on both the deepening inequality of society and the carbon-related transition to net zero. I am the co-chair of the World Resources Institute. I was one of the founders of Social Finance [a nonprofit focused on getting private-sector resources to address social and environmental challenges], so conservation and the environment and poverty are critical factors that I care deeply about. It's consistent with Generation, and the partners of Generation are often quite involved in other philanthropic activities. Last year 97 percent of the employees of Generation participated in one way, shape, or form in philanthropic activities.

DR: Any other outside interests, hobbies, or sports that take your time or interest?

DB: My family does for sure, and I love sports. I am an avid Green Bay Packers and Detroit Tigers fan. That does take some of my time and sometimes can result in frustration.

DR: How do you think ESG investing will likely change in the future?

DB: We must do a better job defining sustainability and ESG. We must drive towards a greater understanding of how to report around sustainability, both understanding companies as well as the impact of the portfolio. We need to raise standards around what it means to use sustainability and ESG. This goes back to the question about greenwashing.

There is a sense that sustainable investing is always a win-win. It's not. There are trade-offs often. The challenge is that it doesn't lend itself to simply a box-checking exercise. It's more complicated than that. We're going to have to drive to greater understanding, greater standards, and greater rigor in terms of how we think about sustainability and ESG.

DR: Any role models that you've had in the ESG-focused world?

DB: The man who comes to mind is a man by the name of John Elkington. He founded a number of sustainability initiatives. He's a serial entrepreneur. His most recent company is called Volans. I would say he's the dean of sustainability. Generation is quite aware that when we started 18 years ago, there were probably a dozen other founders of the sustainability movement that started way before us who deserve a lot of credit. We were early to it, but there are even earlier pioneers whom we have great admiration for.

ACKNOWLEDGMENTS

Like my prior books, this one is the result of many people working collaboratively with each other and with me, and I would like to acknowledge their hard work and valuable contributions. Without their efforts, this book would obviously not have been possible.

To begin with, all of the interviewees deserve my gratitude and appreciation for agreeing to be interviewed and for later reviewing and approving the interview transcript. For the book, I did interview a fair number of individuals who, in the end, could not be included in the book for space limitation reasons. However, the insights from these other interviews were absolutely invaluable in enabling me to understand better the field of their investment expertise. I was able to include a number of those interviews in the audio version of this book, and appreciate those interviewees consenting to participation in that format.

As with my prior books, Simon & Schuster could not have been more helpful in getting the book from concept to final product. In particular, I would like to thank for their support and continuing interest Jonathan Karp, Simon & Schuster's CEO, and Dana Canedy, Simon & Schuster's senior vice president and publisher. And as with my prior books, I could not have had a better, more supportive, and more encouraging editor than Stuart Roberts. Stuart's editing skills are truly world-class. Stuart's efforts were buttressed by the equally skilled editing of Stephanie Frerich, who in time succeeded Stuart as principal editor.

My relationship with Simon & Schuster was initially made possible by Washington's favorite lawyer, and my law school colleague of more than four decades, Bob Barnett. He has many more important clients than me, but he has always provided me with ready access to his experience and judgment, for which I am quite grateful.

The book also could not have been produced without the unstinting efforts of Jennifer Howard, who has worked with me as well on my prior books. She was, as always, indefatigable in reviewing the interview transcripts and trying to help edit them into a readable and interesting text. Her suggestions about how to make the interviews work better for the reader were invaluable.

My dedicated and long-serving personal staff members also deserve a great deal of credit for keeping this undertaking on track. Foremost among them is my renowned chief of staff of more than thirty years, MaryPat Decker, who encouraged me to pursue publishing this book and made certain that the requisite interviews were scheduled in person or virtually (and rescheduled, as was often necessary). Laura Boring and Amanda Mangum, who have worked with me respectively for 17 and eight years, were indispensable in preparing the texts for my introductory pieces, and for otherwise doing everything they could to make the book writing and preparation processes work smoothly (while also performing their many other responsibilities).

I also am indebted to Trenton Pfister, my tireless research assistant, for working to confirm the enormous number of facts contained in my introductions and the interviews.

Many of these interviews were, by necessity, done virtually, and I could not have had a more efficient technology consultant than Mandeep Singh Sandhu. Everything that had to be taped under his supervision was done flawlessly. No technical glitches or failures, which would certainly not have been the case if I had been in charge of the technical aspects of the interviews. Fortunately, my team did not ever allow that to occur.

While most of the interviews for this book occurred specifically for this book, there were some that had been part of a television show I host on Bloomberg TV, *Bloomberg Wealth with David Rubenstein*. For her help in making those interviews possible, and for her help as well with those transcripts, I am indebted to that show's extremely talented and effective producer, Kelly Belknap. I am also grateful for the support of Mike Bloomberg and Al Mayers, the executive at Bloomberg who oversees the television and radio programming.

I was trained as a lawyer, and was new to the investment world when I helped to found The Carlyle Group in 1987. I have learned a great deal about investing over the years, and tried to provide some of that learning in this book. But a good deal of what I have learned comes from my co-founders, Bill Conway and Dan D'Aniello, who deserve the lion's share of credit for helping build Carlyle into one of the world's largest and most successful global investment firms. Of course, I have also learned much about investing from the considerable number of other investment professionals who have worked or still work at Carlyle (most especially Ed Mathias, who helped raise Carlyle's capital), but special gratitude is owed to my co-founders. Without them, I might have had to return to the practice of law, which would not have been a plus for me or my former clients.

I have also learned a fair bit about investing from watching the investment activities of my family office, Declaration Capital, which invests in areas typically not pursued by Carlyle. Brian Frank leads that office and has done an outstanding job building it over the last five years, and I am indebted to him for helping to educate me about investment matters not covered traditionally by Carlyle.

I have also benefited from serving on the investment committees of the Institute for Advanced Study, the Memorial Sloan Kettering Cancer Center, the Smithsonian Institution, and the National Gallery of Art, and appreciate the educational experience provided to me from those organizations' dedicated professionals. From serving on the board of trustees at Duke University, the University of Chicago, and Johns Hopkins University and as a fellow of the Harvard Corporation, I have also learned a good deal about the investment world, even though my responsibilities there did not include direct investment committee membership.

Finally, I want to thank Josh Lerner, a true private investment expert and the Jacob H. Schiff Professor of Investment Banking at Harvard Business School, for his review for accuracy of parts of this book.

All author proceeds from the book will be provided to the Johns Hopkins Children's Center, the Children's National Hospital in Washington, and the Boston Children's Hospital.

No doubt there will be some mistakes or errors in this book. As the author, I deserve the blame for whatever might not be accurate in this book. I worked hard to make certain that every fact and statement was checked, but mistakes do occur and they can fairly be placed at my doorstep.

INDEX

ABOUT THE AUTHOR

DAVID M. RUBENSTEIN is cofounder and cochairman of The Carlyle Group, one of the world's largest and most successful global investment firms.

Mr. Rubenstein is chairman of the boards of the John F. Kennedy Center for the Performing Arts, the Council on Foreign Relations, the National Gallery of Art, the University of Chicago, and the Economic Club of Washington; a fellow of the Harvard Corporation; a trustee or director of Memorial Sloan Kettering Cancer Center, Johns Hopkins Medicine, the Institute for Advanced Study, the National Constitution Center, the Brookings Institution, the World Economic Forum, Lincoln Center for the Performing Arts, and the American Academy of Arts and Sciences. He has served as chairman of the boards of Duke University and the Smithsonian Institution, and cochairman of the board of the Brookings Institution. Mr. Rubenstein is an original signer of the Giving Pledge and a recipient of the Carnegie Medal of Philanthropy and MoMA's David Rockefeller Award.

Mr. Rubenstein is the host of *The David Rubenstein Show: Peer-to-Peer Conversations* on Bloomberg TV and PBS and *Bloomberg Wealth with David Rubenstein* on Bloomberg TV, and the author of *The American Story: Conversations with Master Historians* (Simon & Schuster, 2019) and the *New York Times* bestsellers *How to Lead: Wisdom from the World's Greatest CEOs, Founders, and Game Changers* (Simon & Schuster, 2020) and *The American Experiment: Dialogues on a Dream* (Simon & Schuster, 2021).

A native of Baltimore, Mr. Rubenstein is a 1970 magna cum laude graduate of Duke University, where he was elected to Phi Beta Kappa. Following Duke, he graduated from the University of Chicago Law School in 1973. Prior to cofounding Carlyle in 1987, Mr. Rubenstein practiced law in New York and in Washington, and during the Carter administration he was deputy assistant to the president for domestic policy.